APPLICATIONS OF NATURAL LANGUAGE TO INFORMATION SYSTEMS

Applications of Natural Language to Information Systems

Proceedings of the Second International Workshop
June 26-28, 1996, Amsterdam, The Netherlands

Edited by

R.P. van de Riet
Vrije Universiteit, Amsterdam, The Netherlands

J.F.M. Burg
Vrije Universiteit, Amsterdam, The Netherlands

and

A.J. van der Vos
Vrije Universiteit, Amsterdam, The Netherlands

1996

IOS
Press

Ohmsha

Amsterdam, Oxford, Tokyo, Washington, DC

ISBN 90 5199 273 4(IOS Press)
ISBN 4 274 90102 5 C3000 (Ohmsha)
Library of Congress Catalogue Card Number: 96-76771

Publisher
IOS Press
Van Diemenstraat 94
1013 CN Amsterdam
Netherlands

Distributor in the UK and Ireland
IOS Press/Lavis Marketing
73 Lime Walk
Headington
Oxford OX3 7AD
England

Distributor in the USA and Canada
IOS Press, Inc.
P.O. Box 10558
Burke, VA 22009-0558
USA

Distributor in Japan
Ohmsha, Ltd.
3-1 Kanda Nishiki - Cho
Chiyoda - Ku
Tokyo 101
Japan

PRINTED IN THE NETHERLANDS

Preface

Bringing together *D*ata*B*ases, including all what belongs to its broader field of information systems, and *N*atural *L*anguage, in particular techniques around lexicons, is the theme of the workshop *NLDB* which a year ago, for the first time, was successfully held in Versailles and which will now be held at the Vrije Universiteit in Amsterdam.

More and more people begin to understand that there is a close connection between the field of information systems, including communication aspects, and the field of linguistics. They can profit from each other very much. In information systems one realizes more and more that the applications involve (common) knowledge stored in lexicons, in linguistics one uses more and more techniques from the area of databases. The abbreviation ICS will be used here for Information and Communication Systems.

In the past, consulting databases or getting answers in natural language was a dream for many users. Nowadays, this is an accessible convergent point, mainly due to the large progress of research in natural language and to the development of new technologies which allow the storage of real semantic electronic dictionaries. Each aspect of the life cycle of the information system can be improved by using natural language techniques: the specification, validation, design, simulation, implementation and conflict resolution of databases, of their application programs, and of the database query languages. New software engineering research techniques and methods are used, allowing natural language-based program specifications.

The 35 papers which were submitted, were indexed in one of the categories, mentioned below. The members of the program committee (PC) had indicated their areas of expertise and papers were distributed accordingly. To get a more homogeneous evaluation of the refereeing process referees with conflicting reports were confronted, by e-mail, with these conflicts. After that the members of the PC obtained a version of the evaluation of all papers (without the names of the referees). Two other iterations took place after which the PC Chairman made the final decisions. It was felt that this was a good process; purely done by e-mail: efficient, but regrettably without the traditional dinner.

Below, the themes are listed with two numbers: the first one indicating the number of submissions, the second one indicating the number of papers selected.

Natural language interfaces for database querying	4 - 3
Natural language as a specification interface for design of ICSs	5 - 2
Paraphrasing the design of ICSs as conceptual schemas in NL	3 - 2
Natural language for the validation of specifications of ICSs	1 - 0
Linguistic aspects of view integration	3 - 3
Conceptual modelling and linguistic knowledge	7 - 4
Use of linguistic tools and electronic dictionaries	4 - 2
Textual databases, indexing and retrieval	0 - 0
Generating texts from structured data	0 - 0
Generation of natural language texts from formal specifications	1 - 0
Semi-formal interfaces for interacting with databases	0 - 0
Hypertext facilities for database querying	3 - 3
Indexing and retrieving	4 - 3

In closing, we want to thank all members of the PC who did the refereeing work, offered suggestions for the workshop and gave their prestige to the Workshop, so that we have a nice attendance. Also we want to thank a number of additional referees. We are very grateful to the two key-note speakers: Peter Chen, who invented the E-R Model, which is such a good interface between people and Data Bases, and Gerald Kristen, who founded the company KISS which uses so much Natural Language to make this interface concrete, indeed *NL* for *DB*.

Finally, we want to thank our sponsors: KISS B.V. and Elsevier Science B.V. for their support.

Amsterdam, June 26, 1996.

Reind van de Riet   Hans Burg   Bram van der Vos

Workshop Committees

Organizing Committee

Hans Burg (Chairman)	Vrije U. Amsterdam, The Netherlands
Mokrane Bouzeghoub	PRiSM, U. of Versailles, France
Jon Atle Gulla	GMD Darmstadt, Germany
Anton Nijholt	U. of Twente, The Netherlands
Reind van de Riet	Vrije U. Amsterdam, The Netherlands
Bram van der Vos	Vrije U. Amsterdam, The Netherlands

Program Committee

Reind van de Riet (Chairman)	Vrije U. Amsterdam, The Netherlands
Ana Paula Ambrosio	U. of Goias, Brazil
Elisa Bertino	U. di Milano, Italy
Mokrane Bouzeghoub	PRiSM, U. of Versailles, France
Janis Bubenko	U. of Stockholm, Sweden
Hans Burg	Vrije U. Amsterdam, The Netherlands
Isabelle Comyn-Wattiau	Essec, France
Roland Dachelet	Inria, France
Jan Dietz	Delft U. of Technology, The Netherlands
Frank Dignum	Eindhoven U. of Technology, The Netherlands
Paul McFetridge	Simon Fraser U., Canada
Christian Fluhr	CEA, France
Sabine Geldof	Vrije U. Brussels, Belgium
Jon Atle Gulla	GMD Darmstadt, Germany
Henri Habrias	U. of Nantes, France
Kees Koster	U. of Nijmegen, The Netherlands
Jean-Noël Meunier	PRiSM, U. of Versailles, France
Elisabeth Métais	PRiSM, U. of Versailles, France
Anton Nijholt	U. of Twente, The Netherlands
Erich Ortner	U. of Konstanz, Germany
James Pustejovsky	Brandeis U., USA
Anne de Roeck	U. of Essex, UK
Bram van der Vos	Vrije U. Amsterdam, The Netherlands
Hans Weigand	U. of Brabant, The Netherlands
Chien-ho Wu	NDMC, Taiwan

Additional Reviewers

J.H. ter Bekke	G. Guerrini	Frank Lehmann	Alain Vailly
P. van Bommel	Rainer Hammwoehner	Bruno Schienmann	
A.N.W. Dahanayake	Ron Kaplan	Ans A.G. Steuten	

Sponsors

Elsevier Science B.V.
Kiss B.V.

Contents

Information Retrieval

Natural Language Database Interfaces

Conceptual Modeling with Linguistic Knowledge

Linguistic Aspects of Database View Integration

Applications of Natural Language to Information Systems
R.P. van de Riet et al. (Eds.)
IOS Press, 1996

English, Chinese, and ER Diagrams

P. P. Chen
Computer Science Department
Louisiana State University
Baton Rouge, LA 70808, U.S.A.
E-mail: chen@bit.csc.lsu.edu

1 Extended Abstract

Entity-Relationship (ER) diagramming technique has been used as a graphical technique for modeling the real world. In our daily life, we use natural languages to describe the real world. Therefore, it is of interest to both the theoreticians and practitioners to examine the similarities and differences of the ER diagramming technique and natural languages so that we can get a better understanding on what is a more natural way for a human being in a certain cultural environment to model the real world. It also helps us to add more useful features to the existing modeling techniques such as the ER diagram to make them more natural and more powerful.

In a previous work of the author [1], the main correspondence relationships between ER diagram structures and English grammar structures have been identified. The following are some examples: A "common noun" in English usually corresponds to an "entity types/set" in ER diagrams, while a "proper noun" usually corresponds to a "specific entity". A "verb" usually corresponds to a "relationship". An "adjective" corresponds to an "attribute of an entity" while an "adverb" corresponds to an "attribute of relationship". The "gerund" and "clauses" structures also have corresponding structures in ER diagrams. In short, there are quite a few one-to-one correspondences between ER diagram structures and English grammar structures.

In this paper, we will look at another major natural language, the Chinese. In particular, we will look at the construction principles of Chinese characters. Each Chinese character is an ideogram. There are quite a few principles of constructing a Chinese character. Here, we select some of them which are of interest to modeling and computer professionals and synthesize them into the following set of principles:

1. "Physical Resemblance Principle": the principle of building an ideogram which is an icon representing the major and special physical attributes of the thing in the real world.

2. "Subset Principle": the principle of adding a special graphical construct to an exiting ideogram to become another ideogram. This corresponds to adding a constraint to an entity type to produce a entity subtype.

3. "Composition Principle": the principle of making a new ideogram by putting two or more ideograms together. This is similar to the "aggregation" concept in ER diagram.

4. "Group Principle": This is a special case of the "composition principle" in which all the component ideograms are the same.

5. "Commonality Principle": The principle of constructing a new ideogram with the semantic meaning of the common features of the things or concepts represented by the component ideograms.

6. "An-Instance-of-a-Type Principle": The principle of constructing a new ideogram representing a thing or a concept which is an instance of a type represented by a component ideogram.

In the paper, we will attempt to identify what is missing in the existing ER diagramming technique and what features could be added to improve it. In some sense, English which has a stronger and more well-defined grammar structure than Chinese can be used a model for building large ER diagrams. Chinese which has an ideogram-based character set (vs. English which has a phonetic- based character set) can provide us guidelines on how to design a graphical modeling technique. It can also provide guidelines for the design of graphical icons on Windows systems, which is a direction for future research.

In conclusion, natural languages and ER diagrams are all modeling techniques. A lot of good concepts can be learned from different natural languages in order to improve graphical modeling techniques such as the ER diagramming technique.

References

[1] P. P.-S. Chen. English Sentence Structure and Entity-Relationship Diagrams. *Information Systems*, 29:127–149, 1983.

Applications of Natural Language to Information Systems
R.P. van de Riet et al. (Eds.)
IOS Press, 1996

Understanding Business Language

G.J.H.M. Kristen
Kristen Information & Software Services (KISS) B.V.
The Netherlands

1 Outline

One of the main problems in business today is that the mutual understanding of persons and information systems of an organisation is relatively low. The reason for this is the rather technical focus to information supply of the past decades. Information supply is mainly seen as a technical problem of developing new programming languages, database management systems and computer hardware. Despite all developments the communication aspects of the organisation itself have been neglected heavily.

The presentation introduces a methodology for improvement of the communication between project members and business people by making use of object oriented principles based on the concepts of our natural language. As a result the level of understanding between the different project members increase. With help of these object oriented concepts more projects are delivering the requested functionality in time and within the planned budgets.

The presentation explain globally why grammatical concepts are important for specification of the business objects and business actions. As such the natural language can be seen as the critical element in the process of communication about business objects with the business people.

In order to get a consistent framework for modeling, the grammatical concepts have been enclosed in the KISS-method for object orientation. The modeling process is supported by the KISS-DOMINO game. The KISS-DOMINO game is especially made for simulating the interactive communication between the different project members. As a result the interaction improves the quality of the specification process and speeds it up. The next step is the generation of a fast prototype for interactive specification of the functionality asked. The quality of the specifications can now be checked directly and omissions have to be added in the initial models.

The presentation shows the importance of our natural language for modeling and structuring information supply of the organisation on a large number of aspects.

2 Curriculum vitae

Gerald Kristen is founder and general manager of KISS, the Netherlands, a consulting firm specializing in object orientation. He founded KISS in 1990 and he and his colleagues consult, train and develop in the KISS-method for object orientation. Next to articles about object orientation and natural language approaches to system engineering, Gerald Kristen is also author of the book "Object Orientation, the KISS method", Addison-Wesley, 1994.

The KISS-method is evaluated by the independent IT-Research organisation Butler-Bloor as the best systems-development method that exists currently: "It originates from individual work by Gerald Kristen who can be classified as one of the best methods authors in the world. His OO method represents a genuine intellectual achievement in its simplicity, usability and completeness. Gerald has taken the ideas of object orientation and used them as a means of gathering information and meaning from everyday language. He uses KISS for designing information systems in an incremental fashion, which is entirely practical and easily understood by the systems professionals. It is both elegant and ingenious."

Gerald Kristen studied Business Engineering at the Technical University of Eindhoven and Master of Business Administration at the Catholic University of Leuven.

References

[1] G. Kristen. *Object Orientation: The KISS-method: From Information Architecture to Information System.* Addison-Wesley, 1994.

Applications of Natural Language to Information Systems
R.P. van de Riet et al. (Eds.)
IOS Press, 1996

Natural and Formal Languages in the Development of Information Systems

A. T. Berztiss
Department of Computer Science, University of Pittsburgh, Pittsburgh, PA 15260, USA
(e-mail: alpha@cs.pitt.edu; fax: +412-624-8854)
and
SYSLAB, University of Stockholm

Abstract. We attempt to determine the rightful roles for natural and formal languages in the development of information systems. In so doing we address three issues. First, we give a set of guidelines for reducing ambiguity in the writing of natural language requirements. Second, we consider domain modeling in terms of patterns defined in natural language, and relate requirements, domain models, and formal specifications. Third, we relate domain modeling to our earlier work on queries as a means of constructing conceptual models.

1. Introduction

Formal languages have fixed syntax and semantics, there is no ambiguity, but attempts at translating formal expressions into cognitive concepts often result in failure. An expression may get misinterpreted or it may defy comprehension altogether (quite advanced students in the author's courses have been at a complete loss when confronted with the Z schema "efficient TN" on p. 75 of [1]). Natural languages have fluid syntax and semantics, are notoriously ambiguous, but a natural language statement is rarely beyond the comprehension of a competent speaker of the language. Unfortunately, even carefully crafted natural language statements are ambiguous: the requirements for a library system that were given to prospective participants in a workshop on software specification and design [2] provide a good example. An analysis by Jeanette Wing [3] disclosed several ambiguities; we have extended this list [4, pp. 130-131]. If we can have misinterpretations in both formal and natural languages, then it appears to make little difference which is being used. This in not quite so. While a formal language statement *inherently* has only one valid interpretation, a natural language statement may have several. It is therefore essential that an initial natural language requirements statement be accompanied by the equivalent formal specification.

Since both types of languages present problems, we should try to improve matters with respect to one or both. We have attempted to improve the readability of formal specifications with our specification and prototyping language SF (for examples of SF specifications see [5] and [4, pp. 176-195]). We have also given some guidelines to be followed in writing natural language requirements [4, pp. 136-137]. This work is extended in Section 2. In Section 3 we introduce a software development model that is to determine when to switch from natural to formal language.

Recently Alexander's work on patterns in architecture [6] has become adapted to software design [7]. The patterns are defined in natural language. We are taking the view that patterns are to be the basis of domain models for information systems. Section 4 is a discussion of domain modeling, and in Section 5 we relate requirements and domain models, and consider the place of natural language in this. In particular, our work on queries in the construction of conceptual models [8, 9] is integrated with domain modeling in Section 6. Section 7 contains some conclusions and suggestions for further work.

2. Guidelines for natural language requirements

A *requirement* for a software system is generally a natural language statement for which it can be established whether the software system does or does not satisfy it. Thus, "the system is to allow determination of the average length of borrowing for any copy of a book in the library" is a requirement; "the system is to be user-friendly" is not a requirement – we call it an *expectation.* Requirements gathering produces a list of *wishes.* Some of the wishes are requirements, others are merely expectations. A requirements document may contain both requirements and expectations. We propose a set of guidelines to improve the quality of requirements documents.

Traceability. For each statement on the wish list indicate its source. This is to allow clarification in case there arise difficulties with the interpretation of a statement.

Vocabulary. Replace overworked terms, define uncertain terms, and avoid synonyms. An example of an *overworked* term is "book", which can be used in at least two senses, as in "last year this publisher put out thirty-seven books; the publisher has 200,000 books in its warehouse." In the first sense the appropriate term is "title"; in the second it is "copy". The term "age" is *uncertain* – the author found that in a single insurance office it meant age last birthday, age next birthday, or age nearest birthday. The library requirements of [2] contain the terms "borrow" and "check out" – although it is likely that the two terms have exactly the same meaning, i.e., that they are *synonyms*, the use of different terms suggests that they could have different interpretations.

Partition. The wish list is to be partitioned into four groups of statements, where the first three groups relate to requirements, and the fourth consists of expectations. The three groups of requirements relate to (A) structure of the information base for the application, (B) changes to the information base, and (C) the mode of operation of the system, such as access rights, and nonfunctional characteristics of the system.

Disambiguation. This is to be an explicit step in requirements analysis. A statement could be paraphrased by several people in order to establish whether a uniform interpretation is being given to the statement. If the paraphrases show differences of interpretation, the source of the statement is to be consulted. If the source is not available, an attempt should be made to establish why the statement is part of the requirements – this should help to pick the correct interpretation. A requirement should not be very terse. With some degree of redundancy it becomes easier to establish the intended meaning.

Definiteness. Some statements may at first appear to be expectations, but, on further reflection, they can be turned into type C requirements. This happens when a test is devised for showing that the system satisfies a statement. The test usually takes the form of a benchmark – a benchmark for usability is described in [10].

Visualization. Requirements of type A should be illustrated by means of an Entity-Relationship (ER) diagram [11] or an object-type diagram [12]. A natural language paraphrasing tool for ER diagrams has been developed [13]. Comparison of the output of this tool with the initial requirements document may show some inconsistencies that are to be removed. Type B requirements relate for the most part to the state changes that are permissible for an object, e.g., a copy of a book in a library may be in the states of available, checked out, being repaired, etc. The requirements also tell under what conditions a state change is to take place. All permissible state changes can be shown by a state-transition diagram.

3. A software process model

No matter how high the quality of a natural language requirements statement, at some point in system development there has to take place a switch from natural language to formal language. The question is when this is to happen. We shall try to arrive at an answer by looking at Figure 1, which shows a software development process model for information systems. It is a modification and extension of a model we introduced in [14].

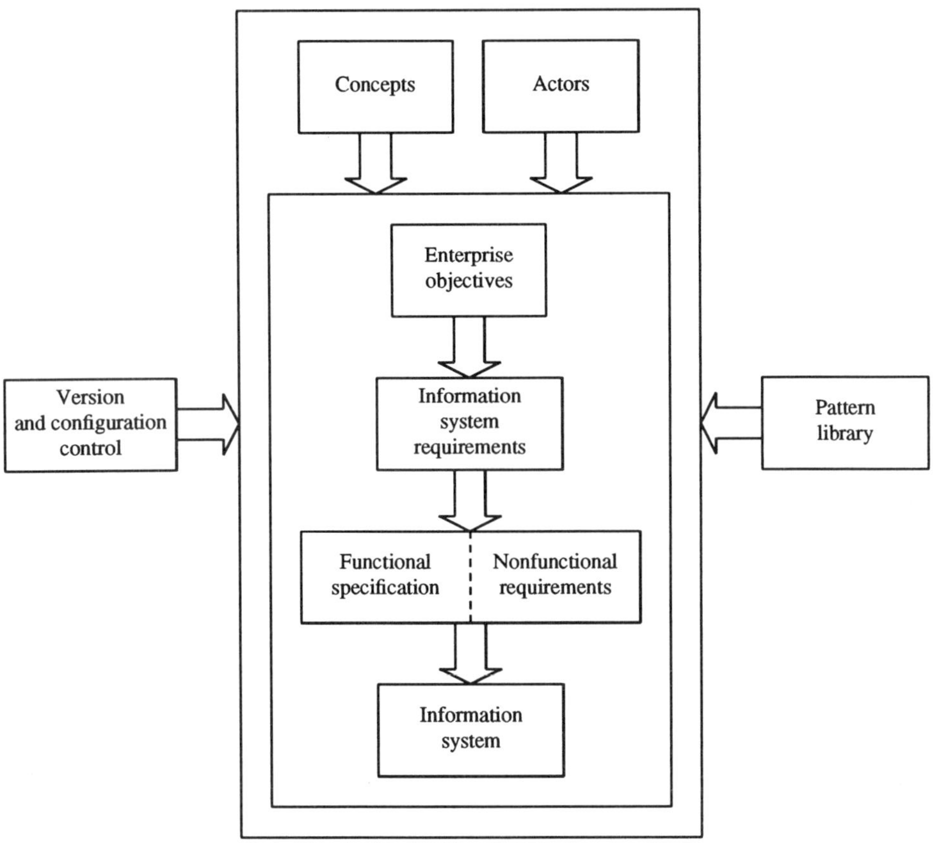

Fig. 1 — A software process model

System development begins with an examination of the objectives of an enterprise, and, in our context, ends with an information system. The objectives determine what systems are to be developed. If the development of a system is not explicitly driven by the objectives, the system still has to be consistent with the objectives. Objectives are invariably expressed in natural language, and so are the information system requirements that give shape to what is expected of the information system – these requirements relate to both functional and nonfunctional characteristics of the system.

Nonfunctional requirements remain expressed in natural language, but, under our process model, functional requirements are to be converted into a formal specification, which means that they are to be expressed in a formal language. A very important component of our model is represented by the pattern-library box. The pattern library will be discussed in greater detail in Section 5. Here we merely indicate that some of the components of the system are to be obtained from the pattern library – for the time being we leave it open whether patterns are to contribute to requirements or specifications, i.e., whether they are to be expressed in natural or formal language.

The more enclosed a box, the more specific its role in the process. The pattern-library box is not enclosed, which means that this component is not influenced by what particular software product is being developed. Neither is version and configuration control. Several versions of the system can be generated, and, during the lifetime of a particular version, it is represented in different forms, such as requirements, design, and code. There must always be a clear understanding of which version a particular representation belongs to (version control), and that all representations of a version are consistent (configuration control). The two remaining components are somewhat dependent on the application – the software process is defined in terms of various concepts, which may depend on the type of software being developed, and different roles in the process are allocated to actors, which can be people or software tools.

4. Domain modeling

Developers of information systems have been constructing domain models for a long time, under various designations, such as conceptual models, enterprise models, and business rules. Since about 1981 others have also become interested in domain analysis and domain models – for surveys of such work to about 1991 see [15, 16]. There is still confusion regarding the term *domain*. Glass and Vessey [17] ascribe some of the confusion to a lack of distinction between application domains, i.e., problems to be solved, and implementation domains, i.e., tools, representations, and methods that are to help solve the problems. This confusion we try to eliminate with our process model – actors and concepts relate to the implementation domain; the pattern library relates to application domains.

We have found no need to define domain as such. The real interest is in domain knowledge and domain models. In the broadest sense, *domain knowledge* relates to a discipline or occupation, such as chemical engineering, accounting, or management, and it is the entire corpus of data, rules, and processes that characterizes the discipline. Some of it is codified in standards and handbooks, but most of it is distributed in the collective memory of practitioners of the discipline. A *domain model* is an abstraction that consists of only those parts of the domain knowledge that are relevant to an application or a family of applications, and the purpose of *domain analysis* is to develop appropriate domain models.

A domain model can cover an entire discipline, but for the development of information systems we want a narrower focus – our interest is in a process such as order fulfillment, or a procedure for dealing with a particular situation, e.g., an exception. This is in keeping with the emphasis that business reengineering puts on processes (see, e.g., [18]). A *process model* defines a business process, and a *situation model* is concerned with individual tasks that form part of processes, as well as with communication between tasks, which may belong to a single process or to several separate processes. In addition, we introduce an *enterprise model*. Its relationship to domain knowledge is not clear-cut in that part of an enterprise model expresses enterprise objectives as formulated by top management, and the objectives need not be tied to domain knowledge. We shall not discuss this model further here.

As we intimated earlier, some domain knowledge may be expressed as patterns [7]. In terms of patterns, a domain model can be regarded as an application-specific adaptation of a set of patterns. Note that the patterns of [7] relate to the software process, i.e., they define implementation domains, but, as we shall see in the next section, patterns can equally well define application domains.

We are mainly interested in domain models composed of patterns for their ability to foster reuse. It appears that despite high claims for software reuse, in reality software reuse is not widely practiced [19]. We ascribe this in some measure to a concentration on code reuse, and make the claim that reuse of requirements or specifications is much more effective than code reuse. Some experience with our specification and prototyping language SF substantiates this claim (for an outline of SF see, e.g., [4, pp. 176-195]). For example, it took the author no more than 15 minutes to convert an SF specification of a software system for controlling the kind of high-tech baggage lockers one sees in some French railway stations into a specification of a software system for vending machines. We now need a systematic way for developing and organizing pattern libraries.

5. Requirements and domain models

We introduce two specific patterns, which have their origin in two widely different domains. This is to illustrate the versatility of the approach. One of the patterns defines a reservation process, the other defines a process for dealing with an exceptional situation in a safety-critical application. The reservation pattern belongs to the domain model of rental processes, where "rental" is given a very broad interpretation. In a general sense, the pattern can relate to a rental car, a library book, a hotel room, a concert seat, a restaurant table, etc. The general pattern is described by the following capsule summary:

> *Reservation*. A customer makes a reservation of a rental object for a length of time starting at an indicated date and/or time. Variants of the basic pattern include (a) group reservations, (b) indication of just the desired starting point and no indication of the length of rental, (c) no indication of a starting point, as in the case of a library book that is currently checked out to some other borrower, (d) confirmed reservation, (e) overbooking, in anticipation of a cancellation, (f) no prior reservation, with the arrival of a customer interpreted as a reservation, (g) in case of shortage of rental objects, a customer may be put into a wait line, but be allowed to make a reservation if the shortage is no longer in effect, (h) for some applications, the rental site and the return site of a rental object may differ. The credit-worthiness of a customer may have to be established as part of this pattern.

This pattern can be specialized to any one of the applications we listed above. The task we have selected here is the reservation of a rental car. A specialization follows a fixed format, made up of five components. They define the mode of initiation of a task, steps that comprise the task, changes to the information base caused by the task, other tasks that may be initiated by this task, and (optionally) notes – they refer to special aspects of the task that do not fit in under the other headings.

Pattern: *Reservation of rental car.*

Triggered by: Customer communication, including the arrival of a customer at the rental desk, or the wait-lines pattern.

Activities:

(a) If customer requests a car of a particular type, check the availability of such a car for the requested period at the indicated rental site.

(b) If car of type requested by customer not available, or customer does not ask for a particular type, suggest a car of an available type.

(c) If triggered by the wait-line pattern, notify customer next in line of the possibility of making a reservation.

(d) If a reservation is made, encourage a customer to make this a confirmed reservation.

Information base changes:

(a) If a reservation is made, enter customer details and car details into the information base.

(b) If the car is to be returned to a different site, make an appropriate entry in the information base for that site.

Affects:

(a) The pattern *Wait lines*, if no car that satisfies a customer's wishes is available, and the customer elects to be put on a wait list.

(b) The pattern *Payment*, if this is a confirmed reservation.

Notes: Overbooking is not practiced by this rental-car company. A "reservation" effected by a customer just showing up at the rental desk is to be treated as a confirmed reservation.

In a different context, we have a pattern to deal with a situation in which a meter has been registering the same value over an extended period of time. Here the general formulation is:

> *Stuck meter.* A meter has been observed to give the same reading over an extended period of time. A determination is to be made whether the meter is stuck.

In this case the capsule summary is already quite specific. The problem has three parts: determination that the meter readings do not change, a perturbation of the system that is to cause a change in the meter reading, and restoration of the system to the state it had before the perturbation. If the meter is stuck, then a corrective action is to be undertaken.

Pattern: *Stuck meter.*

Triggered by: Observation that k successive readings of the meter give the same value. The value of k and the interval between successive readings is to be supplied by a domain expert.

Activities:

(a) Perturb the system, which, if the meter is not stuck, should result in a change of the meter reading. The nature of the perturbation is to be specified by a domain expert.

(b) A short interval after the perturbation, check whether the meter reading has changed, and restore the system to its original state. The restoration process is to be specified by a domain expert.

Information base changes: A reference reading has to be saved against which the current reading is to be compared, and a count of successive readings that are the same is to be maintained.

Affects: The pattern *Meter out*, if the meter continues to give the same value after the perturbation.

Notes: The corrective action to be taken in accordance with the pattern *Meter out* is to take precedence over Activity (b).

The question now arises whether the pattern library is to be made up of patterns left in their natural-language form, or whether we should maintain a library of formal specifications of patterns. Our recommendation is that each pattern be defined in both forms – the natural language form would allow requirements to be defined in terms of patterns, and when the functional requirements have to be transformed into a specification, this is achieved by gathering up the formally defined versions of the patterns. Since this paper is to deal primarily with natural languages and information systems, we shall not include here SF specifications corresponding to our patterns. The SF specification of *Stuck meter* can be found in [20].

Now consider the development of an information system for a restaurant. Since we already have the patterns for the rental-car system, we should make use of them. This we did, with good results. The change of the natural language version of the reservation pattern took less than six minutes, and the change of the SF specification only slightly longer. Thus our objective has been achieved: – we have a natural language requirements statement for each specific application to serve as the basis for discussion between the sponsors and the developers of an information system, and an equivalent formal statement that serves as the official defining document of the system. Moreover, since formal specifications in some languages are executable, the reliability of the specification is inherited by the implemented system.

One of the problems affecting software reuse is the difficulty of finding appropriate components in a reuse library. Here, because the pattern library for the development of information systems has a hierarchical structure, retrieval is not a problem. At the top level of the hierarchy we have general categories, such as rentals, order fulfillment, and customer service. This level serves as an index leading to the next level at which these categories become checklists, composed of the capsule summaries. Some of the components of the checklist for rentals: reservation, cancellation, return, lease-purchase, overdue item, inventory management, and transaction trends. Next, an entry in a checklist can point to specializations or merely to a refinement, e.g., the reservation pattern has numerous specializations, but the stuck-meter pattern has only one.

6. Queries and domain models

The recommended procedure for developing an application is to extract from the pattern library a general catalog of patterns that cover a broad domain, e.g., the rental domain. From this library are extracted those patterns that are relevant for the particular application – for example, not all the patterns that relate to car rentals relate also to the management of restaurant tables. Each such pattern may have several specializations in which it has been adapted for particular applications. The specialization that is closest to the new application is selected, and it is adapted for the new application in both the natural language and formal versions.

However, situations arise in which the conceptual model underlying an application is not well understood. Then the task is to explore the domain of the application thoroughly, and develop patterns appropriate for the application. Also, because patterns are primarily concerned with the process structure of an information system, they refer to the information needs of an application only in an indirect way, by telling how the information base will be affected by the activities.

Therefore, the definition of the information base for an application should be a separate activity from the definition of processes. We find the use of natural language queries to be very helpful in the definition of the information base. The requirements analyst requests that queries be formulated by prospective users of the system, and uses these queries to arrive at the definition of an appropriate information base. The fact that natural language is ambiguous is an advantage here. Because they can have different interpretations, natural language queries can suggest improvements in conceptual models.

Let us take a specific query: "How tall are Swedes?" First we have a homonymity problem, but this is easily resolved – Swede as a person is capitalized; swede as a kind of turnip is not. Much more difficult is the determination of what is meant by Swedes as persons, and this is a conceptual rather than a linguistic problem. We could have any of the following interpretations, which is not an exhaustive list: citizens of Sweden, people who identify themselves as Swedes, people whose parents belong to one of the previous two categories, residents of Sweden, people born in Sweden. This suggests that a set of persons could have several partitions based on "nationality" – by citizenship, by country of birth, etc.

Next, "tall" is a fuzzy concept, so the response here should be a height value. The query suggests that the information base should contain heights of people, and the proper response to the query appears to be an average height. But should the average be based on the adult population alone? What does adulthood mean in this particular context? Should there be two averages, one for men and one for women? Should the average be based on every member of the population, or on a representative sample? After the appropriate decisions have been made, the answer to the query could be given as follows: "The average height of current residents of Sweden who were born in Sweden and have reached the age of 18 is x for males and y for females." This leads to the inclusion of sex and date of birth as attributes of people, and, possibly, the partitioning out of a smaller representative sample population from the total population.

There is considerable difference between the queries "How tall are Swedes?" and "Are Swedes tall?" In [8] we discussed the subjective nature of the tallness concept, and recommended that responses to queries that contain subjective concepts be given in a context. For example, "Are Swedes tall?" cannot be answered with just "yes" or "no", and responding with average heights is not adequate either. Average heights should be shown together with average heights of other populations for comparison so that users of the information system can make their own subjective judgements of whether Swedes are tall. This can be carried too far – users do not want to be overwhelmed with information they may regard irrelevant. We call this the reference problem, and we refer to the determination of how exhaustive the answer to a particular query should be as the reference decision.

7. Conclusions and suggestions

The primary purpose of our investigation has been to establish the proper role of natural language in the design of information systems. Let us summarize the contributions of this paper, and indicate areas in which further research has to be undertaken.

1. We have developed a set of guidelines for the writing of natural language requirements for information systems. The purpose of the guidelines is to reduce ambiguity.
2. We have shown that a library of patterns can support very rapid construction of new information systems, and have defined a development process for informations systems based on this library.
3. We suggest that patterns be defined in both natural and formal languages for reasons of understandability and exactness, respectively.
4. We find that natural language queries formulated by prospective users provide very useful inputs during the definition of the structure of the information base of the system.
5. Automatic translation of a natural-language pattern into SF would be difficult, and is not recommended because the natural-language pattern could easily be misinterpreted in this process. But people can also misinterpret. A software tool that translates a pattern from SF back into natural language would therefore be very useful. Differences between the original natural-language pattern and the pattern generated by the tool would indicate possible misconceptions.
6. As an extension of the above, an SF pattern could be translated into a natural language other than the language from which it derives. This approach is preferable to direct translation between natural languages because it greatly reduces the number of translation systems required. Moreover, the complexity of each such system is also reduced: provided SF uses standardized natural-language naming conventions, translation from SF to Italian, say, should be much less of a problem than translation from English to Italian. This is important as internationalization of software is being given greater attention (see, e.g., [21-23]). The standardization of SF naming conventions is a task for the future.
7. The reference problem is very difficult. Our initial suggestion is that users should participate interactively in reference decisions, the participation to be supported by a software tool, but this topic should be thoroughly studied before a decision is reached on how best to approach the reference problem.

References

[1] Hayes, I. (Ed.), *Specification Case Studies.* Prentice-Hall, 1987.

[2] Harandi, M.T. (Ed.), *Proc. 4th International Workshop on Software Specification and Design.* IEEE Computer Society Press, 1987.

[3] Wing, J.M., A study of 12 specifications of the library problem. *IEEE Software* **5**, 4 (July 1988), 66-76.

[4] Berztiss, A.T., *Software Methods for Business Reengineering*. Springer-Verlag, 1995.

[5] Berztiss, A., Formal specification methods and visualization. In *Principles of Visual Programming Systems*, S.-K. Chang (Ed.), Prentice Hall, 1990, 231-290.

[6] Alexander, C., *The Timeless Way of Building*. Oxford University Press, 1979.

[7] Coplien, J.O., and Schmidt, D.C. (Eds.), *Pattern Languages of Program Design*. Addison-Wesley, 1995.

[8] Berztiss, A.T., Imprecise queries and the quality of conceptual models. In *Information Modelling and Knowledge Bases V*, H. Kangassalo, H. Jaakkola, T. Kitahashi, A. Markus (Eds.), IOS Press, 1994, pp. 256-270.

[9] Berztiss, A.T., and Matjasko, K.J., Queries and the incremental construction of conceptual models. In *Information Modelling and Knowledge Bases, VI*, H. Kangassalo, H. Jaakkola, S. Ohsuga, B. Wangler (Eds.), IOS Press, 1995, pp. 175-185.

[10] De Waal, B.M.E., and Van Der Heiden, G.H., The evaluation of user-friendliness in the design process of user interfaces. In *Human Factors in Information Systems Analysis and Design*, A. Finkelstein, M.J. Tauber, R. Traunmueller (Eds.), North-Holland, 1990, pp. 93-103.

[11] Chen, P.P., The entity-relationship model: toward a unified view of data. *ACM Trans. Database Syst.* **1** (1976), 9-36.

[12] Rumbaugh, J., Blaha, M., Premerlani, W., Eddy, F., and Lorensen, W., *Object-Oriented Modeling and Design*. Prentice-Hall, 1991.

[13] Dalianis, H., A method for validating a conceptual model by natural language discourse generation. In *Advanced Information Systems Engineering*, LNCS no. 593, P. Loucopoulos (Ed.), Springer-Verlag, 1992, pp. 425-444.

[14] Berztiss, A.T., and Bubenko, J.A., A software process model for business reengineering. In *Information Systems Development for Decentralized Organizations*, A. Solvberg, J. Krogstie, A.H. Seltveit (Eds.), Chapman & Hall, 1995, pp. 184-200.

[15] Arango, G., Domain analysis - from art form to engineering discipline. *Proc. 5th International Workshop Software Specification and Design*. IEEE Computer Society Press, 1989, pp. 152-159.

[16] Neighbors, J.M., The evolution from software components to domain analysis. *Int. J. Software Eng. Knowledge Eng.* **2** (1992), 325-354.

[17] Glass, R.L., and Vessey, I., Contemporary application-domain taxonomies. *IEEE Software* **12**, 4 (July 1995), 63-76.

[18] Davenport, T. H., *Process Innovation: Reengineering Work through Information Technology*. Harvard Business School Press, 1993.

[19] Frakes, W.B., and Fox, C.J., Sixteen questions about software reuse. *Comm. ACM* **38**, 6 (June 1995), 75-87, 112.

[20] Berztiss, A.T., Unforeseen hazard conditions and software cliches. *J. High Integrity Systems* (1996), in press.

[21] Digital Corporation, *Digital Guide to Developing International Software*. Digital Press, 1991.

[22] Taylor, D., *Global Software — Developing Applications for the International Market*. Springer-Verlag, 1992.

[23] Kataoka, Y., Morisaki, M., Kuribayashi, H., and Ohara, H., A model for input and output of multilingual text in a windowing environment. *ACM Trans. Information Systems* **10** (1992), 438-451.

Applications of Natural Language to Information Systems
R.P. van de Riet et al. (Eds.)
IOS Press, 1996

Analyzing Informal Requirements Specifications: A First Step towards Conceptual Modeling

J.F.M. Burg* and R.P. van de Riet
Department of Computer Science
Vrije Universiteit
Amsterdam, The Netherlands
{jfmburg,vdriet}@cs.vu.nl

Abstract. Information and Communication System development processes start with specifying the requirements in an informal way. The resulting requirements specification is a natural language document that forms the basis of all future activities, like analysis, design and implementation. In the analysis phase an abstract representation of the requirements is specified, in order to understand the real intentions of the users and to highlight the aspects that are important for the final implemented system. This abstraction step, or Conceptual Modeling, is certainly not a trivial one, and includes decisions about what kind of information should be modeled and how this should be done. In this paper we shall mainly focus on how to deal with the informal requirements specification in order to facilitate the conceptual modeling process, independently of the modeling techniques used. This Natural Language Analysis includes re-structuring the natural language document in standard sentence structures, using linguistic knowledge from a lexicon and defining one integrated structure to represent lexical as well as conceptual structures.
Keywords: Requirements Specification, Lexicon, Conceptual Modeling, Grammatical Analysis, Information and Communication Systems

1 Introduction

When a software development process is started, i.e. a problem has been identified and its solution involves a software product, the first task is to *elicit* knowledge from the domain and its users. Several approaches to accomplish this iterative and incremental task are treated in [25]. One of the resulting documents of this knowledge elicitation process is the informal requirements specification written in natural language, that mainly describes the required functionality of the software product under development.

In this paper, we focus on the *functional* requirements, which are descriptions of the desired service of the intended system, while *non-functional* requirements describe the constraints that are placed on the system, its environment and the system development (like security, availability, performance, etc.) [25].

The *ambiguous*, *incomplete* and *inconsistent* nature of the informal requirements document probably causes several problems. The commonly accepted solution is to

*Supported by the Foundation for Computer Science in the Netherlands (SION) with financial support from the Dutch Organization for Scientific Research (NWO), project 612-123-309

abstract, and formalize, the information from the requirements specification in conceptual models. The graphical nature of these models gives more insight in complex structures of the problem domain, while the support of CASE-tools avoids redundancy and inconsistency within and among models. The models and their (semi-) formalized equivalents are also useful inputs for the design and implementation phases of the software development process.

The abstraction step or conceptual modeling, is not a trivial one, and includes decisions about what kind of information should be modeled and how this should be done. Section 2 defines the concepts to be modeled. The main focus of this paper is however on how to deal with the informal requirements specification in order to facilitate the conceptual modeling process, independently of the modeling techniques used. Existing approaches are presented in Section 3. In Section 4 the integration of the sentence structures, the lexicon structures and the conceptual modeling structures is highlighted as an important aspect of this abstraction process and some related problems and solutions are presented. The concluding sections include related and future work.

2 Modeling Concepts

In this section the concepts that have to be modeled for an adequate abstraction of a problem domain are defined. In [25] three cornerstone concepts of conceptual modeling are defined, which are interrelated in Figure 1.

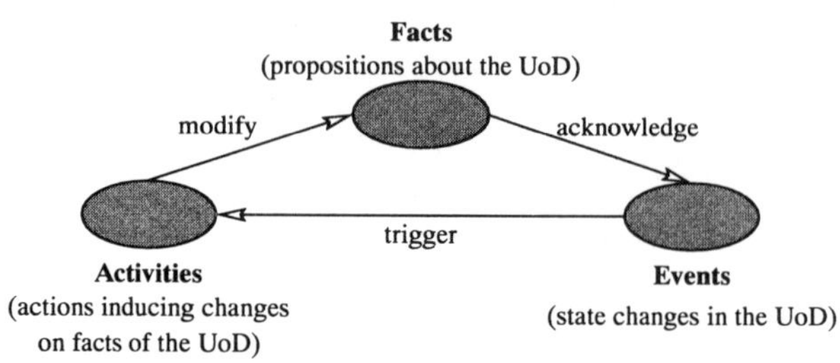

Figure 1: Relationships between Conceptual Modeling Concepts [25]

Based on these cornerstones, on experiences with some widely spread analysis methods (e.g. [29, 38, 21, 22]) and on [30] we think analysts should look after the following conceptual modeling concepts in natural language requirements specifications:

- object/class: (an abstraction of) something in the problem domain
- attribute: a property of an object
- standard relationship: an association between two or more objects. Special relationships include inheritance (*'a book is a document'*) and aggregation (*'a chapter is part of a book'*)
- action/event: 'incidents' taking place in the problem domain (*'lending a book'*)

3 Approaching Natural Language Specifications

In this section an overview of approaches to *discover* and *identify* candidate concepts like objects (or classes), relationships, actions and attributes is presented. Although all analysis techniques and methods contain subsets of these concepts, most of them do not clearly describe ways of identifying them in the informal problem domain specifications. Several stages of the maturation process of this identification task can be distinguished:

1. In the early days of entity-relationship modeling (ER [13]), only some heuristics were available to find candidate concepts: looking for nouns would yield entities, examining verbs would lead to relationship discoveries, etc. Even some modern object-oriented modeling approaches (e.g. [29] and [38]) still rely on these heuristics.

2. In order to give more structure to these heuristics, *Natural Language Analysis* [14, 34] was introduced as a method to produce an ER model from a text written in natural language. Although this 'method' does not consist of a fixed sequence of steps, some heuristics are available:

   - Transform the user sentences into **elementary sentences**, that contain only one main verb.
   - Find **common nouns** in the elementary sentences, because they usually represent an ER entity type.
   - Find **transitive verbs** in the elementary sentences. They usually indicate an action.
   - Identify **adjectives** that usually represent an attribute of an ER entity type.
   - Identify **adverbs** that usually represent an attribute of a relationship.

   Because a natural language analysis of a complete requirements document would yield a number of irrelevant candidate concepts, the analysis could be concentrated on a small number of highly relevant sentences. One set of such sentences are the queries that the system will have to answer (**query analysis**). A generalized approach is called **natural language analysis of transactions**, in which the required system transactions are identified and submitted to the natural language analysis. A scenario-based analysis [11] (or use-case [21] or transaction sequence [38] approach) should be used to identify the transactions.

3. A more complete approach, that is based on linguistic grammars, is **grammatical analysis** that is included in the KISS method [22]. The grammatical analysis consists of several steps:

   a. Transform the user sentences into **structured sentences**, each one consists of two parts:

      i. **main structure:** subject, predicate, direct (i.e. active) object, preposition, indirect (i.e. passive) object

      ii. **special grammatical elements:** adjectives, adverbs, nominal predicates, gerunds, attributive adjuncts

In a current KISS project, called GRAMMALIZER[1], these structured sentences, or *grammatical meta-structures* are topic of research.

b. Make a list of candidate objects and subjects, which are defined in the KISS terminology as:
   i. $\text{object}_{\text{KISS}}$ are all objects (or: entities) that perform or suffer actions
   ii. $\text{subject}_{\text{KISS}}$ are all objects that perform actively one or more actions

c. Make a list of candidate actions

d. Make a list of synonyms (two words for the same concept) and rename possible homonyms (one word for two concepts)

e. Make a list of nominal predicates (e.g. *'a book is a document'*)

f. Make a list of gerunds and nominalizations (verbal nouns like *'paying'* and *'payment'* respectively). The nominalizations are not officially included in the KISS method yet.

g. Make a list of genitives (e.g. *'the value of the order'*)

Every item on the resulting lists has to be evaluated by the analyst. Based on this evaluation some items will remain on the lists, others will disappear. These lists are combined into descriptions of objects, actions, functions, gerunds and subjects (Table 1). In [18] a similar approach is described as part of their

Primitiva	Descriptions
Object	Name, Synonyms, Description, Suffering actions, Is_a objects, Genitive objects
Action	Name, Synonyms, Objects suffering an action, Changes in objects, Derived gerunds, Permitted subjects
Function	Name, Description, Responsible subject, Inspectable objects
Gerund	Name, Derived action, Action specifications
Subject	Name, Synonyms, Peformed actions, Responsibility

Table 1: Final Lists of Grammatical Analysis (KISS [22])

grammar based modeling method. This **syntactical analysis** also transforms user sentences into a unifying format, containing subject, predicate, direct object and preposition group and leads to the recognition of a set of object types, a set of action types and the involvement and responsibility of object types. In [31] a methodology is presented that maps natural language constructs into ER-representations and in [28] linguistic patterns are defined which form a set of basic sentence structures in which all natural language sentences can be expressed. These approaches are both based on syntactic analysis.

4. In the COLOR-X project, we advocate **semantic analysis** as an additional step, in which the *meaning* of the words is annotated to them. These meanings are found in a supporting lexicon. This approach tackles the possible problems of homonyms in a more adequate way, and also gives more information about the concepts, like ontological (e.g. *'to lend'* means *'to give something temporarily'*), structural (e.g. transitive verbs require a subject as well as an object to be

[1] GRAMMALIZER is a project in which KISS, the Katholic University of Brabant and we participate, and which is financially supported by Senter, project DIB508313.QID.

specified) and inter-conceptual (e.g. *'to borrow'* has as a complementary antonym *'to return'* and as a perspective antonym *'to lend'*). [4, 3] already mentioned the need for syntactic, semantic as well as real world knowledge to fully understand a natural language document and to correctly transform it to conceptual models.

Lexicon We see the lexicon as the central repository of all terminology and related linguistic elements that we need to describe communication in and about the world we live in. As such, it is much more than a list of terms. The lexicon contains the concepts that make up our communications, and it defines the relationships between these concepts. To access the information contained in the lexicon a Lexicon Management System should be built upon it. We think the lexicon to be a multi-level repository, based on the specificity, or refinement, of the concepts found at each level. Most of the times the refinement levels are [9]:

(a) lexical knowledge, at the moment we use WordNet [27], which is the result of an ongoing research program at Princeton University in the representation of lexical information. It consists of four semantic networks, one for each of the major parts of speech (nouns, verbs, adjectives and adverbs). Each node in the semantic network for a part of speech represents a concept, conveyed by a set of synonyms **synset**. The links in the semantic network represent various lexical relationships between synsets.

(b) domain-specific knowledge, which consists of concepts and relationships between these concepts that are typical for the domain (like a library-domain), but their specific meaning can not be found in the lexical knowledge level.

(c) application-specific knowledge, which further refines the information available at the domain-specific level. The meaning of the concepts and relationships between the concepts found at this level, is not valid for the domain or company as a whole, but it is specific for the corresponding application, which uses this meaning. This latter level of knowledge consists of different sets, which are not necessarily disjoint, belonging to separate applications.

It is striking to notice the similarities between our notion of a multi-level linguistic repository and Yourdon's "30-30-30"-rule for identifying basic entity objects for a certain application, which says [38]:

> 30 percent of the basic entity types are generic, 30 percent are industry-specific, 30 percent are environment specific, and the remaining 10 percent cannot be readily categorized at all.

Another aspect of the COLOR-X approach is the fact that its underlying formal language, CPL (Conceptual Prototyping Language [16]), is based on Functional Grammar (FG [17]). FG is a formalism to capture the deep structure of natural language sentences. So, instead of using arbitrarily chosen structured sentences, we have adopted the general formal FG structures, as the basic input of the overall analysis process.

Although the COLOR-X approach is supported by automatic tools, some improvements are still possible. One of the most obvious but also rather difficult improvements is to automatize the knowledge acquisition process [35, 26, 2], which involves automatic parsing of the general natural language specifications.

4 Integrated Meta-Structures

In the previous section some approaches to acquire the important knowledge from natural language specification were presented. The most advanced approaches, that consist of a combination of the syntactic (or grammatical) as well as semantic analysis (e.g. COLOR-X), are suffering however from a mismatch problem between the different (meta-) structures involved:

- **sentence level**, i.e. structured sentences (KISS [22]), or FG [17]
- **lexicon level**, i.e. WordNet [27]
- **conceptual model level**, i.e. CPL [16]

The problem is caused by the proposed methods, which first re-structure the natural language sentences of the requirements specification in for example structured sentences, then combine these structures with the knowledge found in the lexicon to verify their correctness and finally transform these combined structures in conceptual models. It's obvious that there are two cases of mismatching structures.

There are two solutions to this mismatch problem: defining transformation rules to transform one structure into another one, or defining one general underlying structure that replaces all three existing different structures. In this paper we propose CPL as an integrating structure.

Conceptual Prototyping Language The CPL language has been developed as a specification language as close as possible to natural language, by basing it on Functional Grammar [17], but formal enough to specify the requirements of an information and communication system in a precise and unambiguous way. The formal semantics, as defined in [16], is based on predicate, modal, deontic and temporal logic. Each CPL construct is translated into some combination of these logics. The general form of a CPL specification is as follows:

Modality : [Tense :] Predication $T_1 \cdots T_n$
[(**id:** $\cdots$)]* [(**sit:** $\cdots$)]*

Modality	= **FACTUAL|MUST|NEC|PERMIT**
Tense	= **ACTION|DONE|PROSP|PERF|PRET**
Predication	= a relation between n terms $T_1 \cdots T_n$,
T_i	= a term denotes a (set of) object(s), that play specific roles.
id	= identification of the objects
sit	= situation in which this CPL specification is supposed to hold

Example: When a company has sold a car to a customer, it has to send a bill to this customer within a week.

MUST: ACTION:
send(**ag**=C in company) (**go**=bill) (**rec**=C2 in customer) (**temp**=T2 in time)
(**id:** T2 = T1 + 1*week)
(**sit: DONE:** sell(**ag**=C in company) (**go**=car)
(**rec**=C2 in customer) (**temp**=T1 in time))

In the next sections the meta-structures of the three central representations, i.e. (structured) natural language sentences, lexicon knowledge and conceptual models, are replaced by CPL specifications.

4.1 Conceptual Model in CPL

In [5, 8, 7, 10] CPL has been used as the formal underlying language for graphical conceptual models (i.e. the COLOR-X Static Object Model and the COLOR-X Event Model). General CPL structures in this approach corresponding with the modeling concepts defined in Section 2, are (classes and attributes correspond with nouns and relationships and events with verbs):

- *attribute:*
  FACTUAL: has_a(**zero** = class) (**pat** = A in attribute)
  (**id:** value_of(A) (type))
- *inheritance:*
  NEC: is_a(class_{sub}) (class_{super})
- *relationship:*
  FACTUAL: [**not:**]
  relationship(< card_1 > $\textbf{role}_1$ = class_1) $\cdots$ (< card_n > $\textbf{role}_n$ = class_n)
- *event:*
  PERMIT|MUST|NEC : [**not:**]
  event(< card_1 > **ag|fo** = class_1) $\cdots$ (< card_n > $\textbf{role}_n$ = class_n)
  [(**id:** constraint) [**and** $\cdots$ **and** (**id:** constraint)]]
  [(**sit: DONE:** event($\cdots$)
  [(**sit: PERF:** event($\cdots$)
  [**and** $\cdots$ **and** (**sit: PERF:** event($\cdots$))))]]]

4.2 Lexicon in CPL

In the lexicon the information about verbs should be stored as:

- verb($\textbf{role}_1$ = noun_1) $\cdots$ ($\textbf{role}_n$ = noun_n)

For each verb the particular roles (or semantic functions, as they are named in FG) should be defined. Although this is a difficult task, because there are many possible uses of a verb. A list of common occurrences of role-combinations can be used as a useful heuristic [17]. Table 2 shows some common occurrences.

Because FG distinguishes between semantic functions, that are important for the 'core' meaning of the verb, and satellites (like man(ner), instr(ument) and time), that give additional information, the definition of verbs is not unnecessarily complex.

Relations between concepts in the lexicon, like hyponymy (is_a), meronymy (has_a or part_of) are stored, respectively, as: [2]

[2] a concept is either a noun or a verb

Type	Roles	Example
action	agent, goal	repair
action	agent, goal, direction	bring to
action	agent, goal, source	take from
action	agent, goal, recipient	give to
process	force, direction	move to
position	positioner, loc	live in
state	zero, location	rest on

Table 2: Combination of Semantic Functions [17]

- is_a(concept_{sub}) (concept_{super})
- has_a(**zero** = noun) (**pat** = noun_{part})

The decision about which semantic functions (or role, like ag(ent), go(al), etc.) a certain noun can fulfill, is based on the *features* (like active, dynamic, telic, etc.) of the semantic function and the noun. A particular noun can only be used for a semantic function if the features of both agree to a certain degree [32, 33]. The information about the features should be included in the taxonomy structure of the lexicon.

4.3 Natural Language Sentence in CPL

Finally, we have to substitute KISS' structured sentences with CPL structures. Table 3 shows the correspondences between elements of the structured sentences and CPL concepts. We have chosen to represent the KISS structured sentences because this approach is an advanced and matured way of identifying the conceptual concepts in natural language texts (Section 3).

KISS' Structured Sentence Element	CPL Concept & Construction
subject	agent
predicate	modality and verb
direct object	goal
preposition & indirect object	semantic function or satellite
adverb	satellite
adjective	has_a(noun) (adjective)
nominal predicate	is_a(noun) (noun)

Table 3: Correspondences between Structured Sentence Elements and CPL Concepts

4.4 Example

In this section a toy example is presented in order to show the advantages of the integrated structure, as being proposed in this paper. As a lexicon we use a prototype, that is in fact an extended version of WordNet. The sentences are taken from the requirements document for a library book circulation system:

> *A member can borrow a book from the library with his pass. The user should return the book within three weeks.*

NL:	A member	can borrow	a book	from the library	with his pass
	⇓	⇓	⇓	⇓	⇓
KISS:	subject	predicate	direct object	indirect object	indirect object + attr. adjunct
	⇓	⇓	⇓	⇓	⇓
CPL:	agent	**PERMIT:** borrow	goal	source	instrument + identifier

Figure 2: Natural Language and its Structured Sentence (KISS) and CPL Equivalents

Figure 2 shows the structured sentence and CPL equivalents of a part of the library description. The CPL equivalents of the natural language sentences are:

PERMIT: ACTION: borrow
(<1> **ag** = member M) (<1> **go** = book B) (<1> **src** = library L)
(<1> **instr** = pass P) (**tmp** = time T1)

MUST: ACTION: return
(<1> **ag** = member M) (<1> **go** = book B) (<1> **rec** = library L)
(**tmp** = time T2)
    (**id:** $T2 \leq T1 + 3 * week$)
    (**sit: DONE:** borrow(<1> **ag** = member M)
      (<1> **go** = book B) (<1> **src** = library L)
      (<1> **instr** = pass P) (**tmp** = time T)
    (**id:** own(<1> **zero** = member M) (<1> **pat** = pass P)))

The process that transforms a natural language document to conceptual models is supported with knowledge from the lexicon. For example, querying WordNet about *'to borrow'* gives:

meaning	:	to get temporarily
verb frame	:	somebody borrows something from somebody

We have developed an extensional layer on top of WordNet that specifies the verb frames in two ways:

1. *semantic functions:* the roles the nouns play in a certain verb frame, like agent, goal, etc. [17]

2. *noun domains:* the verb frame for each verb is extended to include a designation of the allowable noun domains for each role to be filled. In [3, 12] the following domains are distinguished (note: many nouns occur in more than one domain):

   animate - person, institution
   human - programmer, analyst, operator
   process - program, process, algorithm
   data structure - file, record, address
   condition - completion, progress
   location - center, place, side
   measurement - amount, group, precision
   inanimate - desk, chair, book
   machine - computer, disk drive, printer
   data - information, character, document
   event - interrupt, change, overrun
   language - algebra, alphabet, grammar
   state - maximum, minimum, parity

The following resulting CPL structure is retrieved from the lexicon (Figure 3):
borrow(**ag** = human/animate) (**go** = inanimate) (**src** = human/animate).
The next step involves FG's satellites i.e. verify if there are additional satellites necessary to specify the natural language sentence in a complete way. In the example

Lexicon:	somebody	borrows	something	from	somebody
	⇓	⇓	⇓	⇓	⇓
Specific:	agent = human/animate	borrows	goal = inanimate	(from)	source = human/animate

Figure 3: Specifying WordNet's Verb Frames

sentences two possible satellites are: **instr(ument)** (i.e. *'pass'*) and **tmp (time)** (in order to express the constraint *'within three weeks'* the moment in time at which the actions take place are important). A possible decision not to include the instrumental satellite could be the implicit knowledge that any member of a library has a pass.

In [32, 33] verifications are proposed that check that the features of *'a member'* and *'human'* (i.e. human, living and individual), of *'book'* and *'inanimate'* (i.e. concrete and individual) and of *'library'* and *'animate'* (i.e. concrete) correspond. This means that according to the features defined for each concept, the combination *'a member borrows a book from a library'* is correct.

Another kind of knowledge about which the analyst decides interactively if it should be included in the final CPL representation (and thus in the conceptual model) is additional relationships. For example the knowledge, available in the lexicon, that a member is a specialization of a person might be interesting for certain applications. The decision whether or not to include such a relationship should be solely based on analysis criteria and not on implementation ones (like a reduction of the total number of lines of programming code).

The CPL structures obtained by this approach can be visualized using COLOR-X models. Figure 4 (a) and (b) show the static information that is stored about the *'borrow'* relationship, and the dynamic dependencies between the *'borrow'* and *'return'* actions, respectively.

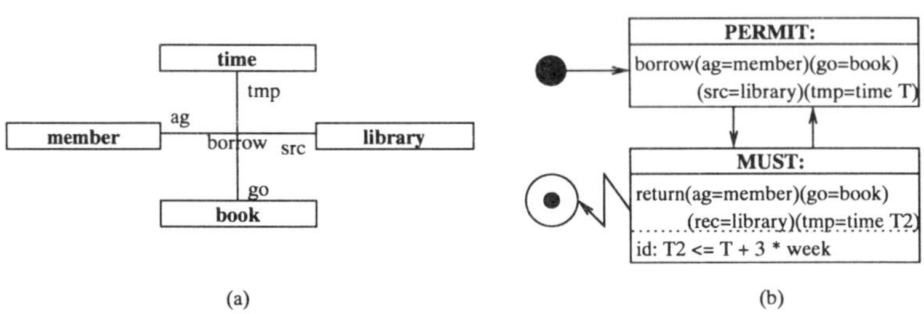

Figure 4: (a) COLOR-X Static Object Model and (b) COLOR-X Event Model

5 Future and Related Work

In this paper we have shown that all three kinds of (meta-) structures (sentence, lexicon and conceptual model) can be expressed in CPL specifications. The main advantages of having one common meta-structure is the seamless integration of information from different resources and the absence of the need for transformation rules.

At the moment we are involved in two projects that run in parallel. The first one concentrates on the use of linguistic theories and tools in the field of conceptual modeling. In the COLOR-X [5, 8, 7, 6, 10, 11] project we have defined two models which are based on CPL. The COLOR-X method involves the use of a lexicon during conceptual modeling, by re-using existing linguistic knowledge about words and constructs. The foundation of CPL on linguistics, makes natural language paraphrasing of the conceptual models possible, as a way of validating these models [36, 1]. Other validation techniques include explanation facilities [19, 20] and prototyping [15, 24].

The other project in which we participate is the KISS' project GRAMMALIZER, in which the first steps of the analysis phase (including conceptual modeling) is supported with linguistic tools. In this project the syntactic (i.e. grammatical) and semantic analysis steps mentioned in this paper are subject to automatization. An integrating structure, like CPL as proposed in the previous section, plays an central role in this automatization process.

References

[1] A. P. Ambrosio, E. Metais, and J.-N. Meunier. The Linguistic Level of the KHEOPS Case Tool. In M. Bouzeghoub and E. Metais, editors, *First International Workshop on Applications of Natural Language to Data Bases (NLDB'95)*, pages 25–39, Versailles, France, 1995. AFCET.

[2] C.A. Argila. Finding and Keeping Good Objects. *The American Programmer*, October 1994.

[3] B. Belkhouche and J. Kozma. Semantic Case Analysis of Informal Requirements. In S. Brinkkemper and F. Harmsen, editors, *Proceedings of the 4th Workshop on the Next Generation of CASE-tools*, Paris, 1993.

[4] W.J. Black. Acquisition of Conceptual Data Models from Natural Language Descriptions. In *Proceedings of the 2nd Conference of the European Chapter of the ACL*, Copenhagen, 1987.

[5] J.F.M. Burg and R.P. van de Riet. COLOR-X: Object Modeling profits from Linguistics. Technical Report IR-365, Vrije Universiteit, Amsterdam, 1994.

[6] J.F.M. Burg and R.P. van de Riet. COLOR-X Event Model: Integrated Specification of the Dynamics of Individual Objects. In M.P. Papazoglou, editor, *The Proceedings of the Fourteenth International Object-Oriented and Entity-Relationship Conference (OO-ER'95)*, number 1021 in Lecture Notes in Computer Science, pages 146–157, Gold Coast, Australia, 1995. Springer-Verlag.

[7] J.F.M. Burg and R.P. van de Riet. COLOR-X: Linguistically-based Event Modeling: A General Approach to Dynamic Modeling. In J. Iivari, K. Lyytinen, and M. Rossi, editors, *The Proceedings of the Seventh International Conference on Advanced Information System Engineering (CAiSE'95)*, number 932 in Lecture Notes in Computer Science, pages 26–39, Jyvaskyla, Finland, 1995. Springer-Verlag.

[8] J.F.M. Burg and R.P. van de Riet. COLOR-X: Object Modeling profits from Linguistics. In N.J.I. Mars, editor, *Towards Very Large Knowledge Bases: Knowledge Building & Knowledge Sharing (KB&KS'95)*, pages 204–214, Enschede, The Netherlands, 1995. IOS Press, Amsterdam.

[9] J.F.M. Burg and R.P. van de Riet. The Impact of Linguistics on Conceptual Models: Consistency and Understandability. In M. Bouzeghoub and E. Metais, editors, *First International Workshop on Applications of Natural Language to Data Bases (NLDB'95)*, pages 183–197, Versailles, France, 1995. AFCET.

[10] J.F.M. Burg and R.P. van de Riet. Syntax, Semantics and Pragmatics of COLOR-X Event Models: Specifying the Dynamics of Information and Communication Systems. Technical Report IR-392, Vrije Universiteit, Amsterdam, 1995.

[11] J.F.M. Burg and R.P. van de Riet. A Natural Language and Scenario based Approach to Requirements Engineering. In *Natuerlichsprachlicher Entwurf von Informationssystemen (NEI'96)*, Tutzing, Germany, 1996.

[12] J.F.M. Burg, R.P. van de Riet, and S.C. Chang. A data-dictionary as a lexicon: An application of linguistics in information systems. In B.Bhargava, T.Finin, and Y.Yesha, editors, *Proceedings of the 2nd International Conference on Information and Knowledge Management*, pages 114–123, 1993.

[13] P. P.-S. Chen. The Entity-Relationship Model – Toward a Unified View of Data. *ACM Transactions on Database Systems*, 1(1):9–36, 1976.

[14] P. P.-S. Chen. English Sentence Structure and Entity-Relationship Diagrams. *Information Systems*, 29:127–149, 1983.

[15] A.M. Davis. Operational Prototyping: A New Development Approach. *IEEE Software*, pages 70–78, September 1992.

[16] F.P.M. Dignum. *A Language for Modelling Knowledge Bases. Based on Linguistics, Founded in Logic*. PhD thesis, Vrije Universiteit, Amsterdam, 1989.

[17] S.C. Dik. *The Theory of Functional Grammar. Part I: The Structure of the Clause.* Floris Publications, Dordrecht, 1989.

[18] P.J.M. Frederiks, C.H.A. Koster, and Th. P. van der Weide. Object-Oriented Analysis using Informal Language. Technical Report CSI-R9516, Computing Science Institute, University of Nijmegen, December 1995.

[19] J.A. Gulla. *Deep Explanation Generation in Conceptual Modeling Environments.* PhD thesis, University of Trondheim, Trondheim, 1993.

[20] J.A. Gulla and G. Willumsen. Using Explanations to Improve the Validation of Executable Models. In C. Rolland, F. Bodart, and C. Cauvet, editors, *The Proceedings of the Fifth International Conference on Advanced Information System Engineering (CAiSE'93)*, number 685 in Lecture Notes in Computer Science, pages 118–142, Paris, France, 1993. Springer-Verlag.

[21] I. Jacobson. *Object-Oriented Software Engineering: A Use Case Approach.* Addison-Wesley, 1992.

[22] G. Kristen. *Object Orientation: The KISS-method: From Information Architecture to Information System.* Addison-Wesley, 1994.

[23] G. Levreau, E. Métais, and J-N. Meunier. Database Schema Design: A Perspective from Natural Language Techniques to Validation and View Integration. Arlington, Texas, USA, 1993.

[24] O.I. Lindland and J. Krogstie. Validating Conceptual Models by Transformational Prototyping. In C. Rolland, F. Bodart, and C. Cauvet, editors, *The Proceedings of the Fifth International Conference on Advanced Information System Engineering (CAiSE'93)*, number 685 in Lecture Notes in Computer Science, pages 165–183, Paris, France, 1993. Springer-Verlag.

[25] P. Loucopoulos and V. Karakostas. *System Requirements Engineering.* McGraw-Hill Book Company Eurpope, 1995.

[26] L. Mich and R. Garigliano. A Linguistic Approach to the Development of Object Oriented Systems using the NL System LOLITA. In E. Bertino and S. Urban, editors, *Proceedings of the International Symposium on Object-Oriented Methodologies and Systems (ISOOMS'94)*, pages 371–386, Palermo, Italy, 1994.

[27] G.A. Miller, R. Beckwith, C. Fellbaum, D. Gross, K. Miller, and R. Tengi. Five Papers on WordNet. Technical report, Cognitive Science Laboratory, Princeton University, 1993.

[28] C. Rolland and C. Proix. A Natural Language Approach for Requirements Engineering. In P. Loucopoulos, editor, *Proceedings of the 4th International Conference on Advanced Information Systems Engineering.* Springer-Verlag, Manchester, 1992.

[29] J. Rumbaugh, M. Blaha, W. Premerlani, F. Eddy, and W. Lorensen. *Object-Oriented Modeling and Design.* Prentice-Hall International, Inc., Englewood Cliffs, New Yersey, 1991.

[30] A.G. Sutcliffe, W.J. Black, and P. Loucopoulos. System Specification Semantics: Defining the Knowledge captured by Structured System Development Methods in Conceptual Models. In E.D. Falkenberg and P. Lindgreen, editors, *Information System Concepts: An In-Depth Analysis.* Elsevier Science Publisher B.V. (North-Holland), 1989.

[31] F.S.C. Tseng, A.L.P. Chen, and W-P. Yang. On Mapping Natural Language Constructs into Relational Algebra through E-R Representation. *Data and Knowledge Engineering*, 9:97–118, 1992.

[32] A.J. van der Vos and R.P. van de Riet. A First Semantic Check based on Linguistic Information for State Transition Diagrams. Technical Report IR-372, Vrije Universiteit, Amsterdam, 1994.

[33] A.J. van der Vos, R.P. van de Riet, and J.A. Gulla. Verification of Conceptual Models based on Linguistic Knowledge. In *First International Workshop on Applications of Natural Language to Data Bases (NLDB'95)*, pages 151–165, Versailles, France, 1995. AFCET.

[34] R.J. Wieringa. Requirements Engineering: Frameworks for Understanding. Technical report, Vrije Universiteit, Amsterdam, 1995.

[35] Y. Wilks and S. Nirenburg. Steps Towards Automated Knowledge Acquisition. In N.J.I. Mars, editor, *Towards Very Large Knowledge Bases: Knowledge Building & Knowledge Sharing (KB&KS'95)*, pages 97–102, Enschede, The Netherlands, 1995. IOS Press, Amsterdam.

[36] C.-H. Wu and D. Flynn. NALABA: A Natural Language Based Integrity Requirements Validation System. In *First International Workshop on Applications of Natural Language to Data Bases (NLDB'95)*, pages 167–182, Versailles, France, 1995. AFCET.

[37] N. Yonezaki. Natural Language Interface for Requirements Specification. In Y. Matsumoto and Y. Ohno, editors, *Japanese Perspectives in Software Engineering*, pages 41–76. Addison-Wesley, Singapore, 1989.

[38] E. Yourdon, K. Whitehead, J. Thomann, K. Oppel, and P. Nevermann. *Mainstream Objects: An Analysis and Design Approach for Business*. Prentice-Hall, 1995.

[39] G.P. Zarri. Knowledge Acquisition from Natural Language Documents for Large Knowledge Bases. In N.J.I. Mars, editor, *Towards Very Large Knowledge Bases: Knowledge Building & Knowledge Sharing (KB&KS'95)*, pages 103–113, Enschede, The Netherlands, 1995. IOS Press, Amsterdam.

Applications of Natural Language to Information Systems
R.P. van de Riet et al. (Eds.)
IOS Press, 1996

Paraphrasing as a Technique to Support Object-Oriented Analysis

C.F. Derksen, P.J.M. Frederiks*, Th.P. van der Weide
Department of Information Systems, University of Nijmegen
Toernooiveld 1, NL-6525 ED Nijmegen, The Netherlands
{caspard,paulf,tvdw}@cs.kun.nl

Abstract. The goal of the information analysis process is to derive the information grammar which describes the communication language within some application domain. This process involves both domain experts and system analysts. Since good communication between these two partners is essential, a proper common language should be chosen. Natural language seems to be a good candidate for this purpose.

Two essential activities of the analysis process are modeling the application domain, and validating the resulting models. In this paper the focus is on validation. We consider object-oriented analysis models and paraphrase them by sentences in natural language. The paraphrasing process is automatically supported by the Grammar Workbench using the AGFL formalism to describe the information grammar. This results in a prototype for paraphrasing analysis models.

Keywords: object-oriented analysis, natural language, information grammar, validation, paraphrasing, AGFL.

1 Introduction

In the modern way of thinking about information systems, the communication between man and machine is more and more directed towards using natural language ([25], [11]. [1]). As a consequence, the analysis process of the application domain is more directed towards the communication language within the application domain (also referred to as Universe of Discourse, or UoD for short). The goal of the analysis phase then is to derive the so-called *information grammar* ([24]) which describes this communication language. Modern analysis techniques thus are focusing on inferring the information grammar from concrete examples of communication within the application domain. An advantage of this approach is that (intermediate) results can be validated by the domain expert readily, as each intermediate result corresponds to a (partial) grammar for sentences in the language spoken in the UoD. As a result, the communication between domain expert and system analyst will also be based on natural language. Sample sentences are provided by the domain expert and processed by the system analyst, while modeling results are paraphrased to get sentences which can be validated by the domain expert. The purpose of this paper is to sketch such a paraphrasing mechanism.

*Corresponding author.

In this paper we discuss the contribution of some basic object-oriented analysis models to the information grammar. Our concern basically is with the information structure, ignoring such things as constraints on populations of this structure. This allows us to restrict the information grammar to a context-free grammar. From this grammar sample sentences can be produced automatically. This provides the opportunity for obtaining an (intermediate) description of the application domain which can be validated by the domain expert. An additional advantage of using grammars is that parsers can be generated automatically. Such a parser can be used to test the pragmatics of the future information system, i.e. it can check the way a user wants to communicate with the information system (rapid prototyping). As a result, the information grammar can be seen as an executable specification, making the information grammar comprehensible ([14]). Note that ambiguous sentences will also be detected by the parser. For some related work the reader is referred to [2, 3, 16, 22, 26]

This paper has the following structure. Section 2 contains a discussion about the usage of natural language for object-oriented analysis. Some well-known object-oriented analysis models are sketched together with a direction to obtain these models. Furthermore, the relation between information grammars and the AGFL formalism is made. In section 3 the AGFL formalism and the Grammar Workbench, are introduced. An application is shown in section 4. Section 5 contains some conclusions and suggestions for future research.

2 Object-Oriented Analysis using Grammars

This section discusses the nature of information grammars. We present how an information grammar may be derived, and its relation to object-oriented analysis models. Furthermore, a context is introduced in which these models can be paraphrased.

2.1 Underlying perspective

Almost all modern modeling techniques have as point of departure a description in natural language of the world to be modeled. This description is referred to as the *initial specification*, and is provided by so-called *informed users* (domain experts). Ideally, this initial specification is a precise specification from which system developers can derive the required information system.

Using natural language for problem specification is not new in the field of computer science. Already in the early seventies syntactic-oriented programming methods, like step-wise refinement, were introduced, see e.g. [8, 20]. The step-wise refinement method verbalizes the problem top-down using simple control structures like `IF THEN ELSE FI`. A natural language approach to information modeling is not new either. The conceptual data modeling techniques NIAM ([24, 9]) and PSM ([13, 5]) are based on such an approach. For these techniques the goal of the modeling process is to derive the grammar that governs the communication within the application domain, the so-called *information grammar*. This grammar can be depicted as an information structure diagram. The verbalization of the elements of the information structure diagram forms the base for the terminal symbols for this grammar.

A major advantage of the linguistic approach is that (intermediate) results can be validated by the informed user readily, as each intermediate result corresponds to a (partial) grammar for sentences in the language spoken in the UoD. The rationale behind the linguistic approach to information modeling is a scheme of base axioms describing the cognitive identity of domain experts and system analysts. Base axioms as such fall outside the scope of this paper, for more information see [23], [28] and [10].

2.2 Building the Information Grammar

As stated in [27] the philosophy behind a method *does* affect the way of working and the way of modeling of this method. Traditionally, three aspects of a (natural or artificial) language are distinguished: *syntax*, *semantics* and *pragmatics*. Our approach is to exploit syntactical aspects as much as possible, although some semantics may be necessary for the modeling process. The domain expert is held to be responsible for the semantic part. The way of working during the analysis phase can be divided in the following stages (for a more elaborate discussion, see [10]):

1. Collect significant information objects from the application domain.
2. Verbalize these information objects in a common language (expert language formulations).
3. Reformulate these formulation in a unifying format (reformulated expert language formulations).
4. Abstract rules and facts from reformulated expert language formulations (information grammar and population).
5. Interpret and visualize the information grammar (analysis models).
6. Paraphrase analysis models.

These stages are repeated until the paraphrasing of the formal specification (the analysis models) matches the informal specification. Stage 1 and 2 of this way of working are performed by the domain expert solo. The reformulation of the expert language formulations, stage 3, is based on interaction between analyst and domain expert. The tasks of stage 4 and 5 are performed by the analyst, who is appointed for this job mainly! Finally, the paraphrasing phase in stage 6 is performed by the system analyst and validated by the domain expert.

2.3 Object-oriented analysis models

During the modeling process sample sentences are analyzed according to several grammatical perspectives, leading to a number of abstractions of the informal specification. Each abstraction provides a specific view on the nature of the application domain, and results in a corresponding model. The models together compose the conceptual model of the UoD. The following analysis models may be distinguished in object-oriented analysis. These models have been inspired by some models of the KISS method ([19]):

1. the *(object) action involvement model.* This model describes the types of objects and actions that have been determined from the informal specification, and states which object types are involved in what action types. It is also indicated which object type is responsible for each action type.

2. the *(object) property model.* This model deals with static aspects of the application domain, by modeling *properties* of object types.

3. the *(object) life model.* This model considers the application domain from a historical perspective, and describes for each object type the *course of life* of its instances.

In this paper we restrict ourselves to these models. On an ad hoc basis, we will also pay some attention to other aspects of object-orientation (such as specialization and generalization). For more details, see [10].

2.4 Concrete Grammars versus Abstract Grammars

As pointed out in section 2.1 our point of departure is a specification in natural language. This specification can be seen as an instance of a *concrete language*, e.g. the English language. The underlying deep structure is to be captured by an *abstract grammar* ([21]). In information system terminology this abstract grammar is referred to as the information grammar. The derivation of the information grammar from a concrete grammar is referred to as *abstraction.* Given a concrete and abstract grammar, sample sentences in concrete language can be *transduced* to sentences in the abstract language and vice versa. We will term the reverse transduction as *ornamenting.* In best case these transductions are performed automatically. However, still a lot of work has to be done to achieve such an ideal situation.

The restricted form of information grammars (corresponding to the analysis models, see previous section) can be expressed by context-free grammars. In the field of information modeling it is customary to *visualize* information grammars graphically e.g. ER ([4]), NIAM ([24]) and PSM ([15]). Graphical representations are also referred to as analysis models. System analysts and designers are familiar with these kind of models. However, domain experts may have difficulties in understanding those models. This causes a gap between system analyst and domain expert. For validation purposes the analysis models may be *paraphrased*, leading to a description in natural language (see figure 1). In section 4 fragments of an information grammar are presented in the AGFL formalism.

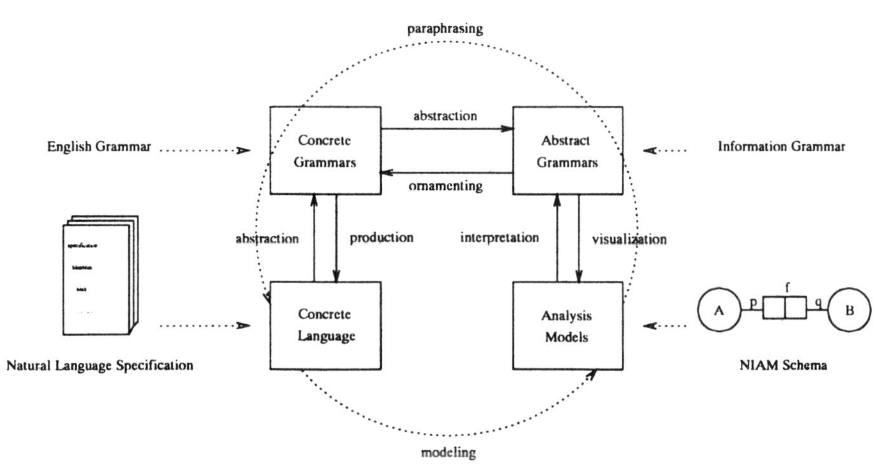

Figure 1: Using grammars in the analysis phase

3 A Short Introduction to AGFL

Originally, the AGFL (Affix Grammars over Finite Lattices) formalism ([17]) has been developed for the description of natural languages. In this section a brief introduction to the AGFL formalism and its implementation is given.

3.1 The AGFL formalism

Affix Grammars are a family of two-level grammars where the first level consists of context-free *production rules* extended with *affixes* and the second level defines the *domains* of these affixes. AGFLs are a particularly simple form of Affix Grammars, in which restricted context-free *affix rules* generate finite domains for each affix.

In order to introduce AGFL we need some terminology. An affix rule consists of a *nonterminal affix* followed by a double colon followed by a series of *affix alternatives* separated with semicolons followed by a point. An affix alternative consists of either a *terminal affix* or a nonterminal affix.

A production rule consists of a *nonterminal* followed by a single colon followed by a series of *alternatives* again separated with semicolons and followed by a point. An alternative consists of a possibly empty series of *members* separated with commas. A member is either a nonterminal or a terminal enclosed in quotes. A nonterminal consists of a *head* and an optional *display.* A display is a series of *affix expressions* separated with commas and enclosed in braces. An affix expression is either a nonterminal affix or a concrete set of terminal affixes.

The following grammar shows two affix rules with two alternatives each and two production rules with one alternative each.

```
rel  :: I; R.
prod :: B; P.

TO PRODUCE (prod, R):
  PRODUCER (prod), "in the role of", PRODUCER, "produces", RECORDING.
TO PRODUCE (prod, I):
  RECORDING, "is produced by", PRODUCER (prod), "in the role of", PRODUCER.
```

Nonterminal `TO PRODUCE (prod, R)` consists of a head `TO PRODUCE` and display `(prod, R)`.

Given some *start* nonterminal, sentences are produced by repeatedly replacing a nonterminal with one of its alternatives. In AGFL, affixes are used for enforcing agreement between parts of speech. The *consistent substitution rule* demands that in an alternative all occurrences of the same affix must obtain the same value. This value should be a nonempty set of terminal affixes for which rewriting succeeds. Using affixes in order to express various constraints such as uniqueness, cardinality, etcetera and representing object hierarchies with affix rules is still an interesting subject of investigation.

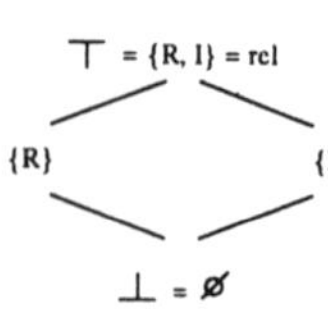

Figure 2: The lattice of values for the affix `rel`

In AGFL, affix rules determine power-set lattices over over the affix domains with intersection as only operation. The lattice for the affix `rel` is shown in figure 2. The top element `rel` of the lattice can be seen as the union of all possibilities (the values may be `R` or `I` or or their combination). During rewriting the set of possible values of an affix may be narrowed down to a smaller set by intersection with other affixes. However, an affix may not assume the empty set, the bottom element of the lattice, as value.

The generative power of AGFLs does not exceed the power of context-free grammars. However, AGFLs have better descriptive properties and allow quite efficient implementation. In practice, the limitations imposed on AGFL do not turn out to be to restrictive for describing natural languages ([18]).

3.2 The AGFL system

The AGFL system consists of a collection of software systems for natural language processing and grammar development. Here, we will describe the Grammar Workbench (GWB) and the GEN parser generator.

The Grammar Workbench is an environment for the development of grammars in the AGFL formalism. Its purposes are to allow the user to edit grammars, to perform consistency checks on a grammar, to compute grammar properties, to assist in performing grammar transformations and to generate example sentences. In our experiment as described in section 4 we are particularly interested in the GWBs capability to generate example sentences from a grammar in AGFL. The ideas behind the Grammar Workbench and its implementation are elaborated in [7, 6].

The GEN parser generator[1] generates a parser for a possibly ambiguous or left recursive grammar in the AGFL formalism. Real life applications require a grammar to use large lexical databases (*lexica*) in an efficient way. Therefore, GEN optionally invokes its integrated lexicon system which compresses a lexicon and builds an index for fast access. During lexical analysis the parsers generated by GEN try to identify the categories of each word in an input sentence in the lexicon. If lexical analysis succeeds, the parser will generate all parse trees according to the grammar. These parse trees can be translated (transduced) to other representations depending on the application domain. For instance, one could experiment with transduction of queries in restricted natural language to expressions in the query language LISA-D ([12]). However, at this moment transduction is still under implementation.

4 An Elaborated Example

In this section we first present the information grammar of the so-called music example ([10]) as an AGFL grammar. Then we demonstrate how this is paraphrased using the Grammar Workbench. Finally we give a short introduction to the parser generator.

The music example is described by the following informal specification:

> *This example deals with persons subscribing for the academy of music. The names and birth dates of persons are administrated. A person who can play an instrument (vocals are also an instrument) can set up a band. Both bands and instruments have names. After a band has been set up, persons may join this band. Persons can also leave a band. A song is written by one or more persons. Each song has associated a song name. Several bands have*

[1]The GEN parser generator and its description can be obtained at the AGFL www-site at `http://www.cs.kun.nl/agfl/`

the opportunity to record some of these songs. Some of these bands will produce these recordings themselves or with help of one or more persons. For each recording a date and a tape number is assigned. A band does not exist any more when it is disbanded. Persons who unsubscribe the academy are not considered anymore.

In this example the following object types, represented as nonterminals, can be distinguished:

```
BAND, INSTRUMENT, PERSON, RECORDING, SONG
```

Furthermore, we have the following action types:

```
TO DISBAND, TO JOIN, TO LEAVE, TO PLAY, TO PRODUCE, TO RECORD,
TO SET UP, TO SUBSCRIBE, TO UNSUBSCRIBE, TO WRITE
```

Since more than one object type can perform the action type TO PRODUCE, i.e. PERSON and BAND, a generalization of these object types is introduced and called PRODUCER. Furthermore, the course life of object type PERSON indicates a specialization MUSICIAN in a natural way (see [10]). The nonterminal TO BE is used to summarize all generalizations and specializations (object hierarchy):

```
TO BE: BAND, "is a producer.", PERSON, "is a producer.",
       MUSICIAN, "is a person.".
```

Since the action type TO PRODUCE may be performed by object types BAND and PERSON, both being producers, we introduce the following affix rule:

```
prod :: B ; P.
```

Next we consider the action involvement grammar which describes the relation between object types and action types. For example the active sentence, *band records song*, has as object types *band* and *song*, related by action type *to record*. Object type *band* is *responsible* for the execution of action type *to record* whereas object type *song* is *involved* in that action type. The sample sentence also can be formulated in a passive way, i.e. *song is recorded by band*. Using both active and passive sentences for paraphrasing results in the generation of better readable texts.

Before the action involvement grammar is presented action type TO PRODUCE will be discussed in some more detail. There are two variants, the active formulation (coded as R) and the passive formulation (coded as I). These two variants are expressed in another affix rule (see also section 3):

```
rel :: I ; R.
```

Augmenting action type TO PRODUCE with affixes prod and rel results in the following production rules:

```
TO PRODUCE (prod, R):
  PRODUCER(prod), ", in the role of", PRODUCER, "produces", RECORDING.
TO PRODUCE (prod, I):
  RECORDING, "is produced by", PRODUCER(prod), ", in the role of", PRODUCER.
```

The rest of the action involvement grammar is described in the following way:

```
TO DISBAND: BAND, "disbands".

TO JOIN (R): MUSICIAN, "joins", BAND.
TO JOIN (I): BAND, "is joined by", MUSICIAN.

TO LEAVE (R): MUSICIAN, "leaves", BAND.
TO LEAVE (I): BAND, "is left by", MUSICIAN.

TO PLAY (R): PERSON, "plays", INSTRUMENT.
TO PLAY (I): INSTRUMENT, "is played by", PERSON.

TO RECORD (R): BAND, "records", SONG.
TO RECORD (I): SONG, "is recorded by", BAND.

TO SET UP (R): MUSICIAN, "sets up", BAND.
TO SET UP (I): BAND, "is set up by", MUSICIAN.

TO SUBSCRIBE: PERSON, "subscribes".

TO UNSUBSCRIBE: PERSON, "unsubscribes".

TO WRITE (R): PERSON, "writes", SONG.
TO WRITE (I): SONG, "is written by", PERSON.
```

From the music example the following properties are recognized, encoded via the label types:

```
B_NAME, I_NAME, P_NAME, B_DATE, R_DATE, TAPE_NR, S_NAME
```

The relation between the object types and their properties is described by the object property grammar. The nonterminal `TO HAVE` is used to summarize all static aspects of the UoD:

```
TO HAVE: BAND, "has band name", B_NAME, ".",
         INSTRUMENT, "has instrument name", I_NAME, ".",
         PERSON, "has person name", P_NAME, ".",
         PERSON, "has birth date", B_DATE, ".",
         RECORDING, "has recording date", R_DATE, ".",
         RECORDING, "has tape number", TAPE_NR, ".",
         SONG, "has song name", S_NAME, ".".
```

Object types can be responsible for, and involved in several action types. The order in which action types may be performed by an object type is expressed by the life grammar. The course of life of object type `BAND` is expressed by the nonterminal `LIFE OF BAND`:

```
LIFE OF BAND: TO SET UP (rel) , ". Then", C_ONE, ". Then", TO DISBAND, ".".
```

The symbol `C_ONE` is an auxiliary nonterminal, refined as follows:

```
C_ONE: "repeatedly", TO RECORD (R), "or", TO JOIN (I), "or",
                     TO LEAVE (I), "or", TO PRODUCE (B,R).
```

Auxiliary symbols result from the translation of the control structures, such as *selection* and *iteration*, that are used to affect the order in which action types can occur in the course of life of object types. The symbol `C_ONE` results from an *iteration-selection* symbol. For more details the reader is referred to [10]. The rest of the life model is presented without discussion:

```
LIFE OF INSTRUMENT: C_TWO, ".".
C_TWO: "repeatedly", TO PLAY (I).

LIFE OF PERSON: TO SUBSCRIBE , ". Then", C_THREE,
                ". Then", TO UNSUBSCRIBE , "." , PERSON ACTS AS MUSICIAN.
C_THREE: "repeatedly", TO WRITE (R), "or person acts as musician or",
                       TO PRODUCE (P,R).
PERSON ACTS AS MUSICIAN: "person acts as musician means" , TO PLAY (rel) ,
                         ". Then", C_FOUR, ".".
C_FOUR: "repeatedly", TO SET UP (R), "or", TO JOIN (R), "or", TO LEAVE (R).

LIFE OF RECORDING: TO RECORD (rel), ". Then", C_FIVE, ".".
C_FIVE: "repeatedly", TO PRODUCE (prod, rel).

LIFE OF SONG: TO WRITE (rel), ". Then", C_SIX, ".".
C_SIX: "repeatedly", TO RECORD (rel).
```

The action grammar, property grammar, life grammar and generalization/specializations together compose the information grammar expressed by the start symbol START via the following rule:

```
START: LIFE OF BAND, LIFE OF PERSON, LIFE OF RECORDING,
       LIFE OF SONG, LIFE OF INSTRUMENT,
       TO HAVE,
       TO BE.
```

The object types are verbalized as follows for this example:

```
BAND: "band".
INSTRUMENT: "instrument".
PERSON: "person".
RECORDING: "recording of", SONG, "recorded by", BAND.
SONG: "song".
PRODUCER: "producer".
MUSICIAN: "musician".
```

Note the special verbalization rule for RECORDING. The reason is that RECORDING is a gerund, i.e. RECORDING is an objectified action type ([10]).

The following nonterminals need further specification:

```
PRODUCER (B): BAND.
PRODUCER (P): PERSON.
```

Finally, we summarize all label instances encountered in the informal specification. In our example no instances can be found. For this example the following instances are added:

```
B_NAME: "The Rolling Stones".
I_NAME: "guitar".
P_NAME: "Keith Richards".
B_DATE: "18 December 1943".
R_DATE: "25 May 1995".
S_NAME: "Street Fighting Man".
TAPE_NR: "11".
```

The label instances can be used to generate fancier sample sentences. From this resulting information grammar, GWB (randomly) generated the following description:

```
band is set up by musician . Then repeatedly band records song or band is
joined by musician or band is left by musician or band , in the role of
producer produces recording of song recorded by band . Then band disbands .

person subscribes . Then repeatedly person writes song or person acts as
musician or person in the role of producer produces recording of song recorded
by band . Then person unsubscribes . person acts as musician means person
plays instrument . Then repeatedly musician sets up band or musician joins
band or musician leaves band .

band records song . Then repeatedly recording of song recorded by band is
produced by band , in the role of producer .

song is written by person . Then repeatedly song is recorded by band .

repeatedly instrument is played by person .

band has band name The Rolling Stones . instrument has instrument name
guitar . person has person name Keith Richards . person has birth date
18 December 1943 . recording of song by band has recording date 25
May 1995 . recording of song by band has tape number 11 . song has
song name Street Fighting Man .

band is a producer. person is a producer. musician is a person.
```

Note that the readability of these generated sentences is not yet optimal and should be improved. However, this example demonstrates the power of a rather simple transduction mechanism.

A second way of validating the information grammar is to generate a parser for this grammar using the parser generator (GEN). With this parser the pragmatics of the information grammar can be tested. In order to be able to accept new person names and band names, the rules for MUSICIAN and BAND are modified as follows:

```
MUSICIAN: PROPER NAME.
BAND: PROPER NAME.

PROPER NAME: $MATCH("[A-Z][a-z]*"), [PROPER NAME].
```

Applying GEN to this simple grammar leads to a parser that allows sentences like:

```
Paul joins The Rolling Stones
```

For this sentence the parser will generate the following parse tree, augmented with some statistics:

```
parsing 1       (0.002 sec.)

START
  TO JOIN(RESP)
    MUSICIAN
      PROPER NAME
        "Paul"
    "joins"
    BAND
      "The Rolling Stones"

printing time was:       (0.010 sec.)

all:     1       (prescan: 0.011 s., parsing: 0.003 s., printing: 0.010 s. )
```

5 Conclusions and Future Research

In this paper we have discussed the role of information grammars for information modeling. Information grammars have been used for (1) describing the structure of the information system (2) describing the communication within the UoD (3) validating the information modeling process. The focus has been on the validation part and applied for object-oriented analysis models.

An implementation of an information grammar has been presented. Furthermore, a small example of testing the pragmatics of an information grammar has been shortly described.

Validation of the information modeling process is worthwhile for future research. In this paper paraphrasing has been used for structural aspects. The AGFL formalism and system seem to be a promising way to achieve more experience in paraphrasing constraints on populations of analysis models.

Acknowledgment

The authors would like to thank Kees Koster for fruitful discussions on the subject of using two-level context-free grammars for paraphrasing information models.

References

[1] J.A. Bubenko. Information System Methodologies - A Research View. In T.W. Olle, H.G. Sol, and A.A. Verrijn-Stuart, editors, *Information Systems Design Methodologies: Improving the Practice*, pages 289–318. North-Holland, Amsterdam, The Netherlands, 1986.

[2] E. Buchholz, H. Cyriaks, A. Düsterhöft, H. Mehlan, and B. Thalheim. Applying a Natural Language Dialogue Tool for Designing Databases. In *Proceedings of the First Workshop on Applications of Natural Language to Databases (NLDB'95)*, pages 119–133, Versailles, France, June 1995.

[3] J.F.M. Burg and R.P. van de Riet. The Impact of Linguistics on Conceptual Models: Consistency and Understandability. In *Proceedings of the First Workshop on Applications of Natural Language to Databases (NLDB'95)*, pages 183–197, Versailles, France, June 1995.

[4] P.P. Chen. The Entity-Relationship Model: Toward a Unified View of Data. *ACM Transactions on Database Systems*, 1(1):9–36, March 1976.

[5] M.A. Collignon and Th.P. van der Weide. An Information Analysis Method Based on PSM. In G.M. Nijssen, editor, *Proceedings of NIAM-ISDM*. NIAM-GUIDE, September 1993. pp. 22.

[6] C. Dekkers, C.H.A. Koster, M.-J. Nederhof, and A. van Zwol. Manual for Grammar WorkBench Version 1.5. Technical Report 92-14, Department of Computer Science, University of Nijmegen, Nijmegen, The Netherlands, July 1992.

[7] C. Dekkers, C.H.A. Koster, M.-J. Nederhof, and A. van Zwol. The Grammar Workbench: A First Step towards Lingware Engineering. In *Proceedings of the second Twente Workshop on Language Technology, Memoranda Informatica 92-29*, pages 103–115, Enschede, The Netherlands, April 1992. University of Twente.

[8] E. W. Dijkstra. *A Discipline of Programming*. Prentice-Hall, Englewood Cliffs, New Jersey, 1976.

[9] L. Dunn and M. Orlowska. A Natural Language Interpreter for the Construction of Conceptual Schemas. In B. Steinholz, A. Sølvberg, and L. Bergman, editors, *Proceedings of the Second Nordic Conference CAiSE'90 on Advanced Information Systems Engineering*, volume 436 of *Lecture Notes in Computer Science*, pages 175–194, Stockholm, Sweden, 1990. Springer-Verlag.

[10] P.J.M. Frederiks, C.H.A. Koster, and Th.P. van der Weide. Object-Oriented Analysis using Informal Language. Technical Report CSI-R9516, Computing Science Institute, University of Nijmegen, Nijmegen, The Netherlands, December 1995.

[11] P.J.M. Frederiks and Th.P. van der Weide. From a File-Oriented View to an Object-Oriented View. Technical Report CSI-R9601, Computing Science Institute, University of Nijmegen, Nijmegen, The Netherlands, January 1996.

[12] A.H.M. ter Hofstede, H.A. Proper, and Th.P. van der Weide. Formal definition of a conceptual language for the description and manipulation of information models. *Information Systems*, 18(7):489–523, October 1993.

[13] A.H.M. ter Hofstede, H.A. Proper, and Th.P. van der Weide. Grammar Based Information Modelling. Technical Report CSI-R9414, Submitted for publication, Computing Science Institute, University of Nijmegen, Nijmegen, The Netherlands, October 1994.

[14] A.H.M. ter Hofstede and Th.P. van der Weide. Formalisation of techniques: chopping down the methodology jungle. *Information and Software Technology*, 34(1):57–65, January 1992.

[15] A.H.M. ter Hofstede and Th.P. van der Weide. Expressiveness in conceptual data modelling. *Data & Knowledge Engineering*, 10(1):65–100, February 1993.

[16] P. Johannesson. Supporting Schema Integration by Linguistic Instruments. In *Proceedings of the First Workshop on Applications of Natural Language to Databases (NLDB'95)*, pages 41–56, Versailles, France, June 1995.

[17] C.H.A. Koster. Affix Grammars for Natural Languages. In H. Alblas and B. Melichar, editors, *Attribute Grammars, Applications and Systems*, volume 545 of *Lecture Notes in Computer Science*, pages 469–484, Berlin, Germany, 1991. Springer-Verlag.

[18] C.H.A. Koster, and E. Oltmans (Eds.). Proceedings of the first AGFL Workshop. Technical Report CSI-R9604, Computing Science Institute, University of Nijmegen, Nijmegen, The Netherlands, January 1996.

[19] G. Kristen. *Object Orientation, the KISS Method: From Information Architecture to Information System.* Addison-Wesley, Reading, Massachusetts, 1994.

[20] L.G.L.T. Meertens. Program text and program structure. In P.G. Hibbard, S.A. Schuman, editor, *Constructing quality software*, pages 271–283, Amsterdam, May 1978. North-Holland. IFIP WG 2.1/WG 2.4 Working Conference, Novosibirsk.

[21] B. Meyer. *Introduction to the Theory of Programming Languages.* Prentice-Hall, Englewood Cliffs, New Jersey, 1990.

[22] L. Mich and R. Garigliano. A Linguistic Approach to the Development of Object Oriented Systems using the NL System LOLITA. In E. Bertino and S. Urban, editors, *Proceedings of the International Symposium, ISOOMS '94: Object-Oriented Methodologies and Systems*, volume 858 of *Lecture Notes in Computer Science*, pages 371–386, Palermo, Italy, September 1994. Springer-Verlag.

[23] G.M. Nijssen. An Axiom and Architecture for Information Systems. In E. D. Falkenberg and P. Lindgreen, editors, *Information System Concepts: An In-depth Analysis*, pages 157–175. North-Holland/IFIP, Amsterdam, The Netherlands, 1989.

[24] G.M. Nijssen and T.A. Halpin. *Conceptual Schema and Relational Database Design: a fact oriented approach.* Prentice-Hall, Sydney, Australia, 1989.

[25] J. Preece, H. Sharp, D. Benyon, S. Holland, and T. Carey. *Human Computer Interaction.* Addison-Wesley, Reading, Massachusetts, 1994.

[26] C. Rolland and C. Proix. A Natural Language Approach For Requirements Engineering. In P. Loucopoulos, editor, *Proceedings of the Fourth International Conference CAiSE'92 on Advanced Information Systems Engineering*, volume 593 of *Lecture Notes in Computer Science*, pages 257–277, Manchester, United Kingdom, 1992. Springer-Verlag.

[27] G.M. Wijers. *Modelling Support in Information Systems Development.* PhD thesis, Delft University of Technology, Delft, The Netherlands, 1991.

[28] J.J.V.R. Wintraecken. *The NIAM Information Analysis Method: Theory and Practice.* Kluwer, Deventer, The Netherlands, 1990.

Applications of Natural Language to Information Systems
R.P. van de Riet et al. (Eds.)
IOS Press, 1996

Exploring Fact Verbalisations for Conceptual Query Formulation

A.H.M. ter Hofstede[1], H.A. Proper[2,3] and Th.P. van der Weide[4]

Abstract. An increasing number of conceptual modelling techniques use verbalisation of sample data to derive a model for the given universe of discourse (the problem domain). The underlying assumption is that by elaborate verbalisation of samples taken from the universe of discourse one can elicit an overview of the concepts relevant for the universe of discourse and their interrelationships. In each of these approaches, information modelling is considered as a process leading to some form of an information grammar that describes the expert language; the language used to communicate in the universe of discourse.

In this article we start by discussing a mechanism to support these verbalisations and associated information grammar. We then show how to mine the richness of the verbalisations in the context of a conceptual query language. It is shown how these verbalisations lead to formulations that closely resemble the expert language.

1 Introduction

When developing an information system using a conceptual modelling approach, usually the first task is to derive a complete model of the underlying universe of discourse. A wide range of modern conceptual modelling techniques initiate this task by verbalising sample forms, cases, etc. taken from the universe of discourse. This verbalisation process is usually conducted in close cooperation with domain experts. Examples of such approaches are the ER variation discussed in [6], NIAM and Object-Role Modelling (ORM) ([10]), OMT ([16]), and the KISS method ([14]).

In recent years, research has been conducted where principles from linguistics are applied to improve the underlying theoretic foundations of these verbalisation based approaches ([9], [7], [6]). The underlying assumption is that by elaborate verbalisation of the samples from the universe of discourse, a complete overview of the structure and

[1]Department of Computer Science, The University of Queensland, Brisbane, Australia 4072, arthur@cs.uq.edu.au.

[2]Cooperative Information Systems Research Centre, Faculty of Information Technology, Queensland University of Technology, GPO Box 2434, Brisbane, 4001 Australia, erikp@icis.qut.edu.au, http://www.icis.qut.edu.au/~erikp/.

[3]Research Discovery Unit, Research Data Network Cooperative Research Centre, The University of Queensland, Level 7, Gehrmann Laboratories, Brisbane, 4072 Australia, http://www.dstc.edu.au/RDU/.

[4]Computing Science Institute, University of Nijmegen, Toernooiveld, 6525 ED Nijmegen, The Netherlands, tvdw@cs.kun.nl, http://www.sci.kun.nl/afdis/persons/tvdw/tvdw.html.

rules in the universe of discourse can be obtained. The verbalisations resulting from this initial step are consequently used as input for the actual design of the conceptual model.

In this article we only focus on information modelling aspects of conceptual modelling. Therefore, we use verbalisations to derive the so called *information model*. In the next section we argue that an information model essentially provides a crude grammar of the language spoken by the communication partners in the universe of discourse (the expert language). The challenge presented in this article is to re-use the verbalisations in the formulations of queries, thus bringing the resulting query language closer to the language of the users.

This challenge was born out of frustration with the formulation of queries in SQL. After all the trouble modellers and users have gone through in verbalising samples from the universe of discourse, it comes as an anti-climax if users (and database administrators) still have to use SQL to formulate queries, and even more, have to refer to the actual tables to access the information. This frustration has fueled the development of so-called *conceptual query languages* such as RIDL ([15]) and LISA-D ([11]).

The focus of this paper is both on a discussion of verbalisation of samples provided during the analyses phase, as well as on the application of these verbalisations in the context of a conceptual query language. The structure of the paper is as follows. In section 2, the basic philosophy of verbalisation based modelling techniques is addressed, with a special focus on Object-Role Modelling (ORM). Section 3 then discusses how an information grammar, and associated query language, is derived from these verbalisations. This is followed in section 4 by a brief discussion of a way to support users in query formulation processes, and the use of such a conceptual query language as a feedback mechanism for natural language query interfaces. For a more elaborate, and formal, treatment of the ideas discussed in this paper, refer to [12].

2 Fact Verbalisation as a Basic Philosophy

The point of departure for Object Role Modelling (ORM) is a description of the communication in the universe of discourse in terms of a set of sample sentences ([10]). The effect is that an information system does not represent the objects of the real world but rather the *facts* known about these objects. The facts themselves are composed of references to these objects. This is what earned ORM the predicate *fact oriented modelling*. Objects are referenced by their properties. A fundamental principle of ORM is therefore *fact orientation*, stating that each state of a universe of discourse can be fully described (characterised) by facts. From these facts the fact types (in ER terminology: relationship types) can be derived.

An important issue for information modelling is the balance between completeness and the absence of ambiguities and redundancy. Therefore, samples need to be restricted to what is referred to as *ORM Normalform*. In [10], this normal form and its rationale is exposed in full detail. The restriction to normal form enforces the use of elementary sentences and requires values to be fully typed. As a result, each of these elementary sentences represents a valid sentence, a *fact formulation*, in the expert language; albeit in a rather awkward style. The resulting sets of (normalised) sentences describe a restricted subset of the expert language. This language is referred to as the *normalised infor-*

mation language. The conceptual schema of the universe of discourse can be regarded as a crude grammar of this latter language. This entails the following language inclusions: normalised information language $\subseteq$ expert language $\subseteq$ natural language. At present, the existing commercial ORM CASE-Tool InfoModeler is able to take sentences of the normalised format as input and convert this to a first draft of the conceptual schema ([3]).

In our view, two of the remaining research challenges:

1. Build tools to aid humans in the verbalisation of facts from the universe of discourse in ORM Normalform. Such a tool could use its linguistic knowledge to propose possible normal forms. Promising results in this direction can be found in e.g. [9] [7], and [6].
2. Enhance the conceptual schema modelling language with constructs that allow for alternative, and more natural, verbalisations of facts to enrich query (and result) formulation.

This article is concerned with the second challenge. We will provide a mechanism that allows us to generate alternative and more natural verbalisations (with preferences) of a single (deep structure) fact. Normally, a conceptual query language is only able to approximate the *normalised information language* in its naturalness. Using alternative verbalisations we will be able to better approximate the *expert language*. This richer language is called the *information language*, and its underlying grammar the *information grammar*. With this language we would have:

normalised information language $\subseteq$ information language $\subseteq$ expert language $\subseteq$ natural language

Simply allowing any question that can be formulated in the expert language as a query would introduce interpretation problems due to the inherent ambiguity of natural language. Therefore, our extensions are focussed on a controlled way to do this without introducing a mechanism that is prone to ambiguity. In a later section we briefly discuss the idea of building a natural language query interface that takes a query formulated in the expert language and tries to find all possible interpretations of this query in terms of queries formulated in the information language. These interpretations can then be shown to the user; leading to a natural dialogue between users and the information system.

The query language that is derived from the information language is a refinement of the existing conceptual query language LISA-D ([11]. The original version of LISA-D was strictly based on the *normalised information language*. The information grammar, which forms the base of the enriched LISA-D, is built from a lexicon and a set of grammar rules. Both the lexicon and grammar rules consist of application dependent and application independent parts.

3 The Information Language

From the sample sentences which result from the analysis phase, the verbalisation and denotation of instances can be derived as well. The resulting verbose representation of instances can be used by the information system in user dialogues. Most importantly, query formulations may benefit by improved instance denotation. Update of instances, as well as presentation of query results, can both be improved using an elegant verbalisation mechanism. In addition, sample instances may be verbalised and shown to the user as a means to validate models (see e.g. [8]).

3.1 Verbalisation in ORM schemas

Before discussing the basic verbalisation functions for an ORM schema, we first introduce our running example. In figure 1, the information model of a presidential database is depicted. As ORM and its notation has now been widely published ([10]) we refrain from a detailed explanation.

Any ORM information model contains two key components: *types* ($\mathcal{TP}$) and *roles* ($\mathcal{RO}$). Types come in two important flavours: *object types* and *fact types.* Each fact type has associated (or can bee seen to consist of) a set of roles from $\mathcal{RO}$. The two type flavours possibly overlap as the type Marriage illustrates. This is an example of an *objectified fact type.* All types in an ORM schema have a name, which is recorded by the function $\text{ONm} : \mathcal{TP} \rightarrow \mathcal{NM}$, where $\mathcal{NM}$ is a set of names. Roles also receive a name of their own. This name is referred to as the *participation* name. They are provided by the function $\text{PNm} : \mathcal{RO} \rightarrow \mathcal{NM}$. Roles of different fact types may have identical participation names. However, two roles of the same fact type must have different participation names. Roles ($\mathcal{RO}$) may also have a *reverse participation name,* $\text{RNm} : \mathcal{RO} \rightarrow \mathcal{NM}$ which verbalises the decomposition of the fact type into the components involved. As an example, consider figure 2. There we have: $\mathcal{TP} = \{A, B, C, f\}$, and $\text{Roles} = \{p, q, r\}$. This is a fragment from the presidential database model, with the following names:

$\text{ONm}(A)$ = Person	$\text{PNm}(p)$ = with	$\text{RNm}(q)$ = obtained by
$\text{ONm}(B)$ = Nr of Voters	$\text{PNm}(q)$ = in	$\text{RNm}(q)$ = with
$\text{ONm}(C)$ = Election	$\text{PNm}(r)$ = leading to	$\text{RNm}(q)$ = obtained in
$\text{ONm}(f)$ = Election results		

Participation names are usually omitted from schema diagrams. The actual schema diagrams usually feature the fact verbalisations that follow from the sample verbalisations. These verbalisations correspond to mix-fix predicate symbols. For instance, the verbalisation: The person with name 'Eisenhower D.D.' has the nr of voters 10000 in the Election '55' has as underlying mix-fix predicate: ... has ... in ... . These mix-fix predicate symbols are captured formally by the relationship: $\text{MFix} \subseteq \mathcal{NM}^{+} \times \mathcal{RO}^{+} \times \{\texttt{Short}, \texttt{Possesive}\}$.

There are two forms of fact verbalisations. The **Short** form is used for the verbalisation without possessive forms. For instance, $\text{MFix}([\text{has, in}], [p, q, r], \texttt{Short})$ is a short form verbalisation for the fact type in figure 2. which with proper object type names filled in leads to: Person has nr of voters in election. The second form allows us to formulate facts in the **Possesive** format. An example would be be: $\text{MFix}([\text{who has a, in an}], [p, q, r], \texttt{Possesive})$, which would lead to (with proper articles added): A person who has a nr of voters in an election. Mix-fix verbalisations for an n-ary fact type are always given as $n-1$ (non-empty) strings with 'holes' (the '...') in which instance denotations can be substituted. So we always have: $\text{MFix}([\alpha_1, \ldots, \alpha_m], [p_1, \ldots, p_n], x) \Rightarrow m = n - 1$ making them mix-fixed infix verbalisations. This means that a formulation like President 'Clinton' and Person 'Hillary' are married

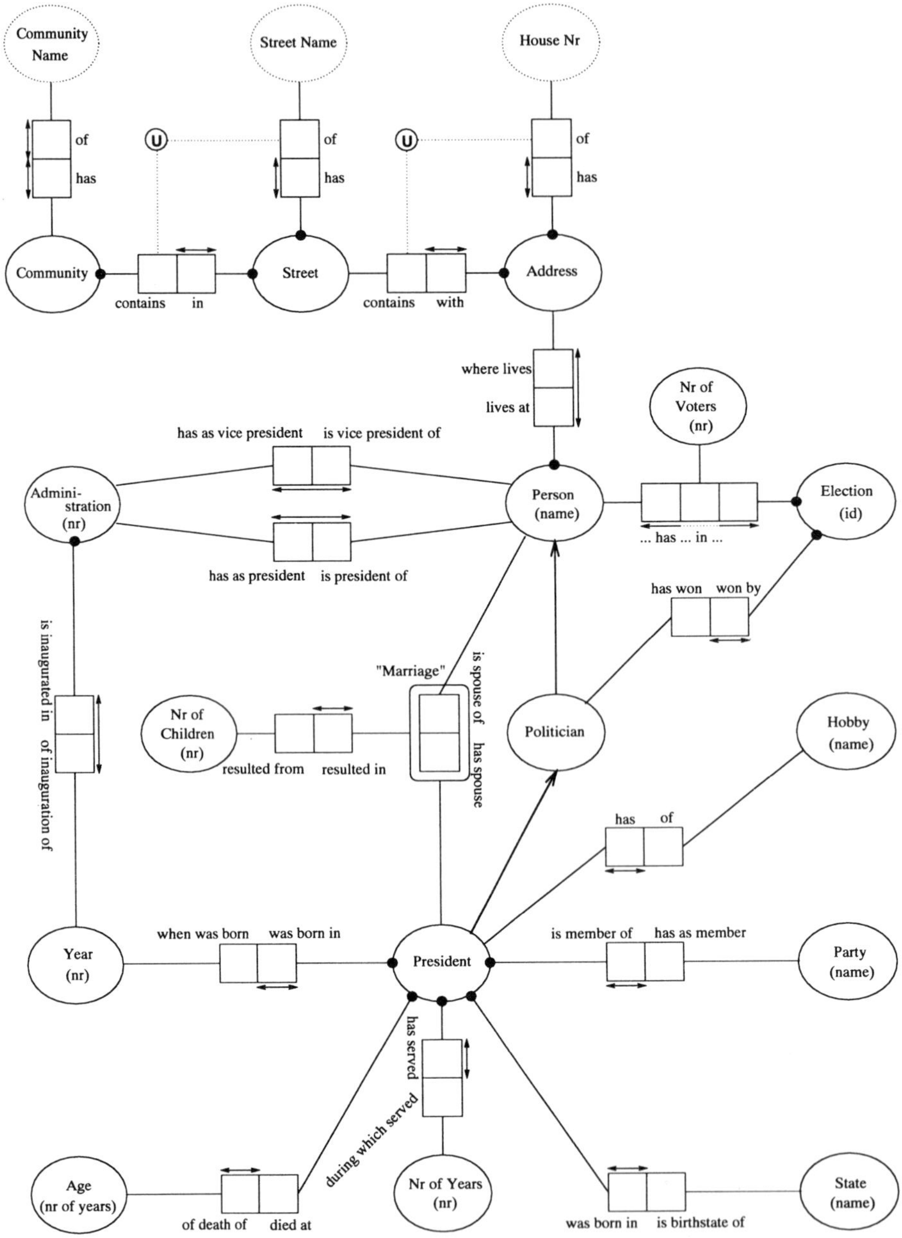

Figure 1: The presidential database information model

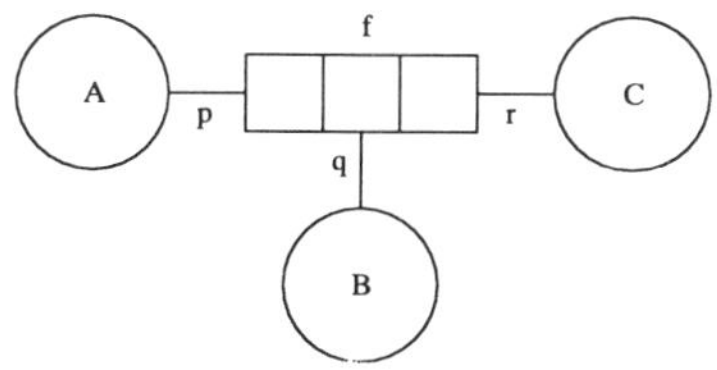

Figure 2: Example model before naming

is not allowed, since the underlying mix-fix predicate is: ... and ... are married which consist of 2 holes and 2 strings (should be 1). The reason for this limitation is that the mix-fix predicate verbalisations are not intended as a verbalisation mechanism for instances (these are discussed in subsection 3.3), but rather as a mechanism to verbalise transitions through fact types. In particular higher (> 2) order fact types. Verbalisation of transitions through fact types are absolutely essential for the formulation of longer queries in LISA-D that span multiple fact types. An example of such a longer query is: LIST An administration which has as president a person who has a nr of voters [which is >= 1000000] in an election which spans two fact types.

In a next step, we will try to define one single verbalisation form in a more elementary linguistic format from which the different verbalisation formats can be generated. For this, we will be looking at the use of functional grammars as a generic format ([9], [7]).

3.2 *Building the Information Grammar*

Using the names provided by ONm, PNm, RNm, and MFix in the formulation of queries and constraints will yield expressions that are close to their original formulation in natural language. However, one should realise that we by far do not obtain the richness of a natural language. This apparent disadvantage, however, comes hand in hand with the advantage that the inherent ambiguity of natural language is absent.

Designers of conceptual query languages necessarily have to perform a delicate balance act between on the one side the requirement to define a mathematically based and unambiguous language, and on the other side the need to define a language that is close to natural language. The result is a language in which expressions have a clear intuitive meaning as the expressions are close to natural language, but which handles 'sluggish' when formulating expressions. Interpretation of the word 'sluggish' depends on one's background. From a natural language point of view, the resulting language is certainly not flexible and elegant. When looking from an SQL point of view though, the resulting language is highly flexible, orthogonal, and closer to one's intuition. Finally, by adding tool support helping users in the query formulation process, the 'sluggishness' of the language should be dramatically lessened.

The basis for the information language is the lexicon, assigning a meaning to the names given to concepts in the information structure. The meaning of names is administered by the relation Lexicon $\subseteq \mathcal{NM} \times \mathcal{PE}$ where $\mathcal{PE}$ are so-called path expressions. The path expression language is defined in full detail in [11], and basically corresponds to a path oriented version of the relational algebra that utilises the graph nature of information structures. This language is used as the semantic base of LISA-D.

The lexicon is filled from three sources. The names of the concepts in the information structure are the first source:

1. Names of types themselves: ONm(x). For example: president.
2. Type names preceded by an appropriate article: Article(x, k) ONm(x). Examples are: the marriage and a person. The articles, like: *the*, *an*, *a*, of a type is presumed to be provided by the function: Article : $\mathcal{TP} \times \{\texttt{Undetermined}, \texttt{Determined}\} \rightarrow \mathcal{NM}$ Though articles can be specified manually, linguistic tools to automatically generate articles do exist.
3. Fact participation names: PNm(x). For instance: is spouse in.
4. Reverse fact participation names: RNm(x). For instance: with spouse.

The second source are generic keywords for standard constructs in an information structure, like bridge types, collection types, sequence types, etc. In this article we will not discuss these keywords in detail. Finally, the third source of keywords are the constants, like 'Ford G.R.' To build the actual language from the lexicon, a number of construction mechanisms is used. The most important one is concatenation, which comes in two flavours. Firstly, we can simply juxtapose words from the lexicon: Election leading to election results obtained by person. The second flavour of concatenation allows us to use the mix-fix predicate verbalisations. On each position of a mix-fix predicate an existing sentence may be inserted, thus creating more complex sentences. To avoid ambiguities, we sometimes need to add brackets. An example of such a case is: An administration which has as president a person who has a nr of voters [WHICH IS >= 1000000] in an election, which is built using the mix-fix predicate verbalisation ... has ... in ... for the election results fact type.

Besides concatenation, a number of other construction mechanisms exist. For example, operations like union and intersection, predicates, and comprehension schemes. A detailed discussion of these language constructs can be found in [11]. To allow for the introduction of more compact and convenient verbalisations, LISA-D also supports a macro mechanism. An interesting aspect of this mechanism is that it allows for the specification of arbitrary fix-point queries ([12]).

3.3 Denotation of instances

To support the denotation of instances, in particular instances of complex object types, it is assumed that each object type has associated a number of verbalisation rules. We have designed a scalable verbalisation mechanism that allows us to define elegant and situation specific denotations of instances. Verbalisation rules specify how object instances are represented in the universe of discourse. As this is the preferred way to denote instances as used by the parties involved in the universe of discourse, it makes sense to ensure that in the communication with the information system these denotation styles can be used as well.

Element verbalisations usually omit explicit verbalisation of typing information. For example, we would use 'J.F. Kennedy' in the presidential database example if only referring to 'J.F. Kennedy' as a person. When referring to this person as a president, this would become president 'J.F. Kennedy'. This way of treating typing information, and using it only when needed, is a convention used in natural language that keeps sentences readable. However, when we integrate the element verbalisations in the LISA-D language, special care must be taken not to introduce ambiguities this way. In some situations explicit typing must simply be added.

Verbalisation rules are treated as meta-rules in the sense of two-level grammars (see e.g. [17]). They are instantiated by a population of the information structure. As a result, with any population a concrete verbalisation grammar can be associated. For our running example, we have the following default verbalisation with regards to the fragment dealing with people's addresses:

$$
\begin{aligned}
\langle \textsf{Community}: x \rangle &\twoheadrightarrow_1 \langle \textsf{Community name}: \textsf{Community name of Community } x \rangle \\
\langle \textsf{Street}: x \rangle &\twoheadrightarrow_1 \langle \textsf{Street name}: \textsf{Street name of Street } x \rangle \text{ , } \langle \textsf{Community}: \textsf{Community contains Street } x \rangle \\
\langle \textsf{Address}: x \rangle &\twoheadrightarrow_1 \langle \textsf{House Nr}: \textsf{House Nr of Address } x \rangle \; \langle \textsf{Street}: \textsf{Street of Address } x \rangle
\end{aligned}
$$

The first rule states that an instance x of type Community is verbalised by a Community name. This community name is determined by Community name of Community x, i.e. the community name of community x. To denote a street, the house number and street name are denoted first. This is followed by a ',' and the community name. This leads to a denotation of addresses in the following format: *1 Toernooiveld, Nijmegen*. In some countries, this is not the accepted style to write addresses. For example, in some countries the preferred style to write this address is: *Toernooiveld 1, Nijmegen*. What makes this case special is that while a street is identified by a street name (Toernooiveld) and the community name (Nijmegen), the house number needs to be placed in between. To obtain this kind of verbalisation we need to introduce two additional (partial) verbalisation rules for Street.

$$
\begin{aligned}
\langle \textsf{Street}: x \rangle &\twoheadrightarrow_2 \langle \textsf{Street name}: \textsf{Street name of Street } x \rangle \\
\langle \textsf{Street}: x \rangle &\twoheadrightarrow_3 \langle \textsf{Community}: \textsf{Community contains Street } x \rangle
\end{aligned}
$$

Note that the subscripts 1, 2, and 3 of the right arrows ($\twoheadrightarrow$) reflect the preference on the verbalisation rules. However, there is more to this numbering than meets the eye. This is explained in more detail in [12]. For this article it suffices to simply presume that the numbers provide the preference, where 1 has a higher preference than 3.

If we also change the verbalisation of Address to:

$$
\begin{aligned}
\langle \textsf{Address}: x \rangle &\twoheadrightarrow_1 \langle \textsf{Street}: \textsf{Street contains Address } x \parallel 2 \rangle \; \langle \textsf{House nr}: \textsf{House nr of Address } x \rangle \text{ , } \\
& \langle \textsf{Street}: \textsf{Street contains Address } x \parallel 3 \rangle \\
&\twoheadrightarrow_2 \langle \textsf{House nr}: \textsf{House nr of Address } x \rangle \; \langle \textsf{Street}: \textsf{Street of Address } x \rangle
\end{aligned}
$$

the desired verbalisation style is obtained. Using $\langle t : P \parallel l \rangle$ we express the preference to use verbalisation rule l for type t in the context of the given rule P.

Fact types also have associated verbalisation rules. For fact types it is also very useful to introduce partial verbalisations, which only verbalise part of a fact instance; focusing on a number of aspects only. For example, the participation of a person in an election, irrespective of the numbers of voters, may be verbalised as:

$$
\begin{aligned}
\langle \textsf{Election results}: x \rangle &\twoheadrightarrow_2 \textsf{the participation of } \langle \textsf{Person}: \textsf{has Election results } x \rangle \\
& \textsf{in } \langle \textsf{Election}: \textsf{with Election results } x \rangle
\end{aligned}
$$

In the inheritance hierarchy, the default is that verbalisations are inherited downward. However, the inherited verbalisations may be overriden. In case of the running example, the verbalisation of instances of President differs from the verbalisation of instances of Person. The following example shows how this can be handled.

$$\begin{array}{rcl}
\langle \mathsf{Person} : x \rangle & \rightarrow_1 & \langle \mathsf{Politician} : x \rangle \\
\langle \mathsf{Politician} : x \rangle & \rightarrow_1 & \langle \mathsf{President} : x \rangle \\
 & \rightarrow_2 & \mathsf{politician}\ \langle \mathsf{Person} : x \rangle \\
\langle \mathsf{President} : x \rangle & \rightarrow_1 & \mathsf{president}\ \langle \mathsf{Person} : x \rangle
\end{array}$$

4 Computer Supported Query Formulation

In this section, we study as an example application how an integrated workbench could be built that tries to combine the formality and completeness of LISA-D with the freedom of natural language querying. A query workbench should contain a set of integrated and complementary tools, each of which supports a part in the query formulation process. We propose such a workbench to have at least the following tools: *Query by Navigation*, *Natural Language Querying*, and *Query by Construction*. In the remainder of this section we briefly highlight each of these tools.

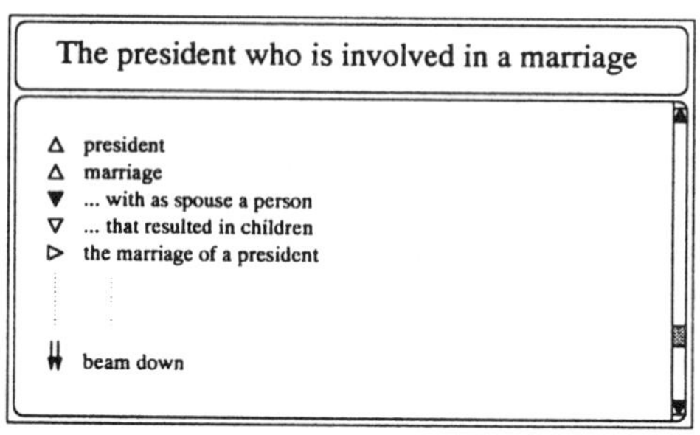

Figure 3: A Query by Navigation session

Query by navigation is a mechanism that has been succesfully used in the context of information retrieval ([1], [5], [4]). Its application in the context of query formulation on structured databases has been reported before in e.g. [13]. In figure 3 a fragment of a query by navigation session is shown. The central idea of query by navigation is to let users navigate through the graph spanned by the information model, meanwhile familiarising themselves with the information available, and gradually formulating part of their query. In figure 3, the user has arrived at the president who is involved in a marriage, and can now refine the focus to e.g. the president who is involved in a marriage with as spouse a person, or further enlarge their focus to president.

A language like LISA-D is clearly better suited for non expert users to specify their own queries, then a language like SQL. However, due to its unavoidable formality, LISA-D as such may still be regarded as too limiting for end users. Therefore, it makes sense to also include a natural language front end. Given a query in full natural language, this query could be interpreted as a path expression using the verbalisations specified with the conceptual schema.

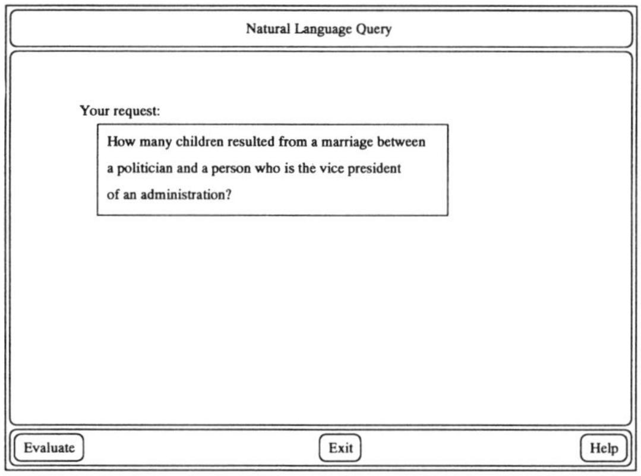

Figure 4: A natural language query

In figure 4 an example natural language query is given. This query is ambiguous in that it is not clear to which person the who is the vice president of an administration refers to. The system would therefore be able to interpret this query in at least two ways. By translating each of these interpretations to a path expression (the semantic domain of LISA-D), and then re-verbalising these path expressions, we could built a feedback system that enables the system to have a natural dialogue with users. In figure 5 the system shows the different interpretations to the user.

The query by navigation tool and the natural language front end together still do not allow users to build queries with all kinds of complex operators. It is clear that query by navigation as such does not support this. Natural language querying will support this only to some extent. Formulating a query requiring a fix-point for its evaluation can be very tedious when using natural language. This is not a flaw of query by navigation or natural language querying. The aim of these two tools was respectively to help users explore the stored information, and to allow them to formulate queries in their own words.

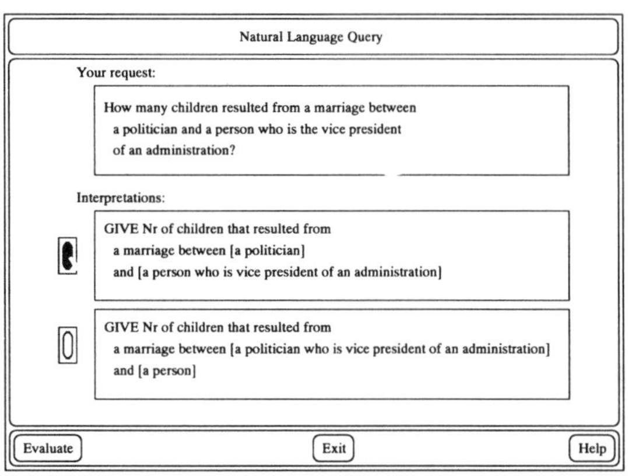

Figure 5: Resolving ambiguities by re-verbalising interpretations

To support the formulation of arbitrarily complex queries, we therefore need a tool that basically provides a syntax directed editor. An example of this is shown in figure 6.

This *Query by Construction* tool basically provides a query workbench. Query 'snippets' that either result from a query by navigation session, or natural language query, can be dragged onto the query workbench where they can be combined into complex queries using an array of operations. The power of such a query workbench is obviously the combination of tools.

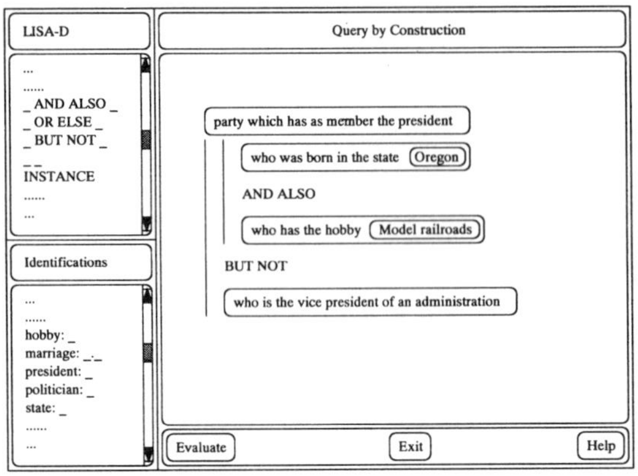

Figure 6: Example query by construction session

5 Conclusions & Discussion

Focus in this paper has been on grammatical aspects of conceptual data modelling, where we did not yet dare venture into the area of linguistics. The latter step will be part of future research in an attempt to further improve the naturalness of LISA-D and instance verbalisations. We have shown how the use of verbalisations allows information systems to communicate with users in a language that more closely resembles their language. Query results can be presented in a more user-friendly format. The verbalisation mechanisms described in this paper are very liberal.

Future research now focuses on three issues. The first issue is the automatic support of the first phase, i.e. the automatic processing and refinement of the sample verbalisations. Secondly, we intend to specify verbalisation information in a more generic format to allow more flexible use in LISA-D. This generic format would have to correspond to what in [2] is called the logical form. In [2] a distinction is made between an actual natural language sentence, its logical form, and the final representation. For LISA-D the final representation would be the underlying path expression language. Functional grammars would be a possible candidate to introduce this logical form.

Finally, we are also studying how verbalisations can help in advertising databases in a networked environment; characterising the contents of a database.

Acknowledgements

The work reported in this paper has been funded in part by the Cooperative Research Centres Program through the Department of the Prime Minister and Cabinet of Australia.

References

[1] M. Agosti, A. Archi, R. Colotti, R.M. Di Giorgi, G. Gradenigo, B. Inghirami, P. Matiello, R. Nannuci, and M. Ragona. New prospectives in information retrieval techniques: a hypertext prototype in environmental law. In *Online Management 89, Proceedings 13th International Online Information*, pages 483–494, London, United Kingdom, 1989.

[2] J. Allen. *Natural Language Understanding.* Benjamin Cummings, Redwood City, California, 2nd edition, 1995.

[3] Asymetrix. *InfoModeler User Manual.* Asymetrix Corporation, 110-110th Avenue NE, Suite 700, Bellevue, WA 98004, Washington, http://www.asymetrix.com, 1994.

[4] R. Bosman, R. Bouwman, and P.D. Bruza. The Effectiveness of Navigable Information Disclosure Systems. In G.A.M. Kempen, editor, *Proceedings of the Informatiewetenschap 1991 conference*, Nijmegen, The Netherlands, 1991.

[5] P.D. Bruza. Hyperindices: A Novel Aid for Searching in Hypermedia. In A. Rizk, N. Streitz, and J. Andre, editors, *Proceedings of the European Conference on Hypertext - ECHT 90*, pages 109–122, Cambridge, United Kingdom, 1990. Cambridge University Press.

[6] E. Buchholz, H. Cyriaks, A. Düsterhöft, H. Mehlan, and B. Thalheim. Applying a Natural Language Dialogue Tool for Designing Databases. In *Proceedings of the First Workshop on Applications of Natural Language to Databases (NLDB'95)*, pages 119–133, Versailles, France, June 1995.

[7] J.F.M. Burg and R.P. van de Riet. COLOR-X: Object Modeling profits from Linguistics. In *Proceedings of the KB&KS'95, the Second International Conference on Building and Sharing of Very Large-Scale Knowledge Bases*, Enschede, The Netherlands, 1995.

[8] H. Dalianis. A method for validating a conceptual model by natural language discourse generation. In P. Loucopoulos, editor, *Proceedings of the Fourth International Conference CAiSE'92 on Advanced Information Systems Engineering*, volume 593 of *Lecture Notes in Computer Science*, pages 425–444, Manchester, United Kingdom, 1992. Springer-Verlag.

[9] F.P.M. Dignum and R.P. van de Riet. Knowledge base modeling based on linguistics and founded in logic. *Data & Knowledge Engineering*, 7:1–34, 1991.

[10] T.A. Halpin. *Conceptual Schema and Relational Database Design.* Prentice-Hall, Sydney, Australia, 2nd edition, 1995.

[11] A.H.M. ter Hofstede, H.A. Proper, and Th.P. van der Weide. Formal definition of a conceptual language for the description and manipulation of information models. *Information Systems*, 18(7):489–523, October 1993.

[12] A.H.M. ter Hofstede, H.A. Proper, and Th.P. van der Weide. Grammar Based Information Modelling. Technical Report CSI-R9414, Submitted for publication, Computing Science Institute, University of Nijmegen, Nijmegen, The Netherlands, October 1994. Electronically available as: http://www.icis.qut.edu.au/~erikp/articles/Grammar.ps.

[13] A.H.M. ter Hofstede, H.A. Proper, and Th.P. van der Weide. Computer Supported Query Formulation in an Evolving Context. In R. Sacks-Davis and J. Zobel, editors, *Proceedings of the Sixth Australasian Database Conference, ADC'95*, volume 17(2) of *Australian Computer Science Communications*, pages 188–202, Adelaide, Australia, January 1995.

[14] G. Kristen. *Object Orientation, the KISS Method: From Information Architecture to Information System.* Addison-Wesley, Reading, Massachusetts, 1994.

[15] R. Meersman. The RIDL Conceptual Language. Research report, International Centre for Information Analysis Services, Control Data Belgium, Inc., Brussels, Belgium, 1982.

[16] J. Rumbaugh, M. Blaha, W. Premerlani, F. Eddy, and W. Lorenson. *Object-Oriented Modeling and Design.* Prentice-Hall, Englewood Cliffs, New Jersey, 1991.

[17] A. van Wijngaarden, B.J. Mailloux, J.E.L. Peck, C.H.A. Koster, M. Sintzoff, C.H. Lindsey, L.T. Meertens, and R.G. Fisker. *Revised Report on the Algorithmic Language ALGOL 68.* Springer-Verlag, Berlin, Germany, 1976.

Applications of Natural Language to Information Systems
R.P. van de Riet et al. (Eds.)
IOS Press, 1996

An Information Retrieval Approach to Locating Information in Large Scale Federated Database Systems

R. Richardson and A. F. Smeaton
School of Computer Applications
Dublin City University
Dublin, Ireland

RR@BroadCom.ie and asmeaton@CompApp.DCU.ie

Abstract. In large scale federated database systems (FDBS) there is a need for users to be able to locate information of interest from among the export schemas of database systems in the federation. This must be done by having those who provide export schemas also provide descriptions of the contents of those schemas but the problem then is matching information requests against schema descriptions with a reasonably high degree of precision. In this paper we describe our approach to this problem which involves using a vocabulary from a knowledge base, sense-disambiguating polysemous words and using the knowledge base as a structure from which we estimate the semantic similarity between words. These semantic similarity values are used in computing degrees of overlap between a user's query and the schema descriptions. In the paper we describe the design for a FDBS system, FEDDICT, which achieves the goal of allowing a more flexible match between query and schema description. As with other researchers who have addressed the same problem, we have found it impossible to evaluate our approach empirically on either real or synthetic data environments but we have evaluated the effectiveness of our matching algorithm in an image caption retrieval application. The results of these evaluations show that our approach yields improvements in the caption retrieval environment which has exactly the same characteristics to that to be expected in a large scale federated database system.

Keywords: FDBS, Semantic Similarity, Knowledge Base, Federated Dictionary

1 Introduction

Computing for the modern business world must be able to handle the sharing of data that arises from corporate take-overs and mergers, acquisitions and other cases leading to globally distributed enterprise data. Providing database operations in environments of large numbers of independent heterogeneous database systems is a real challenge and we are slowly embracing an architecture of having these linked together, initially through gateways [28] and then through a tighter integration of database components. In such environments and in cases where the data to be accessed is not local, there are two broad approaches to locating information and providing access. These approaches are the tightly coupled Federated Database (FDBS) approach and the loosely coupled FDBS approach, respectively.

The term federated database was first introduced in [13] and is defined in [24] as a collection of co-operating but autonomous heterogeneous database systems. In a FDBS there is no centralised control since component databases control access to their own data and this control extends to deciding which data is to be made globally available. Component database administrators produce what is known as an export schema which describes what data in their database is to be made available to other databases in the federation. Federated schema(s) are then built by combining the export schemas. The method of building the federated schema(s), i.e. through schema integration or import, coupled with the knowledge of who has responsibility for their creation and maintenance determines the category of the resulting FDBS. Simply stated, in the tightly coupled approach a central authority, commonly referred to as the federated database administrator, is responsible for creating federated schemas and the process itself takes the form of schema integration. In the loosely coupled approach each user is the administrator of his/her own federated schema and the process of developing federated schemas is through schema import.

Research into heterogeneous distributed databases has traditionally investigated approaches to sharing data among a small number of component databases. In such an environment the integration of all export schemas to form one or more federated schemas, as in the tightly coupled FDBS approach, seems quite reasonable. Similarly the issue of "knowing what is out there" for users of loosely coupled systems is not really significant since it can be assumed that the amount of information the user has to know is kept at a reasonable level. However, as the number of databases grow the environment becomes less amenable to both these approaches. In the case of the tightly coupled approach the complexity involved in integrating perhaps thousands of export schemas would be enormous not to mention the practically intractable problem of maintaining database integrity across the federation given the freedom of component databases to update their local data at will. It is similarly unreasonable to assume that a user of a loosely coupled FDBS will always know exactly what he/she is looking for and what each database contains in an environment that consists of up to thousands of databases.

In the remainder of this paper we describe the design for a federated dictionary referred to as FEDDICT, to aid in overcoming the problems associated with locating information in large scale loosely coupled FDBSs. The next section introduces the problem we tackle in more detail and discusses the knowledge base and semantic similarity estimators we have developed. Following that we outline the design and implementation of FEDDICT. Section 4 presents the results of our evaluation and experiments. In section 5 we give a brief overview of related research and the final section presents the conclusions and our recommendations for future research.

2 Locating Information in a Federated DBMS

There is a consensus in [25], [5] and [8] that the problems of locating and relating information from within a large number of inter-connected autonomous heterogeneous databases is a major open research issue. The problem extends to finding the range of subjects about which information is stored in the federation. Most commercially available systems [8], provide users with the ability to scan the available data sequentially but this is, however, impractical for large systems. In a separate analysis of the state of federated databases, [6] describes how locating information is achieved in two steps. First, the requesting database consults the federation dictionary for existing databases and available schemas, and secondly, imports all known schemas (whenever possible) and browses through them for a certain information type. This is quite possibly inadequate and certainly undesirable if there are tens (not even hundreds or thousands) of such schemas.

It would appear that in order to make progress, we need a system which can identify the location of specific data when given imprecise identifiers, (i.e. identifiers which don't refer to the names of structures within which data are stored). In light of the problems raised due to size it seems impractical that the item of data sharing should be import schema objects. Given the possibly huge amounts of data globally available, users could not be expected to be aware of the names of individual import schema objects nor would it be possible to allow users to browse through all export schemas. Furthermore, there will also be a lack of standardisation in the naming of schema objects across databases and it would not be unusual to find objects such as 'Table051', 'cde090', etc. These names do not in any way reflect the nature of the information contained within data structures. It is thus necessary to tackle the problem at the conceptual level, that is to allow users to refer to information of interest in terms familiar to them.

Information retrieval (IR) is a discipline in which vague or imprecise user queries are matched against text documents in order to rank those documents likely to be relevant to the user's information need. The conventional approach to IR is to compute a measure of similarity between a query and each document based on the co-occurrence of keywords or index terms in both. A known inadequacy with this approach is that our natural language is rich enough to allow the same concept to be expressed using different words or word combinations [26].

For example,

- warehouse employee shift assignments
- stores personnel work rota

both refer to a description of working hours for people who work in the warehouse department yet in the two descriptor phrases there are no words common to both expressions.[1] Within information retrieval the approach taken to address this problem is through query expansion whereby the original information need as expressed in a query is refined by using, for example, synonyms from a thesaurus [11]. The problem we address in this paper is essentially the same problem but in a completely different application and the approach we take is to measure the semantic distance between descriptor terms using a knowledge base of terms and term relations. Furthermore we restrict the use of terms in the system to those from our knowledge base thus enforcing a restricted vocabulary.

The knowledge base we used in our work was derived from WordNet and in the following subsections we provide a more detailed description of how our KB was constructed and our semantic similarity functions were derived.

[1]Admittedly some of this is due to American v English use of the English language.

2.1 WordNet as a Knowledge Base

WordNet is the product of a research project at Princeton University which has attempted to model the lexical knowledge of a native speaker of English, [16], [17], and [3]. The system has the power of both an on-line thesaurus and an on-line dictionary, and much more. Figure 1 illustrates some of the different kinds of relationships that WordNet has and also the range of information covered. Information in WordNet is organised around logical groupings called synsets. Each synset consists of a list of synonymous word forms and semantic pointers that describe relationships between the current synset and other synsets. A word form can be a single word or two or more words connected by underscores, (referred to as collocations). The semantic pointers can be of a number of different types including:

- Hyponym/Hypernym (IS-A/HAS A)
- Meronym/Holonym (Part-of/Has-Part)
- Meronym/Holonym (Member-of/Has-Member),
- Meronym/Holonym (Substance-of/Has-Substance)

In our work we only use the nouns from WordNet, ignoring the verbs, adjectives and adverbs. This leaves us with c.60,000 word forms of which more than half are single words and the remainder collocations. This is adequate for our task.

The initial form of our KB consisted of a number hierarchical concept graphs, (HCGs), constructed directly from WordNet. The root concepts of the HCGs were chosen as result of a set of experiments to determine what root concepts would, as a group, provide maximum coverage of the nouns in WordNet whilst minimising the degree of overlap between HCGs. The motivation for creating HCGs was purely efficiency in order to make the computation more manageable and as we will see later we have not sacrificed effectiveness in any way.

The root nodes of the set of 11 HCG we have used which achieves this coverage is as follows :

-Entity	-Psychological_feature
-Location	-Shape
-Abstraction	-State
-Event	-Act
-Group	-Possession
-Phenomenon	

The resulting HCGs ranged in size from 43950 unique concepts (Entity) to 688 concepts (Shape). While we would have preferred a more even balance across HCG size, we believe the disparity in the HCGs we use does not cause any major problem. However, the big disadvantage with the initial HCGs is the fact that neither links nor nodes in the HCGs are weighted and so an automatic link weighting mechanism was developed so WordNet links could be meaningfully used in a conceptual distance function. Details of this weighting mechanism can be found in [20].

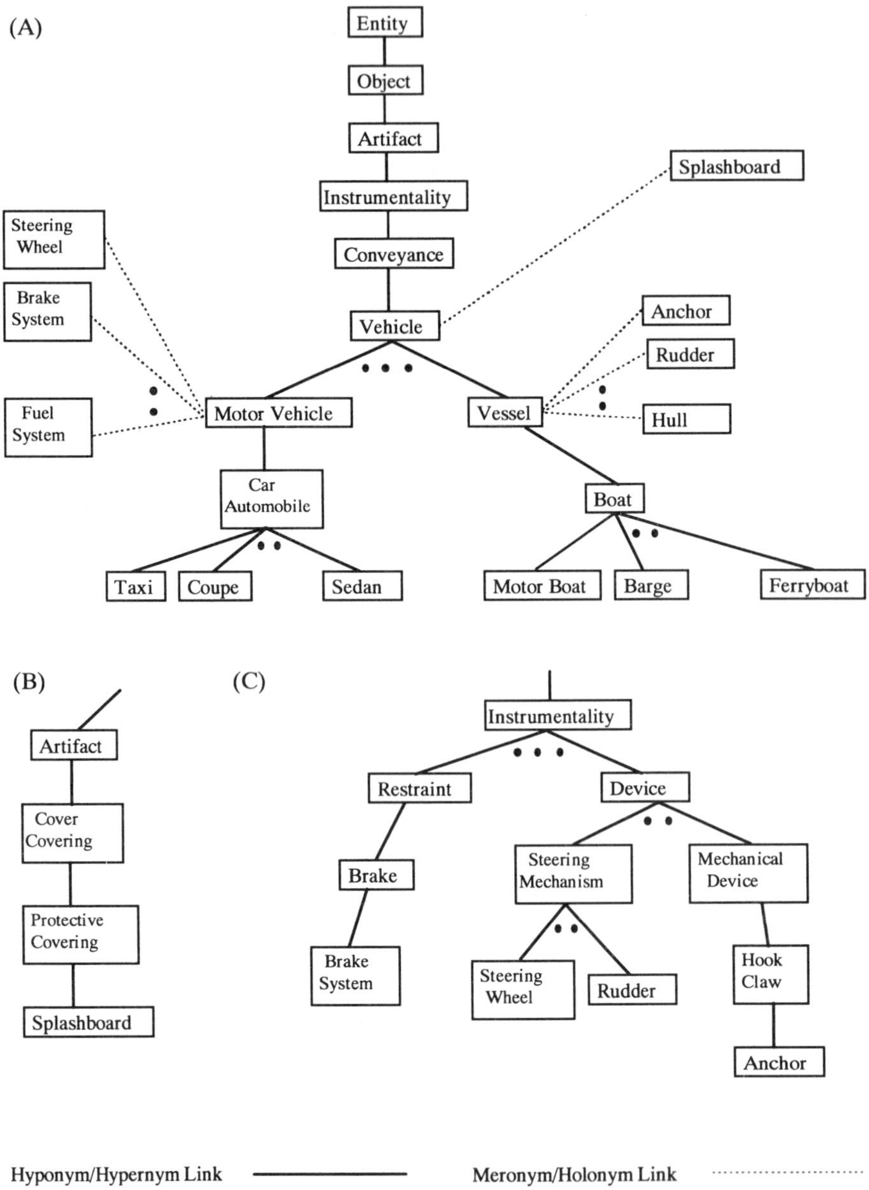

Figure 1 : Extract from the WordNet System

2.2 Semantic Similarity

A number of approaches to measuring conceptual similarity have been taken in the past. Tversky's feature based similarity model, [29], is arguably the most powerful similarity model to date however, its applicability in FEDDICTs situation would require a much richer knowledge base than we have available. Although a WordNet-derived knowledge base is quite thorough in its coverage of concepts, the number of semantic relation types connecting these concepts is considerably less than would be required for use by a feature based similarity model. As such, we opted to employ an information based approach to estimating semantic similarity between words based on work carried out by Resnik, [18] and [19]. The semantic similarity of concepts is estimated using the distributional behaviour of classes of words in a large text corpus. Resnik views noun synsets as a class of words where the class is made up of all words in a synset as well as words in all directly or indirectly subordinate synsets and conceptual similarity is considered in terms of class similarity. The similarity then between two classes is approximated by the information content of the first class in the noun hierarchy that subsumes both classes. The information content of a class is approximated by estimating the probability of occurrence of the class in a large text corpus. As such, the similarity of two classes of words, c_1 and c_2, can be expressed as:

$$\mathrm{Sim}(c_1, c_2) = \max_{C_i} \left[\log \frac{1}{P(C_i)} \right]$$

where C_i is the set of classes dominating or superordinate to both c_1 and c_2, $P(C_i)$ is the class probability of class c_i, and is the information content of class C_i. In our work we took 278 Mbytes of text from the Wall Street Journal, tagged this with a parts-of-speech tagger to detect occurrences of nouns, or word occurrences which were potentially nouns, and used the frequency of occurrence of WordNet nouns and collocations to compute the information content of synset classes in our HCGs.

The information based semantic similarity estimator measure is not without weaknesses. Perhaps foremost is the fact that this technique ignores information in WordNet that may be useful namely that only the synonym and IS-A relations are used while the other relation types, which are used effectively by the adapted Rada-like conceptual distance approach, are unused. A second weakness is apparent in the method we used to calculate the information content of classes whereby many polysemous words will have an exaggerated information content value. If one takes for instance the polysemous word 'bank', then the information content for this word will include all occurrences of the string 'bank' occurring as a noun in the corpus, regardless of meaning. This is due to the fact that we did not, and indeed cannot yet automatically distinguish WordNet word senses from free text with any degree of accuracy above 65% [21]. This net result of being unable to distinguish word senses gives the same exaggerated information content value to a 'commercial bank' as to a 'river bank'. To further complicate things, given the fact that the information content of a class is defined in terms of the information content of its subordinate classes, superclasses of classes containing polysemous words are similarly over-valued. This disregard of ambiguous words is a particular problem given the fact that classes in WordNet refer to particular senses.

3 The Underlying FDBS Operation

Having introduced the word-based similarity estimator which we use in FEDDICT, we will now give an overview of how this would operate within FEDDICT and of how FEDDICT would fit in with the overall operation of a large scale FDBS. Achieving interoperability in a FDBS environment is a task that is performed in two phases. The first phase consists of finding the target databases that are most likely to hold information of interest and the second phase consists of querying the information stored there, [4]. Due to the broad scope of this operation, our research is more concerned with the first phase of the problem, locating the databases. However, FEDDICT could, for instance, be used in conjunction with the negotiation protocol outlined in [1] or an inter-database communication method introduced in [14]. Such a negotiation protocol would be based on the use of quasi copies of data. Exactly how up to date the copy is could be determined by negotiation between the requesting user, (the importer), and the user who owns the requested data, (the owner).

In order to allow potentially interested importers to determine the semantic contents of an exporter's schema rather than the syntactic aspects like table and column names, an exporter must provide a description of those contents. This is done by having the exporter describe its database in terms of natural language. Naturally some guidelines for DBAs registering schemas would need to be in place in order to impose a certain consistency of style, length of description, etc.. A post-processor ensures that only terms (either single words or collocations) known to our KB are used in these descriptions. Furthermore, when polysemous terms are used in the export schema description the user is asked to disambiguate each of these into one or more intended word senses. For example, the word *match* can mean

- a peer of equal standing
- a piece of wood used for lighting a cigarette for example
- a sporting contest or competition
- a couple, who live together
- a duplicate or a double
- ...etc.

while the word *table* can refer to

- a four-legged piece of furniture
- a raised piece of land with steep edges
- an arrangement of data
- ...etc.

When using words like these it is important to determine which sense is intended as the semantic similarities between the *piece of furniture* and the *arrangement of data* senses of "table" with the *vertical arrangement of data* sense of the word "column", will be very different. With the present state of language engineering it is not possible to automatically disambiguate a word sense given its context with 100% accuracy especially in the FDBS application where there will be so little context or surrounding words, anyway. For applications like document retrieval where some noise is tolerable this may be adequate and there may be more statistical information available as the corpus will be larger but in the FEDDICT application where we require very high precision, manual word sense disambiguation is the only option. While this may seem like a disadvantage it is not such an overhead. A DBA will be obliged to provide a textual description of the schema being exported anyway and the sense disambiguation process itself is not cumbersome. We sense-disambiguated a collection of over 2700 image captions of approximately the same length as schema descriptions, over a 3-week period with the captioning and sense disambiguation process taking an average of 2.5 minutes per caption. Our experiences found that using sense disambiguation was in fact reassuring to indexers as it raised their confidence level in the descriptions they provided. This would be true for DBAs also.

When a user becomes interested in searching the federation for database components of interest, (s)he specifies this interest as a natural language statement and once again only terms known to our KB are allowed in this query. Manual sense disambiguation takes place once again if necessary. The task of the database locator is to search the descriptions of export schemas to find schemas which may be of interest to the importer. How exactly this matching is done we shall see in the section on evaluation.

To see where the FEDDICT database locator fits into the overall operation of a federated DBMS, the following steps are involved:

- The first step is for the owner of each export schema to publish it in the manner described above and using to FEDDICT's KB as a controlled vocabulary in this operation.

- At some point in the future an importer may become interested in a piece of information. A user 'query' is constructed using natural language terms from FEDDICT's KB and this query is compared with stored descriptions of export schemata. FEDDICT's semantic similarity estimators between term are employed in this process.

- Once the importer determines the location of the owner site in whose data it has an interest, it sends the owner a message containing an access request, (typically complete with an estimation of querying rate, coherency and selection conditions).

- When the owner site receives the request, it computes the cost of granting a quasi-copy and decides whether to allow access or not. If access is granted, the requested is translated into a standard format unit (SFDU), [14], and copied to the importer site where it is translated into that site's native data format. Updates can be received and the copy updated according to the agreed terms of sharing.

At any point subsequent to this the importer can shut down the maintenance of its quasi-copy of the exporter's data and withdraw its interest in that data.

4 Evaluation

In our research into locating and relating data in large scale FDBSs we have proposed a conceptual level approach, that is to allow users refer to database information of interest in terms familiar to them while allowing a degree of flexibility in matching through the use of semantically-based word distances. In the formulation and implementation of our approach we endeavoured to develop a generic information processing system, independent of any specific application like FEDDICT. In retrospect we found that evaluating our system in an FDBS application was very difficult and it is not difficult to imagine the kind of problems associated with creating a synthetic artificial environment for a large scale FDBS. Fortunately, the number of applications to which a concept level approach could be applied is enormous (e.g. document retrieval, information filtering, multimedia caption retrieval, generation of hypertext links, etc.). In our evaluation we concentrated on the question "Would it work ?", i.e. firstly is the WordNet derived KB capable of being used as a domain independent controlled vocabulary, and secondly are the information based and conceptual distance similarity estimators accurate as concept level comparison mechanisms.

After wrestling with the problems of setting up a synthetic FDBS environment in which to do our testing, we carried out our evaluation a multimedia caption retrieval application. For this we used a database of 2714 image captions each with an average of 5.9 WordNet indexing terms, some of which were collocations (phrases). This is comparable to the size one could expect in a FDBS. Each image was manually indexed using the FEDDICT KB as a controlled vocabulary and sense-disambiguated during the indexing process. Functionally this corresponds precisely to the situation a database exporter would have when describing a database schema to be exported except that in a FDBS the entire system would be distributed. A set of 47 user queries was collected and relevance assessments from the users were gathered yielding about 10 relevant captions per query, again what one could expect in a FDBS. Evaluation was performed by computing precision values at standard recall points.

Our experiments assigned a score to each caption and ranked captions by these scores. In the following descriptions, a query $Q = \{q_1, \ldots, q_m\}$ is matched against a caption $C = \{c_1..c_n\}$ and $\text{Sim}(t_1, t_2)$ is the information based similarity between terms t_1 and t_2. Our baseline run was to compute a caption score by expanding each query and caption term in the collection by including synonyms from the synset and these results are given as run1. In run2 we computed a caption score based on using the n x m similarity values between all combinations of query terms and caption terms. We then applied a threshold similarity value, θ, and used only similarities above this, in order to remove noise. This can be formalised as

$$\text{run2}(Q, C) = \frac{\sum_{i=1}^{m} \sum_{j=1}^{n} \text{Sim}'(q_i, c_j)}{k}$$

where

$$\text{Sim}'(x, y) = \begin{cases} \text{Sim}(x, y), & \text{if } \text{Sim}(x, y) > \theta \\ 0, & \text{otherwise} \end{cases}$$

where and k is a count of the number of similarities used in the computation. Run3 is a bit more complicated in that for each query term we determine the best-matching caption term, sum these similarity values and normalise by the number of query terms and for each caption term we determine the best-matching query term, sum the similarities and normalise by the number of caption terms, and we add these respective similarities. Formally this is given as

$$\text{run3}(Q, C) = \frac{\sum_{i=1}^{m} \max\left[\text{Sim}(q_i, c_j)\right]}{m} + \frac{\sum_{k=1}^{n} \max\left[\text{Sim}(q_l, c_k)\right]}{n}$$

where $j = 1, \ldots, n$ and $l = 1, \ldots, m$. The precision values at standard recall points for the 3 runs are given in Table 1. This is a fairly standard way in information retrieval

	Run1	Run2	Run3
Precision at Recall values:			
0.00	.584	.434	.670
0.10	.530	.363	.620
0.20	.472	.316	.555
0.30	.436	.261	.481
0.40	.404	.240	.460
0.50	.389	.230	.447
0.60	.295	.163	.370
0.70	.253	.131	.333
0.80	.238	.122	..305
0.90	.208	.105	.249
1.00	.190	.098	.219
Av P over all	.323	.206	.405

Table 1: Precision-Recall performance figures

experimentation to evaluate the effectiveness of a retrieval strategy. More detailed results of the performance of caption retrieval can be found in [27].

We conclude from these results that our approach to matching information requests against descriptions of objects works well when there is little information available as with the caption application. The image caption retrieval environment is exactly the same situation as with the case of descriptions of structured data in an FDBS application. Descriptors of shareable data in a FDBS would be very similar to those used for describing images in our caption retrieval application as both would have descriptions which are short and terse and in both cases the queries would also be short. In both applications the scope for relevance feedback or interactive searching would be great. We thus propose that our approach to image caption retrieval involving word-word semantic distances would work well when applied to the problem of locating and relating information in a large scale FDBS.

5 Related Research

The problem of locating information of interest from a federated database system is one which is still not widespread but is looming as database technology progresses. There are many gateway products in the market which connect clients to server databases and there are commercial FDBS products like InterViso [28] which provide a value layer above simple connectivity. These handle views, transactions, model translation, simple name mapping, etc. The more complex name mapping problems where different names are used for like data, etc., are handled by having human designers who perform this mapping and thus with a system like InterViso, the role FEDDICT would have played is taken by a human database administrator.

Research in the area of using a system to help in locating data started with the FINDIT system developed by Bouguettaya, [4]. The approach followed in FINDIT was to use a knowledge base (KB) as a kind of controlled vocabulary which could be employed by users to describe shareable information as well as information requests, just as we have done in FEDDICT. However, FINDIT was not implemented or tested and the existence of the KB was simply assumed. Also, no provisions were made for the very real problem of ambiguity in the use of language. Bates points out in [2], "the probability of two persons using the same term in describing the same thing is less than 20%", and Furnas et al. found that "..the probability of two subjects picking the same term for a given entity ranged from 7% to 18%", [10]. Thus we can see that if a database locator which caters for short descriptions of schema exports and also for short queries is to be useful it must have in-build capabilities to handle variations in word usage.

In subsequent research, Merz and King describe the architecture and design of a FDBS query facility referred to as DIRECT, [15]. DIRECT uses textual descriptions of items in different databases to locate and relate data items across several component databases. A simple keyword search is used to identify semantically similar items. Obviously this leaves the system open to all the problems we mentioned above of two users using two different terms to describe the same thing. Also, they report, the "data descriptions are not sufficient" for the purposes of identifying data. Finally, Bright et. al, [9], report on a system referred to as SSM (Summary Schemas Model). As with FINDIT, SSM employs KB as a controlled vocabulary however unlike FINDIT, the problem of natural language ambiguity is addressed in SSM. Rogets thesaurus is used as a knowledge base and a conceptual distance function is used to compare the semantic similarity of concepts used in the descriptions. Although an evaluation of the system, in terms of whether it actually "works" is not reported they say of Rogets thesaurus :

> "Rogets provides only the most basic semantic relations, and the vocabulary is somewhat dated. In particular, Roget's hypernym (IS-A), links are not as meaningful as they could be ..." [9]

and they conclude of their conceptual distance function:

> "SDM (Semantic Distance Measure), sophistication is currently limited by the available systems taxonomy. A more complex taxonomy (with more linguistic information), would allow more variation and control over SDM calculations. The SDM function is the core function that applies the power of the system taxonomy to provide semantically meaningful results to users ..." [9].

Both the SDM and FEDDICT systems make use of a KB as a controlled vocabulary and use a semantic similarity function to estimate the equivalence of natural language concepts. However, whereas SSM employs Rogets thesaurus as its KB we opted for a KB derived from the WordNet lexical database as WordNet contains considerably more semantic information and has a far broader coverage than Rogets Thesaurus. The greater number of semantic links in WordNet and its sheer size (more than 60,000 nouns) allowed us to develop a semantic similarity function more sophisticated than SSMs semantic distance function. Greater sophistication itself is not a justification for anything however what we have done here is evaluated how well our method performs in a FEDDICT-like environment, given the impossibility of experimenting with a real FEDDICT as such large FDBS do not yet exist. We do not know of similar evaluations of alternative approaches to locating information in a federated database dictionary.

6 Conclusions

The research outlined in this paper addresses open research problems in the area of large scale loosely coupled FDBSs. It has been recognised that one of the most challenging problems that faces the database community is achieving an interoperable environment for the ever increasing number of autonomous and heterogeneous databases [7], [25] and [9]. In line with these findings, this paper describes a proposal for the prototype federated dictionary, FEDDICT. FEDDICT employs a domain independent KB and two semantic similarity estimators to allow a concept-level approach to the problem of locating information of interest in the federation. This enables users to find information of interest to them without a priori knowledge of the space of information and databases.

Evaluations of our approach were conducted using a multimedia caption retrieval application and the results of our evaluation show our approach works well in situations where there is little descriptive information available. This are exactly the characteristics encountered in the problem of locating data in a large scale-scale FDBS.

Future work includes an investigation into further development of the negotiation protocol, an attempt to make progress on a more direct evaluation in a FDBS environment and more detailed study of the performance of our semantic similarity estimator in such a FDBS application. In addition we hope to re-do some of the creation of a KB from WordNet and to use adjectives and verbs, as well as nouns, in the new version.

Acknowledgements:

The authors wish to acknowledge the help given by John Murphy during this research and first author acknowledges funding support from IBM IISL Ltd.

References

[1] R. Alonso, and D. Barbara. *Negotiating Data Access in Federated Database Systems.* Princeton University, Research Report CS-TR-160-80, June 1988.

[2] M. Bates. *Subject Access in Online Catalogs: A Design Model.* Journal of the American Society for Information Science, 11, 357- 376, 1986.

[3] R. Beckwith, G.A. Miller, and R. Tengi. *Design and Implementation of the WordNet Lexical Database and Searching Software.* Working Paper, Princeton University, 1993.

[4] A. Bouguettaya, R. King and K. Zhao. *FINDIT : A Server Based Approach to Finding Information in Large Scale Heterogeneous Databases.* First International Workshop on Interoperability in Multidatabase Systems, Kyoto, Japan, April 7-9, 1991, 191-194.

[5] A. Bouguettaya. *A Dynamic Framework For Interoperability in Large Multidatabases.* University of Colorado at Boulder, Boulder, Colarado, May, 1992, Ph.D. Thesis in Computer Science.

[6] A. Bouguettaya and R. King. *Large Multidatabases: Issues and Directions.* IFIP, DS-5 Semantics of Interoperable Database Systems, Volume 1, Australia, Nov. 16-20, 1992, 53-64.

[7] A. Bouguettaya and R. King. *The Universal Database: The World-wide Conglomeration of Heterogeneous Autonomous Databases.* Submitted for Conference Publication, 1993.

[8] M. W. Bright, A. R. Hurson, and S. H. Pakzad. *A Taxonomy and Current Issues in MultiDatabase Systems.* IEEE Computer, Mar 1992, 50-59.

[9] M. W. Bright, A. R. Hurson, and S. Pakzad. *Automated Resolution of Semantic Heterogeneity in Multidatabases.* ACM Transaction on Database Systems, Vol. 19, No. 2, June 1994, 212-253.

[10] G. W. Furnas, T. K. Landauer, L. M. Gomez,, and S. T. Dumais. *The Vocabulary Problem in Human-System Communication.* Communications of the ACM, Vol. 30, No. 11, November 1987, 964-971.

[11] A. Ginsberg. *A Unified Approach to Automatic Indexing and Information Retrieval.* IEEE Expert, 8(5), 46-56, 1993.

[12] D. Harman. *Overview of the Second Text Retrieval Conference (TREC-2).* Information Processing & Management, 31(3), 271-289, 1995.

[13] D. Heimbigner and D. McLeod. *A Federated Architecture for Information Management.* ACM Transactions on Office Information Systems, 3(3), 1985, 253-278.

[14] W. Litwin, L. Mark and N. Roussopoulos. *Interoperability of Multiple Autonomous Databases.* ACM Computing Surveys, Vol. 22, No. 3, Sept 1989, 267-293.

[15] U. Merz and R. King. *A Query Facility for Multiple Databases.* ACM Transactions on Information Systems, Vol. 12, No. 4, October 1994, 339 - 359.

[16] G.A. Miller, R. Beckwith, C. Felbaum, D. Gross, and K. Miller. *Introduction to WordNet An On-line Lexical Database.* International Journal of Lexicography, Vol. 3, No. 4, 1990, 235 - 244.

[17] G.A. Miller. *Nouns in WordNet A Lexical Inheritance System.* International Journal of Lexicography, Vol. 3, No. 4, 1990, 245 - 264.

[18] P. Resnik. *Selection and Information: A Class based Approach to Lexical Relationships.* PhD. dissertation at the University of Pennsylvania. Also appears as Technical Report 93-42, November 1993.

[19] P. Resnik. *Semantic Classes and Syntactic Ambiguity.* ARPA Workshop on Human Language Technology, Princeton, March, 1993.

[20] R. Richardson, A.F. Smeaton, and J. Murphy. *Using WordNet for Conceptual Distance Measurement.* Proceedings of the BCS-IRSG Colloquium, Glasgow, March 1994.

[21] R. Richardson. *A Semantic-based Approach to Information Processing.* Ph.D. thesis, School of Computer Applications, Dublin City University, 1994.

[22] R. Richardson and A.F. Smeaton. *Automatic Word Sense Disambiguation in a KBIR Application.* The New Review of Document and text management, Vol. 1, 299-320, 1995.

[23] M. Sanderson. *Word Sense Disambiguation and Information Retrieval.* Proceedings of the 17th International Conference on Research and development in Information Retrieval (SIGIR94), 142-151, Dublin, July 1994.

[24] A. P. Sheth and J. A. Larson. *Federated Database Systems for managing Distributed, Heterogeneous, and Autonomous Databases.* ACM Computing Surveys, Vol. 22, No. 3, Sept 1990, 183-236.

[25] A. Silberschatz, M. J. Stonebraker, J. Ullman. *Database Systems : Achievements and Opportunities.* Communications of the ACM, Vol. 34, No. 10, October 1991, 110-120.

[26] A.F. Smeaton. *Progress in the Application of Natural Language Processing to Information Retrieval Tasks.* The Computer Journal, 35(3), 268-278, 1992.

[27] A.F. Smeaton and I. Quigley. *Experiments on Using Semantic Distances Between Words in Image Caption Retrieval.* to appear in Proceedings of the 19th International Conferecne on Research and Development in Information Retrieval (SIGIR96), Zurich, 1996.

[28] M. Templeton, H. Henley, E. Maros and D.J. van Buer. *InterViso: Dealing with the Complexity of Federated Database Accesses.* VLDB Journal,4, 287-317, 1995.

[29] A. Tversky. *Features of Similarity.* Psychological Review, 84, (4), 1977, 327 - 352.

Applications of Natural Language to Information Systems
R.P. van de Riet et al. (Eds.)
IOS Press, 1996

Metalinguistic formulas and semantic representation of knowledge in training simulators

Ghyslaine LE BAIL
lebail@irit.fr
Raymond COUSIN
Patrice CAPDEVILLE
IRIT, 50, Chemin des maraichers
31077 TOULOUSE CEDEX, France
cousin@irit.fr

Abstract. The general purpose of our research is to design suitable tools for the requirements of design engineers of knowledge bases so as to realise and use training simulators. One of our objectives is to construct and improve a computational architecture receiving the semantic knowledge about comprehension of utterances, generation of explanations and reasoning in knowledge based systems. Another objective is to express the structural representation of utterances thanks to the new idea of metalinguistic formulas.
Keywords : natural language, knowledge representation, semantics, training simulator, metalinguistic formulas

1 Introduction

The realization of a training simulator based on knowledge bases borrows techniques and knowledge from different fields such as computational linguistics (natural language interface), cognitive psychology (simulation of human reasoning), cognitive ergonomy (interfaces fitted to users). The construction of such a system is based on a partnership between two (or more) artificial agents (concept of communicating agents in multi-agent systems) or between an artificial agent and an human agent (expert, learner). This construction is directly dependent on the modelling of context in which the communication takes place and the implementation of interaction between both partners : comprehension of human utterances, communication of messages from system (request or generation of explanations), exchange of information between two artificial agents (during the simulation of an intelligent process for instance).
In general, the existing applications deal with only one type of interaction. The aim of our research is to enable different types of interaction to exist in the same computational structure. In order to achieve this ambition, our attempt is to carry out three complementary objectives :

- Constructing and improving a computational architecture receiving the semantic knowledge about comprehension of utterances, generation of explanations and reasoning in a knowledge based system.

- Making the communication between artificial agents observable by means of metalinguistic formulas in applicative language. These formulas express the structural representation of natural language semantics.
- Using metalinguistic formulas in the process of production of natural language utterances : intermediate representation between the structural representation of an utterance and its natural language expression.

In this paper, we will present the structural representation of semantic knowledge linked to a context (linguistic agents, semantic roles). We will also introduce the transformation of this representation into metalinguistique formulas.
In section 2, we will develop the general problematics about training simulators and we will refer to concrete applications in natural language processing (NLP) having tackled some of the interactions mentioned beforeed. In section 3, we will consider in section 3 our approach in relation to objectives investigated before describing (4) our computational architecture, a model named ABCD (Archistructure of dynamic knowledge bases). The description of a semantic representation of contextual knowledge about a universe will be the object of the section 5.

2 General problematics

The general purpose of our research is to design suitable tools for the requirements of design engineers of knowledge bases so as to realise and use training simulators. In the face of the ever increasing complexity of such systems, it is necessary to simplify the cognitive contribution of the user thanks to a communication in a high level language closely related to natural language and the job oriented language specific to a microworld. This microworld or universe U can be discovered by the end-user thanks to the simulation of U. This simulation of universe also involves a communication between agents in the training system.
The modelling of the communication process leads to the construction of structures fitting as well as possible the mechanisms underlying an exchange between a human agent and an artificial agent or between two artificial agents. These mechanisms are the comprehension of natural language utterances, reasoning and generation of utterances.

- The comprehension of texts in natural language is compared to the construction of semantic representations produced during the semantic interpretation run.
- In order to be capable of reasoning, it is necessary :
  - to take into account the inferential phenomena involved in language understanding (especially for the discovering of implicit knowledge)
  - to go through a process of deduction based on the properties of some relations (transitivity, symmetry, reflexivity, ...) [9]
  - to interpret the text according to its context of utterance and the reference world (or conversational context).

  To realize this, the semantic representations must be integrated into the general knowledge of the system.

- The generation of utterances occurs after a user request or with the aim of giving explanations. The main thing is indeed the ability to justify what the system did in a given situation so that the end-user can understand the sometimes complicated reasoning of the simulator. It is also important to give the system the opportunity of explaining what it can do and what it cannot do.

The modelling of a conversational context, the flexibility of systems (integration of new knowledge, knowledge evolution) and the faculty of giving explanations are problems approachable according to two points of view : to keep the classic modularization in lexical level, syntactic level and semantic level, or to develop computational architectures based on a totally different functioning.
The first point of view is interesting as regards the results of systems but it does not actually tackle the cognitive modelling of understanding [8].
The second point of view, which seems promising to us, attends to the use of interactions between modules and develops theoretical tools, at the knowledge representation level as well as at the computational architecture using them.

Research about NLP has long been devoted to the study of the structure and meaning of single sentences. This step is essential, but after the construction of internal representations of sentences, it is necessary to integrate them into a broader structure beyond the level of sentence which represents a higher level of comprehension [8]. This concerns the search by reasoning of links existing between the different elements of a text as well as the links between the text and its context.
Instead of building the semantics of the sentence which would be a kind of description of the signification of one element, this sentence must be replaced in its context [5].

Sowa's conceptual graphs support many systems of NLP. They have been used especially for the semantic representations of sentences (Kalipsos, [6], 1991). Kalipsos exploits the interactions between the lexical, syntactic and semantic modules, but allows a feeble consideration of the context of utterance. Furthermore, as regards the evolutivity in a knowledge base, it seems difficult to describe the rearrangements of the semantic content inherent in the process of understanding and reasoning with conceptual graphs [7].
Regarding the links between an utterance and its context, systemic grammars of Hallidayand Winograd have focused on the functional organisation of language (i.e. organisation into systems) and the relations existing between the form of the text and the contexts (conversational context or context of utterance) in which the text can appear. Various complementary points of view are considered in this type of grammar : the system of mood (main, declarative or affirmative proposition), the system of linguistic agents (agent, object, ...), the thematic system (what we talk about) and the informative system (the determination of the known and the unknown regarding the structure of the sentence). The strong point of this representation is the integration of processing syntactic, semantic and pragmatic together; its weak point is its application to only very limited universes.
The same weak point is to be found in augmented transitions networks (ATN) (Wood 1970, Winograd 1983) : an ATN having a wide linguistic coverage is difficult to write.

The mechanisms of understanding and utterance are often respectively compared to analysis and production of NLP. Far from being unaware of NLP techniques (lexical, syntactic, semantic and pragmatic aspects), our approach is directed towards their integration into a huge representation, representation in which both the dynamic and evolutive aspect of knowledge linked to reasoning mechanisms will be taken into account. The implementation of training simulators meeting these requirements led us to the construction of a shared structure for understanding, utterance and reasoning in a new computational architecture called ABCD (Archistructure of dynamic knowledge bases).

3 Our approach to natural language processing

The NLP, as a means of communication, aims at making the relation between the user and the computer more human, easier and user-friendly. The interactive use in question is established in a training situation. Communicating agents are interadapted at the same time to a situation in a place and a time given [1]. In our training system, the analysis of natural language utterances or rather understanding of natural language utterances, is meant for the interpretation of utterances in comparison with a knowledge base and then their translation into metalinguistic formulas (cf. Figure 1).

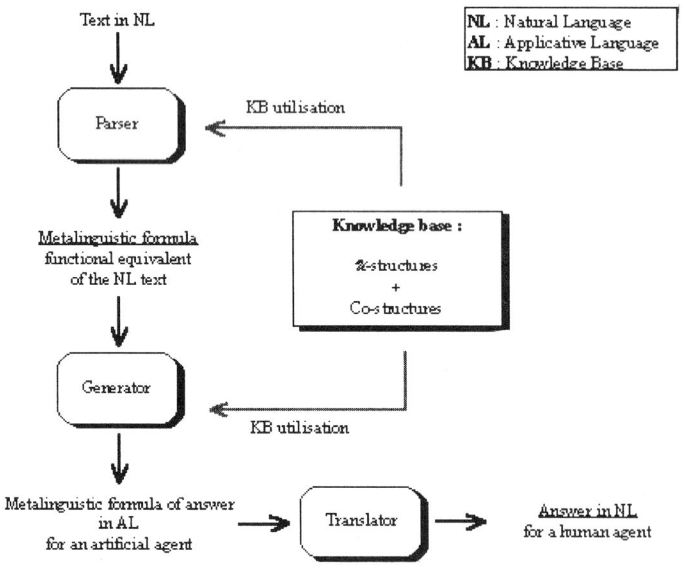

Figure 1: Integration of metalinguistic formulas in NLP

The interpretation process produces semantic representations that place the **linguistic agents** of the sentence and the relations between linguistic agents. The syntactic representations necessary to interpretation need not be complex [7]. The parsing can be restricted to the recognition of the mains syntagms open to receive the semantic roles played by linguistic agents.

The **metalinguistic formulas** obtained by the translation of semantic representations, independent from language, are expressed in a type functional language (whose the use will be explained in subsection 5.1). So, the formulas represent the functional equivalent of the sentence in natural language on which inferences and reasoning will be applied to.

The generation of utterances concerns among other things, an answer to queries from users or explanations about a reasoning of the simulator. For a query, the equivalent formula in applicative language is confronted with the knowledge base contents. The system works out an answer with the same formalism that must be converted into a text in natural language.
These objectives led us on the one hand, to improve the "host structures" for the knowledge about context, and on the other hand, to develop automatic mechanisms of knowledge exploiting so that the system can perform some reasoning and produce explanations.

4 The ABCD model : computational structures for cognition

The structuring of knowledge is a technique which aims at establishing a correspondence between the real world and a symbolic formalism that can be processed by the computer. "To structure" means to move from observed world to its knowledge and vice versa. The result of a structuration is called computational structure for cognition.

4.1 An intuitive and graphic approach

The structuring of the knowledge about a universe is carried out according to the ABCD model. In order to uniformly translate all the sides of knowledge concept, the HBDS model (Hypergraph Based Data Structure, [3]) is used in a repetitive way to form the ABCD model. The basic concepts of class, attribute and relation feature in the HBDS model.
A **class** (C) is an entity that gathers some elements (or instances of class) having the same characteristics. The instances of class (IC) differ from each other by the value of their attributes.

> *Example* : In Figure 2, the class PERSON contains a single IC whose the value of the attribute Christian name is Paul.

The **relations** (R) reflect the interactions between the entities of a same universe. An occurrence of relation (OR) expresses a particular relation between two classes. An OR is oriented, binary and can have some attributes. The instanciation of an OR between two IC is an instance of occurrence of relation (IOR).

> *Example* : <to_walk> is a relation. This relation has a single occurrence between the class PERSON and the class PLACE and a single IOR between the IC Paul and the IC street.

An **attribute** (A) is an entity pointing to a special characteristic, a property, a way of being or doing that a human perceives or builds and assigns to a class or a relation. The attributes describe qualitative states.

> *Examples* : The class PERSON possesses two attributes Christian name and name. The class PLACE also has the attribute name.
> The relation <to_own> has an attribute date specifying the beginning date of possession. A particular attribute "called deictic" attribute is linked to the relation <to_walk>; it refers to the IC dog.

4.2 The concept of structure

The concept of structure is a concept higher than those of class, attribute and relation. A structure is a graph of which the nodes are shown by classes and the arcs by occurrences of relations. Two types of structures exist in the ABCD model :

- **U-structures**, conceived by the users of the training simulator,
- **co-structures**, conceived by the designers or experts of universes.

A user-structure or U-structure is the collection of facts relating to a situation. The user conceives his universe by declaring some classes, relations, attributes and other instances of concepts (cf. Figure 2). All U-structure is then the expression of the static component of knowledge concerning the modelled universe.

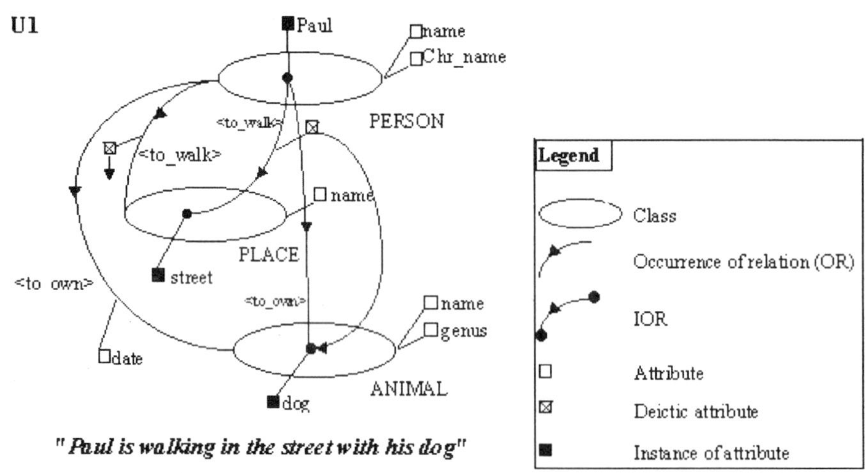

Figure 2: Example 1 of U-structure

More than one U-structure can be associated with an utterance. We left the user some freedom of modelling insofar as he keeps to the basic rules of construction (examples of rules of construction : every class has only one occurrence, no more than one same OR between two classes, ...). Figure 3 is an other U-structure for the sentence *"Paul is walking in the street with his dog"*.

U-structures are not sufficient to model a universe U; it is necessary to associate with them some particular constructions or co-structures which are defined by ABCD designers to run U-structures. Co-structures make possible the association of metaknowledge (properties, definitions, methods) to U-structures concepts. Their functioning is also programmed by designers. Co-structures are the basis of transformation of data (or facts) featuring in U-structures into knowledge [4].

Examples :

- $S, co-structure of U-structures or meta-structure
- $D, co-structure of definitions,

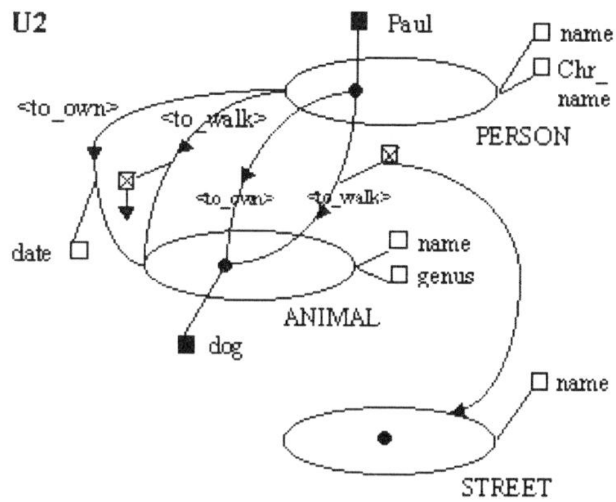

"Paul is walking in the street with his dog"

Figure 3: Example 2 of U-structure

- $G, co-structure of grammar,
- $I, co-structure of interfaces,
- $R, co-structure of rules.

Thanks to the structural logic of ABCD, all data contained in a U-structure are instanced in the suitable co-structures. On the one hand, these data, converted into knowledge, reveal several kinds of semantic links between components of the universe represented by the user : it is the "computational aspect" of structures. On the other hand, the exploiting mechanisms of knowledge contained in co-structures enable us to compare them to genuine coprocessors.
U-structures and co-structures are combined and complement each other to represent both static and dynamic aspects of knowledge on U, thus converting databases into knowledge bases.

5 A semantic and dynamic representation of contextual knowledge

The understanding of general mechanisms characterising the representation of a context of utterance involves the taking into account of different levels and types of metaknowledge shared into co-structures.
Concerning the automatic natural language processing, both semantic and definitional points of view will be tackled (co-structures $S and $D).

5.1 The meta-structure $S

We were first interested in the development and improving of a host structure to describe some situations extracted from the real world. Reasoning, mainly about signification, will be led from these descriptions.
The co-structure $S is the semantic representation of situations on users' universes. It gathers knowledge about U-structures and expresses the properties inherent in elements

from an operative point of view. $S makes explicit the semantics of different constituents of U-structures with respect to the user's aims, thus increasing the abilities of knowledge exploiting.
Like every structure, $S contains classes, relations and attributes. $S classes are divided into three groups :

- classes of U-structures elements (CC, CR, CIOR, ...)
- classes of "associators" (CS)
- the other classes (class of properties of relation, class of descriptor of method, ...)

A list of the main classes is presented in Table 1.
From a semantic point of view, classes of associators allow experts to link the information (in the form of attributes) specific to the association of two elements : for instance, the domain of definition of the attribute name for the classes PERSON and ANIMAL (cf. Figure 4).

Table 1: Main classes of $S

CC	Class of classes
	□ Attributes:name, type ∈ {*animate, inanimate, ...*}
CSRC	Class of associators relation-class
CR	Class of relations
	□ Attributes : name, type ∈ {*action, state, ...*}
CSAC	Class of associators attribute-class
	□ Attributes : domain of definition
CA	Class of attributes
CSAR	Class of associators attribute-relation
	□ Attributes : domain of definition
CIOR	Class of IOR
	□ Attributes : act of language ∈ {*will, belief,..*}, form ∈ {*affirmative, negative*},tense
CSIORR	Class of associators IOR-relation
CIC	Class of instances of class (IC)
CSICC	Class of associators IC-class
	□ Attributes : alias —*refers to IC without using the values of classes attributes*
CV	Class of values
CSAV	Class of associators attribute value
CSICV	Class of associators IC-value
CSICIOR	Class of associators IC-IOR
CSIORV	Class of associators IOR-value
CAD	Class of deictic attributes
CIAD	Class of instances of deictic attributes
CPR	Class of properties of relation
CSPR	Class of associators property-relation
CDMR	Class of methods descriptors of relation

The relations of $S, or $S-relations are functions which inform us about **semantic roles** (in the same sense as Fillmore's semantic cases) of $S-classes elements (cf. Table 2). They bring out the relations of meaning existing between these elements.
A semantic role is played by a linguistic agent. A **linguistic agent** (LA) is defined as a being (animate or not) who is committed to an action and plays a certain role according to his relationship with this action and other linguistic agents.

So, in the sentence "*Paul is walking in the street with his dog*", "*Paul*" is committed to an action in which he plays the role of agent (we have called this role <who>). The

Table 2: Some relations of $S

<who>	Animate LA who achieves or satisfies a U-relation.
<what>	Animate or inanimate LA on which a U-relation is directed
<auxiliary>	Inanimate LA which contributes to the achievement of a U-relation
<where>	U-relation location with variants <where_begin>, <where_end>
<when>	Temporal location of a U-relation with variants <when_begin> and <when_end>
<benef>	Animate or inanimate LA a U-relation with the type action is intended
<means>	Concrete inanimate LA by means of which a U-relation with the type action can be performed
<accomp>	Animate LA with whom a U-relation with the type action is performed
<what>$^{-1}$	Inverse of $S-relation <what> with a U-relation with the type action
<where>$^{-1}$	Inverse of $S-relation <where>
<who>$^{-1}$	Inverse of $S-relation <who>
<benef>$^{-1}$	Inverse of $S-relation <beneficiary>
<sub>	$S-relation of subordination between two IOR.

action takes place in a spatial setting "*in the street*" (<where>) and accompanied by a co-partner "*his dog*" (<accomp>) (cf. Figure 4).
The same LA can play different roles. An animal can be a patient (<what>) in the sentence "*A person owns* **an animal**") or a co-partner (role <accomp> in the sentence "*A person is walking with* **an animal**"). Conversely, several LA can play the same role : for instance, the role <who> in the sentence "**Peter** *and* **Paul** *are walking in the street*".

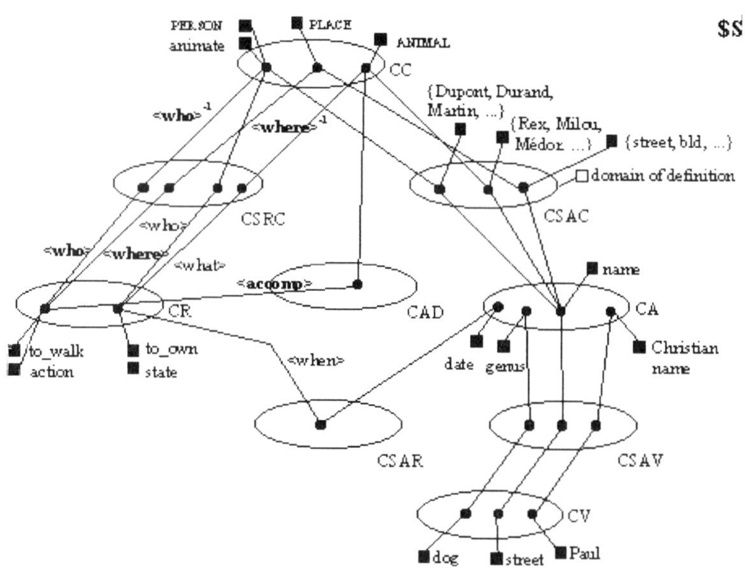

Figure 4: Extract of the meta-structure $S associated with the U-structure U1

The getting of information contained in co-structures is possible thanks to an applicative language called ALECX for Applicative Language for Set, Conceptual and refleXive processing in logic. ALECX is a language especially conceived for an ABCD architecture. Metalinguistic formulas are used as a means of communication between

artificial agents.
Let us assume that an agent want to know the semantic roles of several U-structures components : the semantic role of U-structure elements is obtained by calling the ALECX function role. The application of semantic roles (which are functions) to U-relations produces its LA.

Examples :

- The query "what is the semantic role of PERSON regarding the OR **to_walk** between the classes PERSON and PLACE ?" is written in ALECX :
role (PERSON, to_walk(PERSON, PLACE)) ? =<who>
- What is the role of PLACE regarding the same OR ?
role (PLACE, to_walk(PERSON, PLACE)) ? =<where>
- Which are the classes fulfilling the role <who> regarding the relation **to_walk** ?
who (to_walk) ? = PERSON
- Which are the relations having the class PERSON for agent ?
who^{-1}(PERSON) ? = {to_walk, to_own}

Metalinguistic formulas also make appear the types (class, relation, attribute, instance) and the semantic roles of U-structures elements representing utterances.
Thus, for the utterance "*Paul is walking in the street with his dog*", the following metalinguistic formula is obtained from Figures 2 and 4:

UTTER(**to_walk**[=(present,CIOR.tense), =(affirmative,CIOR.form)],
=(role[=(PERSON.Chr_name,**Paul**],<who>),
=(role[=(PLACE.name,**street**)],<where>),
=(role[=(ANIMAL.genus,**dog**)],<accomp>))

Because of its design, the co-structure $S allows us to take into account many syntactic and semantic notions such as :

- subordination ($S-relation <sub> of the class CIOR),
- negative form (attribute **form** of the class CIOR),
- paraphrase, notably thanks to properties of relation (for instance, the U-relation <to_marry> is a symmetric relation),
- significant semantic features as animate, inanimate, concrete, no concrete, ...(attributes of the class CC),
- synonymy and antonymy,
- nominalization,
- effects of speech from LA points of view : the active form (<who> point of view), the passive form (<what> point of view), the form by ellipsis of <who> (<auxiliary> point of view in the sentence "**The key** *opens the door*" for example).

As we are going to see, the interaction between $S and $D allows us to represent synonymy, antonymy, hyperonymy and nominalization.

5.2 $D, the co-structure of definitions

The different meanings of a word are usually specified by the means of definitions [2] :

- definition by reference to synonyms
  Examples : to walk = to go on foot, dog = bow-wow
- definition by reference to antonyms
  Examples : absolute = not relative
- definition by reference to hyperonyms
  Examples : park = public garden, doggy bag = bag proposed to customers in restaurants to take away the food they have not eaten.
- definition by nominalization
  Examples : driver, driving → to drive, walking, walker → to walk

Some of these definitions are references to $S elements such as nominalization, synonymy and antonymy. An illustration for the nominalization of the verb "*to drive*" is given in the Figure 5. So, in $D, the IC driving represents the nominalization of the IC to_drive in $S-class CR, and the IC driver represents the pair of IC in the class CSRC associating PERSON and VEHICLE by the relation to_drive.

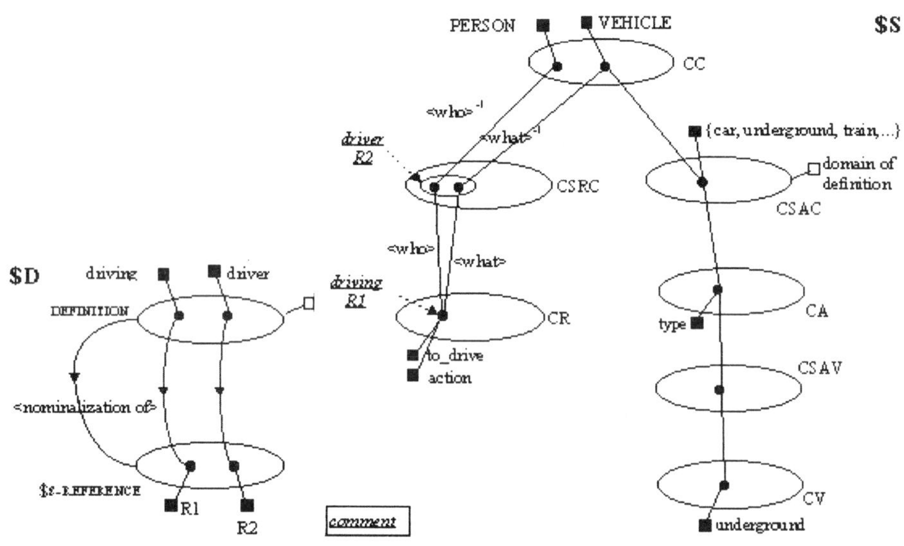

Figure 5: Definition by references to $S elements

Definitions by reference to hyperonyms are represented by the means of metalinguistic formulas (ALECX function *DEF*).

Example : given the definition of "*foreman*" : "*person who supervises a site*"
DEF (foreman, [PERSON](p), [SITE](s), to_supervise(p,s))

Through the examples above we have seen that it was possible to represent schematically some semantic aspects of sentences (linguistic agents, semantic roles), vocabulary (definitions), and how artificial agents could exploit U-structures and co-structures with the applicative language ALECX.

6 Conclusion

The possibility of establishing a dialogue between artificial agents during the simulation of a universe is the main objective of our research on training simulators.
From this point of view, we work on a strategy to take into account various knowledge using a metalinguistic formulation of interactions between agents.
The first point conducted us to the construction of a computational structure including knowledge linked to utterance understanding, generation of explanations and reasoning in a training simulator. We have shown the interesting features of the ABCD model through structural and metalinguistic representations of some utterances in natural language. ABCD seems to be the adequate model on the one hand for the representation of semantic aspects of utterances, and on the other hand for the discursive exploiting of structural representations of utterances thanks to our language ALECX.
Considering the second point, we think that the transformation of ABCD schemas into metalinguistic formulas will simplify exchanges between artificial agents and in the end, the transition from an utterance in natural language to a structural representation of this utterance and vice versa.

References

[1] Marie-France Blanquet Intelligence artificielle et système d'information ESF Editeur, 1994

[2] Gerrit Burket, Peter Forster "Representation of Semantic Knowledge Term Subsumption Language" Lexical Semantics and Knowledge Representation, Proceedings of the first SIGLEX Workshop, Berkeley, CA, USA, June 1991 Lecture Notes on Artificial Intelligence (LNAI 627) J. Pustejovsky, S. Bergler (Eds), Editions Springer Verlag, 1991

[3] Francois Bouillé "Un modèle universel de banque de données simultanément partageable, portable et répartie" Thèse, avril 1977

[4] Raymond Cousin "Processeur coopératif d'acquisition et de représentation des connaissances" Colloque, Rabat, Maroc, 1994

[5] Jacques Jayez L'inférence en langage naturel Editions Hermès, 1988

[6] Jean-Francois Nogier Génération automatique de langage et graphes conceptuels Editions Hermès, 1991

[7] Francois Rastier, Marc Cavazza, Anne Abeillé Sémantique pour l'analyse : de la linguistique à l'informatique Editions Masson, Collection Sciences cognitives, 1994

[8] Gérard Sabah L'intelligence artificielle et le langage, Tome 2 : Processus de compréhension Editions Hermès, 1989

[9] J.T. Sykes, V. Konstantinou, P.L.R. Morse "Extracting Explicit and Implicit Knowledge from Natural Language Texts" ICCI'94, Conceptual Structures, Current Practice, Proceedings of the 2nd International Conference on Conceptual Structures Lecture Notes on Computer Science (LNCS 835) Editions Springer Verlag, 1994

HypER: An Extended E/R Model With Hypertext Facilities

Gilles Levreau, Mokrane Bouzeghoub
Laboratoire PRiSM
Université de Versailles Saint-Quentin en Yvelines
Gilles.Levreau@prism.uvsq.fr
Mokrane Bouzeghoub@prism.uvsq.fr

Abstract. During the database development process several information sources are used to extract the knowledge which is necessary to understand the semantics of the database application. Much of this knowledge exists in informal representations such as forms, high level specifications, natural language sentences and semi-formal requirements. However no conceptual model captures 100% of the source information, either because the data model is not sufficiently rich or because the information is not relevant to the database implementation. Hence, much information is lost during the design process. Therefore, it is important that this lost information should be kept somewhere in order to facilitate maintenance by providing documentation and by keeping an affiliation link between the formalised knowledge and the source it originated from. To do so we propose to connect to the conceptual model (i.e. an extended ER model) hypertext facilities which do not necessarily enhance the expressiveness of the data model, but provide an elegant way of documenting conceptual schemas by introducing meta data as part of objects and relationships.
Keywords: database design, semantic models, hypertext, design documentation

1 Introduction

During the database development process several information sources are used to extract the knowledge which is necessary to understand the semantics of the database application. Much of this knowledge exists in informal representations such as forms, high level specifications, natural language sentences and semi-formal requirements.

Designers analyze these sources, extract what is meaningful with respect to the database being built, and express it as concepts of a conceptual data model. This latter plays a central role in this activity - it drives the design process and imposes the type of knowledge to represent, depending on its basic concepts and structuring rules. Therefore, the richer the data model is in concepts, the more it captures meaning about the application. This is why many authors propose extensions to conceptual models in general, and more specifically to the Entity/Relationship model. They provide means to capture, at the conceptual level, additional semantics represented by constraints, action rules [20] and temporal aspects [21], enabling designers to capture and structure the relevant information that defines as completely as possible the database semantics.

However no conceptual model captures all of the source information, either because the data model is not sufficiently rich or because the information is not relevant to the database implementation. Hence, much information is lost during the design process, as depicted in Figure 1. Many documents or fragments of texts are abstracted into portions of the schema and design decisions are made in such a way that only the future implementation of the schema seems to be important. Unless imposing a rigorous discipline of documentation (an old challenge never reached), only some designers remember the links between the final database schema and its sources (and for how long ?). However, for the maintenance, this lost information may be useful, even necessary, especially when the database schema needs to be modified.

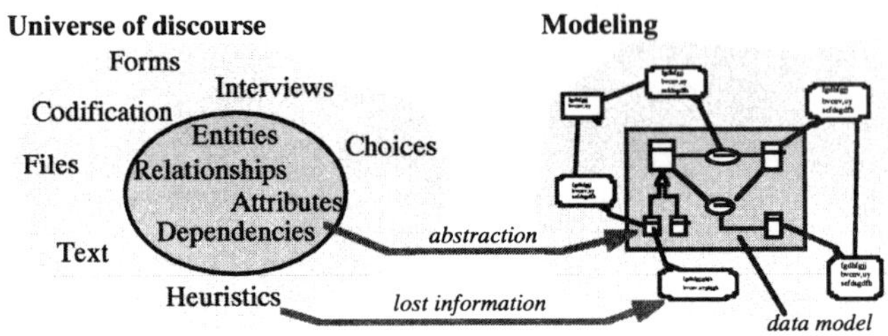

Figure 1: abstraction of the universe of discourse with loss of information

This information could also be helpful during the view integration process and during the database querying process by novice users. Integrating separate database views pose a number of problems related to users perceptions of the real world, to the terminology used, and to the comprehension of the data models. Providing documentation by hypertext facilities enhance understanding of the database schemas and lead to a better integration process. Before querying databases, novice users may need documentation about the semantics of the content of these databases. A certain level of documentation about entities and attributes can be used to explain their semantics or even the quality of the corresponding data (i.e. last updates, null values, added or relaxed constraints, etc.).

Therefore, it is important all this information should be kept somewhere in order to facilitate maintenance by providing documentation and by keeping an affiliation link between the formalised knowledge and the source it was originated from. As the nature of part of this information excludes its integration in the data model, we propose to surround the conceptual model (i.e. an extended ER model) by hypertext facilities, as depicted in Figure 2. The hypertext is considered as a means of keeping track of information otherwise lost during the design process. Hypertext nodes enable the representation of complex and even unstructured documents. Hypertext links are especially well adapted to handle the rich connectivity underlying such information. Nodes and links also enable simple, direct, and rapid access to related pieces of information. For example, they can connect an entity in the conceptual data model to the original fragment of text from which this entity has been abstracted. This allows visual and rapid checking of the semantics and the coherence of the database schema.

Introducing hypertext facilities in the conceptual model does not necessarily enhance the expressiveness of the data model, but it provides an elegant way of documenting conceptual schemas by introducing meta-data as part of the objects and relationships. This combination of models (referred in the following as the HypER model) allows the formal specification of a database schema and its corresponding documentation. Besides entities and various relationships and constraints, HypER schemas can contain nodes describing forms, graphics, texts or even formal or semi-formal descriptions such

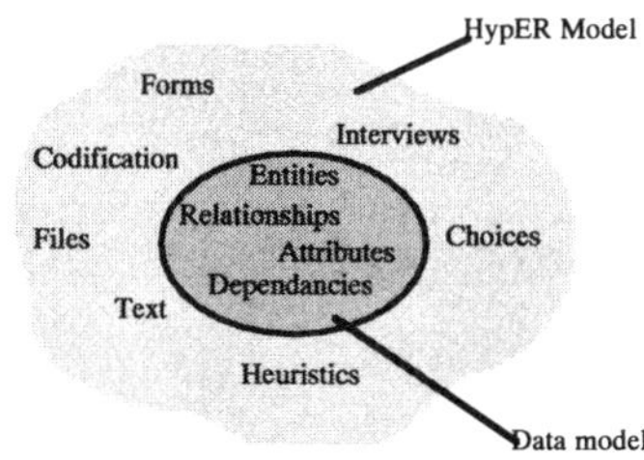

Figure 2: the HypER model as a layer around the data model

as code in a given programming language or rules and directives on how to understand and to use the conceptual schema. The HypER model has been implemented in Kheops, a CASE tool developed in a project at Versailles University.

Section 2 of this paper presents the formal conceptual model of Kheops, on top of which the hypertext facilities are built. Section 3 presents the HypER graphical editor, which provides the hypertext facilities. Finally, section 4 analyses this model with respect to related works.

2 Kheops Conceptual Data Model

KHEOPS is a CASE tool which provides many functionalities for database applications engineering, such as diagrammatic editors, code generators, knowledge extractor from natural language, paraphrasor of database schemas, view integrator, etc. The conceptual data model underlying this CASE tool is an extended E/R model which includes object-oriented features such as complex objects, inheritance and behavior. This section summarizes the fundamental concepts of our conceptual model and their corresponding graphical representation. This model has evolved through the years to permit the design of either relational databases [2], object-oriented databases [3] or active databases [17].

2.1 Concepts

The fundamental concepts of our conceptual data model include entities (or objects), types, classes, attributes and many kinds of relationships such as aggregation, generalization, association, reference and message. Classes are sets of entities that have the same type and the same behavior. Types are simple or complex data structures; they may characterize either classes or attributes. The dichotomy between a class and a type allows to distinguish between a set and its properties.

The model allows the specification of binary or n-ary relationships which may both have attributes and operations. Among the relationships, we can highlight some whose semantics is recognized uniformly in most applications, such as aggregations, generalizations, references and messages. Aggregation describes an entity as a composition of other entities. Generalization describes a class as a union of other classes. A reference is a static invocation of an object by another object, using its identifier. A message is sent from an entity (sender) to another entity (receiver) so as to ask the receiver to perform one of its operations. A message has attributes which represent the specification of actual parameters of the called operation.

The behavior of objects and relationships is specified by two complementary aspects: (i) operations which can be performed on them, and (ii) rules which capture integrity constraints and management laws (business rules, derivation rules, active rules, etc.). Integrity constraints complement the structural description of the database. They enable to specify properties the database must comply with to be consistent.

2.2 Diagrammatic representation of the model

Graphical representations play a central role in conceptual modeling. They allow an easy communication between designers and users in one hand, and between designers and implementors in another hand. Although they are not able to represent 100% of the formal model, they are considered as a convenient support for knowledge acquisition and for conceptual reasoning about the application. Following many authors and design methodologies, we can use E/R diagrams to give a graphical representation to our model. A class is represented by a box which contains the entity name, its attributes, its operations and the corresponding constraints.

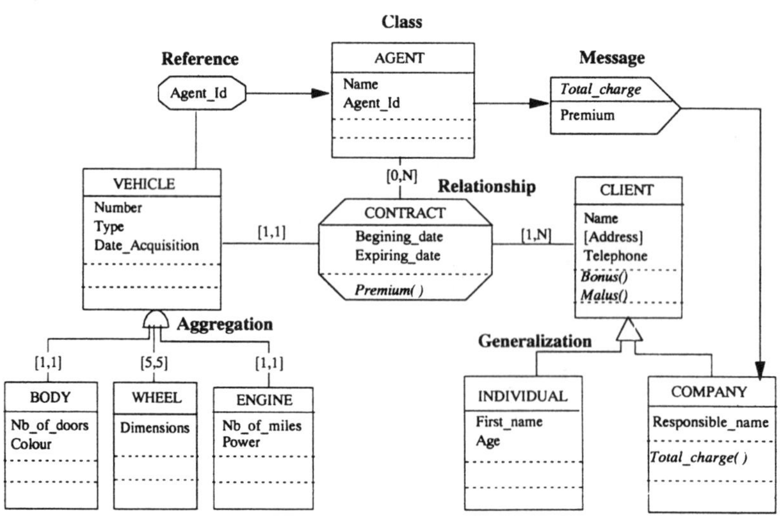

Figure 3: Example of an extended E/R diagram

Figure 3 shows part of the graphical representation of the conceptual schema of an insurance company. The class CLIENT has the attributes name, address, telephone and two operations bonus and malus. It has two subclasses, INDIVIDUAL and COMPANY. The relationship CONTRACT involves the classes AGENT, CLIENT and VEHICLE. A VEHICLE has three components BODY, WHEEL and ENGINE. An AGENT may send a message total_charge to a COMPANY. A VEHICLE has a reference to the attribute agent_id of an AGENT.

This graphical representation does not represent all of the specification of the insurance company, the remaining or the complete specification could be given by a textual representation.

3 HypER

Besides the data model briefly presented in the previous section, Kheops provides a hypertext layer to document schemas built with this data model. The hypertext layer provides, to some extent, a kind of formal model for documentation. This could be considered as a rational way for documenting and maintaining database applications.

The graphical editor of HypER schemas enables to edit extended E/R diagrams and to attach or access related documentation through hypertext links. Using graphical displays supplies functionalities otherwise impossible with a printed version of E/R diagrams. Displaying on screen introduces a third dimension of navigation which allows to master the complexity of large database schemas. Common techniques used with graphical displays, such as multiple windows and scroll bars, can be applied to the representation of the model. For example, an entity with a long list of attributes would clutter the sheet of paper, whereas the use of scroll bars make it possible to have all the attributes readily at hand.

In the remainder of this section we present the hypertext concepts of HypER with a typical use of the graphical editor during the design process. The section ends with an enumeration of the different issues met by the use of hypertext.

3.1 Basic concepts of HypER

The HypER model includes the hypertext concepts of nodes and links. Nodes are linked to each other and form a network. Both nodes and links are typed. The type of a node indicates the nature of the information it contains (e.g. graphics, free text). The type of a link indicates the nature of the relationship between the nodes it links (e.g. annotation, mapping). We distinguish four main types of nodes:

- Free Text nodes: these nodes contain a textual documentation which can be made in natural language or in a jargon specific to a given domain. For example, as a free text document, one can have a page of comments which explains the meaning of an entity in a given database schema. This kind of document could eventually be structured into chapters, sections and paragraphs.

- Formal Text nodes: these nodes contain various specifications ranging from high level specifications (e.g. Z specification, first order logic specification or abstract data type specification) to source code written in a programming language.

- Graphics nodes: these nodes contain graphical documents such as ER diagrams, data flow diagrams, administrative forms or even informal diagrams. A given diagram could be represented as a bitmap or a PostScript file. Besides the graphical aspect, part of these diagrams are characterized by a formal semantics which can be described by formal text nodes.

- Audio Video nodes: these nodes contain numeric information which represents sound or pictures describing a dynamic comment of the data model.

Among nodes of each type, we can distinguish nodes containing interpretable documents and nodes containing non interpretable documents. Interpretable documents are compilable documents; their semantics is understood by the Kheops system. Non interpretable documents are not compilable documents; their semantics is not known by the system. Interpretable documents are composed using the different interfaces provided by Kheops, such as the graphical editor, the natural language parser or the formal language compiler. These documents are stored in two different ways: in their original formats (image, free text or structured specification) and as semantic networks which represent their semantics. Non interpretable documents are just represented in their original format; at most, they are characterized by a basic type, like bitmap or sound. Examples of these documents are interviews, comments, or various graphics.

Figure 4 summarizes the types of nodes of HypER, with an example for each of them. In the last column is the graphical representation associated with each type of node. This representation enables us to represent the hypertext network as a graph of nodes and links (such as in Figure 6).

type of node	interpretable	non interpretable	graphical notation
free text	specification in natural language	comments	comments
formal text	specification in formal language	Z specification	Z specif
graphics	E/R diagram	data flow diagrams forms	E/R
audio/video		interview	interview

Figure 4: types of nodes

The types of links supported by a hypertext system greatly influence the ease of use and usefulness of the hypertext facilities. If links reflect the semantics of the application domain, then users spend less additional cognitive effort trying to understand the meaning and wondering which link they should follow [9]. Thus, we have to understand what specific tasks users expect to perform, the data they manipulate, in order to provide support for these tasks and representation for this data. Four types of links are considered in HypER:

- Documentation links: a link of this type points to a document considered as a comment to a given concept of the database schema. For example, a free text page can be associated to a database constraint to explain its meaning and use.

- Paraphrasing links: a link of this type points to a document which is considered as a paraphrasing of the content of the original document. For example, a natural language text can be associated to a conceptual schema to explain the semantics underlying the data structure. Kheops is able to paraphrase automatically conceptual schemas described in an extended E/R model.

- Mapping links: a link of this type relates a concept at a certain level of abstraction to another concept (or others concepts) at another level of abstraction. For example, a conceptual entity expressed in E/R model could be mapped to one or several relations of the relational model. A cardinality of a conceptual relationship could be implemented as a checking procedure associated to a trigger.

- Reference links: a link of this type is a generic link which allows to relate any pair of nodes. Its semantics usually depends on the application. For example, we use this kind of link to represent cross-references between a given database schema and the programs which operate on it.

Not all combinations of types of nodes and links have a meaning. For example, paraphrasing links lead only to free text nodes containing natural language sentences. Figure 5 summarises the valid combinations for links whose source anchor is a node containing an E/R schema. For each type of destination node we mention an example of interpretable node and another one of uninterpretable node. Note that destinations of mapping and reference links are either interpretable nodes or nodes that can be generated by Kheops. This is because these links refer to concepts of the data model. Thus, in order to compute these links it is necessary that the meaning of the destination node be known to Kheops. That is, Kheops must know the relation between the contents of the node and the conceptual data schema.

dest. node \ link		documentation	paraphrasage	mapping	reference
free text	natural language				
	comments				
formal text	formal language				
	Z specif.				
graphics	E/R				
	picture				
audio/video					

specialized by user (origine, annotation, ...)

Figure 5: valid combinations of nodes and links

Figure 6 illustrates the various nodes and links of HypER and their connection to the conceptual data model. In this example, links annotation are a specialisation of the documentation link type.

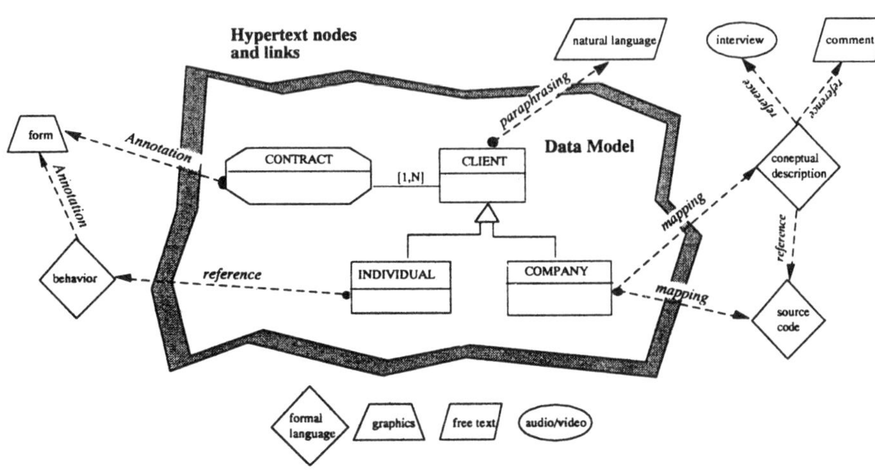

Figure 6: Example of nodes and links types in HypER

3.2 HypER in use

In this section we describe typical uses of the hypertext facilities. These facilities could be mainly used for three different purposes: (i) documentation and report generation about the meta knowledge, (ii) validation of the design process, (iii) evolution and maintenance.

The documentation activity is traditionally centered around a repository which contains meta data. The HypER model could be considered as a way of organising and accessing the repository. Each concept of the database schema (entity, relationship, attribute, operation or constraint) should be carefully and precisely documented in order to be used during the validation process or during maintenance. HypER schemas could serve as basic material to elaborate technical reports for database administrators or project leaders.

As an illustration, let us consider the example depicted in Figure 7. The inner part contains a conceptual schema which describes clients ordering products. Some of the concepts of the schema have a specific origin, described here in the annotations in the outer part of the figure. For example, the concept ORDER has been created as an entity because in the universe of discourse there was a file containing the clients orders, which led the designer to abstract it as an independent object. The entity PERIOD does not even correspond to an object of the universe of discourse being modelized: it has been added afterwards when statistics on products sales were needed. Such explanations are prone to oblivion, whereas they justify the design choices, and thus could help understand and validate the schema. Keeping track of them through hypertext links provides a powerful way to both organise them and then help access them.

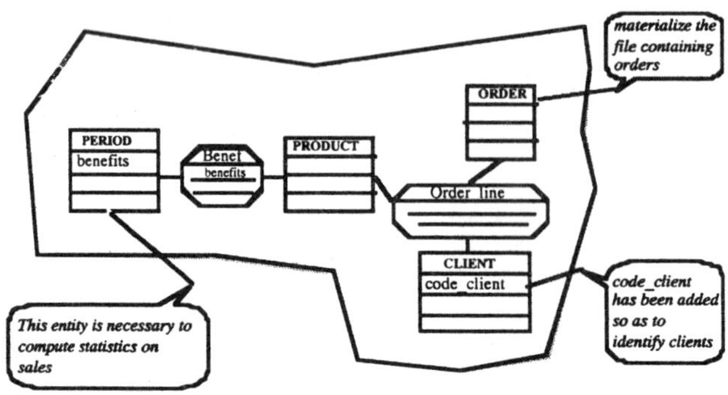

Figure 7: documentation of the conceptual schema

Figure 8 shows a database schema with the related documentation accessed through documentation links. In this figure, links have been materialized with their labels which indicate their corresponding types, and the content of each node is displayed in a separate window.

The validation process consists on one hand in checking that the conceptual schema corresponds to the universe of discourse. The validation of database schemas is a difficult task because it directly refers to the semantics of words and concepts. A clear and precise documentation is thus fundamental to enhance the understandability of the schemas. Kheops makes it available through documentation links. In addition, paraphrasing techniques are often used to generate a simple text from high level or technical specifications. These free texts are attached as comments to the corresponding schema. Kheops provides paraphrasing links, accessed through the paraphrasage entry

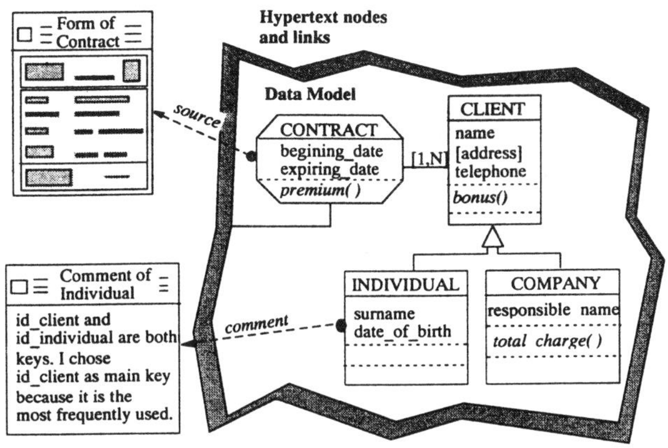

Figure 8: links involved in the documentation process

of an entity menu. Choosing it generates a description of the entity in natural language. Figure 10 shows a window containing the paraphrasage of the description of the entity CLIENT.

It is also necessary to validate the design process, that is to check that the relevant design choices have been made along all steps of the design process. As an explanation, let us consider the example depicted in Figure 9. The conceptual schema mention that the two entities EMPLOYEE and CHILD are specifics of the entity PERSON. As the concept of generalization does not exist in the relational model, it has to be transformed. Three solutions are identified : solution a consists in adding a role to the entity PERSON to distinguish whether it is an employee or a child, solution b consists in implementing the entity PERSON as a view which is a union of the sets of employees and children, and solution c consists in keeping all three entities and adding an attribute to employees and children which refers to their instance as a person.

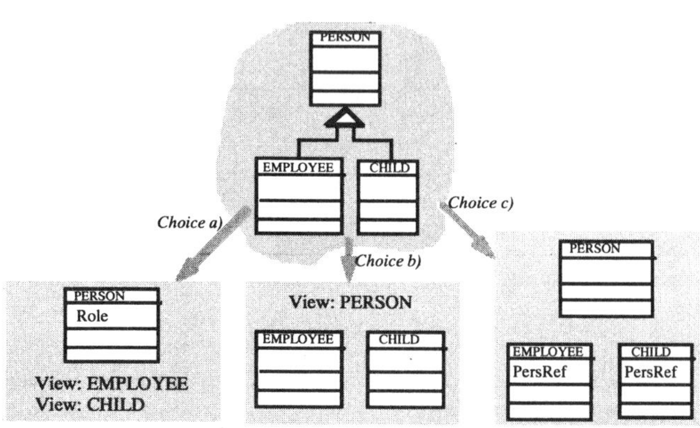

Figure 9: example of design choice

During the design process, many such choices have to be made in order to complete the implementation of the database. The relationships between two levels of abstraction are not always obvious. For example, cardinalities, which have no direct equivalent in object- oriented database languages, are implemented as checking methods. It is thus useful to offer designers a tool that enables them to step through the tree of design choices and browse the related documentation, so as to understand and validate these choices. This can be done by means of mapping links from an object at one level of abstraction to the corresponding objects at another level of abstraction, with documentation links commenting the transformation. Concerning the example of Figure 9, if solution b, say, has been chosen, then a mapping link from the entity Person to the view computing it indicates the transformation. Documentation written by the designer and attached to the view with a documentation link can give the reason of the choice.

Figure 10 depicts the types of links that are useful during the validation process. Paraphrasage and documentation links help understand the schema. Reference links help check that there are no inconsistencies among graphical and textual specifications, by hilighting all occurrences of a particular concepts through all specifications. For example, on Figure 10, the graphical specification mentions the date of birth of individuals, while the textual specification a management rule refers to the age of individuals. The designer might chose to keep track of only one of the attributes.

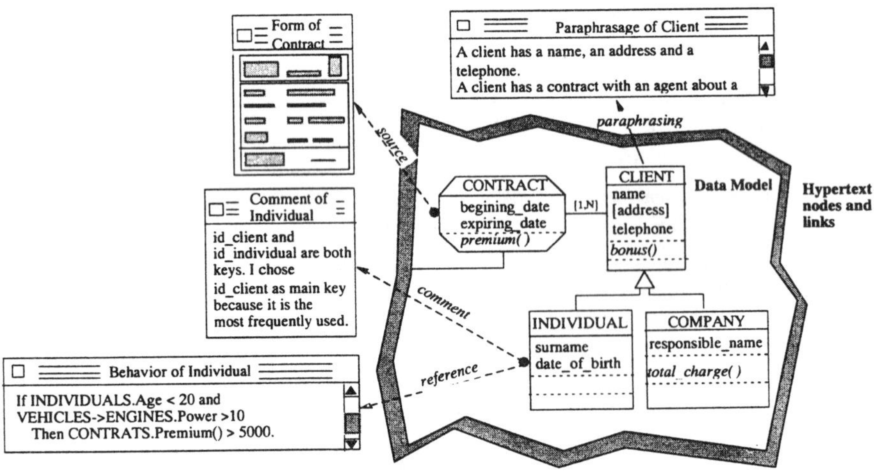

Figure 10: validation of the design process

Maintaining a database schema is a difficult activity. Many problems related to update propagations and coherence make the process complex and risky. People in charge of the database maintenance are usually different from those who designed the database schema. Besides, the conceptual diagram plays a central role in the maintenance process, it needs precise documentation which keeps track of the design decisions and the various transformations from the external specification to its implementation. Once the conceptual schema is validated, the system generates the source code implementing it. A mapping link, accessed through the source code entry of entity menus, leads to the implementation of an element of the schema (provided that the code generation has been performed). The reverse link can serve as graphical documentation of the source code. Figure 11 shows a window containing the C++ source code corresponding to the entity CLIENT. One of the challenge of HypER is to associate to the technical documentation an impact search functionality which allows the database administrators to predict the effect on the database of any change in the real world or technical environment.

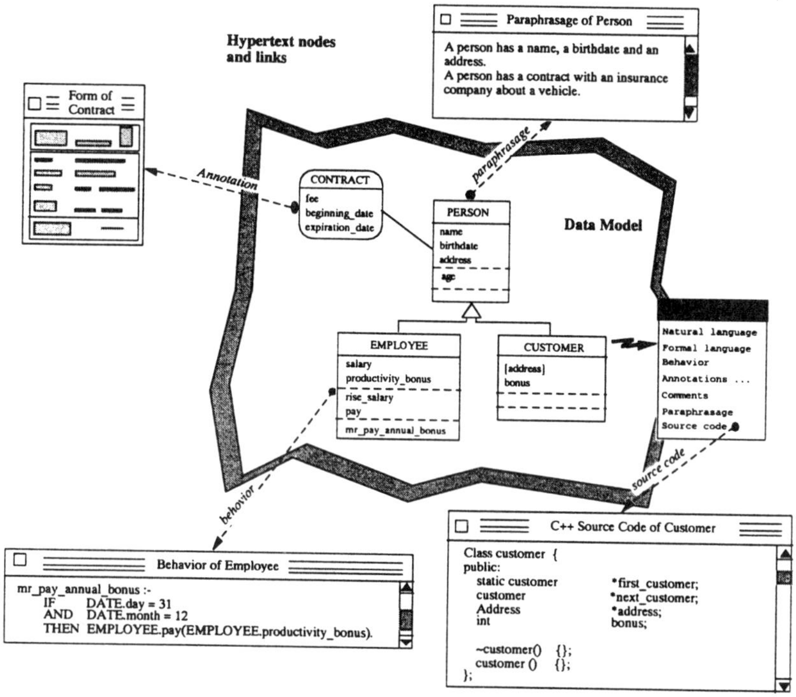

Figure 11: data schema and related nodes

3.3 Issues with hypertext nodes and links

The very freedom of navigation provided by hypertext links generates the often pointed out disorientation problem [12] [10]. In hypertext documents, users have to choose which link to follow, and remember where they are in the information network. These processes create additional cognitive overhead, and give way to disorientation.

A solution widely used is to provide a map of the hypertext network. But often these maps have a simplistic model, with only nodes and links, and do not provide enough information for the user to understand the network [22]. In this paper, we propose the ER diagram as a means of giving an idea of the overall structure of the application being designed. It provides a starting point to navigate in the information space, the semantics associated with the model giving an idea of the hypertext network.

The search techniques provided by most hypertext systems force users to skim through data which is not pertinent to their search. Users have to read this data in order to decide whether it is pertinent or not, adding cognitive overhead. Hypertext systems usually provide search facilities based on textual search or on queries involving keywords. Textual searches are based on syntactic methods, and thus lack the semantics necessary to select the pertinent data. For example, let us imagine I search all sentences mentioning the attribute address of the entity Person. A mere textual search would display any sentence mentioning an address, even an address of a company. Keywords enable to capture semantics, but are attached to objects which are not fine-grained enough, such as nodes and links, to answer precisely to the search above. Links provided by Kheops can be seen as a search method which takes into account the nature of the value being searched. For example, traversing the natural language link from the attribute address of the entity Person will display only those sentences which mention this specific attribute.

Another way usual search techniques return non-pertinent data is due to the nature of nodes. When node content is static, searches return pointers to locations in nodes, for example by opening a node and highlighting the result. This technique is appropriate when users need information about the context of the search result, like the part of a program using a variable. However, in the case of declarative specifications, only the sentences mentioning the searched object need to be displayed. Thus, Kheops extracts the pieces of information about the concept, groups them into a virtual node which exists only as long as the window displaying it exists, linearizing them in a single document. This way, users do not have to examine through every node and decide which next to read [13]. This has the additional benefit of displaying close to each other related pieces of information otherwise scattered in several documents, thus highlighting inconsistencies [18].

4 Related works

Since the ER model has been presented, many extensions have been proposed. They are concerned with capturing more semantics at the conceptual level. For example, they provide means to represent aggregation and generalization [19], integrity constraints, action rules [20] and temporal aspects [21]. They now adapt the model to object-oriented databases, with concepts such as operations attached to objects, and messages [7] [4]. However, by their very nature, these models enable to record only what will be implemented, not the documentation which goes with it.

Several database management systems and information retrieval systems have integrated hypertext functionalities [14] [23] [15]. In these systems, hypertext links are provided as a facility to access data. They enable users to browse in an hypertext fashion the set of objects resulting from a query. However, the hypertext functionalities are not intended to be used during the database design process. We benefit from solutions to problems in common, though, like using virtual nodes and links.

We have benefited from research on CASE tools, too. Hypertext systems have now been used for several years in the domain of software engineering, mostly for their support of the rich connectivity between components and for their capacity to handle many types of information. Several prototypes have been implemented, which focus on specific aspects of software engineering. Dynamic Design [1] and DIF [11] help manage the interconnections of software components, including documentation. Worf [5] provides help during the maintenance process. ICICLE [6] augments the formal code inspection process with computer-aided help and guidance. [8] propose hypertext links as a help to select components from reusable libraries.

However, most of these systems provide environments for programming with C language. The general software life-cycle and the database design process have much in common, but the artefacts handled are different and require appropriate management facilities. For example, to fully understand the use of a variable in a C program, it is necessary to see the part of the program where the variable is used. On the contrary, in Kheops, textual specifications are declarative, so understanding the use of a specific object requires only that the user see the sentences which actually involve this object. Displaying only these sentences require additional treatments, and this problem is not tackled in the systems mentioned above.

Hypertext links is one of the means we chose to capture and keep the information not stored in the conceptual schema. Kheops natural language interface translates the sentences into a semantic network, and stores the linguistic information in a dictionary. This linguistic information, which does not appear in the conceptual schema, is useful for later steps, though [16]. It helps paraphrase an ambiguous ER schema and helps reduce the complexity of the view integration algorithm.

5 Conclusion

In this paper we presented HypER, a model integrating an extended ER model and hypertext facilities. The hypertext facilities are used to keep track of the documentation involved in the design process. The links are accessed from the HypER graphical editor.

The hypertext links to external documents depend on designers creating them. However, designers often undergo demanding time pressures because of tight deadlines. Therefore they give up the activities which are not strictly necessary to make the application works. It is illusory to think that under these constraints, designers will spend time on building the documentation if this task is too long and difficult. Thus, it is essential that the creation of links be a task as fast and easy as possible. But the documents to link might have formats which makes the linkage difficult. For example, designers might argue by electronic mail about a part of the schema, and it would be nice to be able to link the mails to the related elements of the schema (in fact, the reverse would be nice, too). A solution is to store the objects in a shared database, accessible from all applications and tools, so that all tools access the objects through a common interface. The database should be part of the operating system, thus easing the communication of objects between tools. But such operating systems, which are necessary to build a true comfortable hypertext environment, are still a research issue.

References

[1] Bigelow, J., *"Hypertext and CASE"*, IEEE Software, March 1988.

[2] Bouzeghoub, M., Gardarin, G., Mtais, E., *"SECSI: An Expert System for Database Design"*, Proc. of the 11th VLDB Conf., Stockholm, Sweeden, 1985.

[3] Bouzeghoub, M., Metais, E., *"Semantic Modelling of Object-Oriented Databases"*, Proc. of the 17th VLDB Conf., Barcelona, Spain, Sept. 1991.

[4] Bouzeghoub, M., Gardarin, G., Valduriez, P., *"Objets. Du C++ Merise Objet"*, Ed. Eyrolles, 1994.

[5] Brade K., Guzdial M., Steckel M., Soloway E., *"Whorf: A Hypertext Tool for For Software Maintenance"*, Int. Jal of Software Engineering and Knowledge Engineering, Vol. 4, no. 11, March 1994.

[6] Brothers L., Sembugamoorthy V., Muller M., *"ICICLE: Groupware For Code Inspection"*, CSCW 90 Proc., Oct. 1990.

[7] Coad, P., Yourdon, E., *"Object-Oriented Design"*, Prentice-Hall, 1991.

[8] Creech M.L., Freeze D.F., Griss M.L., *"Using Hypertext in Selecting Reusable Software Components"*, Hypertext'91 Proc., Dec. 1991.

[9] De Young, L., *"Linking Considered Harmful"*, in *"Hypertext: Concepts, Systems and Applications"*, Proc. of European Conf. on Hypertext, Versailles, France, Nov. 1990.

[10] Dillon, A., Mc Knight, C., Richardson, J., *"Navigation in Hypertext: a Critical Review of the concept"*, Human-Computer Interaction Interact'90, Ed. Diaper et al, 1990.

[11] Garg, P.K., Scacchi, W., *"A Hypertext System to Manage Software Life-Cycle Documents"*, IEEE Software, May 1990.

[12] Halasz, F. G., *"Reflections on NoteCards : Seven Issues for the Next Generation of Hypermedia Systems"*, ACM Hypertext'87 proc., Chapel Hill, N.C., Nov. 87.

[13] Ichimura, S., Matsushita, Y., *"Another Dimension to Hypermedia Access"*, Hypertext'93 Proc., Seattle, 1993.

[14] Jerke, K.H., Szabo, P., Lesh, A., Rbler, H., *"Combining Hypermedia Browsing with Formal Queries"*, Human-Computer Interaction, Interact'90, North-Holland, 1990.

[15] Lucarella D., Parisotto S., Zangi A., *"MORE: Mutimedia Retrieval Environment"*, Hypertext '93 Proceedings, Seattle, 1993.

[16] Métais, E., Meunier, J.N., Levreau, G., Language *"Database Schema Design: A perspective from Natural, Techniques to validation and View Integration"*, 12th Int. Conf. on E/R approach, Dec. 1993.

[17] Nagui-Raïss, N., *"A Formal Software Specification Tool Using the Entity-Relationship Model"*, 13th Int. Conf. on E/R approach, 1994.

[18] Nanard, J., Nanard, M., *"Should Anchors Be Typed Too ? An Experiment with MacWeb"*, Hypertext '93 Proc., Seattle, 1993.

[19] Smith, J.M., Smith, D.C.P., *"Databases Abstractions: Aggregation and Generalization"*, ACM Trans. on Database Systems, Vol.2, no.1, pp 105-133, June 1977.

[20] Tanaka, A.K., Navathe, S.B., Chakravarthy, S., Karlapalem, K., *"ER-R: An Enhanced Model with Situation-Action Rules to Capture Application Semantics"*, 10th Int. Conf. on the E/R Approach, Oct. 1991.

[21] Theodoulis, C., Loucopoulos, P., Wangler, B., *"The Entity Relationship Time Model and the Conceptual Rule Language"*, 10th Int. Conf. on the E/R Approach, Oct. 1991.

[22] Thüring, M., Haake, J., Hannemann, J., *"What's Eliza Doing in the Chinese Room? Incoherent Hyperdocuments and how to avoid them"*, Proc. of Hypertext '91, Dec. 1991.

[23] Watters C., Shepherd M.A., *"A Transient Hypergraph-Based Model For Data Access"*, ACM Trans. on Inf. Sys., Vol. 8, no. 2, pp 77-102, April 1990.

Applications of Natural Language to Information Systems
R.P. van de Riet et al. (Eds.)
IOS Press, 1996

Audio Facilities for Hypermedia Consultation

S.Djennane and F.Sedes
I.R.I.T - S.I.G
Universite Paul Sabatier
118,Route de narbonne
31062 Toulouse France
djennane@irit.fr -and- *sedes@irit.fr*

Abstract. This paper presents the problem of extending hypertext concept to audio hypermedia one, specifying an architecture for a speech hyperbase get-at-able for instance by blind or visually impaired people. The purpose of such systems is to make the user able to "navigate" through a set of heterogeneous information, along personalized links, mainly using the sound modality.
The enactment of an interface for audio consultation of a hyperbase in natural language must take into account the new paradigm of the spatiotemporal representation in sound space, since the information space creation process and the navigation are different from the ones associated to the visual context.
Keywords: Hypermedia, Audio Interface, Natural Language, Navigation, Annotation.

1 Introduction

The notion of hypertext refers to a set of textual data shown on an electronic medium available for consultation in different ways (Bush,1945): unlike "classical" documents that are linear, information is split into different nodes connected by links. Its reading is based on a route among these links to go from a node to another : this allows the user a mode of consultation by navigation (Nielsen,1990). The concept of "hypermedia" corresponds to the extension of the concept of hypertext to take multimedia information into account. A hypermedia document groups together a set of multiple information (text, sound, picture) that can be consulted according to multiple routes. The fragments of hypermedia documents can also be restituted in different forms: visual, tactile or sonorous. Hypermedia systems are generally based on graphic interfaces essentially implementing pointing-tools and 2D designation devices (mouse, tactile screen, light pen,...).
This paper presents the reflection undertaken in the context of the extension of the hypertext concept to the sound hypermedia one and the consultation problems which are closely linked to the user's perception: sound is volatile, nonpersistent, contrary to pictures; on the other hand, it diffuses and is perceptible even though the receiver and the sender are not facing each other (Cf.Table 1). These spatial and temporal components imply the user's presence and his synchronous reaction.
Thus, the speech/audio interfaces are sequentially made out, whereas visual ones can be globally apprehended: "here", for example, becomes "now". The user must pick up the order as it goes by.

As the ear does not move in a sound space as the eye in a visual one, the concept of navigation, fundamental in hypermedia systems, must be reanalysed and adapted : the vision of the web "from above" is replaced by a vision "from inside" of the "labyrinth". In this project, the problem of extension of the hypermedia database by audio component can be defined by the new paradigm of the interaction with the user: *How to restitute the spatiotemporal representation of the hyperbase in sound space?*
The first particularity of our project lies in the use of audio input/output devices for managing the hyperbase and user's annotations, as well as implementing the access mechanisms during their consultation. Not many hypertext systems use the audio component for the hyperisation and consultation processes at once: we can mention (Muller,1991) who defined the concept of sound documents, Free Style (Gillares,1992), a system allowing vocal annotations on written documents and HyperSpeech, a project in which the consultation interface only uses the sound modality.
The second particularity lies in using natural language vocal commands for man-system interactions. Our system offers the possibility to express such commands: it translates them, recognises them and finally executes them. Indeed, the system reacts by restituting vocal respons to find out transaction execution state.
In this paper, we first present the specific problem of this project. The hyperbase modelling and construction process, lying on the conversion of the electronic linear document into a hypermedia one, is described: this process consists of a structural analysis followed by a hyperisation phase based on the document tree diagram deduced from the structural analysis. We finally detail the functionalities the consultation vocal interface must offer, taking into account the sound modality specificity.

2 Some elements about sound modality and its specificities

Recognition systems for oral input allows to recognize word sequences pronouced by user according to a given grammar. Their implementation requires a learning associated to the speaker.
Synthesis systems for sound output can take different forms, each one owning its own characteristics:noise, music, or speech.
Two synthesis processes exist: digitized speech and text-to-speech synthesis.

- *Digitized speech:*The cards manipulating it are based on a preliminary numerical recording of the sound to be restored. The internal representation quality permits the restitution of natural tone and posody. This process can be extended to other signals: noise, music,...This technique requires important storage capacities.

- *Text-to-speech synthesis:*This type of synthesis lies on the transformation of a text in a sequence of phonemes (the shortest unit of sound of a language: 36 in french), and then the generation of speech by restitution of this sequence. These cards allow to synthesis an unlimited number of sequences given under their orthographic form. Voice quality remains average in spite of the improvements done. Such cards are used in systems of database access by phone and systems of screen review for the blind.

A state of the art of the sound modality allows us to have an idea of the specificities and limitations inherent to applications integrating it. In our project, the audio component must operate not only as an input (control language, requests,...) but also as an output (information reproduction in all its forms, whatever the type of the information may be). Any visual element (picture, diagram, icon,...) has to be dubbled by a textual description associated to a sound component for restitution. The choice of a storage/restitution strategy for textual information presents us with a problem: Text-to-speech synthesis or digitilized voice ?

	Sound	**Text**
Nature	Volatile	Persistant
Perception	Partial	Global

Table 1: Sound vs Text

3 Hyperbase Construction Process

The interface multimodal nature and the information type multiplicity confer the property of multimedia database on the information collection.
Moreover, the database continuously evolving, the hypertext approach seems to fit the need of cooperative tasks of creation and enrichment of it, while ensuring its consistency: information sharing, reusing, versioning. Such a collection can then be viewed as a single database integrating shared information units.
These principles are implemented into the hyperbase within which the document content is split into nodes related by links. The so built links are used for searched information accessing. Classically, a graphic representation of the hyperbase is given by its "web" illustring the hypergraph of the set of documents.
The basic concepts that have been implemented are:

- A *Concrete Node* is an atomic node of elementary information (called *Information Unit*),
- An *Abstract Node* is built by aggregation on concrete and/or abstract nodes; it allows to refer the set of nodes that compose it, and so traduces the information logical structure.
- A *Structural Link* is an implicit link (hierarchical) between an abstract node and its "son" nodes (concrete and/or abstract).
- A *Referential Link* corresponds to a pointer embedded within a node, which cross-refers to another node or a part of node (called a region) : these links are used for implementing bibliographic references, footnotes,...
- An *Anchor Point* is the position where a link is defined by its name, its link ends,
- An *Anchor* is a link end. It can be a source one or a destination one according to the role it plays.
  The two previous terms are equally used when the anchor point of link appears in the source anchor of this link.
- A *Region* corresponds to a part of a concrete node directly accessible and identifiable thus, allowing to speed up positioning during consultation.

3.1 Document Treelike representation based on structural analysis

The general integration process of a linear multimedia document into a hypermedia database consists in (Cf. Figure 1):

- recognition of the document structure, in order to get a representation of its tree structure completed by typographic motifs,
- hyperisation that transforms the tree structure into a graph one,
- storage into the hyperbase.

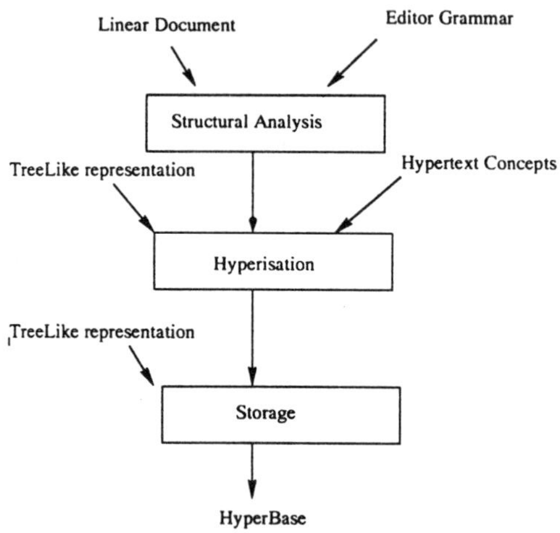

Figure 1: Integration of linear documents

The tree representation can be given according to different document representation standards such as SGML (Standard Generalized Language) (ISO8879), HyTime (ISO10744), HTML (HyperText Mark-up Language), ODA (Open Document Architecture) (ISO8613),... The interest of using a standard is to make it possible to parse the document structure unambiguously thanks to the grammar rigour.
Thus, the only initial constraint is that the document must be self-described i.e, it had to contain tags identifying its structure for its decomposition, which would be impossible otherwise. The SGML standard has been choosen for document description. An SGML document is constituted with a reference to its structure description, done within the DTD (Document Type Definition), and the document content itself. The DTD is common to a whole collection of documents having the same structure. The generation of an SGML document lies on a syntactic and semantic analysis of the source document, possibly associated with the corresponding DTD generation applying to the whole collection documents.

3.2 Hyperisation Process

The system deduces the hypermedia structure of the treelike representation relabelling its nodes: the concrete nodes are determined from leaves. All the ascendants of a concrete node constitute abstract nodes: the structural nodes of the tree become thus

abstract nodes. Structural links are deduced, between a concrete node and an abstract node, or between two abstract nodes. Referential links are characterized by an origin (an anchor point) and a destination (node, or region).
The so generated hyperdocument only expresses the explicit structure of the document given by tagging (references between parts of documents, bibliographic references, footnotes,...). This representation is completed by deduced nodes and links such as indexing links from keyword recognition.
The hyperised document is then integrated into the hyperbase, updating the author index, table of contents. (Chrisment,1993).MoreOver, the SGML document analysis makes possible to granulate information retrieval at the finest level. The granularity level is determined by hyperisation process, according type of information (text, speech, sound, picture and text associated,...). Let us comment Figure 2: After hyperisation,

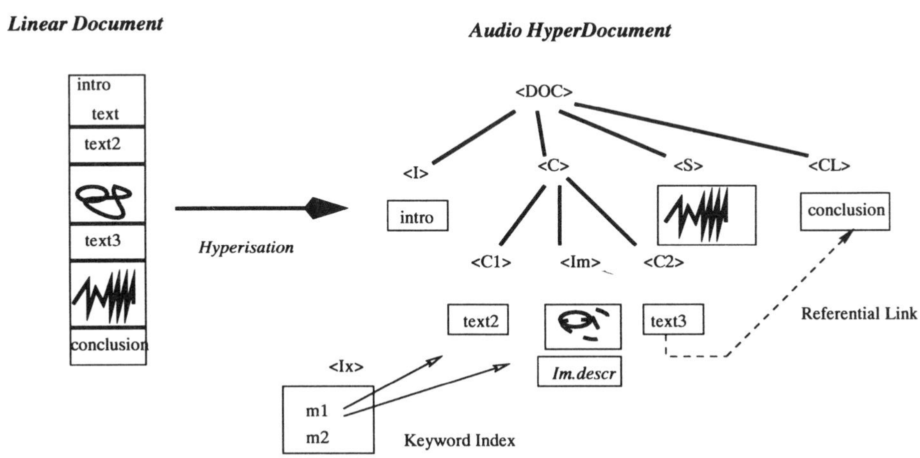

Figure 2: An audio Hyperdocument and its generation

the hyperdocument $\prec DOC \succ$ is composed by an introduction $\prec I \succ$, a set of chapters $\prec C \succ$, by a sound information $\prec S \succ$ and by a conclusion $\prec CL \succ$. The set of chapters is itself composed by a chapter $\prec C1 \succ$, a picture $\prec Im \succ$ and a textual description associated, and by another chapter $\prec C2 \succ$. The keyword index , $\prec Ix \succ$ associates a list of buttons related to nodes or regions to each keyword.

3.3 The data model

An object-oriented semantic data model has been choosen for modelling multimedia documents. This kind of modelling is well adapted to represent complex objects. It consists of extending classical data types to multimedia ones, implementing aggregation in abstract nodes (object composition) and generalisation/specialization (inheritance). This led us to design a metamodel of the hyperbase integrating the previous basic concepts seen at section 3 (Cf.Section 3). An hyperdocument consists thus of a root of logical structure tree. The root node is either an abstract node or a concrete node if we consider in the latter case that the whole document can sometimes be stored as well. For this reason, we introduced the **X** symbol between the multiple inheritance

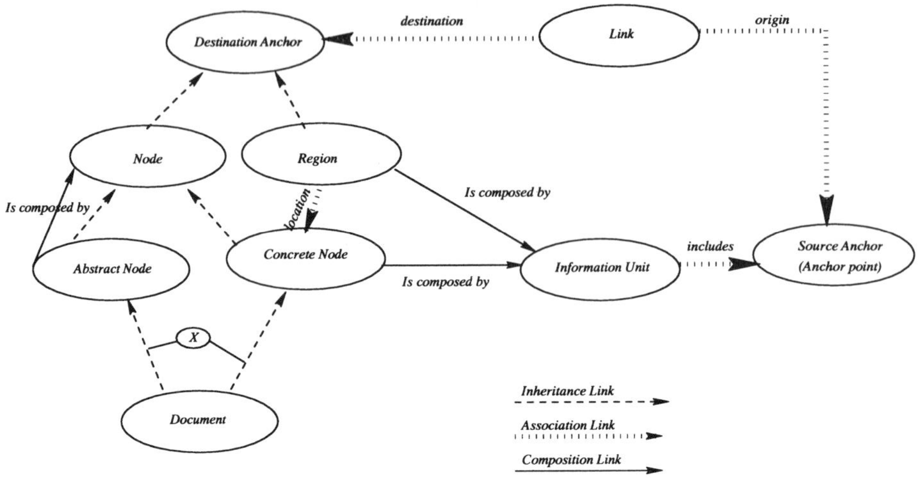

Figure 3: The basic MetaModel

links joining the superclasses *"Abstract Node"* and *"Concrete Node"* to the subclass *"Document"* (exclusive link).
Futhermore, the node can be referred by referential links as well as the region. Because they can be directly referred, corresponding classes (i.e *"Node"* and *"Region"*) are represented in this model as specializations of the *"Destination Anchor"* class.
A concrete node content is split into information units (instances of *"Information-Unit"* class). These ones may include anchor points of referential links. In this model the source anchor of a link is included in the information unit in which the "link anchor point" appears.
We can also, enrich the data model to take in account our study specific aspects that are: (Cf. Figure 4)

1. Information typing because managing multimedia information, we specialize the object class "Information Unit" that can be *Image, Text, or Sound.*

2. Annotations inserted into nodes or links in order to explain their content; an annotation node is indissociable from its author that can make it public or private. We consider, then, an object class annotation.

It is important to mention that the object class "Annotation" is different from other classes, the way it represents objects that have a dynamic behaviour. This is due to the fact that the annotation objects are not defined during hyperbase construction process, but created step by step (by users) during the hyperbase exploitation step.

4 Hyperbase exploitation

The hyperbase constructed by hyperisation process represents the static part of the system , all aspects related to its content exploitation represents the dynamic one. Our aim is to make this content accessible by different-profil users. They can if necessary ask

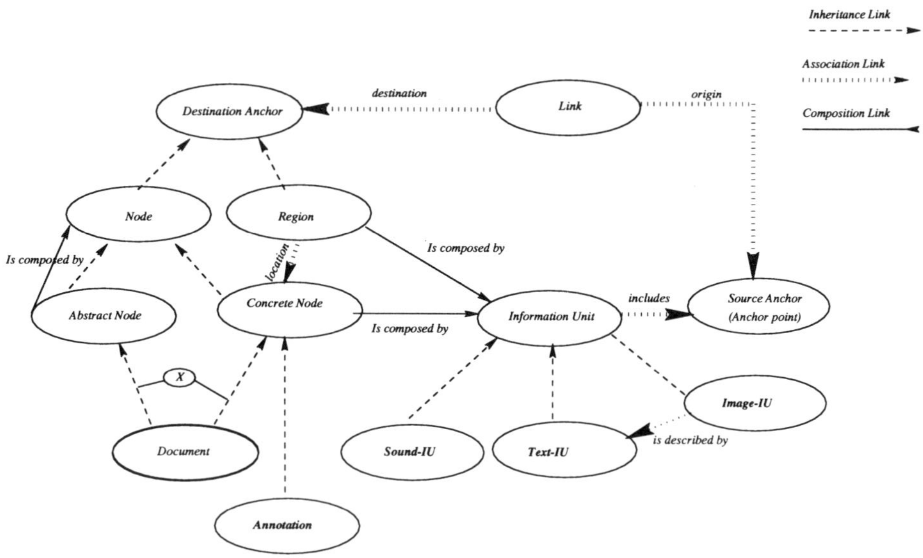

Figure 4: The enriched MetaModel

for an assistance consultation, navigate over the hyperspace but also customise their consultation by annotations.

Mechanisms supporting these functionalities are embedded within a second level we call *dynamic* (by contrast of static). This level cover all reader-type user interventions on the hyperbase. The static part is the result of author-type user handling. Dynamic aspect tiggers second-order link definition associated to hyperbase nodes to satisfy user requests. These kinds of links are called *HYPERLINKS* , second-order links or dynamic links (Cf.Figure 5).

4.1 Marking process

Structural and referential links are automatically determined from hyperisation step. The author or the reader can however intervene on the hyperbase structure and on its content by positioning dialogic or annotation links. We define this additionnal links and nodes as the marking process. Annotations are materialized by marks, implemented by buttons in the consultation stage.

We define two marking types: the author and the reader ones. This distinction is introduced to take into account the user's nature and his access rights towards the hyperbase. The notion of public, shared or private annotations is related to the confidentiality level.

The problem set by the marking process is essentially the identification, restitution and exploitation of marks during sound consultation.

We can give some ideas about the mechanism implemented to manage the audio buttons (materializing the marks), according to the anticipation process. A sound mark alarm is triggered off in order to warn the user. This alarm can come before the mark according to a lapse of time respecting the reaction period to activate it. If the mark

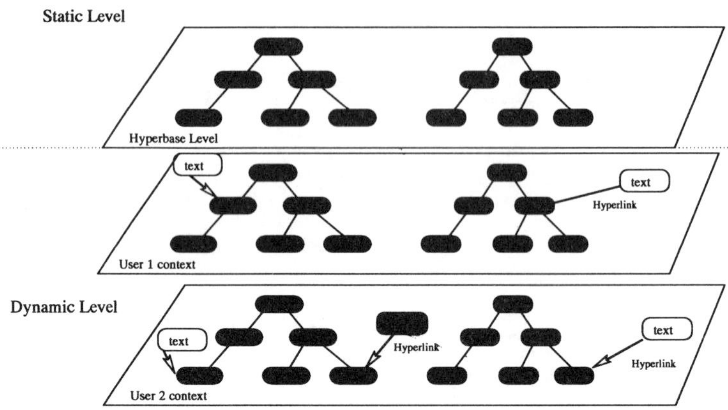

Figure 5: Static level vs Dynamic level and hyperlink definition

is activated, an explanatory comment is made, possibly followed by rerouting selection. The connection to another node occurs at that time. The reaction period can also be considered a posteriori, from the moment when the mark is activated. An a posteriori period must also allow the user to go back over his choice. The adopted strategy must take chronology and synchronization problems into account, when multiple marks are encountered at a given point, in order to avoid overlapping.

4.2 Annotations

Two types of users must be distinguished: the author who creates, organises and supplies the database, and the reader who explores it.

The reader's point of view is not necessarily the same as the author's: indeed, each reader has his own vision of the document he consults, his own characteritics,...The notion of point of view is introduced by means of the possibility to enrich the text by annotations.

Annotations represents customised enrichment that user can bring to a document his is reading (Mazhoud, 1995). It is useful at re-reading document. In an hypertext context, annotation consist of linking a new commentary node to an existing node of the hyperbase. During consultation, annotations are materialised by anchors associated to annotation links.

Annotation problems can be summerized in below: *did the annotation process has to be considered as a particular process and thereby, be traited as well? What kind of mechanisms have to be embedded behind? As for hyperisation process, what granularity is to be consider for annotation (node, region, information unit, character string,...)?.*

4.3 The consultation interface: Audio Navigation

A classical hypertext system (Nielsen, 1990) offers several consultation modes, from sequential reading of the document to navigation. Navigation consists of moving from one node to another through the hypertext web.

Overall views of the hyperbase are given thanks to the graphic illustration of the web representing global as well as local networks: each type of node is materialized by an icon, and the different kinds of links by lines joining these icons.
But this classical image of the web refers to a vision "from above": such a help tool is unexploitable in an audio context. In fact, an audio global "viewing" is impossible because of the sequential discovery process of sound modality. The user only has a vision of the labyrinth "from inside", that is to say a more limited perception, and so he doesn't always know where to head for. In order to allow the reader (i.e. the "listener") to find his way in the hyperbase, we must imagine the equivalent of an audio web. Several solutions can be proposed, all of them based on the principle of marking in order to avoid walking round and round or ending in a cul-de-sac.

4.4 Consultation by menu

Initially, consultation by menu consists in retrieving a node using a menu hierarchy (table of contents). Afterwards, vocal commands make the route possible in order to position oneself on a node of the hyperdocument.
The principle is the following: after the speech restitution of the node, a list of commands is proposed. The user engages vocally (or with keyboard) the command of his choice, and the cycle reoccurs.
After positioning, the system vocally synthesis the list of the next nodes to consult, without proposing the ones already consulted. If there is no next node, the system proposes to go back to one or several levels, according to the underlying treelike structure.
The text-to-speech synthesis can be adopted to utter the commands, and digitized speech, for example, for node content, in order to increase the intelligibility.
Consultation is difficult because of going back and vocal repetition of menus, then the proposed menus should remain fixed. A comment or a tone difference in comparison with the rest of the menu indicates the non active options (analogy with "grey tinted" options of scrolling menus) in order to avoid cycles in consultation paths and dead-ends: indeed, with context-depending lists, in which invalidated links disappear, the reader must simultaneously integrate the dynamic of evolution of the menus conceptually, and how to position himself into the hyperbase. This effort is not obvious and may be translated into a difficulty of "discourse consistency", a loss of the guiding idea that have justified the consultation.

4.5 Audio consultation by navigation

Consultation by navigation consists in using sound marks embedded into the audio sequence corresponding to link activation buttons. In this case, a sound alarm warns the "listener" that a mark is coming. This one has a lapse of time to activate the mark or not. If there is no activation, reading goes on; but he can follow the proposed rerouting or go on if the vocal comment associated to the mark does not interest him.
This navigation is characterized by the introduction of several links. Typing links is used for the choice of the commands synthesized by the system.
Active navigation is based on the notion of dialog boxes by means of which the system proposes a list of vocally synthesized questions. The reader totally or partially gives

the answers using the microphone or the keyboard. The link to tigger is defined dynamically, from the script attached to it. From the answer analysis and the activation of the conditional link, the system suggest a route accompanied by a comment.
A more ambitious but not yet experimented phase consists in implementing an architecture supporting searches by similarity including the sound component (music? noise?...). A simple and interesting experience consists in typing the sound marks semantically differentiating their tones. From a catalogue of these sounds, we can contemplate their searching in the hyperbase, dynamically building, in this way, a consultation route.
In the same idea, sound shades could be implemented for a location "in width" and "in depth" in the tree diagram of the documents. Indeed, the hyperbase has a particular spatial organisation: it could be viewed as a concatenation of hyperdocuments, each hyperdocument being characterized for example by a given sound. So the reader knows in which document he is situated, according to the sound he listens. Moreover, each hyperdocument is hierarchically structured (structural links): for each node, the system indicates by a serie of "bips" the level where it is situated in the tree diagram. The reader can thus find his way according to two orthogonal axes: changes in tones and bips help him to situate himself conceptually when he navigates through the hyperbase via referential links. A colouring of the different spaces by a musical background can also be contemplated.
However, the sensibility of the ear often varies from one person to the other; psychoacoustic studies would be necessary to evaluate the sound representation space of the document.

5 Implementation and Perspectives

The software/hardware architecture of the implemented prototype gives importance to the sound component that requires appropriate devices:

- the input devices are the keyboard and the microphone connected to a speech recognition environment;
- the output ones are a loudspeaker, a digitized speech restitution card, a text-to-speech synthesis card and a braille displayer.

The card ECHOVOX/AR is based on the digitizing storage/restitution of the speech signal. Marking functions (stop and repeat mark) are available. The text-to-speech synthesis card is TELEVOX-PSOLA . The card manager allows to modify delivery, tone and volume. Opening these parameters tends to render different tones of speech which can signify a typography setting-off, a focus in the text,...It can also position prosodic mark and annotations.
The database is implemented under the O2 OODBMS.
Our efforts essentially focus on the validation of the spatio-temporal representation of the hyperbase (logical and visual structure of the documents, database structure,...) with a view to a consultation by navigation based on the sound modality. The strategy of active navigation must be validated more deeply.

6 References

(Bush.1945) V.Bush. *As we may think.* Atlantic Monthly 176, July 1945.
(Calliope,1989) Le calliope. *La parole et son traitement automatique.*Masson, 1989.
(Chisment,1993) C.Chrisment, C.Comparot, C.Julien, P.Y. Lambolez, F.Sedes. *Hyperdocument Structuration, Management and Exchange in an Object-Oriented Database.* 2 rst Symposium on Information Retrieval and Document Analysis. Las Vegas (U.S.A), April 1993.
(Comparot,1994) C.Comparot. *Hyperbase: Formalisation et Architecture.* These de doctorat en Informatique, 1994.
(Gillares,1992) H.Gillares-Galliat. *Dialoguer avec un micro / quand le PC obeira a la voix de son maitre.* Le Monde Informatique, July 1992.
(Lambolez,1992) P.Y.Lambolez, J.P. Queille, J.F. Voidrot. *Using information retrieval technique in Software Maintenance.* Maintenance93 Montreal, 1993.
(Mariani,1989) J.Mariani. *Recent Advances in Speech Porcessing.* Proceedings of ICASSP-IEEE, 1989.
(Martial,1992a) O.Martial, A.Dufresne. *Pour l'acces aux interfaces graphiques par les non-voyants: analyse des representations mentales du bureau.* ERGO-IA'92, 1992.
(Martial,1992b) O.Martial. *AudiCones: Le defi des interfaces graphiques.* Le curseur, September 1992.
(Mazhoud,1995) O.Mazhoud, E.Pascual, J. Virbel. *Representation et Gestion d'annotations.* Hypertexte et Hypermedia, 1995.
(Muller,1991) M.J.Muller, J.E.Daniel. *Towards a Definition of Voice Document.* Proceeding of COIS'90, 1991.
(Nielsen,1990) J.Nielsen. *The Art of Navigation through Hypertext.* CACM'90, March 1990.
(Strempe,1990) U.Strempel. *Presentation of different Types of Talking Newpapers with Special emphasis on ETAB.* Stiftung Blindenansttalt Frankfurt am Main, Germany,1990.
(TextTalk,1990) Texttalk. *Radio-Transmitted daily Electronic Newspaper for the Blind: RATS.* RATS, Sweden,1992.

Applications of Natural Language to Information Systems
R.P. van de Riet et al. (Eds.)
IOS Press, 1996

Hyper-Text generation from databases on the Internet

Sabine Geldof
AI Laboratory - Vrije Universiteit Brussel
Pleinlaan 2,
1050 BRUSSELS BELGIUM
sabine@arti.vub.ac.be

Abstract. In this paper we describe a principled way of generating hyper-text from databases in the context of the World Wide Web. The approach aims at generating multiple texts (i.e. customised to different users and situations) from multiple information sources (mostly databases), in the context of (software) agent based applications. Through a concrete experiment we demonstrate the first step in realizing this aim and we give an outlook on further research along that line.

1 Introduction

The World-Wide-Web (WWW) is a medium for making information widely available and constitutes the basis for the so-called information society. This new infrastructure requires not only the base technology for making information widely available (communication protocols, server and network architectures, etc.) but also techniques for information publishing and maintenance adapted to the highly interactive and flexible communication mode of the WWW. Indeed, as a consequence of the fact that the infrastructure allows for availability of an (almost) unlimited amount of information to a society without physical boundaries, the need arises to manage that information in an effective way. Three aspects of information management are particularly relevant in the context of this paper: making information that is *relevant* at a particular time, accessible in a *useful form* and ensuring that it is maintained *up-to-date*. An efficient service provides the right information at the right time in the right form. These goals can be realised by automatic text generation from information sources.

More and more, databases and information sources in general become accessible to a large public through global networks such as the Internet. They are not anymore targeted to specialised and dedicated users, but intended for the public at large. In that context, the usage of databases becomes critically dependent on more sophisticated natural language processing techniques (NL generation in particular).

We will illustrate this with a real-world experiment: generating an interactive program for Brussels' summer movie festival: Ecran Total. An example of an on-line program page is shown in figure 1.

In comparison to the paper program of the festival, the electronic program shows the information requested by the user, in a form appropriate to the user (e.g. his/her preferred language) and taking into account the time evolution (e.g. past performances are not relevant anymore). The functionality is thus very different from a system like SCHISMA [11], a natural language dialogue system also linked to a database.

Figure 1: Example of a program page in the Ecran Total application

The on-line festival program was published on Internet as an experiment during the festival and a questionnaire allowed to capture feed-back concerning various aspects. The home-page of the festival has been consulted over 500 times. About 30 persons returned the questionnaire, 60% of them are between 20 & 30 years old, 50% replied positive to the question whether the electronic program could replace the paper version. The main arguments of the 46% who replied 'no' were related to the physical nature of the medium (you can take paper with you, you can make annotations, easily show to other people) and to the (still) limited access of Internet for the Belgian citizen. We received no content- related objections against the electronic program. On the contrary, all were very positive about the content and usage of the electronic version, nobody found the information unclear or incomplete. We conclude that the electronic program corresponds very well to the user's information needs and foresee that it will progressively gain popularity over the paper program. The version issued during the festival remains on-line via the home page of our laboratory (http://arti.vub.ac.be/www/research.html) and can still be used to illustrate the idea of an electronic program, while it is partially re-implemented to explore the more principled approach advocated in this paper. Finally, it is used as a first experiment in the context of the MAGICA project (Multi-media Agent-based interactive catalogs), a larger project on the topic of electronic catalogs, involving users in the application areas of tourism and international trade.

We are investigating techniques that allow to take advantage of the opportunities and to cope with the difficulties of the information-rich context that is being created now. Starting from basic technology (template based text generation and calls to databases) implemented in a principled way, we will progressively introduce the enhancements (e.g. user modelling, text generation techniques) that will lead to sophisticated applications (i.e. agent-based information production and presentation). The paper is organized as follows: first we sketch the background of our work, explaining our technological options and referring to other relevant work. Then, these options are made clear through a concrete example that we have implemented. Finally, we conclude with an outlook on further research needed to reach our goals.

2 Background

The short-term goal of our work is to provide tools for authoring interactive catalogs[1] in hypertext format, accessible via Internet and linked to one or more information sources (e.g. databases). Instead of forging all the html page-descriptions by hand (and having to update them in case changes are needed) authors need a way of defining page types which will automatically be realised as concrete catalog pages, ensuring coherence and easy maintainability. A principled approach is a prerequisite since we want to build further on these tools to cope with agent-based interaction. Our long-term goal is indeed the realization of a catalog in which software agents can mediate information, interacting with the personal agent who represents the interest of the user in order to arrive at customised information selection and presentation. A software agent is a small autonomous program related to an owner (a real-world person or organization) who charged the software agent with a specific task. Agents typically communicate with other software agents. A software agent can also be viewed as a persistent process within the agent world which represents the interest of his owner even when the latter is not interacting with the application. In the context of interactive catalogs, the tasks of the software agents are to gather and to present information in a way that is adapted to the user. Increasingly more autonomous software agents will provide the service of an increasingly more sophisticated catalog, where *multiple texts* can be produced (adapted to different situations and users) from *multiple information sources* (if the agent can use information from heterogeneous sources on the Internet).

The remainder of this section is organized as follows: in the next 2 subsections we motivate our basic technological options: template-based text generation and access to information sources via ontological definitions. In the last subsection we situate our work with respect to other relevant work.

2.1 Template-based text generation

The main operational requirements for our catalog -resulting from the use of our authoring tools- are that it be interactive and adaptive to user needs and changing situations (e.g. the time aspect of a festival program or the availability of multi-media materials). Therefore a text generation technique is needed that allows for flexible content definition (determined by a number of parameters) and real time operation over the Internet. Template based text generation satisfies our requirements. Thus, as the user interacts with the catalog, the pages will be generated by templates, completed with information found in the database(s) that are linked to the catalog. Moreover, as suggested by [13],

[1] The festival program used as an example should be considered as a kind of catalog, the latter being a broader concept implying (hyper)textual descriptions of products.

this basic technology can be augmented with specific text generation techniques in order to obtain better quality of text production (e.g. more natural and more coherent texts). At the meta-level, concerned with the question of how these templates are created, we propose an abstract page definition language (cfr. section 3.3), allowing for the use of parameters (e.g. user-language parameter determining the alternative forms of the templates) and of domain terms to be instantiated with information from a database (cfr. section 3.2). The catalog author defines the page types at a high level (including variants according to the relevant parameters) and needs a sufficiently sophisticated means of expression in order to compensate for a full fledged text planning system. We developed a language for that purpose. These abstract page types are then, via CGI-scripts, completed with information from the database and translated into hyper-text mark-up language (HTML). This way of proceeding provides a powerful means to create overall consistency and a particular look-and-feel throughout the catalog.

2.2 Ontology as interface to information sources

Our other technological option concerns the access to the information sources. In the context of proliferation of information on the WWW, sharing and reuse of knowledge and information are important issues. An Internet based information system is committed to the challenge of integrating different information sources. The use of ontologies have been put forward in various contexts ([10], [12] amongst others) as a promising technique. Again, our technological option considers the trade-off between scientific motivation and practical needs for the application. In the context of this project we need only the domain-specific part of the ontology as envisaged by [12]. Access to information sources will always be specified in terms of the ontology defined for the application. An overview of the ontology for our example is given in figure 2 and explained in more detail in section 3.

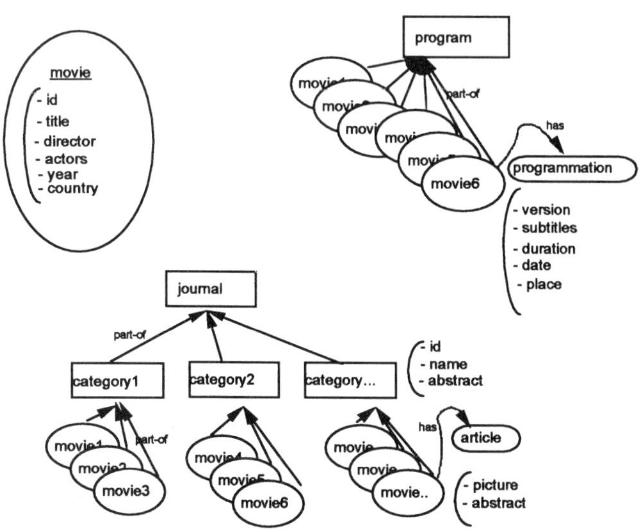

Figure 2: Overview of the movie ontology

The use of ontological terms to refer to data taken from the information sources allows for easy integration of an additional information source and, in the agent-based application, for data exploration by a software agent outside the scope of pre-defined information sources. This means that a software agent should be able to read an ontology of a new information source and to decide whether the data he is looking for can be found in that particular information source.

2.3 Other relevant work

Rather than aiming at an overview of similar work, we focus on the differences and similarities in order to allow for the reader to better situate our work and our technological options (template based text generation and ontology as interface to information sources).

There is a whole range of applied text generation systems based on templates, from basic mail-merge to interactive hypertext. Systems for writing reports (e.g. Austin-Haynes Employee Appraiser) or for automatic letter composition [14] use templates in combination with more or less sophisticated text planning and syntactic realisation techniques to deliver a text. They are interesting for these techniques, but lack the interactive aspect which is needed in the context of our application. IDAS [13] an on-line documentation system for complex, custom-built equipment provides the interactive functionality by generating hypertext from an object-oriented representation which is very similar to our application, however in a non-networked environment. We described a similar experiment (nl. for generating a textual interface to a knowledge based system) in [6] and noticed the need for a dynamic link between the textual presentation and the evolving knowledge system. Commercial tools for creating catalogs on the web (e.g. WebCatalog) often are focused on straightforward projection of a database on the web and do not aim at conceptually sophisticated applications. The system that is closest to our present target is described in [2]. A template based text generation system for personalised medical explanations is linked to an evolving information source, i.c. patients' records. In the present paper we are presenting an authoring methodology to create the same type of application. Cawsey defines patterns of content and text structure with particular conventions on what should be included when explaining different types of issue (disease, treatment, measurement etc..). Similarly, we define page (fragment) types by means of a high-level description language, referring to ontology concepts.

The Fog system [9], generally recognized as the first operational, full fledged text generation system also produces multilingual output from information in databases, although not linked dynamically to the database. It includes a sophisticated text planner and realizer for which reason our system doesn't compare to it (apart from the link db-text). As pointed out above, we had to opt for a template based text generation technique to comply with our operational requirements, still we need sufficiently expressive means for defining these templates so that these can embed the needed refinements in text structure. This is the main challenge of our approach.

In the IGUANA project [4], the issue of interfacing to multiple information sources is tackled in the context of a database querying system. That scope is very different from ours, both from the viewpoint of the resulting application as from the viewpoint of the methodological solution but it starts from the same concern to integrate heterogeneous information sources. Their methodology consists in linking the different information sources to pre-defined views of information, a particular query from the user is then mapped to one of the pre-defined views. Our approach is closer to Gruber's, developed in the context of problems solving systems [10].

3 Dynamic catalog for a movie festival

In this section we will further explain and motivate our technological options through a look at the 'insides' of a concrete application we developed: an electronic catalog for a movie festival.

3.1 Example

The example is taken from an interactive electronic program developed for Brussels' summer movie festival: Ecran Total. The electronic program follows the conceptual scheme of the paper program but offers extended functionalities due to the interactivity of the medium and the dynamic link with the database. Figure 3 shows the home-page of the on-line festival program.

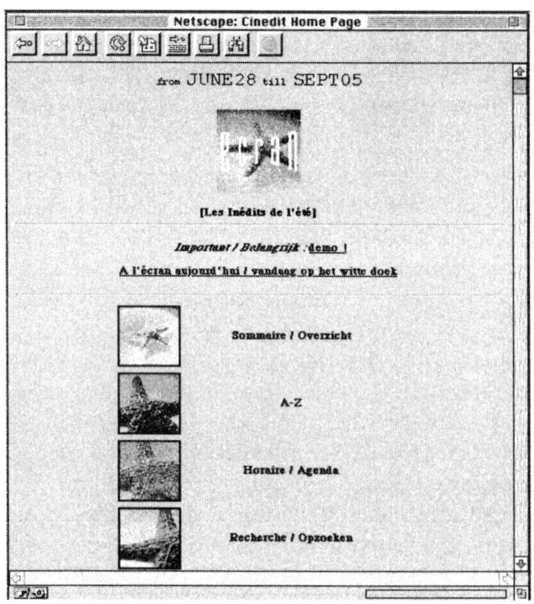

Figure 3: Home-page of the on-line festival program

The main information on festival movies can be found in the journal-pages as the one in figure 1. These can be accessed through various hyper-media links (underlined expressions in figure 1) and contain links to other types of pages (e.g. time-schedules, categories of movies). Figure 4 shows the navigation structure of the on-line program.

The navigation network shows a fairly hierarchical structure: the home-page points to fixed overview pages (festival overview, alphabetical list, time-table, practical information), pointing further to dynamically created pages (category overview, day & week-schedules) finally all pointing to the journal pages. Back-links allow for exploring

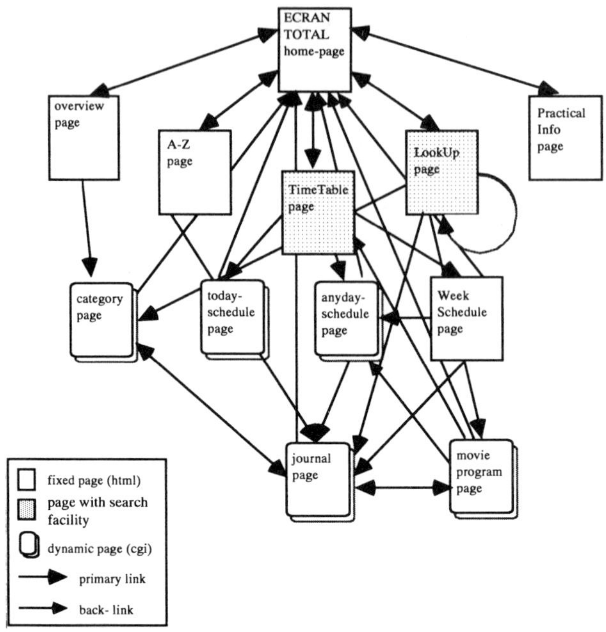

Figure 4: On-line Festival navigation structure

alternatives and there is always a back-link to the home-page of the festival. The search facilities (e.g. on a title or a movie director) allow to access specific information directly. Figure 5 shows an example Look-up page.

The dynamic pages, defined as page types (cfr. infra), are generated by CGI scripts implemented in perl; connections with the msql database are also implemented in perl using a client-server set-up. The hypertext links for dynamic pages consist of tagged URL's including the parameters for the selection and instantiation of the appropriate page template. The perl code corresponding to the page type actually generates the html page, retrieves and fills out data from the database. This dynamicity allows for taking into account various aspects, for instance, time: every time schedule for a movie is built on demand and only the future performances are displayed. The pages can also vary according to the available materials, for instance, the catalog author can define an alternative page type for the case where no movie picture is available. Thus, the electronic program exhibits enhanced functionality w.r.t. to the paper program on at least 2 features: the user is brought immediately to the required information about a movie without having to consult indices with page-numbers and the program evolves in time, as the festival progresses, more and more information becomes irrelevant.

In the next subsection, we will give a more systematic account of the domain structure in the form of an ontology description. The last subsection explains the underlying abstract page type definitions giving rise to the example pages.

3.2 Ontology

An ontology is an explicit specification of a conceptualization [10], which contains the objects, concepts and other entities that are presumed to exist in some area of interest

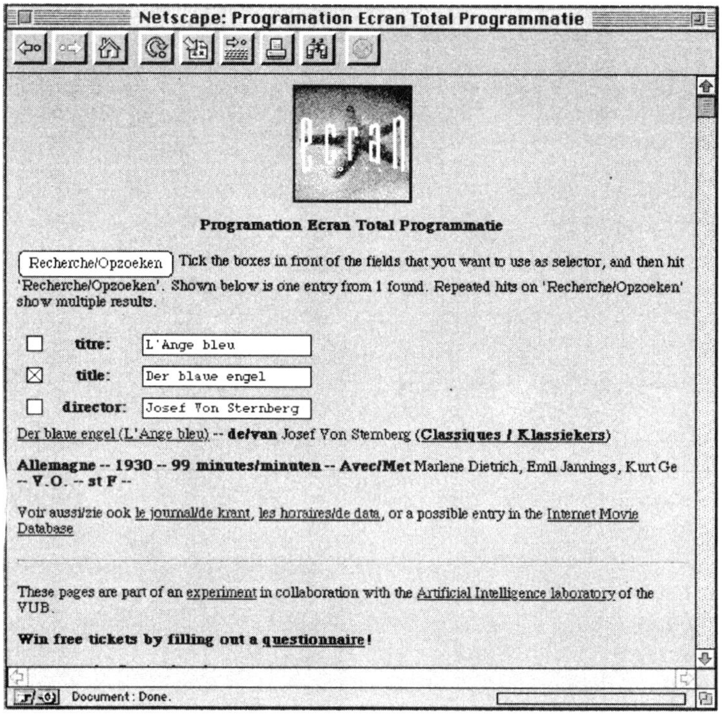

Figure 5: Search facilities in the on-line festival program: Look-up page

and the relationships that hold among them [7].As such, it is broader than a conceptual database scheme, which is related to a particular database. In an application involving multiple information sources and/or databases, the ontology is an integration of different conceptual schemata. Figure 2 shows a graphical representation of the concepts and relationships that matter in our application. The basic object is 'movie', which has a number of associated attributes, 'reference' being the attribute that allows to uniquely identify a particular movie. These movies are organised in 2 larger entities, 'journal', being the thematic organization of the set of movies that constitute the festival, and 'program', the practical organization (i.e. time schedule) of the festival. In either of these organizations, each movie has a concept associated (resp. 'article' and 'programmation') and a number of attributes related to that concept. The latter attributes are not intrinsic to the movie but to the festival they are featuring in. The attributes related to 'programmation' become irrelevant outside the context of this festival (e.g. version, date, time, place), the ones related to 'article' could be reused in other contexts.

The data related to the instantiations of these concepts are stored in the database, which does not follow necessarily the same conceptual schema. This is a first reason for making explicit the ontology. The author of the catalog will use the higher level terms of the ontology (when building abstract page type definitions) rather than the concrete names of database fields in particular tables which might be very cryptic and insignificant to him/her. The mapping between an ontology concept and the place in a particular information source where the instantiations are stored can take various forms, some examples are given in the table below. These mappings are defined using the high level page description language (cfr. infra) but are masked at the conceptual level of catalog authoring.

from **Ontology Concept**	to **Information Source**	= **type of mapping**
director	director in tbl movies	(1) one-to-one
title-of-movie	titre in tbl movies if French title in tbl movies if Engl or Dutch	(2) one-to-many (db fields)
name-of-category	French name in glossary entry for tbl value (eg. CLAS) if French English name in glossary for tbl value (eg. CLAS) if Eng.	(3) one-to-one (db field)-to-many (values in glossary entry)

The simplest mapping is when one ontology concept corresponds to one field in the database (1). If the information is language dependent, the mapping is one-to-many (2). In another case (3), the instantiations of concepts are to be found in another information source (e.g. a glossary): the category a particular movie belongs to, is indicated by a code in the database (e.g. CLAS) and needs to be realised as a full string according to the language (Klassiekers, Les classiques, Classics). Defining these mappings with the page definition language allows to capture these regularities while making abstraction of them at the moment of catalog authoring.

The second reason for making the ontology explicit is that we need to be able to integrate an external information source straigthforwardly. Suppose we want to extend our program with a facility to search movies related to a particular (thematic) key-word. This information is not available in the database built for the purpose of this program, but if we can link to an external database (e.g. the Internet Movie Database, hosted by Cardiff University http://www.cs.cf.ac.uk/Movies/) which defines such keywords, this can be handled conceptually in a clear way by extending the ontology and providing a data- access definition for the newly added term.

The ultimate reason for introducing ontological definitions is that such definitions will eventually be used by software agents to examine new information sources in their quest for information to satisfy the needs of the user. If we want a software agent to perform this task autonomously, we will have to provide agent-readable ontologies. For the moment our ontology is limited to the textual description (for human understanding) but formal definitions and axioms will be needed for agent-based information exploration. A formalism like KIF (Knowledge Interchange Format) intended for the publication and communication of knowledge is a likely candidate [8].

The construction of ontologies requires abstract reasoning that belongs to the field of knowledge modeling and representation. It is an activity that cannot be determined in a step-by-step procedure. Rather than a technique , it is a skill, almost an art. Publications about ontologies concern representation and translation of ontologies, rather than the 'art of ontology building'. Nevertheless, methodologies, tools and strategies proposed in the field of knowledge representation and modeling will undoubtedly contribute to a good and systematic practise of ontology building. For instance, the Componential Methodology and its tool KresT [5] might be appropriate in a task- oriented domain.

Entity-relationship modeling techniques [3] are more appropriate for static domains. Also, COLOR-X [1] seems a promising methodology to use, especially the construction of the static object model (CSOM) and the interface to WordNet are important features w.r.t the integration of different information sources and agent access to ontologies. The mentioned tools and techniques suppose that the ontology is built by a human, which is probably the most realistic option. However, interesting experiments could be done with language-based, automatic domain analysis tools such as proposed by Dinenberg and Levin (this volume).

3.3 *Abstract page type description*

The abstract page definition language is the basis of our authoring tool: it allows for the definition of domain, presentation and catalog primitives and to relate them to each other in a series of page and catalogue structures. Instead of by-hand generation of hyper-media pages, these page and catalog structures will automatically (i.e. through a CGI script) be created and completed with data from the database as to result in the aimed catalog pages. We will illustrate this principle with an example. Consider the movie page shown in figure 1. It is an instance of a page of type 'journal' for a particular movie ('Il Sorpasso' with reference number 30) in one of the supported languages (Dutch). The definition for page type 'journal', refers to a set of page fragments, as shown in figure 6.

```
(define page-type journal (movie)
  <center><FRAGMENT NAME="logo"> <p>
  <FRAGMENT NAME="journal-title"><p>
  <FRAGMENT NAME="link-program">
  <FRAGMENT NAME="link-category" ><p>
  <FRAGMENT NAME="movie-picture" ><p>
  <FRAGMENT NAME="movie-abstract" ><p>
  < hr><FRAGMENT NAME="signature" >
  </center> )
(define page-fragment journal-title

(if (language french)   <b>Journal Ecran Total: <LOOKUP "title-of-movie"><\b>)
(if (language dutch)    <b>Ecran Total krant: <LOOKUP "title-of-movie"><\b>)
(if (language english)  <b>Ecran Total Journal: <LOOKUP "title-of-movie"><\b>))
```

Figure 6: Abstract definition for a page type and a page fragment type

The syntax of the abstract page definition language is closely related to html syntax and thus smoothly integrates with the format statements. For instance, it includes html-like tags for database access (<LOOK UP>) or fragment inclusion (<FRAGMENT>). The statements in abstract page definition language refer, from the conceptual level to the level of instantiated objects by means of 2 mechanisms. First, the ontological concepts (e.g. title-of-movie) are mapped to information source access statements via the meanings definitions (an example of which is given in figure 7).

Second, a mechanism of parameters is provided, exemplified here by the language parameter. At the conceptual level, the parameters are inherited through successive levels of fragment inclusion towards the smallest defined primitives (e.g. from page type 'journal' to page fragment type 'title'). Where necessary, this inheritance can be

```
(define meanings for journal
(category-of-movie
       (lookup in ecran "select category  from journal where movie=$movie"))
(define meanings for movies
      (title-of-movie
      (if (language one-of (english, dutch))
           lookup in ecran "select title from movies where reference=$movie")
       else
   (if ((lookup in ecran "select titre from movies where reference =
                  $movie") eq null)
         lookup in ecran "select title from movies where reference =
                  $movie")
      else  lookup in ecran "select titre from movies where reference =
                  $movie"))
```

Figure 7: mapping of ontological terms to information source access

overridden by an explicit parameter setting. For example, the signature fragment is in english, whether the page is called with dutch, french or english as language parameter. The parameters are instantiated through the URL's of the CGI calls. The page shown in figure 1 is called:
http://arti13.vub.ac.be/cgi-bin/newecran4.pl/PT=journal/movie=30/language=dutch. This brings us to the cgi scripts corresponding to the page fragment definition, as shown in figure 8:

Within the code file, the values of the parameters are passed along through the $PATH variable, (e.g. reference of the movie (30) and the language parameter (Dutch)). These abstraction mechanisms demonstrate that a clear distinction can be maintained between authoring issues ('define page type' and 'define page fragment'), ontological definitions and access to information sources ('define meanings'). This distinction contributes to the modularity of the authoring system and is thus a first step towards our long-term goal (producing multiple texts from multiple information sources, cfr. first paragraph, section 2).

A first aspect is the systematic treatment of customised presentation - generating multiple texts. The example shows how we can easily produce different movie pages according to the preferred language of the user, clearly only one of the possible parameters for customization. Others could be related to the computer infrastructure of the user (size of screen, helper applications ..) or the availability of (multimedia) materials. A second aspect is the transparent integration of multiple information sources. The page definitions make abstraction of the different tables where information can be found. Similarly, the use of an additional external information source would not be reflected at the level of catalog authoring.

4 Conclusion: towards agent-based text production

We have described how we envisage a principled approach to the authoring of electronic catalogs, linked to information sources on the WWW. In view of efficient information management, we propose to author the catalogs as page types defined using a high level language. Such approach allows for parametrisation of the aimed catalogs according to situation determined features (e.g. language of the user). Moreover data, to be retrieved

```
if ($PATH{'PF'} eq 'journal-title') {$query = "select title, titre from movies
          where reference=$PATH{'movie'}";
        $sth = $dbh->Query($query);
        @row = $sth->FetchRow;
        $title = $row[0];
        $titre = $row[1];
        if ($PATH{'language'} eq 'dutch') {$print_title = $title;};
        if ($PATH{'language'} eq 'english') {$print_title = $title;};
        if ($PATH{'language'} eq 'french') {if ($titre eq 'null')
           {$print_title = $title;}
else {$movie = $titre;}; };};

if ($PATH{'PF'} eq 'journal-title') {if ($PATH{'language'} eq 'dutch')
        {print "<b>Ecran Total krant: <A HREF=\"http://arti13.vub.ac.be/cgi-
            bin/newecran4.pl/PT=journal/movie=$PATH{'movie'}/language=dutch\">
        $print_title </A></b> ";  exit};};

if ($PATH{'PF'} eq 'journal-title') {if ($PATH{'language'} eq 'french')
        {print "<b>Journal Ecran Total: <A HREF=\"http://arti13.vub.ac.be/cgi-
            bin/newecran4.pl/PT=journal/movie=$PATH{'movie'}/language=french\">
        $print_title </A></b> ";  exit};};

if ($PATH{'PF'} eq 'journal-title') {if ($PATH{'language'} eq 'english')
        {print "<b>Ecran Total journal: <A HREF=\"http://arti13.vub.ac.be/cgi-
            bin/newecran4.pl/PT=journal/movie=$PATH{'movie'}/language=english\">
        $print_title </A></b> "; exit};};
```

Figure 8: Perl code corresponding to the abstract page fragment definition of figure 6

from the information sources are referred to through ontology terms. Based on these techniques we will extend the application towards agent-based information selection and presentation so that a catalog (e.g. a festival program) becomes truly customised to the user's needs, ranging over a wide spectrum of content and form. More than a useful facility, agent based information presentation will become a necessity in the information society. In order to achieve this long-term objective, further research is needed on innovative user modelling techniques and on the integration of distributed, heterogeneous information sources through machine-readable ontologies. Also, more sophisticated text generation techniques will have to enhance the template-based text generation. These topics are the subject of further research.

Acknowledgements

We are especially indebted to Dr. Walter Van de Velde for extensive co-operation on this experiment and for valuable comments on preliminary versions of the paper. The work reported here was carried out in the context of the CONSTRUCT project funded by the Belgian 'Federale diensten voor wetenschappelijke, technische en culturele aangelegenheden' (DWTC) through the program of 'InterUniversitaire AttractiePolen' (IUAP) and of the MAGICA project, funded by the European Union program Telematics Engineering.

References

1. Burg, J.F.M., Riet, R.P. van de. "COLOR-X: Object modeling profits from Linguistics", in N.J.I. Mars, *Towards very large knowledge bases: knowledge building and knowledge sharing*, IOS Press, Amsterdam, 1995, pp 204-214.

2. Cawsey, A. "Personalised Explanations for Patient Education", *Proceedings of the Fifth European Workshop on Natural Language Generation*, Leiden, The Netherlands , 1995, pp 59-74.

3. Chen, P., "The Entity-Relationship Model - Toward a Unified View of Data", *ACM Transactions on Database Systems*, Vol. 1, No 1, March 1976, pp 9-36.

4. Chuah, Y., Heng, K., Pang, S. "A Natural Language Interface for Querying Multiple Databases Using Predefined Views in a Client-Server Environment", *Proceedings of the First International Workshop on Applications of Natural Language to Data Bases*, Versailles, France, 1995, pp 287-298

5. Geldof, S., L. Steels, W. Van de Velde "COMMET for building Knowledge Systems". *CC-AI* Vol.10, Nr 3 (pp 195-218) Gent, Belgium: Communication & Cognition, 1993.

6. Geldof, S., Van de Velde, W. "Interfacing knowledge: Text Generation fr om Knowledge Systems", VUB AI Memo 95-10, April 1995.

7. Genesereth M.R. and Nilsson N.J., *Logical Foundations of Artificial Intelligence.* San Mateo, CA: Morgan Kaufmann Publishers, 1987.

8. Genesereth M.R. and Fikes R.E., *Knowledge Interchage Format, version 3.0, Reference Manual* Technical Report Logic-92-1, Computer Science Department, Stanford University.

9. Goldberg, E., Driedger, N., Kittredge, R. "Using natural-language processing to produce weather forecasts", *IEEE Expert*, 9(2) 1994, pp. 45-53.

10. Gruber, T. "A Translation Approach to Portable Ontology Specifications", *Knowledge Acquisition*, 1993, 5, pp. 199-220.

11. Hoeven, G.F. v.d., Andernach, J.A., Burgt, S.P. v.d., Kruijff, G-J.M., Nijholt, A., Schaake, J., Jong, F.M.G. de "SCHISMA: A Natural Language Accessible Theater Information and Booking System", *Proceedings of the First International Workshop on Applications of Natural Language to Data Bases*, Versailles, France, 1995, pp 271-285

12. Hovy, E., Knight, K. "Motivating Shared Knowledge Resources: an Example from the Pangloss Collaboration", *Proceedings of IJCAI Workshop on Shared Knowledge*, Chambéry, France, 1993.

13. Reiter, E., Mellish, C. and Levine, J. "Automatic Generation of On-Line Documentation in the IDAS Project", *Proceedings of the Third Conference on Applied Natural Language Processing, Association for Computational Linguistics*, Morristown, N.J. , 1992, pp 64-71 .

14. Springer, S., Buta, P. and Wolf, T., "Automatic letter composition for customer service". In R. Smith and C. Scott (Eds.), *Innovative Applications of Artificial Intelligence 3 (Proceedings of CAIA-1991)*, AAAI Press, 1991

Applications of Natural Language to Information Systems
R.P. van de Riet et al. (Eds.)
IOS Press, 1996

Retrieving Conceptual Models on the Basis of Word Semantics

Jon Atle Gulla
GMD - IPSI
Darmstadt, Germany
gulla@gmd.de

Bram van der Vos
Vrije Universiteit
Amsterdam, the Netherlands
ajvdvos@cs.vu.nl

Ulrich Thiel
GMD - IPSI
Darmstadt, Germany
thiel@gmd.de

Abstract. In the early phases of requirements engineering, inspecting previously constructed conceptual models is important both for reusing specifications and for gaining general knowledge about how similar problems have been solved in other projects. However, as the users at this stage have only vague ideas about the system to be implemented, they are seldom able to specify a query to the CASE repository that is precise enough to capture the relevant conceptual models. In this paper, we present an information retrieval approach that frees the user from knowing the modeling languages used in the repository and helps him retrieve models from other domains that are structurally similar to the one he intends to build. The system exploits the linguistic, semantic properties of the query to suggest what kind of representation he should look for, and it afterwards retrieve all models that are consistent with the query structure and the semantic representations of the words included in the query.
Keywords: model retrieval, lexicon, conceptual modeling, abduction

1 Introduction

A fundamental problem in developing information systems is how to take advantage of the experiences from previous projects. At the design and implementation phases, software libraries and automated support have proven to ease the use of previously constructed design specifications and software routines, and the results so far are promising for the development of information systems as a whole [1, 12]. However, it seems that knowledge transfer from old projects is just as relevant in the early phases of information system development [19, 32]. In requirements engineering, it is useful to have a look at models of other information systems that address either the same problems or related problems that can shed some light on the requirements in the current project. As the people involved in requirements engineering start out with only vague and subjective ideas about the kind of system they are to develop, however, it is difficult to use their initial descriptions to retrieve relevant conceptual models from the CASE environment. It becomes difficult to take advantage of experiences from earlier projects simply because it is not possible to find the previously constructed models that could be helpful. Another problem is that many of the people involved in the requirements engineering phase are not necessarily experts on conceptual modeling languages. Using graphical language-specific query forms, as suggested for example in [17], is questionable both due to the user's lack of knowledge of the semantics of modeling languages and the multitude of languages found in modern (meta-) CASE environments.

The challenge, then, is to provide a model retrieval method that allows very vague and informal queries to be posted. The method should help the user to formulate a complete query, and it should compensate for the user's inability to specify precisely what he wants. The approach suggested in this paper is to take advantage of the deeper semantic representations of the search terms. By means of a semantically rich word lexicon, we construct semantic representations of user's query that can be used to retrieve conceptual models in a two stage process: *(1) From the semantic representation, we suggest possible queries that are formulated in terms of the actual model structures used in the CASE environment. (2) Having a conceptual model pattern with word labels as a query, we search for conceptual models that exhibit the same model pattern and include word labels with structural semantic properties consistent with the original terms.* An advantage of this approach is that the user does not need to know all the representation formalisms used in the CASE environment, since the environment can suggest a formalism on the basis of the linguistic interpretation of his query. Another advantage is that we are able to retrieve not only models including the indicated word labels, but also models that from a semantic, linguistic point of view are structurally analogous with the requested model. Although the representation formalisms used in the paper stem from the PPP CASE environment [8, 9], the technique is by no means restricted to a certain kind of representations. As also alluded to in the paper, the technique fits nicely into other information retrieval techniques and is easily implemented on top of a CASE repository system.

In section 2, we start out by discussing the problems of identifying relevant conceptual models at the requirements engineering phase and explaining why traditional information retrieval techniques are not sufficient for handling these particular problems. Our linguistic, abductive approach to query interpretation is explained in Section 3, whereas the use of linguistic features to match the chosen interpretation with relevant conceptual models is presented in Section 4. The paper concludes with some discussions of project status and future work in Section 5.

2 Conceptual Models and Retrieval Methods

Central at the early stages of information systems development projects is the assessment of the problems at hand and the determination of what information system to build. This requires the involvement of various parties, e.g. systems engineers and domain experts, and all these people have to be able to communicate and work together. Conceptual models are in the requirements engineering phase used to communicate ideas and document system requirements. As opposed to design specifications, they abstract away from technical details and focus on the services and the information that the systems are to provide to their environments. In Davis's words, they represent the *external behavior* of the systems to be developed, whereas design specifications and implementations address the internal behavior [3]. Another view is that conceptual models consitute a *conceptual realm* that bridges the gap between the real-world realm and the datalogical realm [27]. In any case, the models have a clear subjective focus in the sense that they reflect people's perception of the problems and their thoughts about how some computerized support can solve them [14, 28, 35].

CASE environments like PPP store previously constructed models in big repositories [36]. This is intended to encourage the transfer of knowledge and experience from one project to the other, though the exact nature of this transfer is still rather unclear.

One can imagine that old models are simply reused in new projects, just like software components in more traditional software libraries (e.g. [5, 15, 22, 29]), but it might also be that these old models are just forming some kind of background knowledge for the new model. Experiments have been conducted that indicate a considerable improvement of model quality when the modelers can draw analogies to other existing models [7, 18]. Finding these other relevant models at a stage where the requirements for the information system are still informal and fragmentaric, however, is a challenging task that calls for new approaches to information retrieval from CASE repositories.

Looking for relevant conceptual models in the repository, we can take advantage of the models' position as mediators between the users' real world problems and the software routines addressing these problems. This means that the models can be analyzed and searched for from two different perspectives:

Real-world perspective The model is identified on the basis of its relationship to real-world phenomena. This means that the model is described by natural terms focusing on the correspondences to objects and concepts in the application domain. A query like *"give me all models that deal with book loans"* has a clear application domain orientation.

Datalogical perspective The model is identified on the basis of its relationship to computerized structures and behaviors. It is usually described using one of the modeling languages offered by the CASE environment. Searching for ER models, for example, the user can specify a search pattern expressed as a fragment of an ER model.

Due to the very nature of requirements engineering, it is not very realistic to require the model queries to have a complete datalogical perspective [13]. Queries of this kind assume the user to have intimate knowledge of the environment's modeling languages and an ability to specify program structures in the query that match the way these problems have been modeled before. Early in a development project, where people have only fragmentaric and subjective views of the problems, this is not that useful and the real-world oriented queries are more attractive [2]. The real-world perspective allows the user to refer to objects of the application domain in his own language, and it is then the responsibility of the retrieval system to establish a connection between these queries and the structures of the conceptual models in the repository.

A good retrieval system should be able to retrieve the relevant material from the repository (high *recall*) and avoid retrieving the irrelevant material (high *precision*). If datalogical queries are used, the query specification can be compared directly with the representations in the repository, and this simplifies the assessment of relevance. A model can be deemed to be relevant if its semantics — from a datalogical perspective — implies the interpretation of the query. Less strict are techniques calculating the semantic distance between query and model (e.g. [15, 29]), though these techniques all suffer from the strong concentration on program structures and behaviors instead of real-world objects. For real-world queries, which are more interesting in our context, the notion of relevance is not so tangible. A common technique in sofware libraries is to describe the stored representations by means of attributes and categories [2, 5, 22]. A conceptual model is regarded as relevant with respect to a query, if the terms of the query match syntactically with the features describing the model. Various degrees of matching have been defined on the basis of the number of attributes that match and to what extent they match. However, even though some systems use a thesaurus to help the user in finding alternative search terms, the semantics of the terms are not really considered. Since the search terms are not analyzed from the semantic point of view, it is impossible to help the user by suggesting related words or retrieving linguistically related models. In some linguistic approaches, the search terms have been modified or expanded using synonyms, hyponyms, and meronyms from a general-purpose lexicon [26, 34]. This implies that the terms are interpreted as references to real-world objects, though only a very restricted set of semantic properties is considered. For example, searching for a model that deals with books loans, such systems can also present a model that describes the loaning of dissertations, since *dissertation* is a hyponym of *book*.

What these techniques fail to take into account is the fact that the search terms here are only conventional short hands for certain semantic structures. When we request a model about book loans, we are not interested in the labels *book* and *loan* per se, but in the semantic structures associated with these two labels in this combination. We want a conceptual model that can realize these structures, and not a model that can represent two arbitrarily looking words. That is, dissertation loans are relevant to a query about book loans not because *dissertation* is below *book* in some word hierarchy, but because the dissertation model is structurally very similar to an imagined book model. In the same vein, a model describing car rentals is relevant, as this model has to contain many of the same structures as a model dealing with books and loans. Interestingly, as humans we can ourselves easily make these conclusions about relevance, using our intuitive feeling about the meaning of the words included in the query.

3 Linguistic Interpretation of Queries

In our approach, we assume a query for a conceptual model to consist of predicates and arguments. Using a semantically based lexicon, we construct semantic representations corresponding to these queries and use them as inputs to our two-step retrieval method:

1. The semantic representation of the real-world query is transformed into a datalogical query with real-world labels included.
2. The datalogical query and the semantics of the words involved are combined to retrieve models that are structurally consistent with the datalogical query *and* linguistically relevant with respect to the semantics of the words in the query.

In Section 3.1 below, we introduce the semantic linguistic theory used for the representation of queries, whereas Section 3.2 shows how the semantic representations are transformed into datalogical queries. Step 2 of the method is discussed in Section 4.

3.1 Semantic Representations of Query

The semantic representations used in this work come from the *Sign Model (SM)* proposed by Hellan and Dimitrova-Vulchanova [11]. In this theory, the grammar-relevant semantic properties of words and phrases are modeled as conceptual structures in a sign expansion framework. The lexicon assumed in SM is made up of conceptual frames that are not associated with any word category, but can be expanded in different directions to support different words and different subcategorization frames [10]. As an example, both the noun *loan* and the verb *loan* stem from the same lexical entry, and a noun like

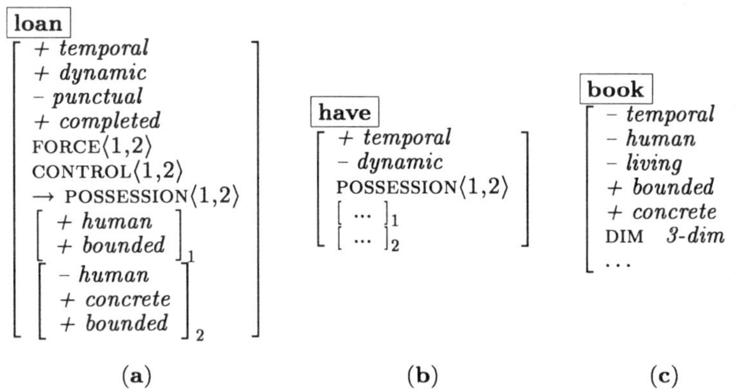

Figure 1: Lexical conceptual representations of *loan*, *have*, and *book*

loaner is generated by combining this lexical entry with the suffix entry *-er*. The actual entries of words, which are not stored in the lexicon, are generated on the fly using a sophisticated system of expansion rules.

The conceptual structures defined represent situations and arguments by means of *aspectual values, semantic relations, selectional restrictions, realizational* and *criterial factors*. Whereas aspectual values provide a semantic classification of situations, the other concepts describe physical properties of the arguments as well as semantic and pragmatic roles imposed on them from the predicate. Realizational and criterial factors are geared very much towards the grammatical realization of words and will not be discussed more here (see [11]). Some examples of expanded conceptual structures representing actual words are found in Figure 1. The boxes on top of the structures are references to the structures. We have omitted the argument specification in (c), as we will not need it in the rest of the paper.

In (a), the conceptual structure for the transitive use of *loan* is shown. The two first aspectual values indicate that a loaning act is a temporally situated, dynamic act. Its dynamic properties is then further specified to be of the durative ([- *punctual*]) and telic ([+ *completed*]) nature[1]. The structure includes two arguments, indexed as *1* and *2*, that are described by means of selectional restrictions and denote the loaner and the thing being loaned, respectively. The semantic relations FORCE and CONTROL marks argument 1 as the source of energy and the controller in the situation, and argument 2 as the entity exposed to this force and control. The arrow in front of POSSESSION means that the situation terminates by a transition to a state in which argument 1 is the possessor of argument 2. The conceptual structure in (b) describes the static ([- *dynamic*]) verb *have*. The first argument is the possessor of the second argument, though neither of them is tied to any selectional restrictions. In (c), *book* is represented as a concrete, three-dimensional, non-living, bounded argument[2].

[1] Since [- *punctual*] implies [+ *temporal*, + *dynamic*], we do not really need to specify all these aspectual values explicitly [33]. We include them here just to avoid any misunderstandings when it comes to the comparison and matching of lexical structures.

[2] *Milk* in *I drink milk every day* is an example of an unbounded argument.

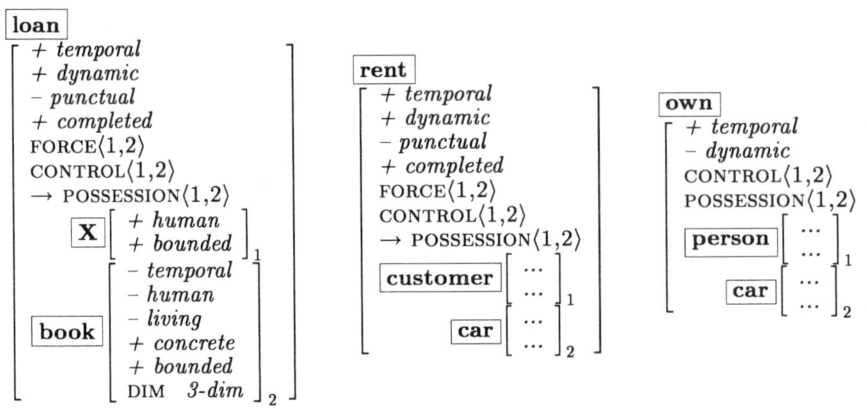

(a) (b) (c)

Figure 2: Generated conceptual representations for (a) the clause *loan(X,book)*, (b) the clause *rent(customer,car)*, and (c) the clause *own(person,car)*

More complex words and phrases are modeled as expansions of the lexical structures. A word like *loaner*, for example, is generated by expanding the structure in Figure 1(a) into an argument, co-indexing the whole structure with argument 1, and marking this argument as an abstracted argument. From a formal point of view, this new structure represents an argument that is defined by argument 1 in the situation prescribed by *loan*. Other typical expansions are the introduction of more detailed aspectual values, the additions of new arguments in the structures, and the inclusion of realizational features for topic/focus assignments [10]. As shown in Figure 2, whole clauses are constructed by unifying the argument frames of the lexical representation of the predicate with the lexical representations of the actual arguments.

3.2 Mapping Semantic Representations to Query Concepts

It is assumed that user's query for a conceptual model is (or can be transformed to be) a list of clause structures, like for example the simple structure *loan(X,book)*, and this list is immediately replaced by its semantic representation. *Loan* and *book* are here single search terms, whereas the semantic structure specifying a model of someone loaning a book is the representation shown in Figure 2(a). In the first step of the retrieval process, we construct possible model patterns based on this semantic representation that can serve as datalogical queries in the next step.

Earlier attempts to construct conceptual models from natural language sentences have emphasized the relationships between word categories and modeling primitives [20, 31]. A verb usually denotes a relationship in an ER model, whereas nouns tend to serve as entities and adjectives as attributes. Special — but unfortunately often ad hoc — methods are introduced for coping with cases that do not fit into this general scheme. Even though suggesting model patterns from term structures is linguistically simpler than automatic conceptual model construction, we feel that this approach does not catch the deeper semantic relationships that are needed for a satisfactory mapping to model constructions. In our approach, we define the linguistic interpretations of modeling primitives by means of logical formulas referring to linguistic conceptual properties. The assumption is that the characteristic properties of a primitive can be analyzed as a partial semantic structure, i.e. as a conceptual frame, and that instances of the primitive have to be semantically consistent with this frame. When a search term matches up with the conceptual frame of a primitive, we know that this term might be understood as an instance of this primitive[3]. However, we cannot be sure that the term *should* be treated as an instance of this particular primitive in the model search. First, we have to make sure that this interpretation can be combined with the interpretations of the other terms to create a coherent and legal model pattern. Secondly, due to the vagueness of many primitives, we have to check if a term can be interpreted as instances of several primitives. For example, in an ER model of a library system, a reader of a book may be either an entity related to the book by some *loan* relationship or a simple attribute of *book*. If several interpretations are possible, the system has to present the different interpretations as different model patterns, and the user can then select the most appropriate one.

Realizing this approach to query reformulation, we make use of an abductive information retrieval technique proposed in [21]. A real-world query is reformulated in terms of datalogical concepts by finding a datalogical query that implies (or explains) the original query. Assuming a theory T that describes the linguistic semantic content of modeling primitives and a semantic representation Q_{RW} of user's query, we look for a set of formulas H (called an hypothesis) so that

$$T \cup H \Rightarrow Q_{RW} \qquad\qquad (T \cup H \text{ is consistent})$$

Some of the rules in T describing the primitives in the PhM modeling language [9] are shown in Figure 3. PhM is an extension of traditional ER models, and the rules show how the instances of the PhM primitives *entity, relationship*, and *attribute* are analyzed with respect to linguistic semantic properties. The predicates *ent_rel/2* and *ent_att/2* can be assumed to denote axioms in the abduction process, whereas the predicate *unify/2* can only be used in the reasoning if the two argument structures unify. The query Q_{RW} is formulated by means of the formulas *semantics/2* and *arg_of/2*, which refer directly to the semantic representation of user's query. The reformulated datalogical query is given by the proof tree for the deduction of Q_{RW}.

Imagine now that the user query *loan(X,book)* is posted. The semantic representation is generated, and this representation is transformed into the following query formulas (the boxes are references to conceptual structures):

$$Q_{RW} = \; semantics(loan, \boxed{\text{loan}}) \wedge semantics(X, \boxed{\text{X}}) \wedge semantics(book, \boxed{\text{book}}) \\ \wedge arg\_of(X, loan) \wedge arg\_of(book, loan)$$

The formulas in Figure 3 are now used to find a hypothesis that would imply that the query above holds. Starting with the query formulas, we use the formulas in T in the reverse direction to find a possible proof for the query. The proof tree is shown in Figure 4(a) and can be understood as the following datalogical query:

$$Q_{PP} = \; rel(loan) \wedge ent(X) \wedge ent(book) \wedge ent\_rel(X, loan) \wedge ent\_rel(book, loan)$$

[3]Similarly, knowledge-based IR systems like RESEARCHER [16], SCISOR [24] and TOPIC/TOPOGRAPHIC [30] employ automatic text analysis procedures to map natural language documents onto unique representation schemes. Since the retrieval process treats NL queries using the same mapping procedure, this underlying representation can be used to retrieve relevant documents.

(1) $\forall Word, \Sigma_0\ \exists \Sigma : conform(Word, \Sigma_0) \wedge unify(\Sigma_0, \Sigma) \rightarrow semantics(Word, \Sigma)$
If a word conforms with a semantic structure Σ_0, the semantic structure representing the word itself must unify with Σ.

(2) $\forall Word : ent(Word) \rightarrow conform(Word, [-temporal, +concrete, +bounded])$
If a word denotes an entity, it has to conform with a concrete, identifiable argument.

(3) $\forall Word : rel(Word) \rightarrow conform(Word, [+temporal, -punctual])$
If a word denotes a relationship, it has to conform with a temporally situated, durative situation.

(4) $\forall Word : att(Word) \rightarrow conform(Word, [-temporal])$
If a word denotes an attribute, it has to conform with a description that does not refer to a temporally situated situation.

(5) $\forall Word : att\_link(Word) \rightarrow conform(Word, [+temporal, -dynamic])$
If a word denotes an attribute link, it has to conform with a temporally situated, static situation.

(6) $\forall Ent, Rel : ent\_rel(Ent, Rel) \rightarrow ent(Ent) \wedge rel(Rel) \wedge arg\_of(Ent, Rel)$
If two concepts are connected by an entity-relationship link, one of them is an entity and the other is an relationship, and the entity concept is an argument of the relationship concept.

(7) $\forall Ent, Att : ent\_att(Ent, Att) \rightarrow ent(Ent) \wedge att(Att) \wedge arg\_of(Ent, Att)$
If two concepts are connected by an entity-attribute link, one of them is an entity and the other is an attribute, and the entity concept is an argument of the attribute concept.

(8) $\forall Ent, Att\ \exists Word : ent\_att(Ent, Att) \rightarrow ent(Ent) \wedge att(Att) \wedge att\_link(Word) \wedge arg\_of(Att, Word) \wedge arg\_of(Ent, Word)$
If two concepts are connected by an entity-attribute link, one of them is an entity and the other is an attribute, and there exists an attribute link whose arguments are made up of these two concepts.

Figure 3: Rules defining linguistic interpretations of the modeling primitives in PhM

Graphically, this query can be represented by the PhM model fragment in Figure 4(b). The proof three (and the query) is based on the hypothesis that *ent_rel(X,loan)* and *ent_rel(book,loan)* hold. In many cases, however, a real-world query can be given different interpretations in terms of datalogical concepts. Consider for example a query like *have(loaner,book)*, which denotes a temporal, static situation. *Have* can here be interpreted as a relationship (rule (3) in Figure 3), though since it is [- *dynamic*], it can also be assumed to be an attribute link (rule (5)). This gives rise to three different interpretations:

$$\begin{aligned} Q_{PP1} &= rel(have) \wedge ent(loaner) \wedge ent(book) \wedge ent\_rel(loaner, have) \wedge ent\_rel(book, have), \\ Q_{PP2} &= ent(loaner) \wedge att(book) \wedge ent\_att(loaner, book), \\ Q_{PP3} &= ent(book) \wedge att(loaner) \wedge ent\_att(book, loaner), \end{aligned}$$

and the user has to select which datalogical query to use in the retrieval. This means that the user is helped by the system in reformulating the NL-based query as a query referring to the concepts stored in the CASE environment. Abduction gives us here a firm logical foundation for dealing with queries that are ambiguous with respect to datalogical concepts. After selecting the appropriate query, the user can of course refine

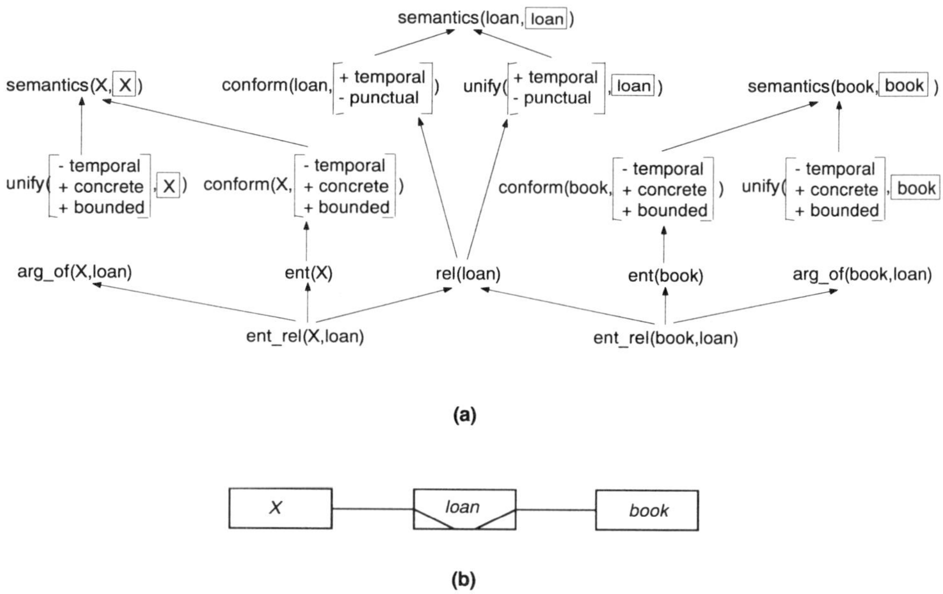

Figure 4: (a) Abducing the query from T (b) Model pattern corresponding to abduction

the query with more detailed information about the model he is looking for. As a final remark, we should also note that the construction of semantic representations enables us to rule out some semantically ill-formed queries, e.g. *loan(X,information)* where *information* is [- *concrete*] and consequently ununifiable with *loan*'s second argument.

4 Retrieving Structurally Similar Models

Having chosen a datalogical query like Q_{PP} above, we can search the CASE repository for PhM models containing *loan* relationships connected to a *book* entity and some other arbitrary entity. In order to retrieve also analogous models, however, we must avoid restricting the search to only the word labels *loan* and *book*. One method is then to substitute synonyms, hyponyms, and meronyms for the words [23], though this does not really address all the semantic properties of the words that affect the way they are modeled. Our concept of analogy is not only rooted in word hierarchies and relations, but also in the underlying semantic properties of the words. A model is deemed relevant to a query if

> *(1) its structure encompasses the datalogical structure of the query,* and *(2) for each corresponding part of their semantic representations, the semantic relations in the query are also in the model and all features and factors unify.*

This technique of comparing semantic representations is based on a linguistic method for model verification suggested in [33]. The semantic representation of a query specifies structural properties that are common to a class of semantically related phenomena. If a model includes a semantic representation that is compatible with the one of the query, we know that the model is related to the query by means of common semantic structures. With the assumption that these semantic structures are reflected in the structure of the conceptual model itself, we have a method for retrieving models that can be useful when the new model corresponding to the query is constructed. For putting the semantic representations properly together, however, the query has to be turned into a datalogical query first. In IR systems, similar problems have attacked using domain-dependent pattern matching [30] or generalization techniques [25].

Consider a model representing a customer renting a car, which is typically modeled as a relationship connected to two entities in PhM. As *car* and *rent* are not related to *book* and *loan* by synonymi or hyponymi, traditional information retrieval systems will find this model fragment irrelevant to the query *loan(X,book)*. Still, there are many structural similarities between car rentals and book loans that also affect the way they are included in conceptual models. If you know how to represent a customer renting a car, you have a starting point for how to represent a customer loaning a book. This similarity is reflected by their semantic representations, which are shown in Figure 2(a) and Figure 2(b). The structures are almost identical, as both indicate a transition to some state in which the argument controlling the situation is the possessor of the other one. Using our compatibility test above, we get that the roles and the features of the model unify with the query, and the model is then presented to the user as a relevant, analogous model. In contrast, a person owning a car is also often modeled by a relationship associated with two entities. If only a model pattern match was used to determine the relevance of a model to a query, a model including persons owning cars would also be retrieved in response to the query *loan(X,book)*. This model is not very useful, though, since owning something does not have this crucial transitional aspect implied in loaning something. This transitional property indicates, for example, that we need dates associated with the loan, mechanisms for establishing and terminating loans, searching routines, etc. Looking at the semantic representation of *own(person,car)* in Figure 2(c), we see that such a model cannot be retrieved using our retrieval method. The possession roles in *own* are not established after a transition and are therefore incompatible with the possession roles included in *loan*. Similarly, a model representing the buying of a car is incompatible because *buy* is a punctual act.

5 Conclusions

The model retrieval approach presented here is intended to support the early stages of software engineering, where domain experts are active and problems are vague and difficult to formalize. Its major advantage is that it lets the user request conceptual models in a vague, formalism-independent way. Requests based on natural language are interpreted using abduction and transformed into alternative datalogical queries. The user selects the query he find most appropriate, refines it if necessary, and submits it to the retrieval system. During the retrieval itself, the deeper semantic properties of the search terms are used to retrieve also models that have different word labels, but are relevant due to their structural analogies.

As the approach is still under development, it is too early to draw any final conclusions about its effectiveness. However, the importance of using analogous models as guidelines in the modeling process is confirmed by experiments [18]. These experiments indicate a considerable improvement when structurally similar phenomena are taken into account, even though the phenomena belong to other domains. A problem with the approach, though, is that the user has to be able to realize the analogy between the models. If completely different word labels appear in the retrieved models, the user might fail to realize the structureal similarities between the models and the query.

Currently, we are working on a CASE project, in which our retrieval method is combined with synthesis techniques to allow a more flexible reuse of representations throughout the whole software development project. Whereas NL-oriented queries are used to request conceptual models from the repository, partly completed conceptual models are in the next round used as queries for design components and software routines.

References

[1] R. D. Banker, R. J. Kauffman, and D. Zweig. Repository Evaluation of Software Reuse. *IEEE Transactions of Software Engineering*, 19(4):379–389, April 1993.

[2] B. A. Burton, R. Wienk Aragon, S. A. Bailey, K. D. Koehler, and L. A. Mayes. The Reusable Software Library. *IEEE Software*, 4(4):25–33, July 1987.

[3] A. M. Davis. *Software Requirements: analysis and specification.* Prentice-Hall, Inc., 1990.

[4] R. A. Elmasri, V. Kouramajian, and B. Thalheim, editors. *Proceedings of the 12th International Conference on the Entity-Relationship Approach (ER'93)*, Arlington, Texas, December 1993. Springer-Verlag.

[5] B. Freitag. A Hypertext-Based Tool for Large Scale Software Reuse. In G. Wijers, S. Brinkkemper, and T. Wasserman, editors, *Proceedings of the Sixth International Conference on Advanced Information Systems Engineering (CAiSE'94)*, pages 283–296, Utrecht, June 1994. Springer-Verlag.

[6] G. Grosz, editor. *Proceedings of the Sixth Workshop on the Next Generation of CASE Tools (NGCT'95)*, Jyväskylä, June 1995.

[7] R. Guindon. Designing the design process: Exploiting opportunistic thoughts. *Human-Computer Interaction*, 5:305–344, 1990.

[8] J. A. Gulla. A General Explanation Component for Conceptual Modeling in CASE Environments. *ACM Transactions on Information Systems*, 14(3), July 1996.

[9] J. A. Gulla, O. I. Lindland, and G. Willumsen. PPP: An Integrated CASE Environment. In R. Andersen, J. A. Bubenko jr., and A. Sølvberg, editors, *Proceedings of the Third International Conference on Advanced Information Systems Engineering (CAiSE'91)*, pages 194–221, Trondheim, May 1991. Springer-Verlag.

[10] J. A. Gulla and S. N. Moshagen. Representations and Derivations in the TROLL Lexicon. In H. Lødrup, I. Moen, and H. G. Simonsen, editors, *Proceedings of The XVth Scandinavian Conference of Linguistics*, Oslo, January 1995.

[11] L. Hellan and M. Dimitrova-Vulchanova. Preliminary Notes on a Framework for 'Lexically Dependent Grammar'. Lecture series at International Summer Institute in Syntax, Central Institute of English and Foreign Languages, Hyderabad, India, July 1994.

[12] E. Henry and B. Faller. Large-Scale Industrial Reuse to Reduce Cost and Cycle Time. *IEEE Software*, 12(5):47–53, September 1995.

[13] V. Karakostas. Requirements for CASE Tools in Early Software Reuse. *ACM SIGSOFT Software Engineering Notes*, 14(2):39–41, April 1989.

[14] D. C. H. Kung. The Behavior Network Model for Conceptual Information Modeling. *Information Systems*, 18(1):1–21, 1993.

[15] D. Lauzon and T. Rose. Task-Oriented and Similarity-Based Retrieval. In R. Juling and D. R. Smith, editors, *The Ninth Knowledge-Based Software Engineering Conference (KBSE'94)*, pages 98–107, Monterey, September 1994. IEEE Computer Society Press.

[16] M. Lebowitz. Intelligent Information Systems. *SIGIR Forum*, 17(4):25–30, 1983.

[17] H. Liu. A Visual Approach to Querying the CASE Repository — A Requirements Analysis. In Grosz [6], pages 143–160.

[18] N. A. Maiden and A. G. Sutcliffe. Exploiting Reusable Specifications Through Analogy. *Communications of the ACM*, 35(4):55–64, 1992.

[19] N. A. M. Maiden. Reuse-Oriented Requirements Engineering in NATURE. *ACM SIGSOFT Software Engineering Notes*, 20(3):90–93, July 1995.

[20] E. Métais, J.-N. Meunier, and G. Levreau. Database Schema Design: A Perspective from Natural Language Techniques to Validation and View Integration. In Elmasri et al. [4], pages 190–205.

[21] A. Müller and U. Thiel. Query Expansion in an Abductive Information Retrieval System. In *Proceedings of Conference on Intelligent Multimedia Information Retrieval Systems and Management (RIAO'94)*, pages 461–480, New York, October 1994.

[22] R. Prieto-Diaz and P. Freeman. Classifying Software for Reusability. *IEEE Software*, 4(1):6–16, January 1987.

[23] A. Puder. Service Trading Using Conceptual Structures. In *Proceedings of International Conference on Conceptual Structures (ICCS'95)*. Springer-Verlag, 1995.

[24] L. F. Rau. Knowledge Organization and Access in a Conceptual Information System. *Information Processing & Management*, 21(4):269–283, 1987.

[25] U. Reimer. Automatic Knowledge Acquisition from Texts: Learning Terminological Knowledge via Text Understanding and Inductive Generalization. In *Proceedings of the Fifth Workshop on Knowledge Acquisition for Knowledge-Based Systems*, 1990.

[26] R. Richardson and A. F. Smeaton. Using WordNet in a Knowledge-Based Approach to Information Retrieval. Technical Report CA-0395, Dublin City University, Glasnevin, Dublin 9, 1995.

[27] C. Rolland and C. Proix. A Natural Language Approach for Requirements Engineering. In P. Loucopoulos, editor, *Proceedings of the Forth International Conference on Advanced Information Systems Engineering (CAiSE'92)*, pages 257–277. Springer-Verlag, May 1992.

[28] A. Sølvberg and D. C. H. Kung. *Information Systems Engineering*. Springer-Verlag, 1993.

[29] G. Spanoudakis and P. Constantopoulos. Similarity for Analogical Software Reuse: A Conceptual Modelling Approach. In C. Rolland, F. Bodart, and C. Cauvet, editors, *Proceedings of the Fifth International Conference on Advanced Information Systems Engineering (CAiSE'93)*, pages 483–503, Paris, June 1993. Springer-Verlag.

[30] U. Thiel and R. Hammwöhner. Informational Zooming: An Interaction Model for the Graphical Access to Text Knowledge Bases. In *Proceedings of International ACM SIGIR Conference on Research and Development in Information Retrieval*, pages 45–56, 1987.

[31] A. M. Tjoa and L. Berger. Transformation of Requirement Specifications Expressed in Natural Language into an EER Model. In Elmasri et al. [4], pages 206–217.

[32] W. Tracz. Where Does Reuse Start? *ACM SIGSOFT Software Engineering Notes*, 15(2):42–46, April 1990.

[33] B. van der Vos, J. A. Gulla, and R. van de Riet. Verification of Conceptual Models based on Linguistic Knowledge. In *Proceedings of the First International Workshop on Applications of Natural Language to Data Bases*, pages 151–165, Versailles, June 1995.

[34] E. M. Voorhees. Query Expansion Using Lexical-Semantic Relations. In W. B. Croft and C. J. van Rijsbergen, editors, *Proceedings of the Seventeenth Annual International ACM-SIGIR Conference on Research and Development in Information Retrieval (SIGIR'94)*, pages 61–70, Dublin, July 1994.

[35] R. Wieringa. Three Roles of Conceptual Models in Information System Design and Use. In E. D. Falkenberg and P. Lindgreen, editors, *Information System Concept: An In-depth Analysis*, pages 31–52. North-Holland, 1989.

[36] M. Yang, A. H. Seltveit, and A. Sølvberg. A Distributed Repository Management System for Formal Conceptual IS Models. In Grosz [6], pages 195–213.

Applications of Natural Language to Information Systems
R.P. van de Riet et al. (Eds.)
IOS Press, 1996

Conceptual Modelling, Indexing and Retrieval for Textual Corporate Knowledge Bases

Gian Piero Zarri
Centre National de la Recherche Scientifique
EHESS - CAMS
Paris, France
zarri@cams.msh-paris.fr

Abstract. In this paper, we suggest that an in-depth exploitation of what could be called the textual component of corporate knowledge can be achieved with the translation of this component into some type of conceptual format. The "metadocuments" obtained in this way can be considered, in fact, as a sort of high-level, conceptual categorisation/indexing of the original NL texts, based on an in-depth representation of their "meaning". We illustrate here the architecture of a prototypical system designed to exploit a knowledge base of metadocuments.
Keywords: Conceptual modelling, Metadocument, Textual corporate knowledge, Knowledge acquisition, Inference techniques

1 Introduction

This paper concerns the construction of a new type of information management systems built up to exploit, in a optimal way, what could be called the textual component of corporate knowledge — i.e., all sort of economically valuable, natural language (NL) documents like news stories, telex reports, internal documentation (memos, policy statements, reports and minutes), normative texts, intelligence messages, etc.

To fulfil this aim, we propose the use (making reference to the usual information retrieval terminology) of enhanced types of document models. As well known, a document model (Boolean models, vector models, probabilistic models ...) is assumed to represent, in some way, the semantic or informational content of the documents under consideration. This implies that, e.g., in the traditional Boolean model, the content of the document will be represented simply by a set of keywords ; a correspondence function will try then to find a match between this set and a query expressed, in turn, by keywords grouped into some form of Boolean combination (i.e., making use of the traditional and, or, not ... operators). We suggest, on the contrary, to make use of (enhanced) document models based on some form of advanced conceptual representation in the Knowledge Engineering style (e.g., semantic nets, frames, conceptual graphs, etc.). This choice should allow to obtain a more reliable representation of the semantic content (i.e., the "meaning") of the original documents, by minimising the information loss which is inherently associated with any modelling task. As a consequence, the precision, recall (and flexibility) rates associated with the correspondence function should also improve.

We call "metadocument" the result of translating into conceptual format the semantic content of an original NL document — this approach can be interpreted as a sophisticated indexing or categorisation technique. Metadocuments can then be stored, e.g., into a knowledge base and, given their role of document models, all the traditional functions of information retrieval, e.g., searching, retrieving and producing an answer (and other functions like the intelligent navigation inside the base) can be directly executed on them. A (to some extent) similar approach is outlined in [1], that too describes a system dealing with the processing of NL documents in a corporate knowledge environment ; however, their approach seems to be more conventional. For a general review of the state-of-the-art in the corporate knowledge management field see, e.g., [2].

In the following, we will describe, in Section 2, the general architecture of the prototype of an information management system for textual corporate knowledge that we have (partially, see next Section) built up thanks to the aid of the European Commission (Esprit project NOMOS, P5330 and LRE project COBALT, P61011) and of the French National Centre for Scientific Research (CNRS). In Section 3, we will introduce succinctly NKRL (Narrative Knowledge Representation Language), the conceptual language we use for the production of metadocuments. In the following Sections, we will comment briefly on the two main blocks of the prototype : the acquisition sub-system, Section 4, and the interrogation sub-system, Section 5. Section 6. will be the "Conclusion".

2 A prototype for dealing with the textual component of corporate knowledge

Fig. 1 gives a very general overview of the architecture of the system we propose. Please note that all the blocks shown in this figure already exist, at least in a prototypical form ; however, the procedures concerning the selection and the activation of the high-level inference procedures, at the bottom, realised in a CNRS context, are still not integrated with the remaining blocks, realised mainly in a NOMOS/COBALT context. All the blocks of Fig. 1 have been implemented in COMMON LISP. In NOMOS/COBALT, we have used as support platform an object-oriented environment : CRL (Carnegie Representation Language) in the NOMOS version, QSL (Quinary Semantic Language) in the COBALT version.

Supposing the integrated system already exists, the original NL documents, on the left, pass through the NL processing modules which constitute the core of the acquisition sub-system. This sub-system executes, essentially, a conversion of the "meaning" of the original documents into NKRL format. The results of this translation activity are stored into the central knowledge base (metadocument knowledge base). Some functions, not shown in Fig. 1 for simplicity's sake, allow browsing and maintenance operations on the contents of the base. Moreover, in order to i) check the correctness of the translation ; ii) supply the user with a means of being informed in real time of the main characteristics of the documents currently analysed, some possibilities of immediate display of the resulting NKRL code have been added in a COBALT context.

The boxes on the right-hand side of Fig. 1 represent the query sub-system of the prototype. The user's queries are, firstly, translated into search patterns or sequences of search patterns — search patterns are NKRL data structures which represent the general framework of information to be searched for, by filtering or unification, within the metadocument knowledge base. The metadocuments can i) directly unify the original query (search pattern) ; ii) unify some new search patterns obtained by inference from the original one, see, below, Section 5. After the (possible) unification of the patterns

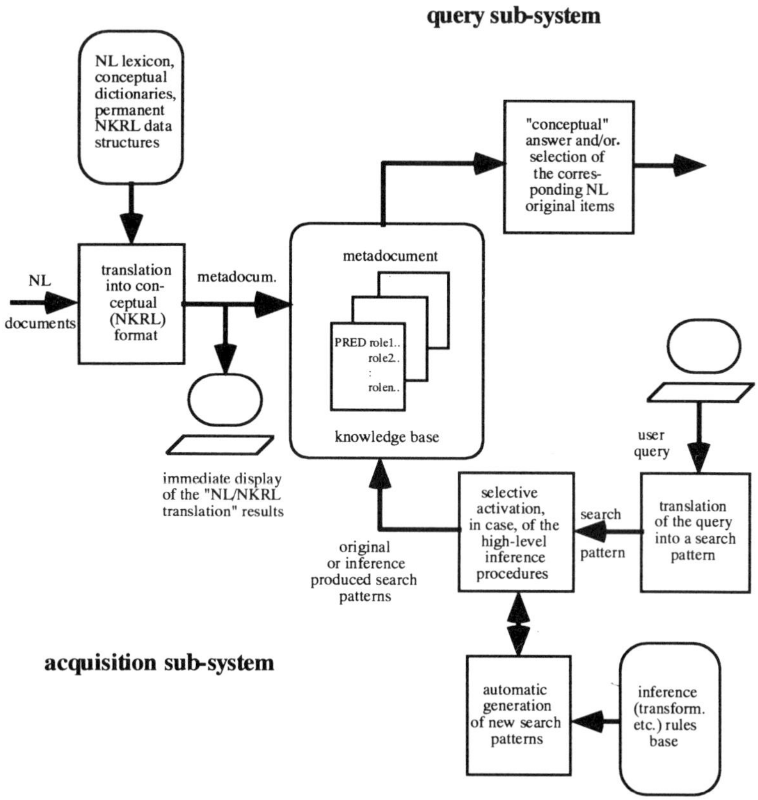

Figure 1: Architecture of the prototype

with one or more metadocuments, these are presented to the user. The output can be shown actually in two different formats, which can also coexist : i) in a concise, tabular format (immediate display) ; ii) as the original NL messages, if they have been stored along with the corresponding metadocuments. We envision the possibility of adding the possibility of showing the results in some type of basic English format.

3 A quick glimpse of NKRL

NKRL (Narrative Knowledge Representation Language) supplies a language-independent description of the semantic content (the "meaning") of non-trivial, NL narrative documents, like the textual corporate documents introduced in Section 1.

NKRL is a two layer language.

The lower layer supplies a set of general tools. It consists of four integrated components.

The descriptive component tools are used to set up the formal, NKRL expressions ("templates") describing general classes of narrative events, like "moving a generic object", "formulate a need", "be present somewhere". Templates encode, therefore, the standard features of various ordinary events and human activities. Templates are structured into a hierarchy, H_TEMP(lates), which can be equated to a taxonomy (ontology) of events.

Templates' instances (called occurrences), i.e., the NKRL representations of single, specific events like "Tomorrow, I will move the wardrobe", "Lucy was looking for a taxi", "Peter lives in Paris", are in the domain of the factual component. Templates and occurrences are characterised by a tripartite format : $(P_i\ (R_1 a_1)\ (R_2 a_2)\ ...\ (R_n a_n))$, where the central piece is a semantic predicate P_i — like BEHAVE, EXPERIENCE, MOVE, PRODUCE etc. — which represents a named relation that exists among one or more arguments a_i introduced by means of roles R_i — like SUBJ(ect), OBJ(ect), SOURCE, etc. From a formal point of view, a metadocument consists, therefore, of the association of several templates and/or occurrences which are tied up by particular binding structures, see [3, 4], that represent the logico-semantic links which can exist between them (the "co-ordination" and "subordination" links, using a metaphor from the domain of natural language).

The definitional component supplies the formal representation of all the general notions, like *physical_entity*, *taxi_*, *location_*, which can be used as arguments in the two components above. Their representations in NKRL terms are called concepts (basically, their data structures can be equated to frames), and are grouped into a hierarchy, H_CLASS(es) — H_CLASS corresponds well, therefore, to the usual concept ontologies.

The instances of concepts, like lucy_, wardrobe_1, paris_ are called individuals, and pertain to the enumerative component.

For more details about the main tools of NKRL — e.g., those allowing the representation of modal or temporal information — see, e.g., [3, 5].

The upper layer of NKRL consists essentially of a catalogue, where we can find a complete description of the formal characteristics and the modalities of use of the well-formed, "basic" templates (like "moving a generic object" mentioned above) associated with the language — presently, about 150, pertaining mainly to a (very general) socio-economico-political context where the main characters are human beings or social bodies. By means of proper specialisation operations, it is then possible to obtain from the basic templates the (specific) "derived" templates that could be concretely needed in the context of a particular, practical application — e.g., "move an industrial process" — and the corresponding occurrences (instances) - e.g., "move, in a well-defined spatio-temporal framework, this particular industrial production from one country to another". In NKRL, the set of legal, basic templates included in the catalogue can be considered, at least in a first approach, see below, as fixed. This means that : i) a system-builder does not have to create himself the structural knowledge needed to describe the events proper to a (sufficiently) large class of narrative documents ; ii) it becomes easier to secure the reproduction and the sharing of previous results.

Please note, however, that (if need be), it is always possible to insert new basic elements in the catalogue. For example if, even in a general context of social interactions, it were absolutely necessary to put special emphasis on everyday life acts like "eating" or "drinking" (which can hardly be expressed by making use of the seven predicates above), we should simply introduce a new predicate in the style of the Schankian INGEST, and add the corresponding new templates (derived, e.g., from the syntactic structures of particular PRODUCE or RECEIVE templates) to the catalogue.

We can now supply, see Fig. 2, a very simple example of NKRL code (a metadocument consisting only of occurrences). It translates a small fragment of news in the COBALT's style : "Milan, October 15, 1993. The financial daily Il Sole 24 Ore reported Mediobanca had called a special board meeting concerning plans for capital increase".

In Fig. 2, c1 and c2 are the symbolic names of two occurrences, instances of NKRL

c1)	MOVE	SUBJ	(SPECIF sole_24_ore *financial_daily*):(milan_)
		OBJ	#c2
		date-1:	15_october_93
		date-2:	
c2)	PRODUCE	SUBJ	mediobanca_
		OBJ	(SPECIF summoning_1 (SPECIF board_meeting_ mediobanca_ *special_*))
		TOPIC	(SPECIF plan_1 (SPECIF *cardinality_several_*) capital_increase_1)
		date-1:	circa_15_october_93
		date-2:	

Figure 2: An example of NKRL coding

templates. MOVE and PRODUCE are predicates ; SUBJ, OBJ, TOPIC (the theme, "à propos of ...", of the event(s) or situation(s) represented in the occurrence) are roles. With respect now to the arguments, sole_24_ore, milan_, mediobanca_ (an Italian merchant bank), summoning_1, etc. are individuals ; *financial_daily*, *special_*, *cardinality_* (which pertains to the *property_* sub-tree of H_CLASS) and *several_* (belonging, like *some_*, *all_* etc., to the *logical_quantifier* sub-tree of H_CLASS) are concepts. The attributive operator, SPECIF(ication), is one of the NKRL operators used to build up structured arguments (or "expansions"), see also, below, Section 5 ; the SPECIF lists, with syntax (SPECIF e_1 p_1 ... p_n), are used to represent the properties which can be asserted about the first element e_1, concept or individual, of the list, e.g., sole_24_ore in occurrence c1, summoning_1 and plan_1 in occurrence c2. *several_* is used within a *cardinality_* SPECIF list in order to provide a standard way of representing the plural number mark, see occurrence c2.

The arguments, and the templates/occurrences as a whole, may be characterised by the addition of determiners (attributes). In particular, the location attributes (lists) are associated with the arguments by using the colon, ":", operator, see occurrence c1. For a recent paper on the NKRL representation of the temporal determiners, date-1 and date-2, see [5].

Please note that the MOVE basic template at the origin of the occurrence c1 is necessarily used to translate any event concerning the transmission of an information ("The financial daily Il Sole 24 Ore reported ..."). It makes use of what is called a "completive construction". Accordingly, the filler of the OBJ(ect) slot in the occurrences (here, c1) which instantiates the transmission template is always a symbolic label (here, ♯c2) which refers to another predicative occurrence, i.e., the occurrence bearing the informational content to be spread out ("... Mediobanca had called a meeting ..."). For other types of NKRL structures (binding structures) allowing to build up complex, second order objects from simple, first order templates and occurrences, see, e.g., [3, 4].

4 The acquisition procedures

The two versions, NOMOS and COBALT, of our NL/NKRL translation system are both based on the use of independent specialists. These are called in sequence, producing a progressive transformation into NKRL structures.

The specialists make use of permanent, common shared data structures. The most important is the lexicon, which is a complex mechanism entailing that each of its NL lexical entries contains morpho-syntactic, semantic and pragmatic information. In particular, three slots, ref-selection, ref-triggering and ref-substitution, may contain pointers towards the "conceptual" dictionaries.

A first dictionary concerns the "selection strategies", i.e., text grammar rules allowing the quick focusing on a particular information to be extracted while ignoring irrelevant elements ; in COBALT, we have used for this task of a commercial product, TCS (Text Categorisation System, by Carnegie Group, U.S.A.). The "triggering strategies" dictionary contains the triggering rules evoked by the lexical entry examined, i.e., the rules allowing the activation of particular templates pertaining to the H_TEMP hierarchy (descriptive component) — the activated templates will supply the general framework of the metadocuments corresponding to the input texts. The triggering rules are a sort of production rules, see below. The left hand side (antecedent part) is always a syntactic condition, expressed under the form of a tree-like structure, which must be unified with the results of the general parse tree produced by the syntactic specialist. If the unification succeeds, the right hand sides (consequent parts) are used to generate well-formed templates.

The last conceptual dictionary is the "substitution strategies" dictionary, where we store the control structures (substitution rules, similar to the triggering rules) allowing to replace an NP (noun phrase group, NL domain), or part of NP, with the corresponding H_CLASS concept(s) or individual(s) (NKRL domain).

With respect now to the specialists, the output of the first specialist of the sequence, the "pre-processing specialist", is a set of distinct sentences which have already been submitted to the morphological analysis. In NOMOS, the syntactic analysis of each (French) sentence was performed by a robust ATN compiler ("syntactic specialist") making use of a Grammaire Francaise de Surface, GSF; syntactic ambiguity was handled i) by using heuristics, see [6] ; ii) by interacting with the user through a friendly interface. In COBALT, we have used as syntactic specialist a morphosyntactic analyser for free (English) texts, SCAM (Surface Categorial Analysis Module) based on an efficient implementation of Categorial Grammar with Unification, CGU, see [7]. The specialist called "separation into morpho-syntactic contexts" has been introduced for the purpose of modularity, robustness and simplicity.

The substitution procedures ("substitution specialist") constitute one of the fundamental steps of the translation process ; they concern the terminal symbols (NL terms) of the syntactic tree, pertaining to the morpho-syntactic context under examination, which are part of a N(oun) P(hrase)'s head. For each one of these terms (NL domain), we must examine the substitution rules stored in the corresponding entries of the "substitution strategies" dictionary, see above, to see if it is possible to replace it with the corresponding concept or individual (NKRL domain). A (unique) NKRL term may also replace the association of several terminal symbols : e.g., it may replace an entire NP group. The output of the substitution specialist is a context expressed as a fragment of parse tree where the leaves can be either NL or NKRL terms.

For example, after this phase, the context corresponding to the "Il Sole 24 Ore" NL fragment examined in the previous Section, becomes equivalent, represented in linear form, to the mixed expression given in Fig. 3, where *financial_daily*, sole_24_ore, mediobanca_, *special_*, etc. are already NKRL terms (concepts or individuals). We do not dwell here on the formal characteristics of the substitution rules : they are handled in a way very similar to that used for the triggering rules, examined below in some details.

The triggering — filling — merging procedures (specialisation procedures), successively carried out by the "generation specialist", represent the core of the translation

"The [*financial_daily*][sole_24_ore] reported [mediobanca_] had called a [*special_*] [board_meeting] concerning [(SPECIF plan_1(SPECIF *cardinality_several_*))] for [capital_increase_1]"

Figure 3: "Mixed" NL/NKRL formulation

engine. These procedures are applied in sequence to the morpho-syntactic contexts — already processed by the substitution specialist — generated by the sentences of the original NL text.

For example, in the formulation of the "Il Sole 24 Ore" fragment which follows from the application of the substitution rules, see Fig. 3, the NL terms "said" and "called" are associated with specific subsets of the triggering rules stored in the "template references" dictionary. We reproduce, in Fig. 4, one of the several triggering rules to which the lexical entry "call" contains a pointer, i.e., one of the rules corresponding to the meaning "to issue a call to convene". This rule allows the activation of the basic template PRODUCE4.12 that will give rise, at a later stage, to the occurrence c2 of Fig. 2. Please note that optional branches under the form "(modifiers (adjs/noun x_n))" — see, in Fig. 4, the branch "(modifiers (adjs x_{31}))" — can be freely inserted in the noun phrases (np) of the syntactic condition to cater for the presence of optional modifiers.

trigger : "call"

syntactic condition :

```
(s (subj (np (noun x1)))
   (vcl (voice active) (v t = x2 = call))
   (dir-obj
    (np (modifiers (adjs x31))
        (noun x3)
        (modifiers (pp (prep about | concerning | ... )
                       (np (noun x4)
                           (modifiers (pp (prep of | for ...)
                                          (np (noun x5))))))))))
```

parameters for the template :

(PRODUCE4.12 (roles subj x_1 obj(SPECIF x_2 (SPECIF x_3 x_{31})) +topic (specifx_4 x_5))
(constr x_3 *assembly_* x_{31} *quality_* x_5*modification_procedures*))

Figure 4: An example of triggering rule

We can remark that the full template is not actually stored in the consequent, given that the H_TEMP hierarchy is part of the common shared data structures, see before. Only the parameters relating to the specific triggering rule are stored in the consequent. For example, in Fig. 4, theli st "constr" actualises the constraints on some of the variables, while others — e.g., the constraints on the variables x_1 (human_being/social_body) and x_4 (planning_activity) — are unchanged.

In this example, the antecedent of the triggering rule effectively unifies the result of the syntactic analysis, thus authorising the instantiation of the template mentioned in the consequent. Moreover, its "antecedent variables", x_n, can capture on the parse tree, during the unification phase, NL or H_CLASS terms which can then be used as specialisation terms for the subsequent filling operations, see [8].

The merge of semi-identical templates, based on a complex unification processes, is the final procedure of the generation specialist. An important innovation proper to the COBALT version of the NL/NKRL translator has concerned augmenting the generation specialist with a special, knowledge-based, PP-attachment module (PP = Prepositional Phrase), see, for some details [8]. The last specialist of the sequence deals with the anaphoric phenomena, see [9], and the calculation of the inter-context logical and semantic links. In this last case, we make use mainly of simple rules activated by the presence of particular syntactic marks, like the existence of co-ordinated sentences linked by NL terms such as or, and, either or when.

5 Using the metadocuments knowledge base for interrogation purposes

Each of the four components of the NKRL language is characterised by the association with a class of proper, basic inference procedures.

For example, the key inference mechanism of the factual component (and the basic inference tool of NKRL) is the Filtering and Unification Module (FUM). The primary data structures handled by FUM are the search patterns that, as already stated, represent (in NKRL terms) the general properties of an information to be searched for, by filtering or unification, within a metadocument knowledge base — a search pattern can be considered an NKRL equivalent of a natural language query, see Fig. 1. For clarity's sake, we reproduce in Fig. 5 the search pattern corresponding to the question : "Which was the theme of the recent board meeting called out by Mediobanca ?" that, obviously, unify with occurrence c2 in Fig. 2. In this figure, we have voluntarily enlarged the scope of the question, by adding more constraints on the OBJ(ect) variable (x). The two dates of Fig. 5 constitute the "search interval" associated with the search pattern : this interval is used to limit the search for unification to the slice of time which it is considered appropriate to explore, see [5].

```
((?w   IS-OCCURRENCE
       :predicate    PRODUCE
       :SUBJ         mediobanca_
       :OBJ          (SPECIF ?x (SPECIF ?y mediobanca_))
       :TOPIC        ?z)
       (1_october_93, 20_october_93)
            ((?x     IS-A (:OR assembly_ adjournment_ dissolution_))
            (?y      IS-A board_meeting)
            (?z      IS-A planning_activity)))
```

Figure 5: A simple search pattern

Please note that the most interesting component of the FUM module is represented by the matching algorithm which unifies the complex structures — like "(SPECIF summoning_1 (SPECIF board_meeting_1 mediobanca_ *special_*))" in occurrence c2 of Fig. 2 — which, in the NKRL terminology, are called structured arguments. In NKRL, structured arguments are built up in a principled way by making use of a specialised sub-language, AECS, which includes four expansion operators, the disjunctive operator (ALTERNative = A), the distributive operator (ENUMeration = E), the collective operator (COORDination = C), and the attributive operator (SPECIFication = S), see [3, 4] for some details. The algorithms for unifying two AECS structured arguments are described, e.g., in [4].

These basic inference mechanisms are used as basic building blocks for implementing all sort of high level inference procedures. For example, inference procedures which have been studied in depth in a CNRS context are the "transformation rules", see [10, 11].

In the database theory, the notion of "transformation" is usually linked with that of "semantic equivalence" between two queries : in a database context, two queries are considered as semantically equivalent if their answer is the same for all database state which satisfy a given set of integrity constraints. This notion is, therefore, used for operations of semantic query optimisation, see, e.g., [12]. In an NKRL context, the notion of transformation acquires a wider significance. NKRL transformations deal with the problem of obtaining a plausible answer from a database of factual occurrences also in the absence of the explicitly requested information, by searching semantic affinities between what is requested and what is really present in the base. The fundamental principle employed is then to transform the original query into one or more different queries which — unlike the transformed queries in a database context — are not strictly "equivalent" but only "semantically close" to the original one.

To give a very simple example, suppose that, working in the context of an hypothetical metadocument database about university professors, we should want to ask a question like : "Who has lived in the United States", even without an explicit representation of this fact in the base. If this last contains some information about the degrees obtained by the professors, we can tell the user that, although we do not explicitly know who lived in the States, we can nevertheless look for people having an American degree. This last piece of information, obtained by transformation of the original query, would indeed normally imply that some time was spent by the professors in the country, the United States, which issued their degree.

Transformation rules are made up of a left hand side — formulation in NKRL (search pattern) format of the linguistic expression which is to be transformed — and one or more right hand sides — NKRL representations of one or more linguistic expressions that must be substituted for the given one. A transformation rule can, therefore, be expressed as : A (left hand side) $\Rightarrow$ B (right hand side). The "transformation arrow", "$\Rightarrow$", has a double meaning :

- operationally speaking, the arrow indicates the direction of the transformation : the left hand side A (the original search pattern) is removed and replaced by the right hand side B (one or more new search patterns) ;
- the standard logical meaning of the arrow is that the information obtained through B implies the information we should have obtained from A.

In reality, the "always true" implications (noted as $B \rightarrow A$, where we assume that the symbol "$\rightarrow$" represents, as usual, the implication arrow) are not very frequent. Most transformations found in real world applications represent "modalised implications". We will note them as $B \Diamond \rightarrow A$, which means "it is possible that B implies A". "$\Diamond$" is the usual modal operator for "possibility", which satisfies then the relation $\Diamond p = \neg\nabla\neg p$ with respect to the second modal operator, "∇ = necessity". An example of modalised transformation is given by the transformation T1 in Fig. 6, which allows us to deal, by using an inference engine based on the FUM module (see [10] for some details), with the informal example above about "university professors" ; as we can see, the antecedent and consequent of T1 are formed by search patterns, slightly simplified here for clarity's sake. Transformation T1 says : "If someone (x) receives a title from an official authority by means of an official document, then it is possible that he has been physically present at that moment in the place (l) where the authority is located". This rule, for example, is not always valid in the case of an university degree (it could be obtained in a correspondence school, etc.). Nevertheless, it is possible to see that, in this case, the semantic distance between an "always true" implication and a "modalised" one is not too important, as it is becomes possible, at least in principle, to change T1 into a true transformation by the addition of a few constraints on the variable p , forinstance the "disequation" : $p \neq <obtainable\_by\_correspondence\_degree>$. More examples, and a complete "theory" of transformations, can be found in, e.g., [10].

```
T1)   EXIST   SUBJ   x: [l] ⇒RECEIVE   SUBJ     x
                                        OBJ      y
                                        SOURCE   w : [l]
                                        MODAL    z
      x = <human_being>
      y = <title_>;  w= <authority_>
      z = <official_document>  ;l  = <location_>
```

Figure 6: A simple example of transformation rule

We can now provide some additional details about the functioning of the query sub-system of the prototype. Coming back to the general architecture of the prototype in Fig. 1 above, we can see that a search pattern may be generated from outside the system when it directly represents, in a deductive retrieving style, the NKRL translation of a query issued by the user — this corresponds to the basic mode of functioning of the query sub-system of the prototype. But, in some cases, it may be also generated automatically from inside the system during the execution of some classes of inference procedures.

Let us consider, in fact, what will happen to a search pattern corresponding directly to a user's NL query when, having used this search pattern in order to ask the knowledge base, we obtain no answer — i.e., we have failed to unify the search pattern with an NKRL item of information which is part of a metadocument — or when, having recovered some information, we would like to know more. In such cases we can consider, as a first hypothesis, to be in a situation where the NKRL image of the information which could supply a plausible answer effectively exists in the central knowledge base, but it may be difficult to retrieve and recognise. Under this hypothesis, we will ask the query system to automatically transform the initial search pattern by substituting it with another "semantically equivalent" pattern, see above.

Unfortunately, the problems associated with the practical utilisation of this type of (implemented) approach are not only technical (construction of appropriate inference engines), but concern mainly the way of i) discovering the common sense rules which constitute the real foundation of the transformation procedures, and ii) formalising them so that we can obtain a sufficient degree of generality. These two activities can be executed *a priori* only to some extent, because the knowledge engineers find difficulty in predicting all the possible practical situations. Concretely, the transformation rules are established often *a posteriori*, by abstracting and formalising (see the explanation-based methods etc. in an Artificial Intelligence context) some procedures empirically found in order to solve particular "cases". This is why we plan to introduce, in a more complete version of the prototype, the possibility of having recourse to Case-Based Reasoning (CBR) techniques, see [13, 14], etc. Given that the "rules", when they exist, are normally considered of a more economic use than "cases", we would like to use the CBR procedures not only for providing the users with a sophisticated and up-to-date problem-solving modality, but also, at the same time, for blazing a trail toward the creation of a practical set of transformation rules to be stored in the rule base, and which will subsume all the different concrete cases used empirically to set up an useful solution.

6 Conclusion

In this paper, we have suggested that an in-depth exploitation of what we have called the "textual component" of corporate knowledge could be facilitated by translating this component into conceptual format (metadocuments). In this case, it becomes possible, in fact, to make use of the textual corporate knowledge according to the specific characteristics of its proper semantic content (its "meaning"). We have then illustrated the general architecture of a prototypical system, implemented to a large extent, for setting up and exploiting a knowledge base of metadocuments, and we have supplied more detailed information about some fundamental building blocks of the prototype.

The different versions of the implemented components have been tested as far as possible, and their performances seem to be satisfactory — e.g., the acquisition subsystem, in the NOMOS version, takes 3 min 16s on Sun SparcStation 1 with 16Mb to process a full article of the French "General Taxation Law" (on average, 4 sentences and 150 wordforms) ; 1 min 06s for the longest sentence. However, it is difficult to provide a full assessment of the performance of the system, given that it has been tested, until now, on relatively small corpora of original documents. For example, in the COBALT project, wa have used a corpus of about 200 candidate news items which have then been translated into NKRL format, and examined through a query system in order to i) confirm their relevance ; ii) extract their main content elements (actors, circumstances, locations, dates, amounts of shares or money, etc.). Of the candidate news, 80% have been (at least partly) successfully translated; "at least partly" means that, sometimes, the translation was incomplete due, e.g., to the difficulty of instantiating correctly some binding structures. We plan to ask the European Commission for a financial aid in order to set up a new, industrial prototype, able to be tested in the environment of a real, industrial user.

References

1. Trigano, P. (1994) "Automatic Indexation and Knowledge Storing", in *Proceedings of the Second International Symposium on the Management of Industrial and Corporate Knowledge - ISMICK'94.* Compiègne: Institut International pour l'Intelligence Artificielle (IIIA).

2. Macintosh, A. (1994) "Corporate Knowledge Management State-of-the-Art Review", in *Proceedings of the Second International Symposium on the Management of Industrial and Corporate Knowledge - ISMICK'94.* Compiègne: Institut International pour l'Intelligence Artificielle (IIIA).

3. Zarri, G.P. (1994) "A Glimpse of NKRL, the Narrative Knowledge Representation Language", in *Knowledge Representation for Natural Language Processing in Implemented Systems - Papers from the 1994 Fall Symposium*, Ali, S., ed. Menlo Park (CA): American Association for Artificial Intelligence.

4. Zarri, G.P., and Gilardoni, L. (1996) "Structuring and Retrieval of the Complex Predicate Arguments Proper to the NKRL Conceptual Language", in *Proceedings of the Ninth International Symposium on Methodologies for Intelligent Systems (ISMIS'96).* Berlin: Springer-Verlag.

5. Zarri, G.P. (1992) "Encoding the Temporal Characteristics of the Natural Language Descriptions of (Legal) Situations", in *Expert Systems in Law*, Martino, A., ed. Amsterdam: Elsevier Science Publishers.

6. Hobbs, J.R., and Bear, J. (1990) "Two Principles of Parse Preference", in *Proceedings of the 13th International Conference on Computational Linguistics - COLING'90*, Karlgren, H., ed. Helsinki: University Press.

7. Wood, M.M. (1993) *Categorial Grammars*. London: Routledge.

8. Zarri, G.P. (1995) "Knowledge Acquisition from Complex Narrative Texts Using the NKRL Technology", in *Proceedings of the 9th Banff Knowledge Acquisition for Knowledge-Based Systems Workshop - KAW'95*, Gaines, B.R., and Musen, M., eds., vol. 1. Calgary: Department of Computer Science of the University.

9. Azzam, S. (1995) "Anaphors, PPs and Disambiguation Process for Conceptual Analysis", in *Proceedings of the 14th International Joint Conference on Artificial Intelligence*. Morgan Kaufmann, San Mateo (CA).

10. Zarri, G.P. (1986) "The Use of Inference Mechanisms to Improve the Retrieval Facilities from Large Relational Databases", in *Proceedings of the Ninth International ACM Conference on Research and Development in Information Retrieval*, Rabitti, F., ed. New York: ACM.

11. Ogonowski, A. (1987) "MENTAT : An Intelligent and Cooperative Natural Language DB Interface", in *Proceedings of the 7th Avignon International Workshop on Expert Systems and Their Applications*, vol. 2. Paris: EC2 & Cie.

12. Chakravarthy, U.S., Grant, J., and Minker, J. (1990) "Logic-Based Approach to Semantic Query Optimization", *ACM Transactions on Database Systems*, **15**, 162-207.

13. Kolodner, J.L. (1992) "An Introduction to Case-Based Reasoning", *Artificial Intelligence Review*, **6**, 3-34.

14. Wess, S., Althoff, K.-D., and Richter, M.M., eds. (1994) *Topics in Case-Based Reasoning* (Lectures Notes in Artificial Intelligence 837). Berlin: Springer-Verlag.

Applications of Natural Language to Information Systems
R.P. van de Riet et al. (Eds.)
IOS Press, 1996

The Fact Extraction Using the Keyfact

Mi-Seon JUN, Se-Young PARK, Man-Soo KIM
Natural Language Processing Section
System Software Department
Electronics and Telecommunications Research Institute
TaeJon, Korea
{msjun,sypark,mskim}@com.etri.re.kr

Abstract. Many information retrieval systems retrieve relevant documents based on exact matching of keywords between a query and documents. We shall show how to extract a fact from a document using an extended concept of keyword, called keyfact which can contain syntactic patterns and semantic information. In second document ranking, predefined keyfact cluster set of the query terms is compared to each relevant document. Because relevant documents are such a small fraction of a collection, this method is different with query expansion retrieval scheme and substantially reduces the computational cost of the experiment.
Keywords : Document Ranking, Fact, Semantic Information, Syntactic Pattern

1 Introduction

Many commercial information retrieval(IR) systems retrieve relevant documents based on keyword matching between a query and documents. There are two problems in using the method. The first problem is that keywords are ambiguous, and this ambiguity is causative of retrieving irrelevant document semantically. Therefore lexical ambiguity has to be resolved. The second problem is that a document is treated as a irrelevant document in spite of a relevant document, for the document does not include the same keywords as query terms. So an original query has to be expanded to semantically related words. The main function of an IR system is to rank relevant documents which satisfies the user's information need. In most retrieval models, the system ranks documents according to their inner product similarity, depending upon keywords in a query. However users are generally not interested in retrieving documents with matching keywords, but with concepts that relevant words or information represent.
Facts are truths in some relevant world. These are the things we want to represent and to search information. One representation of facts is so common that it deserves special mention: natural language sentences. Generally nouns and compound nouns are taken as keywords. Nouns and compound nouns are the most important elements for representing the fact in a natural language sentence. However besides the keywords such as nouns and compound nouns, verbs and adjectives have an important role in a sentence. Using the keywords for an IR system is relatively simple to implement. To extract facts well in a sentence, it is insufficient to use only nouns as keywords. Even in morphological analysis of

a sentence, there are many lexical ambiguities. Furthermore in the syntactic problem, there are too many inflected forms of adjectives and adverbs in Korean. Specially in Korean language, one keyword has 20~30 senses in a dictionary in the worst case. Polysemous words in a query and documents can reduce the precision of a search significantly. Therefore lexical ambiguity has to be resolved. To resolve lexical ambiguity of keywords, we need several information such as keywords, verbs and adjectives. We introduced an extended concept of a keyword, called *keyfact* which can be represented as verb/ adjective, and can contain syntactic patterns and semantic information. We can consider lexical ambiguity of noun and verb.

The verb "쓰다" is a typical Korean polysemy, and has twenty one translatable English verbs such as "write", "spend", "wear", and "adopt" in a Sisa Korean-English dictionary[14]. In another example, the noun "모자" is a typical Korean polysemy. The noun has English nouns such as "mother and child" and "hat". So in our keyfact concept noun and verb/adjective are not independent of each other. If the keyfact can contain syntactic patterns and semantic information such as "모자를 쓰다/wear a hat" and "펜으로 쓰다/write with a pen", then noun which occur with the verb "쓰다" may be thought of as a clue for disambiguating senses. In the same manner, ambiguity of noun is much the same.

The literature generally divides lexical ambiguity into two types: syntactic and semantic[2]. Syntactic ambiguity refers to differences in syntactic category. Semantic ambiguity refers to differences in meanings. A number of approaches have been taken to word sense disambiguation. Lesk uses the Oxford Advanced Learners Dictionary[3] and Weiss uses word co-occurrences[4]. Many researchers used statistic information, semantic information, and both of the information as a knowledge for query expansion. Stiles and Lesk used statistic information of term association from documents. Salton experiments only synonym in the SMART system. Fox experiments five semantic category in the SMART system, and need humane intervention for selecting related words[8]. Above researches did not propose the problem of lexical ambiguity or did not considered automatic lexical disambiguation for query expansion. The ambiguity in a query must be resolved when the query is analyzed. Ambiguous words are not able to effectively expand before the ambiguity is not resolved. Query expansion enhances recall by adding some relevant documents excluded from exact matching. But it degrades precision. In order to improve precision, first the ambiguous word in a query is resolved by using knowledge base, when the query is analyzed. Second keyword concept which is defined as noun or compound noun need to be extend, and verb or adjective must be considered as indexing word. We resolve ambiguous query terms, and then expand unambiguous query terms. There are a wide choice of words to add to a query vector. One can add only the synonyms, or synonyms plus all descendants, or synonym plus parents and all descendants, or synonyms plus directly related words, etc. and any number of child links may be traverse. Expansion by synonyms plus and directly related word is benefit[1]. So we choose the parameter, and expanded queries are consisted with a special relationship FT(Fact Term) as well as semantic relationships using in general thesaurus. Because query expansion is a recall enhancing technique, we used expanded terms of a original query only when compute query-document similarity. So we got high precision rate.

In the following sections, we (1) describe the construction of a keyfact network for ranking the documents; (2) present a visualization of the keyfact network for keyfact retrieval; (3) show how the keyfact network can be used to rank documents and extract a fact; (4) evaluate ranking method to improve retrieval performance; and (5) make suggestions for future research.

2 Keyfact and Keyfact Cluster

The noun is the most important element for explaining the fact. Next we consider the compound noun which is composed of several nouns. The syntactic categories of the next complicated fact are noun phrases. A noun phrase consists of a noun and its modifiers that can be represented as inflected forms of verb and adjective. Korean verb and adjective have much more inflected forms as compared to English and French. The most simple fact(sentence) can be represented by noun(subject) and verb/adjective(predicate). So the keyfact is not independent of case slots, and contains syntactic patterns and semantic information. In this paper, we collected keyfacts and keyfact clusters in Gemong Korean encyclopedia for improved retrieval performance. The encyclopedia has two characteristics. First, it has syntactic characteristic composed of a title word and it's explanation part. Second, it has semantic characteristic that most words in the explanation part are semantically related with the title word. The encyclopedia is good to easily collect words and it's semantically related words of a word. We thought that the encyclopedia is a proper collection for construction of semantic information. The keyfacts extracted from a text can be represented in several forms. The forms have to be designed for easy matching. The keyfact weight is calculated in the same formula for calculating keyword weights based on the keyword frequency. When a user gives a query which contains some keyfacts as well as keywords, our system extracts the keyfacts from the query and tries to match the keyfacts which were extracted from documents. We use an exact matching method and when it fails, a partial matching method will be used. With keyfacts co-occurred with a keyword, we can use these keyfacts for disambiguating the keyword and ranking documents.

A cluster is defined as a set of co-occurring keyfact terms. Co-occurring terms are usually relevant to each other and are sometimes synonyms. For keyfact clustering, we considered the sense definition of the noun in the Gemong Korean encyclopedia. In the simple automatic indexing method, raw terms are analyzed using a stemming algorithm and stop words are removed using a stop list. The stop words are usually prepositions, postpositions, determinants and those that appear too frequently to discriminate any documents. And then it finds an identical inflected verb and gets a basic form of the inflected verb by referencing verb dictionary. Our verb dictionary consists of two parts which are inflected verb form and basic verb form. One basic form can have many inflected form. Therefore inflected form is compared with the input text and basic form is used for disambiguating and ranking. Figure 1 shows one basic form can have many inflected forms. We assigned semantic relationships using in general thesaurus such as BT(Broader Term), NT(Narrow Term), RT(Related Term), HP(Has Part), UF(Used For), and a special relationship FT(keyFact Term). Most thesaurus uses the relationships except FT relationship. FT is defined as relationship between noun and verb/adjective. FT is used for resolving lexical ambiguity in a query and ranking the documents.

inflected forms noun+postposition+verb	**basic form** verb/postposition,noun
차에서 내렸다(got off a car)	내리다/에서,차(get off/a car)
차를 마시다(take tea)	마시다/를,차(take/tea)
차를 탔다(took a car)	타다/를,차(take/a car)
택시로 가다(go by taxi)	가다/로,택시(go/by taxi)
차로 붐비다(was crowded with traffic)	붐비다/로,차(crowd/with traffic)
주위에 몰려들었다(crowded around)	몰려들다/에,주위(crowd/around)
문쪽으로 밀어닥쳤다(crowded through the gate)	밀어닥치다/으로,문쪽(crowd/through the gate)

Figure1: Sample of keyfact

In figure 1, "차를 마시다(take tea) " and "차를 타다(take a car) " have the same keyword "차". The noun **cha** "차" is a typical example of Korean polysemy. This noun has nine meanings such as "vehicle", "tea", "difference", and "for the purpose of" in the Minchungseorim Korean dictionary and two meanings such as "vehicle" and "tea" in Gemong Korean encyclopedia. Therefore it is not easy to analyze the exact meaning from a sentence including polysemy. At first, we define the concept of cluster as a group of keyfacts which co-occur with a specific sense of a polysemy. Some keyfacts appearing in a text are useful for keyfact clustering while others are not. Thus in order to cluster keyfacts effectively, we normalize the clusters obtained by the following processes. we used the weighting by keyfact frequency alone. An appropriate threshold is chosen, and a keyfact which exceeds the threshold 3 are assumed to be connected with a keyword. Followings are normalization results of keyword **cha** "차" in Gemong Korean encyclopedia. For example, the keyword 'vehicle' has 'get off a car' as keyfact and 'bus' as keyword.

vehicle={차에서 내리다/get off a car, 차를 타다/take a car, 택시로 가다/go by taxi, 차로 붐비다/be crowded with traffic, 차로 여행하다/travel by vehicle, 트럭으로 운반하다/carry in a truck, 차를 멈추다/bring a car to a halt, 차를 세우다/ stop a cab, 자가용차를 몰다/drive one' s own car, 버스/ bus, 기차/train, 택시/taxi,...}
tea={차를 끓이다/make tea, 차를 따르다/pour out tea, 차를 마시다/drink tea, 차를 홀짝이다/sip tea, 차가 우러나다/tea brews, 손님에게 차를 대접하다/serve a guest tea, 차를 마시며 이야기하다/talk over a cup of tea, 커피/coffee, 녹차/green tea, 홍차/black tea, 차나무/tea plant, 차거르개/a tea strainer, 컵/cup, ...}

There are too many inflected forms of a adjective and a verb in a text. The keyfacts extracted from a text must be represented in basic forms. The forms have to be designed for easy matching. If a keyfact have the same keyword and the different inflected verb/adjective, it can be represented in the same basic form and will be the same keyfact.

3 Keyfact and Information Retrieval

3.1 System Overview

Our IR system consists of server system and client system. The server platform is a Windows NT 3.5 Server on Pentium, and the client platform is a Windows NT 3.5 Workstation on Pentium. The system uses a HTTPS for Windows NT as a web server, and Netscape navigator for Windows NT as a web browser. The system adopted NCAPI implemented by DDE for the communication between a Netscape navigator and a three dimensional keyfact visualizer[10,11]. Figure 2 shows the server system provides information which is requested by the end-user or information builder. In figure 2, the square shows functional procedure and the circle represents the result of functional procedure. The server has processing engines for information building function and IR. The client system has the browser, and is used by users who want to search information[13]. The types of the IR in the server system can be defined as the natural language retrieval and the keyfact visualization retrieval which are shown in figure 2. In dispatcher function, the user's request is analyzed and is categorized into keyfact visual procedure or natural language query procedure according to the type.

3.2 Keyfact Visualization Retrieval

At recent, WWW has grown up to be the most popular service available on the internet. In spite of its short history, the reason why WWW achieved such a rapid development is that it supports multimedia presentation and hypertext retrieval under an integrated communication environment. The most common browsing object supported by web browsers has a problem in understanding easily the relationship among information because of its simplicity. The latest browsing method is browsing the relations among information in three dimension using a three dimensional web viewer. However the methods can't reflect immediately values changed dynamically and support various functions required for effective browsing. An advanced browser is needed for displaying exactly the relations among information not the information itself, and reflecting immediately the relation updated. In this paper, we provide browsing objects which can describe various relations among information and implement a visualization system which will transform automatically keyfact information into the objects. The information will be described by SGML, which is the standard for the document exchange. Unlike another three dimensional viewers, the system focuses on the visualization of the relations among information, and supports various browsing functions - expanding, shrinking, centralizing, etc. The browsers include keyfact visualizer and natural language interface which serve as helper applications for the typical internet browsers such as Mosaic and Netscape. In Figure 2, the CGI scripts to support the keyfact visualization return index documents or HTML documents after querying with the input data of FORM type from a web browser. The keyfacts construct an appropriate structure to visualize, with the weighted, labeled and many-to-many connected relations among information. We can distinguish a relation from the others by a link-line type and an adjacency by a link-line length. For example, a shorter length may represent the more related relationship. The query invokes three dimensional keyfact browser. Users can retrieve the keyfact network by clicking buttons such as Rotation, zooming, translation, and fly too.

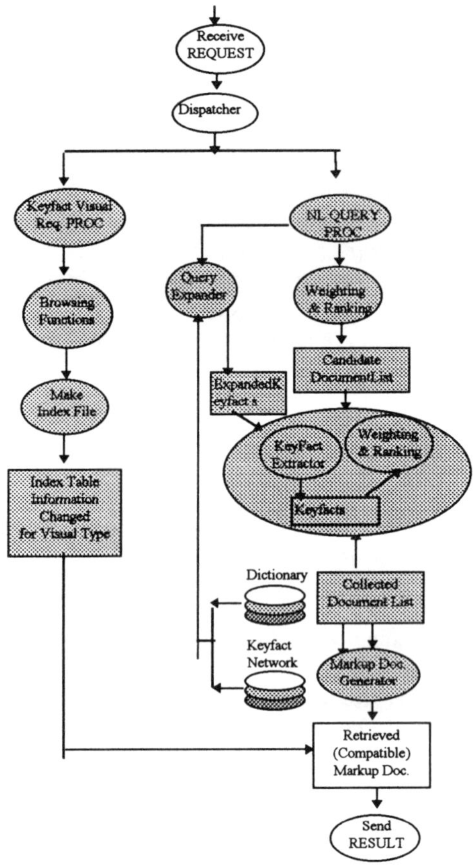

Figure 2: The information retrieval procedure

The graphics operations are performed without communication between the server and a client. The visualization part on a client updates again the visual objects with the information document returned by CCI. Scripts related to the visualization on a server play a role to analyze the posted data and return the document of MIME type through CGI[9,10,11]. If the clicked node is not a nonterminal node, just a web browser shows the list of HTML documents related to the node name by the natural language processing or the keyword processing. In the case of keyword processing, the node name is to be the title in

Gemong Korean encyclopedia. In the case of natural language processing, the node name is to be input of natural language query procedure, and the result is displayed in Netscape browser.

3.3 Natural Language Retrieval

The end-user wants to search the wanted information by the user friendly interfaces. One of those is natural language interface. If the server gets the natural language query, the natural language processing engine is activated. After processing some sequential operation, it creates candidate list, which is replied to client. The procedure of natural language retrieval is as following; First it extracts keyword and keyfact of a query. Second it gets a candidate top-fifty documents. Then the weighting and ranking operation are executed to get the candidate list. In this step, *tf*idf* weighting formula and only keywords are considered. Third it expands the query using the keyfact cluster for more accurate retrieval. Then the *overlap counting* method is executed to the candidate list for weighting and ranking. The document with the greatest number of overlaps between expanded query and a document is in the top of candidate list. Finally the system displays top-ten documents to the end-user.

Disambiguation using Keyfact Cluster

In this paper, some words that exist in a document can be selected by keywords, and some facts that can contain more precise information can be selected by keyfacts. Like this, for more precise natural language processing, we introduced the keyfact. Two examples are given to show how keyfact play an important role in determining the correct meaning.

(1e) What's the difference donkey and horse?
(1k) 당나귀와 말의 차이점은 무엇인가?
tangnagwi-wa **mal**-ui chaichom-un muotinka
donkey and horse the difference what is ?
(2e) What kind of tea can man drink ?
(2k) 사람이 마실 수 있는 차의 종류는?
saram-i masil su itnun **cha**-ui chongyu-nun
man drink can tea of kind what

Even in morphological analysis of a sentence, there are many ambiguities in Korean. As the Korean version in (1k), **mal** "말" is a polysemy and has three meanings such as "horse", "language" and "unit of measure" in Gemong Korean encyclopedia. The raw terms are analyzed by using a stemming algorithm, and the most frequent functional words are removed by using a stop list. Our method decides the specific sense of a given polysemy by calculating the similarity between polysemy of input query and words of predefined keyfact cluster. We can extract keywords such as tangnagwi "당나귀", mal "말" and chaichom "차이점" in a sentence (1k). We can choose "horse" as the correct meaning of mal according to the cluster of tangnagwi. Let's consider the keyfact cluster for 'cha'. If the child's links are limited to depth one, then "make tea", "pour out tea", "drink tea", "sip tea", "tea brews", "serve a guest tea", "talk over a cup of tea", "coffee", "green tea", "black tea", "tea plant", "a tea strainer", and "cup" would be added. Unlike (1k), (2k) involves a keyfact such as masida "마시다/drink" besides keywords such as saram "사람", chongyu "종류" and cha "차". If the sentence (2k) have not had **masida** "마시다", then we can not select "tea" as the correct meaning of the **cha** "차".

Information Filtering using Keyfact Cluster

Given a large amount of data, IR systems must be designed to return the data that the user wants to see. Therefore information filtering is very important part. Our main technical concern is to extract exact meanings from a document. The procedure of natural language retrieval is as following; First it extracts keywords of a query. Second it gets a 50 relevant documents. The relevant documents satisfy the user's information need. Several documents are ranked according to their inner product similarity between the original query and all the documents[5]. A query and all the documents contain both index terms and non-index terms. Index terms consist of only keyword. In order to improve retrieval speed, the IR system employs inverted files. Each document vector uses popular weighting scheme *tf*idf* based on the term frequency and the query vector uses Boolean (1 if the term appears, 0 if not) scheme [5,8]. Following is an example of inverted file. We know that index word '가공식품' occurred in 19 documents, and the word has weighting 40845 in document number 5730.

가공식품 19 5730 *40845* 5481 *40000* 4769 *37005* 4531 *36150* 3294 *48861* 2690 *50622* 24 *40845* 19733 *81689* 19701 *40845* 18122 *47612* 17188 *47612* 16740 34042 16401 *46642* 15298 *68084* 14192 *46642* 12268 *81689* 12265 *40845* 12264 *41870* 12246 *40845*

Documents can then be ranked in order of descending similarity to a query by keyword indexing[5,8]. Third it expands query terms with keyfact terms of predefined keyfact cluster for more accurate retrieval. Fourth each relevant document is compared to cluster set of the query(Second Document Ranking, hereafter). Because relevant documents are such a small fraction of the collection, this process substantially reduces the computational cost of the experiment. SDR provides documents sorted on relevance order by counting overlaps between the retrieved documents and keyfact clusters of the query. The SDR scheme is different with query expansion retrieval scheme[1]. In the query expansion, a new query could be created by adding terms from other documents, as in relevance feedback, or by adding synonyms of terms in the query (as found in a thesaurus). It then returns more documents using the revised query, and terms are consisted keywords. And the user indicates which documents from those returned are most relevant to his query. To calculate similarity, all pairwise combinations between keyfact terms in a query and a document are generated. For each keyfact in the expanded queries, the system enters the document in a hash table; the table is keyed on the document number, and the value is initially 1. If the documents was previously entered in the table, the value is simply incremented. But when the keyfact weighting is calculated, we give an 5 added value to each keyfact not keyword.

The end result is that each entry in the table contains total number of common keyfacts of expanded queries and the document. The table is then sorted to produce a ranked list of documents.

(3e) What is the highest mountain in the world?
(3k) 세계에서 가장 높은 산은 무엇인가?
segye-eseo kachang nopun san-un muotinka
the world in the highest mountain what is

As the Korean version in (3k), **san** "산" is a polysemy and has two meanings such as "mountain" and "acid" in Gemong Korean encyclopedia. Because the sentence (3e) have a keyfact "be the highest", we can select "mountain" as correct meaning of **san** "산". **kachang** "가장" is a polysemy and has several meanings such as "most", "the head of a family", etc. in the Minchungseorim Korean dictionary. Nevertheless **kachang** "가장" is not a polysemy and has one meaning of "the head of a family" in Gemong Korean encyclopedia. Therefore "가장" in all the documents of our test collection Gemong Korean encyclopedia is indexed as meaning of "the head of a family". Given the query "What is the highest mountain in the world ?", when only keywords are applied to ranking documents and the query, D2 is closer to the query : Sim(Query, D1) = 23 versus Sim(Query, D2) = 58. After ambiguity of **san** and **kachang** is resolved, relevant documents are represented as keyfacts and the query are represented as keyfact cluster. Following italic style fonts represent keyfacts, and the others represent keywords. Following results are obtained in SDR.

Query = {*be the highest*, mountain, the world}
D1(the Himalayas) = {the Himalayas, the world, Nepal, China, glacier, winter, wind, summer, climbing, England, the highest mountain, *be precipitous*, *top the mountain*, *climb*}
D2(the head of a family) = {the head of a family, fortune, command, control, family, system, the Orient, the eldest son, inherit a fortune, represent a family, have a authority, system make progress}

Sim(Query, D1) = Mt. Everest + the world + climbing + mountain range + be very high + be precipitous
= 1 + 1 + 1 + 1 + 5 + 5 = 14
Sim(Query, D2) = the world
= 1

When keyfacts are applied to the SDR, D1 is closer to the query : Sim(Query, D1) = 14 versus Sim(Query, D2) = 1. The similarity is based on overlap counts between predefined cluster of input keywords and keyfacts of the document. Keyfact concept has a better performance than keyword concept.

4. Empirical Results

Evaluation of full-text documents retrieval models is based on relevance ranking and it□ measurement of *recall* and *precision* for test collections. Relevance ranking returns an ordered list of relevant documents. Recall is defined as the number of relevant documents retrieved divided by the total number of relevant documents in the collection, and precision is defined as the number of relevant documents retrieved divided by the total number of documents retrieved. Before any evaluation can be performed, the relevance information for each query must be considered. In order to decide which documents were relevant to each query, we spent several months. As a result only 35 queries were used for evaluation. We now address the issue of whether keyfact improves performance when it is applied to the document ranking. Our experiments use the Gemong Korean encyclopedia as a test collection. The test collection comes with a set of natural language queries and a labeling (decided by human experts) that decides which documents are relevant to each query. The collection contains 35 queries and 23,000 documents. Two experiments to evaluate keyfact concept have been run on an IR system called OKSEO at Electronics Telecommunications Research Institute. OKSEO isn't acronym, but is the old name of place, in which the ancestor did research, compilation, and cultural enterprise.

(4e) want to know about speech and language
(4k) 말과 언어에 대하여 알고 싶다
mal-kwa ono-e taehayo alko shipta
speech and language about know want to

Recall and precision values were calculated for each query. The overall performance of an experiment is determined by processing a number of queries, and by computing the average precision over all the queries for each selected recall value. There are two experiments to be compared: experiment 1 and experiment 2. The experiment 1 uses only the keywords without keyfacts in ranking documents. The experiment 2 uses both keywords and keyfacts in SDR. Our system displayed the top 10 terms selected by the *tf*idf* weighting(first ranking) and overlap counting(SDR) as following.

First ranking without keyfacts:	Second ranking with keyfacts :
1 donkey	1 address
2 mule	2 composition
3 zebra	3 subject of writing
4 editorial	4 donkey
5 indirect quotation	5 mule

In the sentence 4k, Korean word "말" has several meanings such as "the unit of measure", "horse", "speech", etc. When we considered only keywords in first ranking step, irrelevant document "donkey" was at the top of ranking and relevant document "editorial" is ranked fourth order. However when we considered both keywords and keyfacts in second ranking step, irrelevant document "donkey" was ranked fourth order. For each query, two retrieval results are compared. In figure3, the resulting graph shows the performance improvement when the keyfact is applied in SDR. The experiment 1 shows about 66% precision in Gemong Korean encyclopedia. In the experiment 2, latent indexing on keyfacts between some retrieved documents and a query provides 22% improvements on the precision performance.

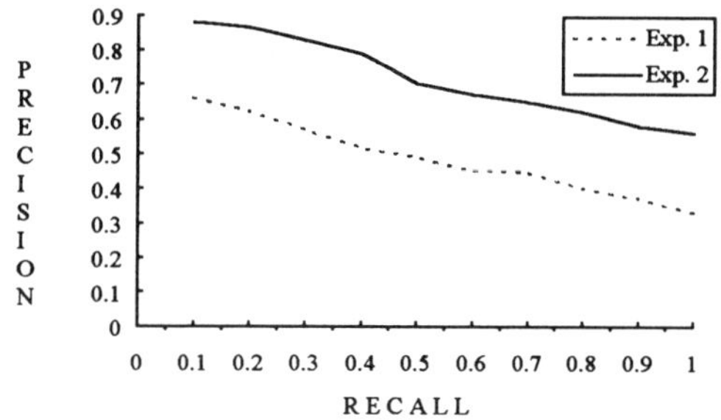

Figure 3: Keyword versus keyfact for 35 queries

5 Conclusions and Future Work

Traditional IR system adopts vectors of weighted term frequencies as representation of documents. The vector space model has some significant problems. It assumes that terms are independent and thus ignores term associations and lexical ambiguity[2,3]. In this paper, we constructed keyfact cluster, which is a new type of thesaurus, to disambiguate lexical ambiguity for natural language retrieval. We implemented three dimensional keyfact network retrieval system for keyfact visualization retrieval. User can easily traverse multi-depth child nodes as well as one-depth child, and retrieve the keyfact network by three argument such as keyword, relationship, and weight in WWW.
We apply the keyfact to the second document ranking, which operates under the assumption that there are any relevant documents for given query in first ranking step. Keyfacts of each relevant document are compared to predefined keyfact cluster set of a query. Because relevant documents are such a small fraction of the collection, this substantially reduces the computational cost of the experiment.

When the collection grows as new documents are added, future research will concentrated on representation and manipulating knowledge(facts). As we look in more detail at ways of representing for more specific, more powerful inference mechanisms that operate on them. In this paper, the query vector uses Boolean scheme. But If the vectors are weighted to give emphasis to keyfacts that exemplify meaning, the system will satisfy the user's information need well.

References

[1]Ellen M.Voorhees, "Query Expansion using Lexical-Semantic Relations". *Proceedings of the Association for Computing Machinery-Special Interest Group on Information Retrieval*, Dublin, 61-69, 1994.

[2]Robert Krovertz and W.Bruce Croft, "Lexical Ambiguity and Information Retrieval". *Association for Computing Machinery Transaction on Information Systems*, Vol. 10, No. 2, 115-141, 1992.

[3]Lesk M., "Automatic sense disambiguation using machine readable dictionaries: How to tell a pine cone from an ice cream cone". *Proceedings of Special Interest Group for Documentation*, 24-26, 1986.

[4]Young S. Han, Young Kyoon Han, and Key-Sun Choi, "Lexical Concept Acquisition From Collocation Map". *Proceedings of a Workshop Sponsored Group on the Lexicon of the Association for Computational Linguistics*, Ohio, 22-31, 1993.

[5]Gerard Salton, *Automatic Text Processing*. Addison-Wesley Publishing Company, New York, 229-271, 1993.

[6]Roy Rada and Judith Barlow, "Document Ranking Using an Enriched Thesaurus". *Journal of Documentation*, Vol. 47, no. 3, 240-253, 1991.

[7]Joon Ho Lee, Myoung Ho Kim, and Yoon Joon Lee, "Ranking Documents in Thesaurus-Based Boolean Retrieval Systems". *Information Processing & Management*, Vol. 30, No. 1, 79-91, 1994.

[8]Yih-Chen Wang and James Vandendorpe, Martha Evens, "Relational Thesauri in Information Retrieval". *Journal of the American Society for Information Science*, Vol. 36, No. 1, 15-27, 1985.

[9]Takuji Imai, "The next-Generation User Interface: From GUI to Multimodal", *NIKKEI Electronics Asia*, September, 1992.

[10]Garrett Arch Blythe, "Netscape's DDE Implementation", *http://home.netscape.com/newsref/std/ddeapi.html*.

[11]David Robinson, "The WWW Common Gateway Interface Version 1.1", *http://www.ast.cam. ac.uk/%7Edrtr/cgi-spec.html*.

[12]K.T. Chong and S.Y. Park, "A Design and Implementation of Information Retrieval System on Information Highways", *Proceedings of International Symposium on Digital Libraries*, 208-213, Aug., 1995.

[13]K.Y. Kim, S.Y.Park, and S.J.Lee, "Automatic Sense Disambiguation for Traget Word Selection", *Proceedings of the 10th Pacific Asia Conference*, 109-113, Dec., HongKong, 1995.

Applications of Natural Language to Information Systems
R.P. van de Riet et al. (Eds.)
IOS Press, 1996

Structured data entry for medical records and reports

Jochen Bernauer, Andreas Benneke, Attila Fueseschi, Martin Urban
Institute for Medical Informatics
University of Hildesheim, Germany
bernauer@med-informatik.uni-hildesheim.de

Abstract. Structured data entry is an approach for acquiring qualitative patient information for the medical record as an alternative to natural language reporting since the latter impedes automatic information analysis and retrieval. The paper outlines a model of data entry and reporting for diagnostic subdomains. It is based on a controlled vocabulary according to a conceptual model for the relevant subdomain expressions. The concept model controls an adaptive interface where the physician can enter his observations and impressions by selecting terms and by composing complex expressions from various menues. The principle operations for structured data entry are concept selection, modification, hierarchical refinement, coordination, and deselection of partial input. The entered data are language independently represented in a concept representation formalism based on conceptual graphs. Formal representations are stored in the medical record and are used for information retrieval. For report generation formal representations are mapped to natural language phrases based on lexical information of the domain concepts and morpho-syntactical rules. The model has been realized in a multi-lingual design for bone scintigraphy, a diagnostic imaging procedure of nuclear medicine. Strengths and weaknesses of the approach with respect to the requirements of medical documentation and reporting are discussed.
Keywords: structured data entry, medical report generation, multilingual text generation

1 Introduction

Documentation and reporting of patient specific information is a routine but time consuming task following diagnostic examinations and surgical procedures. Inspite of the growing application and integration of information technology in medicine most clinical reports are still hand-written, or dictated and typed. This conventional approach is expensive, and results in documents which are opposed to automatic information analysis and retrieval. On the other hand the sublanguage used in conventional reports is very expressive. In order to arrive at structured representations for qualitative patient information there are efforts in recent time aiming at specifications for language-independend representations which the electronic medical record can be built upon [1, 2]. At the same time comprehensive standardized terminology systems for medicine have been developed, for instance SNOMED [3], which are gaining increased expressiveness if combined with methods for formal concept representation.

In principle, there are two competing approaches for arriving at structured patient data:

- conventional free-text documentation and reporting with subsequent automatic analysis and mapping to standardized vocabularies using common formal specifications
- structured data entry based on a controlled terminology and a conceptual domain model with subsequent automatic text generation.

The first approach retains the expressiveness of conventional reporting. However, semantic analysis may be difficult because of the syntactic variety and ambiguity of the sublanguage. The second approach delivers primarily structured information with links to common concept systems through the users input, however at the cost of a constraining vocabulary offering only limited expressiveness.

Experience shows, the more narrow the domain the more there is a chance for structured data entry to succeed. Examples of successful applications for particular diagnostic procedures exist for bone scintigraphy, abdominal ultrasound, chest-X-ray, echocardiography, and pathology [4, 5, 6, 7, 8]. The findings resulting from those procedures are related to a small set of semantic categories (i.e. anatomical structures, morphological or functional abnormalities, disease processes) with a limited set of relevant concepts. Typically, the findings present with a stereotyped structure, and simple sentences or noun phrases are almost adequate verbalizations. However, through the combinatorial nature of the phenomena to be described and the morpho-syntactical variations of the language expressions the application of canned texts is doomed to failure.

2 Architecture of a structured data entry and reporting system

The approach described is to allow the physician to enter the observations and impressions following a diagnostic imaging procedure in a structured way using a controlled domain vocabulary. From the entered findings a text generator produces automatically a natural language report. Through language specific vocabularies and text generators multi- lingual data entry and report generation is achieved. In addition, the system allows for the retrieval of cases from a medical record system by queries using the data entry vocabulary. The proposed approach has a concept-oriented design, takes over methods of formal concept representation and classification, and applies methods of linguistic engineering for multi-lingual text generation. The architecture has been realized for bone scintigraphy, a diagnostic imaging procedure of nuclear medicine for the identification and discrimination of disorders of bones and joints.

The general design is given by Figure 1. The user enters findings on a structured data entry interface which is driven by a concept model of the medical subdomain. For that purpose, it is possible to select and compose complex descriptions by clicking on context-sensitive menues presenting language specific subsets of the domain vocabulary. The entered findings are represented in a formal concept representation language based on conceptual graphs and stored in a medical record system. Patient cases and images can be retrieved by means of automatic classification of queries. Reports are generated by mapping formal representations to language dependent surface structures. This task is supported by language specific lexica and morpho-syntactical rules. The linguistic target structures are complex noun phrases reflecting the telegraphic style of

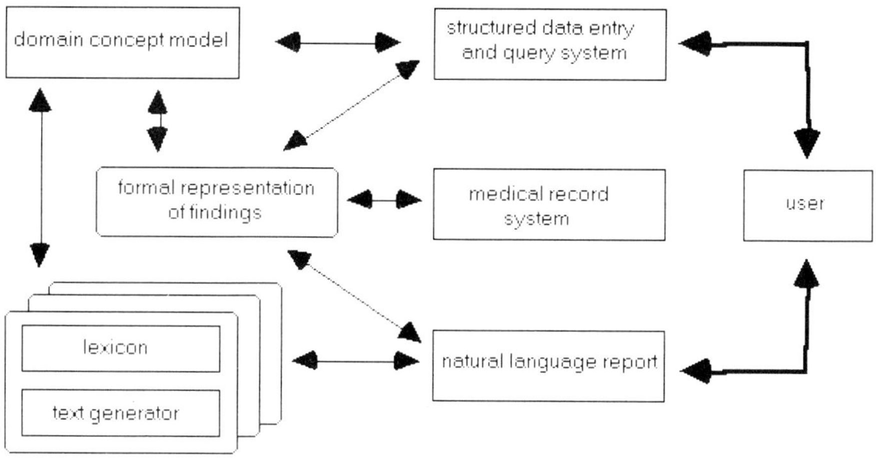

Figure 1: Architecture for a structured data entry and reporting system

professional clinical jargon.

3 Domain concept model

Designing a structured data entry system for report generation in a particular medical domain requires a model of the information to be expressed and entered. A clinical report for a diagnostic investigation typically provides the following components: a section for specifying the patient problem to be analyzed by the study, relevant information about the patients history, the applied procedure and the technical approach, and a section about observations, impressions, and recommendations. In practice, observational and interpretational information is often mingled.

Although conventional reports are phrased using individual terminology sublanguage analysis reveals common conceptual structures addressing concepts from basic semantic categories [6]. Independent of a particular diagnostic procedure those semantic categories are abnormality, topography and disease process. This corresponds to the principle: what can be observed where and why. This principle can be well adopted for the design of a structured data entry system. Typically, a diagnostic procedure focuses on particular body structures, allows for the identification of particular normal or abnormal morphological or functional phenomena which are related to a particular set of disease processes. Bone scintigraphy for instance allows for the identification of kinds of abnormal uptake at bone structures and allows for the differentiation between certain kinds of diseases of bones and joints. Abnormalities visible by echocardiography are for instance spatial alteration of the heart chambers and walls, or motility disorders of walls and valves. The causing processes are specific heart diseases.

Typically the types of abnormality, topography and disease are represented by com-

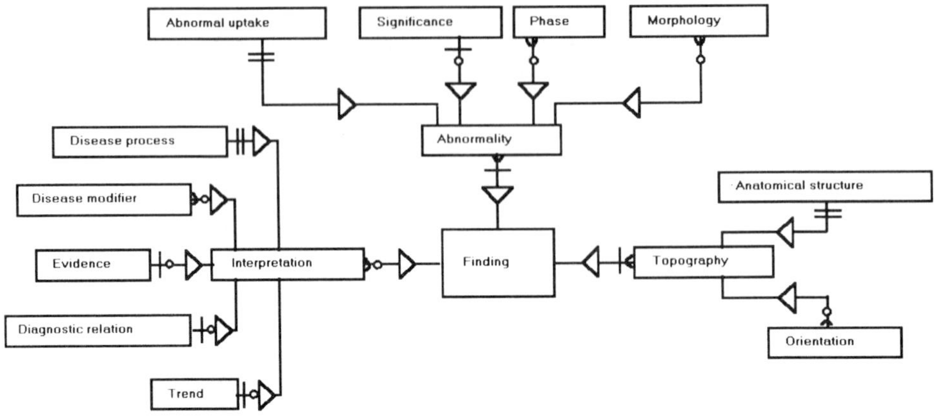

Figure 2: Conceptual model for findings from bone scintigraphy

plex descriptions and are therefore specified by several types of characteristics. In the following the focus will be on bone scintigraphy. A conceptual model for findings in this domain is given by Figure 2. In general, a scintigraphical finding can be specified by the types of abnormality and topography involved and the interpretation given. The type of abnormality is composed by the type of abnormal uptake (increased or decreased uptake), the significance, morphological characterstics and the study phases when the abnormality is observable. The type of topography can be represented by a description of anatomical structures with additional spatial characteristics. An interpretation type refers to a disease process with potential modifiers for evidence diagnostic relation and temporal trend.

The concept system underlying the domain model is organized with respect to generic and partitive relations. These relations support both the navigation through the concept space and the classification of structured findings for case retrieval. The meaningful combination of concepts from the different semantic categories on data entry is controlled by compositional restrictions. Currently the concept system for the bone scintigraphy application has about 1000 entries.

4 The interface for structured data entry

The interface between the concept model and the user are menues presenting the language dependent vocabulary. Figure 3 shows the interface of the scintigraphy system for entering observations and impressions using a German vocabulary, Figure 4 presents the same menues with the Spanish version. The menues for topography and disease have a hierarchical structure.

In principle, the following operations are supported for entering structured data:

- selection of a concept, by clicking on a menue

- concept refinement, by clicking on a menue presenting hierarchically dependent concepts thereby replacing the primarily selected concept.
- concept modification, by clicking on a concept modifying an already selected one.
- concept coordination. This is realized by two different ways. If the menue does not have any subordinate or modificational menues coordination is realized by multiple selection, otherwise a particular button has to be activated indicating the end of entering a complex selection.
- deselection. If a menue does not have any subordinate or modificational menues deselection is realized by repeated clicking the already selected concept. For the deselection of complex selections a particular button has to be activated.

For the composition of complex expressions the semantic relations between the concepts from different menues are implicit and intuitive for the experienced user. For instance, in order to enter the finding "in the early phase and late phase increased focal uptake at the major trochanter and proximal third of the right femur shaft consistent with an acute inflammatory prothesis loosening" the user has to click the following sequence of items (categorial domains in parentheses): "increased uptake" (abnormalities), "early phase" (phases), "late phase" (phases), "focal" (abnormalities modifiers), "lower extremity", "femur", "major trochanter" (hierarchy of topographies), "right" (spatial orientations), "+" (topography coordination), "proximal third of femur" (topography), "right" (orientation), "secondary injury", "prosthesis loosening" (hierarchy of diagnoses), "acute" (diagnosis modifiers), "inflammatory" (diagnosis modifiers), "consistent with" (evidence). Note the different ways for entering a coordination: multiple selection (phases, diagnosis modifiers) if there are no dependent menues, explicit coordination (button "+") for complex selections.

5 Concept representation

The entered findings are represented using language- independent specifications [9]. Concept descriptions are composed by primitive descriptions and semantic relations also called roles (see Figure 5). Formally, a composite concept description consists of a base concept which represents the primary category (genus) of the composite description, and a set of criteria (differentiae) which distinguish the composite description from its primary category. The base concept is either atomic, i.e. can refer to a primitive or defined concept of the domain vocabulary, or composite. A criterion is a 2-tuple consisting of a role symbol and a composite or coordinated concept description. A coordinated concept description consists of a logical conjunctor and a set of concept descriptions to be coordinated.
The formal specification of the finding used in Chapter 4 is:

```
(increased_uptake
        (:has_phase ( ∧   early_phase late_phase))
        (:has_location ( ∧     (major_trochanter (has_orientation right)
                                (femur_proximal_third (:has_orientation right))))
        (:has_morphology focal)
        (:has_interpretation (prosthesis_loosening
                                (:has_diagmod ( ∧   acute inflammatory))
```

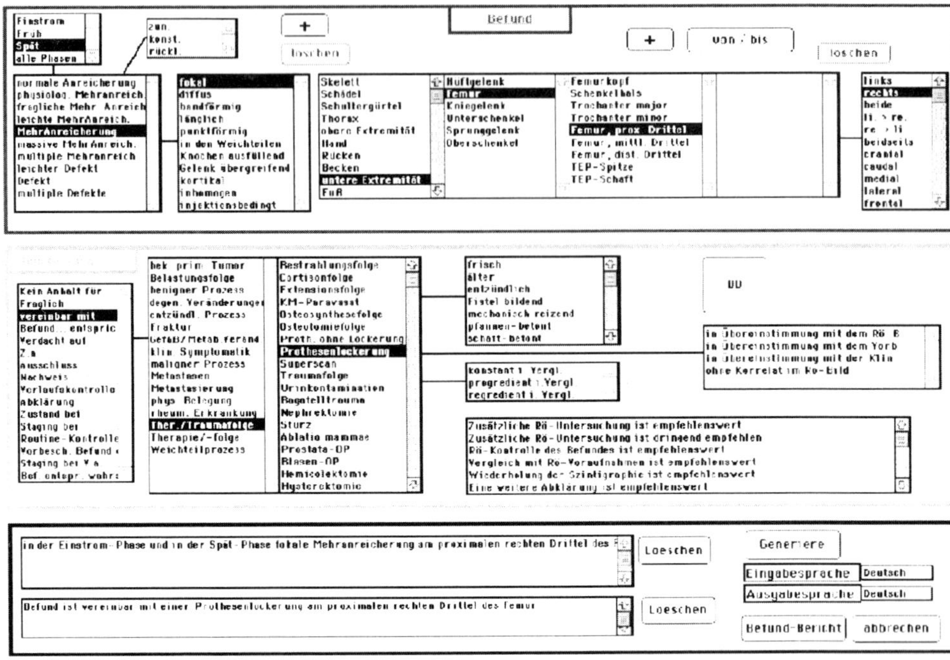

Figure 3: Structured data entry screen for bone scintigraphic findings, German vocabulary

(:has_evidence consistent_with)))

Concept descriptions can be classified automatically using a formal subsumption criterion [10]. This criterion is based both on the generic and partitive relations defined in the concept model and on the structure of concept descriptions. Classification is important for case retrieval under multiple views using the entered findings as case descriptors.

6 Text generation from formal specifications

The task of the text generator is to map formal concept descriptions to grammatically correct language surface structures. This task is supported by language-dependent designations of the domain concepts, default realization rules for roles, language-dependent lexica for nouns and adjectives providing basic grammatical information, and language-dependent morpho-syntactical rules.

6.1 Designation of concepts

Every concept of the domain model is given language specific information. The following considerations focus on the German generation component. The presentation item is the word or word group which is presented in the menues on the user interface. It may be a single word or a word group, and may contain abbreviations or permutations of word order. The presentation item of a concept is independent of the expression

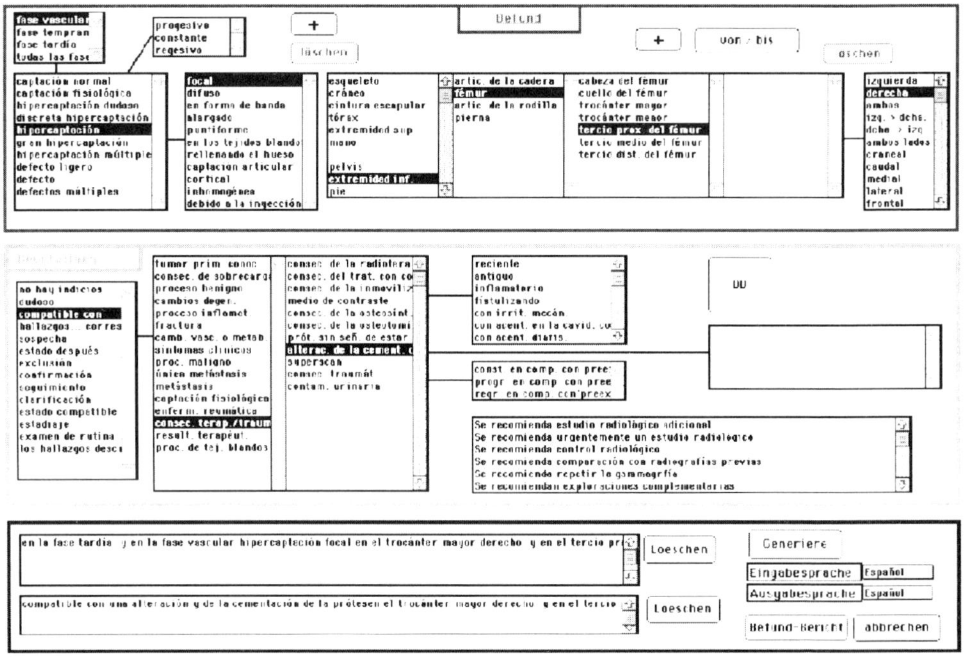

Figure 4: Structured data entry screen with Spanish vocabulary

generated in the report for that concept.
The lexical information for the text generator comprises the following items: the grammatical type indicates the grammatical category of the language expression provided. This is one of noun, adjective, or amorphous expression. For the representation of noun expressions there is a link to a noun entry in the noun lexicon. This item is mandatory. The link represents the noun component which has to be inflected by the text generator. The prefix is the string to which the inflected noun is concatenated. Prefixes allow for an efficient representation of compounds which are very common in German word formation. For instance for the concept "Kniegelenk" (knee joint) "Knie" is represented as prefix, whereas "gelenk" is realized as link to the entry "gelenk" in the noun lexicon. For that reason grammatical information for the noun entry "gelenk" has to be provided only once. Links to adjective entries in the adjective lexicon indicate for the text generator the adjective components of the concept designation. For instance, the lexical representation of the concept "degenerative Veraenderungen" (degenerative chances) has a link to the adjective entry "degenerativ". The amorphous item represents an unalterable component of a noun expression. It is concatenated by the text generator to the inflected noun. For instance, for the concept "Metastase bei Mamma- Carcinom" (metastasis due to mamma carcinoma) "bei Mamma- Carcinom" is represented as amorphous item. The plural tag indicates that the noun expression of the concept is in plural. This is the case for instance for the concept "degenerative Veraenderungen".

The representation of adjectival expressions consists of a link to an adjective entry representing the adjective component which is to be inflected, and an optional amorphous item to which the inflected adjective is concatenated. For instance the adjectival expression "im Vergleich zur Voruntersuchung zunehmend" (increasing compared to

<composite_concept>	::=	(<base_concept> { <criterion> }+)
<base_concept>	::=	<atomic_concept> | <composite_concept>
<criterion>	::=	(<role> <comp/coord_concept>)
<atomic_concept>	::=	*concept_symbol*
<role>	::=	*role_symbol*
<comp/coord_concept>	::=	<composite_concept> | <coordinated_concept>
<coordinated_concept>	::=	(<conjunctor> comp/coord_concept+)
<conjunctor>	::=	$\wedge \| \vee$
{}+ set with > 0 elements		

Figure 5: Syntax of the concept description language

the previous study) the adjective "zunehmend" is represented as link to the adjective lexicon, and "im Vergeich zur Vorunter suchung" as amorphous item, since it is unalterable for the text generator. Finally, amorphous expressions are realized as amorphous items. This applies for adverbial text components of expressions to be generated, or for complex canned texts, as for instance "Eine zusaetzliche Rntgen-Untersuchung ist empfehlenswert" (Additional X-ray study recommended).

The noun lexicon contains for every noun the singular root, and if irregular the plural root. For instance the lexicon entry for "Femurkopf" (head of femur) consists of the singular root "femurkopf" and the plural root "femurkoepf". The inflection type for the singular and for the plural forms control the inflectional suffix. The gender controls the inflection of adjectives and the determiner.
The adjective lexicon contains for every adjective at least the root. The plural tag indicates the pluralization of the noun phrase induced by the adjective - for instance "multiple" or "alle" (all) - the postposition tag indicates an irregular position of the adejctive behind the noun.
The role lexicon contains information about the default realization or roles. The realization of a role considers the grammatical structure of the concept description linked via the role. Potential realizations are adjectival phrase, genitive attribute, prepositional phrase with indication of a particular preposition, or amorphous structure. For instance the roles ":has_morphology" or ":has_diagmod" are assigned a default realization as adjectival phrase, the role ":has_location" is assigned a default realization as propositional phrase with the preposition "an" (at), dative case and definite determiner.

6.2 Morpho-syntactic generation

Through morpho-syntactic generation the formal representation of findings is transformed to language surface structures. In terms of conceptual graphs this includes the verbalization of concepts and roles. Text generation is supported by the lexicon and by morpho-syntactical rules. These rules control firstly the morphology of nouns, adjectives, determiners and prepositions as a function of case, gender, numerus and determiner type, and secondly word order. Text generation is primarily controlled by the rules for the default realization of roles. These rules can be bypassed if the linked concept description has a designation type uncompatible with the default realization.

The target structures of the text generator are complex noun phrases. The grammar

NP	::=	PP∗ Det AP∗ N PP∗ | NP Conj NP
PP	::=	Prep NP
Prep	::=	*preposition+*
Det	::=	*determiner*
AP	::=	Adj | NP Adj | PP Adj
Adj	::=	*adjective+* | *amorphous_itemadjective+*
N	::=	*noun+* | *noun + amorphous_item*
Conj	::=	*conjunction*

Figure 6: Target grammar of the German generator. X∗ means zero or many elements of type X. + means inflectional suffix. amorphous_item means an uninflected word group

for the German generator is given in Figure 6. It reflects the structure of the common language noun phrase with adjectival and prepositional adjuncts and complements [11], but in addition allows for prepositional phrases in front of the determiner. This enables the generation of verb-less sentences in the form of noun phrases which are very common in clinical jargon.

The slots for the concept designations and for the lexica are language specificly defined. The same is with the morpho- syntactical rules for the text generator. The successfull implementation of text generators for German, Spanish and Hungarian based on the outlined principles proves the capacity of the design. Figure 7 presents example reports for these languages.

7 Results

The system has been primarily developed for assisting report generation in a German-speaking environment supported by SIEMENS. The implementation was performed using RDB technology under 4th Dimension. Through multi-center cooperation under the umbrella of European COST B2 - quality assurance in nuclear medicine software - the vocabulary has been translated from German to several European languages (currently English, Spanish, French, Hungarian and Slovenian) and additional text generators have been provided for Spanish and Hungarian. Currently a multi-center and multi-lingual case registry for bone scitigraphy under the World Wide Web is being developed. Patient cases are represented through images, structured findings, clinical information and educational clues. The findings are entered and represented using the outlined multi- lingual data entry environment. Through the text generators language specific case descriptions can be produced. The language-independent representations of findings serve as descriptors which can be classified against user queries. This allows for example to query for cases showing a kind of a benign bone tumor at the spine, retrieving for instance a case of an exostosis (which is kind of a benign bone tumor) at the 5. lumbar vertebra (which is part of the lumbar spine which is part of the spine). This implementation combines C++ and POET OODB.

Fragestellung:

Verdacht auf eine Prothesenlockerung am rechten Hüftgelenk.

Technik:

3-Phasen Skelett-Szintigramm mit 630 MBq 99mTc-MDP

Befund:

In der Früh-Phase und in der Spät-Phase fokale Mehranreicherung am proximalen rechten Drittel des Femur und am rechten Trochanter major. In der Spät-Phase fragliche Mehranreicherung an den beiden Schultergelenken.

Beurteilung:

Befund ist vereinbar mit einer entzündlichen frischen Prothesenlockerung am rechten Trochanter major und am proximalen rechten Drittel des Femur. Fraglich degenerative Veränderungen an den beiden Schultergelenken.

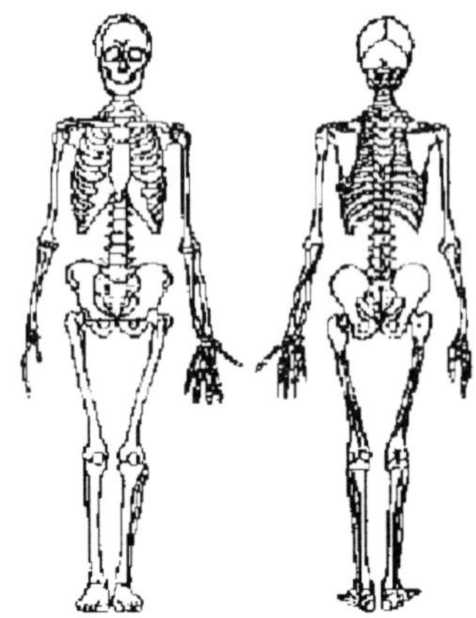

Figure 7: Generated German Report

8 Discussion

The proposed approach aims at the acquisition of qualitative information for the medical record through structured data entry and automatic text generation. This approach is in contrast to conventional dictating and typing which is utmost expressive, but has only a poor potential for the automatic representation and interpretation of meanings. With structured data entry there is a shift of workload to the physican user who has to adapt to a controlled vocabulary presented in a framework according to a conceptual domain model. This working environment is efficient in terms of saving costs and time, and results in structured and comparable information. On the other hand it is exposed to the danger of being constraining the way of thinking and restricting the expressiveness of the sublanguage. For that reason, the success of the approach depends heavily on the construction of a conceptual domain model which fits to the domain dependent expressions to be acquired and represented. Various experiments have shown that this can be achieved for diagnostic procedures in medical subdomains. However, even if these conditions are satisfied it is difficult with the proposed approach to enter referential information, necessary for instance for relating or comparing phenomena with respect to quality, extent or time. In this context it would be very helpful having support for structured editing of findings from previous examinations, since many diagnostic studies are performed in series in order to follow the time course of a patient problem. Also difficult to realize with structured data entry is complex argumentation, or weighing one thing against another. Here, a hybrid solution seems adequate combining both structured data entry and free- text reporting if the complexity of information exceeds the semantic model behind the data entry system.

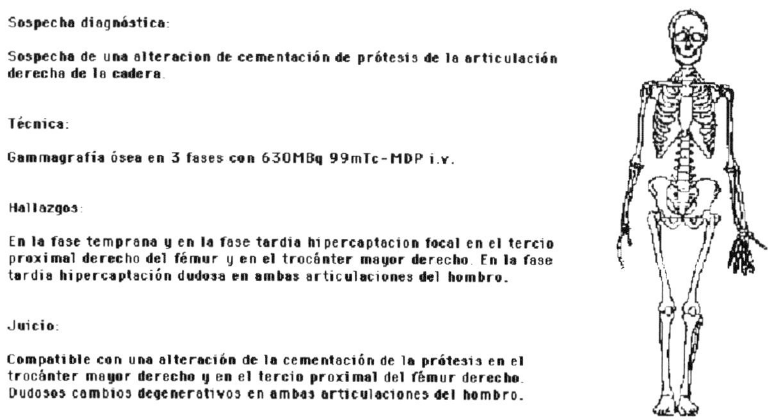

Figure 8: Generated Hungarian Report

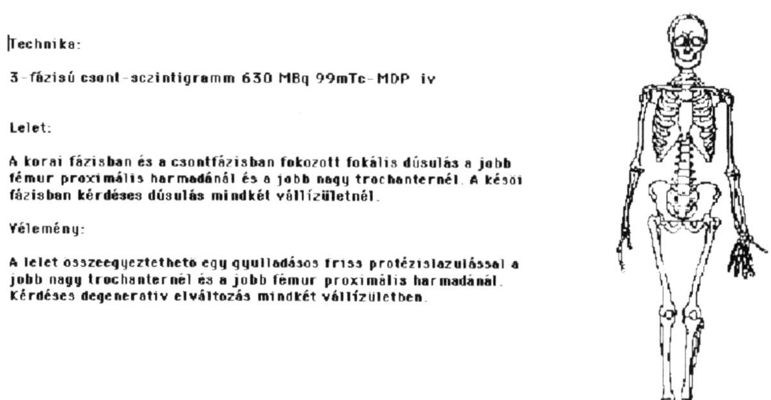

Figure 9: Generated Spanish Report

References

[1] Rector A.L., Glowinski A.J., Nowlan W.A., Rossi-Mori A., Medical-concept Models and Medical Records: Am Approach Based on GALEN and PEN&PAD, Journal of the American Medical Informatics Association. 1995; 2:19-35

[2] Bernauer J. (1991). Conceptual graphs as an operational model for descriptive findings. In: Clayton P.D. (ed.), Proceedings 15th Symposium on Computer Applications in Medical Care 1991, McGraw-Hill, pp 214-218

[3] Rothwell D.J., Côté R.A., Cordeau J.P., Boisvert M.A., Developing a standard data structure for medical language: The SNOMED proposal. In: Safran C. (ed.). Proceedings 17th Symposium on Computer Applications in Medical Care 1993, McGraw-Hill, pp 695-699

[4] Bernauer J.,Gumrich K., Kutz S., Lindner P., Pretschner D.P. (1991). An interactive report generator for bone scintigraphy. In: Clayton P.D. (ed.), Proceedings 15th Symposium on Computer Applications in Medical Care 1991, McGraw-Hill, pp 858-860

[5] Kuhn K., Gauss W., Wechsler J.G., et al., Structured reporting of medical findings: evaluation of a system in gastroenterology. Methods of Information in Medicine, 1992;31:268-74

[6] Friedman C., Cimino J.J., Johnson S.B., A schema for representing medical language applied to clinical radiology. Journal of the American Medical Informatics Association, 1994;1:233-248

[7] Bell D.S., Pattison-Gordon E., Greenes R.A., Experiments in Concept Modeling for Radiographic Image Reports. J Am Med Informatics Assoc. 1994;1:249-262

[8] Moorman P.W., van Ginneken A.M., van der Lei J., van Bemmel J.H., A Model for Structured Data Entry Based on Explicit Descriptional Knowledge. Methods of Information in Medicine 1994; 33:454-63

[9] Sowa J.F. (1984). Conceptual Structures: Information Processing in Mind and Maschine, Addison-Wesley

[10] Bernauer J., Subsumption principles underlying medical concept systems and their formal reconstruction. In: Ozbolt J.G. (ed.), Proceedings 18th Annual Symposium on Computer Applications in Medical Care (SCAMC94), Washington DC, 1994, pp 140-144

[11] Engel U., Deutsche Grammatik, Julius Groos, Heidelberg, 1988

Applications of Natural Language to Information Systems
R.P. van de Riet et al. (Eds.)
IOS Press, 1996

Natural Language Interpretation for Public Administration Database Querying in the TAMIC Demonstrator

Clara Bagnasco
Quinary S.p.A., Via Fara 35, MI, Italy

Paolo Bresciani, Bernardo Magnini and Carlo Strapparava
Istituto per la Ricerca Scientifica e Tecnologica,
I-38050 Povo/Trento, Italy
e-mail: strappa@irst.itc.it

Abstract. In this paper we present the TAMIC demonstrator, a natural language centered interface designed to improve the way an average citizen can access existing information of the Public Administrations. The TAMIC scenario is of an attended desk: interaction is mediated by an unspecialized clerk that interacts with multiple information systems in a transparent manner through the same Natural Language interface. This particular scenario exhibits the potentiality of a Natural Language Interfaces for accessing complex sources of information.
Keywords: Natural Language interface, information access.

1 Introduction

In a recent overview [1] of the field of Natural Language Interfaces to databases (NLI) it has been shown that, although some of the numerous NLI developed in the mid-eighties demonstrated positive characteristics in certain application areas, they didn't gain the expected wide commercial acceptance. The development of graphical and form-based interfaces, and some intrinsic problems of NLI (e.g., opacity on linguistic coverage and conceptual/linguistic failures) are probably the main reasons for the limited success of commercial NLI to databases. However, the technical advancements in various specific areas of NLP have been notable, and many have resulted in a technology mature for new applications. Beside this, a major change in attitude comes from an integrated view of the interface that has been emerging in recent years.

Following these lines of advancement this paper describes the TAMIC [1] (Transparent Access to Multiple Information for the Citizen) project, the aim of which is the realization of a natural language centered interface to substantially improve the way an average citizen can access existing information of the Public Administrations (P.A.). The project has been developed in close collaboration with the users of the system,

[1]The MLAP-TAMIC EU Project ($n^{\underline{o}}$ 63-457) consortium included: QUINARY S.p.A. (Prime Contractor), Istituto Nazionale per la Previdenza Sociale (INPS), Istituto per la Ricerca Scientifica e Tecnologica (IRST), Cap Gemini Innovation (CGInn), Deutsches Forschungszentrum für Künstliche Intelligenz GmbH (DFKI), Istituto di Linguistica Computazionale. A follow-up project has been submitted to the EU.

particularly with INPS, the main Italian public entity for social insurance, and the Autonomous Province of Trento. The first phase of the project, just finished, achieved two important results: first, a in-depth research on user needs has shown that the adoption of a NLI would be suitable for the situation; second, a demonstrative prototype has been realized and a first consensus for the proposed solution was achieved with its presentation to users and to a large number of P.A. managers.

In the present situation of Italian P.A. offices, a citizen who finds himself with the necessity of accessing a data set distributed over several archives must proceed to several successive accesses, each of which provides a subset of the required data, then personally execute the connection of the various gathered data, and finally proceed to distil them and provide a response. This problem has been identified by a variety of studies carried out by the Public Administration in many countries. For example, according to one of these studies, each Italian citizen spends about 20 days per year on bureaucratic matters. Other studies indicate that just now 25% of the Italian citizens need about 30 minutes to obtain one single piece of information from a public administration office, and this time does not take into account travel and the fact that often a bureaucratic case requires access to different offices. The creation of information desks will certainly reduce this waste of time, allowing also an increased transparency with respect to citizens and their cases.

The TAMIC solution is that of an attended desk: interaction is mediated by an unspecialized clerk who interacts with multiple information systems, through the same interface. The clerk can use the interface without knowing the details of the structure of the many different databases involved. Additionally, clerks, who are usually competent only in some areas of P.A., will be able to provide information also on other topics. The TAMIC approach also considers that often one single question will not solve the information problem: one needs to install a kind of dialogue to get to the necessary information, and it is important that also the citizens understand the dialogue between clerk and computer, so that they can collaborate, for instance providing missing data, or exploring alternatives.

In this paper we focus on three aspects that are crucial for the concrete realization of the TAMIC system:

- the integration of the NLI module with standard information access techniques (briefly reviewed in section 2);
- the realization of an intermediate conceptual model (section 4) and its relations with the underlying databases (section 5);
- the transparent access to multiple information systems and the homogeneous access to structurally different databases (section 5).

2 Operational capabilities of the TAMIC system

The TAMIC system consists of an environment for the clerk through which he will be able to interact with the underlying information system. It is presented as a complete interface including a combination of natural language, menus, and graphical aspects. The final setting for validation in the field will see the interface based on a personal

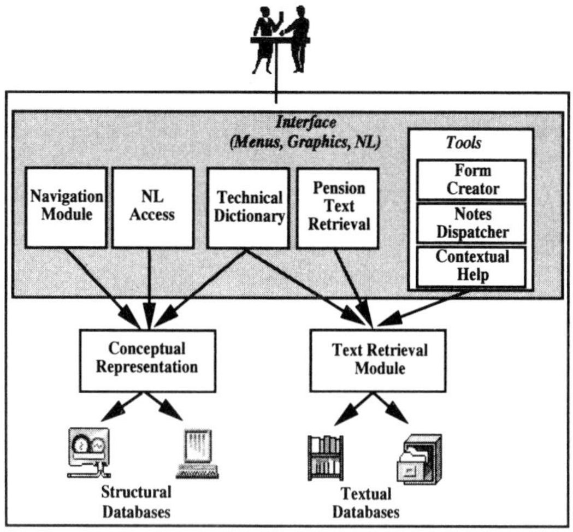

Figure 1: TAMIC main modules

computer connected to the pension system network and with an echo monitor where the citizen will be able to observe and understand the ongoing dialogue between clerk and system. The citizen will ask questions in a clearer way referring to an understandable ongoing dialogue and output data visualized on the screen.

The interface is an integrated environment at two levels: (a) at the level of user actions, it permits the user to pass easily and consistently from one tool to the other; (b) at a deep level it allows the global focus of interaction to be maintained, permitting the integration of browsing and NL access into a single global dialogue modality. Along this line TAMIC helps to overcome the problem of the "teletype approach" provided by earlier NLI that do not exploit the potential of a computer display well enough. In fact, integrating language and graphics to exploit the advantages of both modalities offers a way of enlarging the share of the interactional situation that is available both to the user and the system, overcoming the typical problems of the commercial products. IRST [17, 18], has already successfully experimented the integration of NL modalities (mediated exploration) with graphical browsing of the underlying knowledge (navigational exploration). The whole TAMIC interface yields the following functionalities (see Figure 1):

- *NL access to structured data in the domain.* It includes typed expressions of a relevant subset of natural language (principally complex noun phrases expressions). Linguistic coverage includes quantification, coordination, ellipsis, anaphoric and temporal expressions. Robustness is an important attribute. The NL expressions may be combined with menu based action indications. Replies from the system is directly manipulable. Through mouse based actions one gets more details or other linked information.

- *Browsing of the underlying domains using a graphical interface.* The clerk is able to explore the knowledge available by means of graphical browser. The portion of knowledge actually displayed is used by the system as a context for interpreting NL expressions.

- *Access to textual databases.* TAMIC offers the capability of retrieving written material: technical documents (laws, rules, etc...), which can help the clerk to investigate a particular issue, and material for the citizen which can help him to understand a particular matter.

- *Access to a technical dictionary.* A technical glossary including pension terms is accessible by the clerk who needs to know precise term definitions. The same dictionary is also accessible from the navigation interface.

- *Help tools.* TAMIC provides the clerk with a set of tools integrated in the overall interface.

  An on-line contextual help in the spirit of well known help system available in commercial products.

  A form creator that allows to automatically prepare forms for the individual with relevant data coming from different data bases, so that the form can be printed and given to him for signature, remainder and so on.

  A notes dispatcher to technical offices for questions the clerk can not answer.

The interpretation of requests and other utterances as well as navigational interactions result in interaction with a conceptual model of the domain and of the specific structured available databases. Specific mapping modules, receiving in input a logical form, produce queries to the relevant databases and provide the answers to be dispatched for output presentation.

3 The TAMIC demonstrator

In the preliminary study of the TAMIC project, a demonstrative prototype was developed. It involved some realities of the public administration in Trentino in example areas of the world of work and in particular the "job market" in the province of Trento. In this area there is a rather active structure, the "Agenzia del Lavoro", the main objectives of which are to bring together job offers and requests in a single place and directing job seekers to careers and specific professions with greatest request for personnel. Although having a large information base distributed over various synergetic poles, this structure seems able to exhibit greater potential by integrating its data with those of INPS (social security administration), that, for its own institutional needs, manages a great information flow on companies operating locally and in the job sector. Moreover, the two agencies have similar and complementary aims, as far as job mobility and unemployment generally are concerned, which, in many aspects, come under the "job market" heading. "Prevention and assistance services" were also considered, associated as they are with the job market, even if these are a bit off the main track of the central theme, with the goal of showing system capability to integrate similar information in a single viewpoint: this possibility may be used even in analogous domains, such as, for example, pensions, to integrate information about services managed by different agencies (INPS, Ministry of the Treasury, Province, etc...).

The idea proposed is that of a window attended by an unspecialized employee who may access many computer systems (multifunctional window) through a single interface. The employee interacts with the system in contemporary Italian using the keyboard, and may express himself with some linguistic flexibility. A dialogue – not just isolated sentences – is developed with the computer, without the necessity of the employee knowing the data structures in detail. A citizen may follow the interaction on a second screen, and what happens is completely visible to him, and does not involve symbols or incomprehensible codes.

The demonstrative prototype is in large part the result of applying advanced technologies recently developed in IRST laboratories; a small part of the result comes from simulation. This was developed with direct support of the "users", above all INPS, Agency for Employment of the Province of Trento, and the Government Commissariato.

The citizen that can access the information point can be a job seeker, a personnel hiring agent, an insured worker, a requester or user of unemployment benefits. The dialogue with the clerk may deal with requirements to reach a certain professional level (e.g., work experience and education); job opportunities, even in relation to a specific geographic area; the availability of training courses; names of companies working in certain productive sectors; job openings giving the specific characteristics sought; unemployment benefits needed after factory closings or layoffs; etc. The relevant information for the above mentioned sectors has been collected considering a number of Public Administration Data Bases. Some of them come from the Autonomous Province of Trento, while other come from INPS.

The demonstrator is based on the reuse and adaptation of various existing modules. It must be noted that, in the present implementation of the demonstrator, only a simulation of the use of real database is implemented, that is, a copy of small portions of databases information has been replicated into the knowledge base by hand. In section 5, a technique to *couple* real databases with the knowledge base, in order to allow to uniformly access both KB and DB information, is shortly proposed. It is based on previous works already successfully applied in other IRST NLI demonstrators. In the present implementation of TAMIC this feature has not been fully implemented, due to several technological problems coming from the fact that the P.A. database are typically hosted on non-UNIX and non-Internet connected machines (mainly IBM mainframes), and affording this kind of technical issues is presently out of the scope of the project.

The demonstrator runs on a Sun Sparc workstation with Allegro Common Lisp environment.

4 Natural Language access module

The Natural Language access module of the TAMIC system is based on the so called *Multilevel semantics* approach, which has been proposed [15] as a powerful architecture for semantic analysis. In this approach, interpreting a natural language sentence is a multi-stage process, which starts out with a high-level meaning representation, which reflects the semantic structure of the sentence rather directly. Then translation rules, which specify how the language-oriented semantic primitives relate to the ones that are used at deeper levels of analysis, are applied. One of the advantages of the multilevel approach is that it allows a natural decomposition of complex tasks and the functional modularization of semantic analysis. In concrete applications the definition of the semantics for a level has at least two advantages: (i) modules for specific phenomena could be easily introduced within the appropriate level, provided that the module functions contribute to the definition of the semantics for that level; (ii) a better understanding

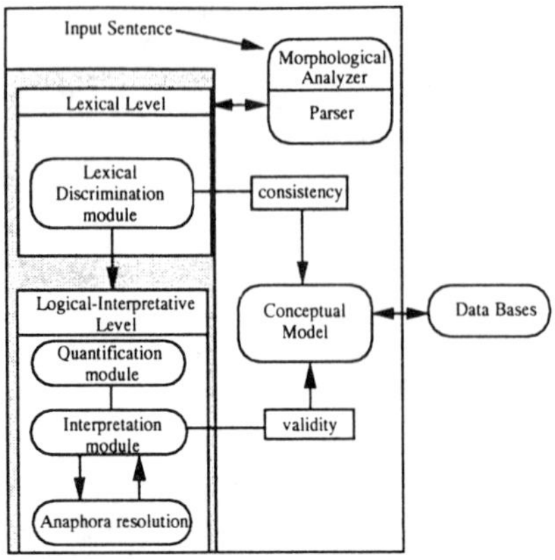

Figure 2: The multilevel architecture for the Tamic system

of the semantic analysis would be allowed: particularly, when a sentence is rejected at a certain level, it would mean that the semantic constraints for that level have been violated. An application of this approach has been used for the realization of the Alfresco and MAIA prototypes, two NLP information access systems developed at IRST [13]. The overall architecture of the NLP module is shown in Figure 2.

The parser used by the TAMIC demonstrator is the WEDNESDAY2 [16] parser. It is a chart based parser which can cope with a large number of linguistic phenomena including declarative, imperative and interrogative sentences, complex relative clauses (and other phenomena connected with so-called long-distance dependencies), idiomatic expressions, various kind of ellipsis, constituent coordination, etc. The parser bases its process largely on information stored in the lexicon.

As far as the semantic analysis is concerned the TAMIC demonstrator includes two levels: the lexical level and the logical-interpretative level. At the lexical level lexical discrimination is computed and a semantic representation of the propositional content of the sentence is produced as output; lexical discrimination is a process by means of which only the sentence readings satisfying given selectional restrictions are selected. When the prepositional content of the sentence is proved to be consistent, the semantic representation produced by this level is passed to the next one; otherwise, if consistency cannot be proved, the whole sentence is rejected.

At the logical-interpretative level specific modules provide a logical form in which both quantifiers and anaphoric ambiguities are resolved. The output is an unambiguous logical form whose predicates are concepts and roles of the Conceptual Model [2], and whose arguments can be variables and instances. As an example, Figure 3 shows the logical form produced by the input sentence "Which requirements for SW engineer does Mario Rossi have?": concepts and roles are capitalized, while constants are in this `typeface`.

Then this form is translated in a query language grounded on the KB concepts to retrieve the actual objects included in the databases that satisfy the sentence. Below we explain how the Conceptual Model is structured and in section 5 we will give more details in coupling the Conceptual Model with the underlying databases.

[2]The structure of the Conceptual Model will be presented in the next section. It is largely defined by means of a knowledge base (KB) using a formalism following the tradition of the kl-one knowledge representation languages [6].

```
(which x (and (Requirement x)
        (Need-req SW-Engineer x))
     (Have-requirement Mario-Rossi x))
```

Figure 3: Logical form produced by the NL access module

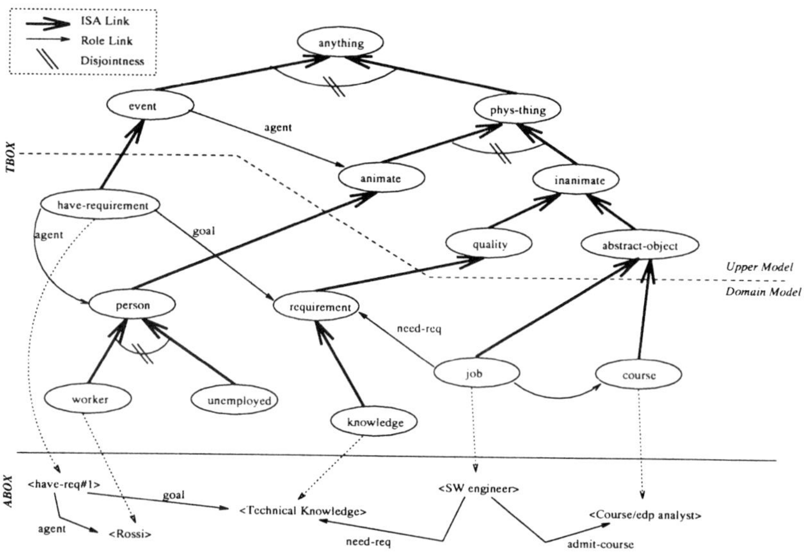

Figure 4: A partial fragment of the conceptual model

4.1 The TAMIC Conceptual Model

The analysis of the meaning of the sentence in the TAMIC architecture is based on a Conceptual Model (see Figure 4), which provides an intermediate representation of the world knowledge which is independent from the actual physical structure of the databases. The design of the Conceptual Model is based on previous experience in the construction of Natural Language information access prototypes developed at IRST [19]. In these experiences we have found it useful to separate a general, linguistically oriented conceptual model (in our terminology the "Upper Model"), from the conceptual model of the actual knowledge of the specific application domain (that we call the "Domain Model"). This separation facilitates the interfacing of the Conceptual Model with the linguistic modules of the system, such as the lexicon and the grammar; moreover, providing a high level of semantic knowledge, the Upper Model is supposed to subsume specific knowledge of the application domain. As Upper Model we adopted the "Generalized Upper Model" (GUM), an already existent ontology specifically designed for Natural Language purposes. GUM has already been used in a number of applicative projects and it is documented in various papers (e.g. [2]). The Upper Model allows to incrementally build a representation of the propositional content of the sentence starting from its components by full composition among its concepts and relations. In addition, GUM provides a full set of selectional restrictions over the participants included in a process, allowing the lexical discrimination process to take place.

The Domain Model is classified (by means of IS-A links) under the GUM. Its realization took a lot of effort and resulted in a complex knowledge base (about 300 concepts and 300 relations). Both GUM and the Domain Model were implemented using the knowledge representation management systems (KRMS) LOOM [14].

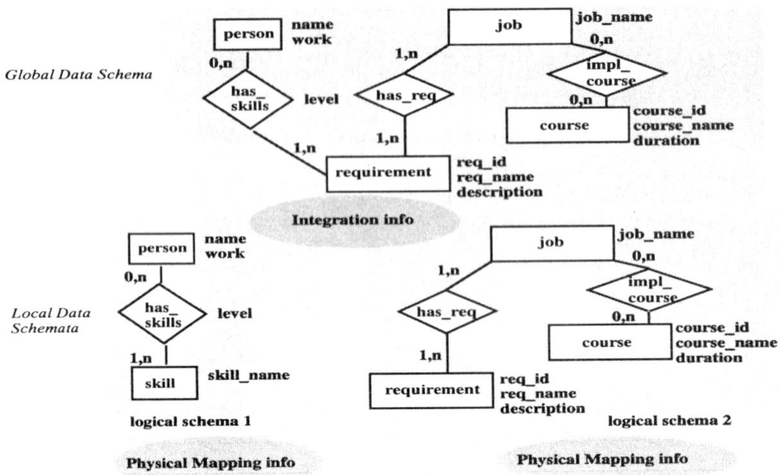

Figure 5: Global Data Schema

5 Multiple Database access

Data access task resolution for P.A. often involves access to different information sources, both physically distant and structurally not homogeneous. Task complexity is very high, as data contained in different databases are not independent: data relating the same logical subject are actually scattered or replicated into different databases.

A solution to the task of making transparent access to multiple heterogeneous databases from a single NL interface can be given by designing three sub modules, that solves the corresponding main sub tasks in which the problem can be logically partitioned:

1. defining an integrated Global Data Schema out of a series of Local Data Schemata (see Figure 5);

2. designing a Data Retrieval Engine able to transform a query to the global schema into a set of queries to the Local Data Schemata;

3. integrating the global data schema and the NL Interface knowledge structure (in TAMIC, the Domain Model), so that a query to the Domain Model is automatically translated into a query to the Global Data Schema.

The definition of an integrated Global Data Schema involves an heavy data modeling phase that must be accomplished in close collaboration with the data administrators. During this phase, the databases containing relevant data that should be delivered to the citizens are selected and deeply investigated. For each relevant database, a Local Data Schema is acquired or produced; the relationships among the Local Data Schemata are analyzed and formalized and an integrated Global Data Schema is produced.

In TAMIC, these tasks are supported by a suite of graphical software tools, that produce a graphical representation of the Local Data Schema out of a particular data source descriptions (DDL file, flat file, data dictionary, etc...) and assist the data administrator in building the Global Data Schema and defining its relationships with each Local Data Schema.

Various elements must be taken into account in order to establish the relationships between each data source and its corresponding Local Data Schema: data sources are of different kinds (e.g., hierarchical, relational, flat files), they reside on particular hosts in particular computer environments, and so on. Such information are formalized into "Physical Mappings", information establishing a correspondence between the logical description of a data source and its actual implementation.

The set of transformation applied to the Local Data Schemata in order to obtain a global data schema are in turn encoded as a set of "Logical Mappings". It is important to underline that the same formalism must be chosen in order to describe both the local and the global schema. In TAMIC, we chose a variant of the Entity-Relationship formalism. Each entity/relationship in the Global Data Schema integrates the information represented by one or more entities/relationships belonging to different Local Data Schemata. Information about the global schema, the physical and the logical mappings are recorded into a relational database, that can be accessed both from the Data Retrieval Engine and from the NL understanding module.

The Data Retrieval Engine uses the Logical Mappings in order to split a query to the Global Data Schema into a set of queries to the Local Data Schemata. Queries to each Local Data Schema are then compiled into a proper set of query programs and executed in the corresponding computer environment exploiting the Physical Mappings. Both the Logical and Physical Mappings are then used in a backward manner in order to integrate query answers.

Once given a global representation of the database inter schema, the task of integrating the Domain Model and the Global Data Schema must be afforded, in order to allow formulating and answering queries via the Knowledge Representation query language. In the TAMIC modular architecture this task involves *coupling* the Domain Model KB with the single virtual relational database. This means that primitive concepts and roles in the KB are made to correspond respectively to unary and binary tables in the global virtual DB [5]. In particular, the so called *tight coupling* technique has been preferred to the so called *loose coupling* approach [11, 5] (that requires a pre-loading of the data from the DB into the KB) because *tight coupling* implements a *on demand* access to the DB. As a result, our implementation allows the following advantages:

- existentially quantified conjunctive queries involving unary and binary predicates can be done;
- no memory space is wasted in the KRMS to keep descriptions of DBMS data;
- answers are given on the basis of the current state of KB and DB, without needing any updating of KB with modified data from DB.

In our approach, the database is considered as a part of the knowledge base, homogeneously extending the assertional part (ABox) used to describe the individuals of the knowledge base and their attributes and properties. As the knowledge base can be queried about individuals described in the ABox by means of *terminology* defined in the terminological part (TBox) of the KB, also the database has to be *coupled* with the terminology, in order to allow a uniform query interface. To this end a mapping between the terminology and the database schema has to be defined. A partial mapping PM between primitively defined terms in the terminology and tables in the global database is defined by the Knowledge Engineer (in collaboration with the data administrators). Using PM also non-primitively defined concepts can be recursively mapped into views

RM((SOME R D)) =
```
SELECT DISTINCT  left
FROM             RM(R)                    if both RM(R) and RM(D) are defined;
WHERE            RM(R).right IN RM(D)
```

Figure 6: A simplified fragment of the recursive partial mapping RM, concerning the translation of a generic SOME-expression of the KB into the corresponding SQL-expression. For simplicity it is assumed that concepts are mapped into unary tables with one column called left, and roles into binary tables with two columns called left and right

of the DB – represented by SQL-expressions – by means of a recursive mapping RM, a fragment of which is sketched in Figure 6 (see [8]).

Basing on *RM*, conjunctive queries involving unary and binary predicates can be answered. Queries are split in their component parts, and each part submitted to the KRMS and/or to the DBMS, after translation into SQL via *RM*. In this way partial answer sets are obtained from the sub-queries, and then *merged* together in an efficient way, in order to avoid combinatorial explosion due to possible spanning of the whole database [7].

As an example of translation, consider the logical form of Figure 3. It can be translated into the following query to the KB (in LOOM syntax):

```
(retrieve (x) (:for-some e
                  (:and (need-req SW-Engineer x)
                        (have-requirement e)
                        (agent e ROSSI)
                        (goal e x))))
```

This query is then translated into the SQL equivalent:

```
SELECT DISTINCT  has-req.requirement
FROM             has-req, has-skill
WHERE            has-req.job="SW-ENGINEER" AND
                 has-skill.person="ROSSI" AND
                 has-skill.requirement = has-req.requirement
```

where the table names **has-skill** and **has-req**, and their field names are given, of course, by the PM function. This translation is obtained by mechanically applying the technique described in [7].

The DBMS will return a list of elements that possibly will be merged with results from the KB (in the case the query was part of a wider query involving also ABox-individuals).

6 Conclusions

We presented first results achieved by the TAMIC project. First, in the proposed setting, in which multiple information sources come from different P.A., the integration of a natural language interface with graphical navigation tools turned out to be an effective way to access the information. Second, a demonstrator has been realized which received a positive validation from a number of P.A. managers.

Future developments include a full implementation of the system, particularly a true access to real databases; a development of the homogeneous NL access both to structural and textual databases; an improvement of the robustness of the system and of its linguistic coverage.

Moreover, we are interested in the prospect of using the TAMIC interface in a multilingual environment. This perspective is of importance both for multilingual areas (e.g., Alto Adige/Südtyrol) and for future international connection of national P.A. information.

7 Acknowledgments

We would like to thank Gigi Rocca and Oliviero Stock for the coordination of the TAMIC project; Alberto Lavelli, Daniela Petrelli, Massimo Zancanaro, and Diego Zamatteo for their contribution to the realization of the TAMIC demonstrator.

References

[1] I. Androutsopoulos, G.D. Ritchie, and P. Thanisch. Natural language interfaces to databases - an introduction. *Natural Language Engineering*, 1(1), 1995.

[2] J. Bateman, B. Magnini, and G. Fabris. The generalized upper model knowledge base: Organization and use. In *Proceedings of KB-KS-95*, Twente, The Netherlands, April 1995. Second International Conference on Building and Sharing of Very Large-Scale Knowledge Bases.

[3] M. Bates, M.G. Moser, and D. Stallard. The IRUS transportable natural language database interface. In L. Kerschberg, editor, *Expert Database Systems*. Benjamin/Cummings, 1986.

[4] R.J. Bobrow. The RUS system. Report 3878, BBN, 1978.

[5] A. Borgida and R.J. Brachman. Loading data into description reasoners. In *Proceeding of ACM SIGMOD*, 1993.

[6] R.J. Brachman and J.G. Schmolze. An overview of the KL-ONE knowledge representation system. *Cognitive Science*, 9(2):171–216, 1985.

[7] Paolo Bresciani. Uniformly querying knowledge bases and data bases. In F. Baader, M. Buchheit, M. A. Jeusfeld, and W. Nutt, editors, *Working Notes of the KI'94 Workshop: KRDB'94 - Reasoning about Structured Objects: Knowledge Representation meets Databases*, number D-94-11 in DFKI Documents, pages 58–62, Saarbrücken, Germany, September 1994. DFKI GmbH.

[8] Paolo Bresciani. Querying databases from description logics. In F. Baader, M. Buchheit, M. A. Jeusfeld, and W. Nutt (Eds.), editors, *KRDB-95: Reasoning about structured objects: Knowledge representation meets databases*, number D-95-12 in DFKI-Research-Report, pages 1–4, Stuhlsatzenhausweg 3, D-66123 Saarbrücken, Germany, 1995. DFKI GmbH.

[9] M.W. Bright, A.R. Hurson, and S.H. Pakzad. A taxonomy and current issues in multidatabase systems. *Computer*, 1992.

[10] C. Collet, M. N. Huhns, and W. Shen. Resource integration using a large knowledge base in carnot. *Computer*, December 1991.

[11] Premkumar T. Devanbu. Translating description logics to information server queries. In *Proceedings of Second Conference on Information and Knowledge Management (CIKM '93)*, 1993.

[12] J.M. Ginsparg. A robust portable natural language database interface. In *Proc. of the 1st ACL Conference on Applied Natural Language Processing*, Santa Monica, California, 1983.

[13] Alberto Lavelli, Bernardo Magnini, and Carlo Strapparava. An approach to multilevel semantics for applied systems. In *Proc. of the 3 rd ACL Conference on Applied Natural Language Processing*, pages 17–24, Trento, Italy, 1992.

[14] R. MacGregor. Inside the LOOM description classifier. *SIGART Bulletin*, 2(3):88–92, 1991.

[15] R. Scha. Logic foundation for question answering. Techical Report MS12.331, Philips Research Laboratory, 1983.

[16] O. Stock. Parsing with flexibility, dynamic strategies and idioms in mind. *Computational Linguistics*, 15(1), 1989.

[17] O. Stock. Natural language and exploration of an information space: The ALFRESCO interactive system. In *Proc. of the 12 th IJCAI*, Sidney, Australia, 1991.

[18] O. Stock, C. Strapparava, and M. Zancanaro. Explorations in a natural language multimodal information access environment. In *Workshop on Intelligent Multimedia Information Retrieval*, Montreal, 1995. IJCAI 95.

[19] O. Stock and The ALFRESCO Project Team. ALFRESCO: Enjoying the combination of NLP and hypermedia for information exploration. In M.T. Maybury, editor, *Intelligent Multimodal Interfaces*. AAAIPress/MIT Press, Menlo Park CA/Cambridge MA, 1993.

[20] User needs and scenario assessment. MLAP TAMIC Project 63057 Technical Report, 1985.

[21] TAMIC final report. MLAP TAMIC Project 63057 Technical Report, 1995.

Applications of Natural Language to Information Systems
R.P. van de Riet et al. (Eds.)
IOS Press, 1996

Natural Language Interfaces for Environmental Data Bases

F. Dinenberg, D. Levin
Russian Research Institute of Artificial Intelligence
Lavrent'eva, 6, Novosibirsk, 630090, Russia
email: {dinen, levin}@ iis.nsk.su

Abstract. The paper presents results of building of NL interfaces for data bases in geoinformational and ecological domains. The types and structures of some data bases supported by governmental agencies of Germany and Russia in environmental area are characterized and exemplified. Elements of the architecture of NL shells implementation and integration are given. Building of NL interface for the geoinformational system MapInfo is described. The presented approaches and systems are based on the experience of automatic natural language processing accumulated during more than 20 years. In particular, this experience resulted in building of InterBASE — a technological support system for automated construction of NL interfaces. The paper outlines the semantic-oriented analysis and other principles and implementation issues of the InterBASE.

1. Introduction

The Russian Research Institute of Artificial Intelligence (RRIAI) and the teams from which it originated have been occupied with the problem of automatic natural language (NL) understanding for more than 20 years [1, 2, 3]. This vast area of research, development and application essentially includes many issues of building NL interfaces for database management systems. A dozen of (not only European) natural languages were used as query languages for many databases of varying content, structure, complexity and DBMS support. The main idea of the approach (which later became very popular worldwide) was a semantic-oriented analysis for queries referred to semantically-restricted subject domains.

The accumulated experience resulted in clear understanding that once a concrete database is given, we can more or less easily construct a practically reliable NL interface for it. The really difficult problem is to make the construction process more regular, so that in the long run it could be performed by many people in the framework of a certain technology. This lead us to the building of the InterBASE* programming environment [4] — a distributed product aimed to support automated creation and improvement of NL shells for a family of market DBMSs.

Further progress in industrial construction and application of NL interfaces could be achieved if the proper niche were found for NL-type interfaces in the broad spectrum of user interfaces. Some features of this niche are as follows:

---

* InterBASE was registered officially as a trademark of RRIAI in Russia in 1991. The same trademark is used by Borland Corp. for a different software product.

- Many non-professional users wish to access the data.
- The subject domain must be of considerable complexity and users' queries must be diverse enough.
- Compatibility with other types of interfaces should be supported together with the possibility to switch to other user modes. There is a promising future of NL-interface application in multimedia environments.

Environmental information system is a good candidate for the real regular usage of NL interface. One of the reasons might be a broad and constantly increasing interest in ecological information. In particular, accessibility of this kind of information becomes of considerable social importance and is supported by some international programs. At present, works on usage of NLI-interfaces are at inculcation stage in two environmental agencies, in Russia — Regional Committee on Ecology and Natural Resources, Novosibirsk and in Germany, — Environmental Ministry of the Land of Baden-Württemberg.

This article presents one of the family of NL interfaces built by our team in the environmental area. The types and structures of some environmental databases are characterized and exemplified. Elements of the architecture of NL shell implementation and integration are given. In particular, an NL interface to the well-known geoinformational system (GIS) MapInfo is briefly described, together with certain specific problems which arise within this kind of application. The last section outlines the semantic-oriented analysis as it was implemented in the InterBASE system.

2. Direct access to geographical and ecological data

This type of NL-interface is illustrated here by an example which concerns a piece of geodata about Germany supported in the GODOT project [5]. The system deals with objects and structures described in Figure 1.

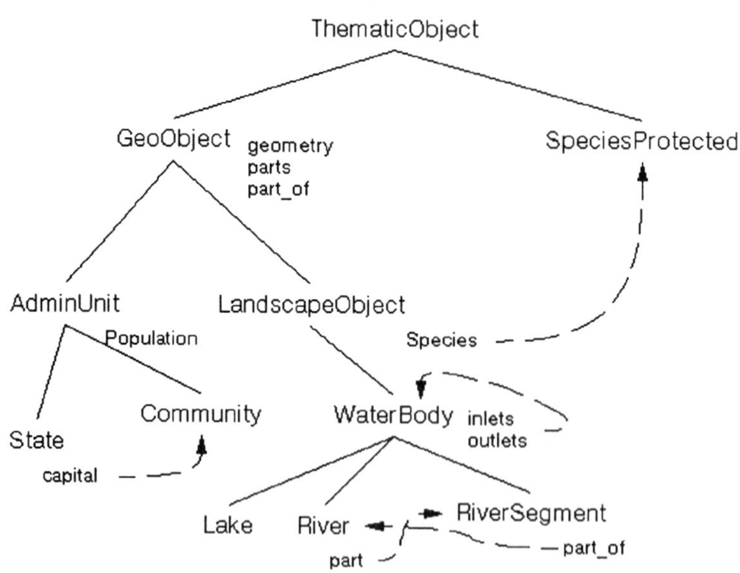

Figure 1

The operational level of data representation is constructed in the relational style as a collection of tables. Here we have the following tables:

STATES — the list of administrative units,
CAPITALS — capitals of states,
LAKES — lakes of states,
RIVERS — rivers of states,
LAKES_SP — species living in lakes,
RIVER-SP — species living in rivers, etc.

Given the structure description together with data files, the InterBASE system is able (see section 3)

- to construct automatically the initial working version of NL-preprocessor,
- to support, if necessary, the process of preprocessor improvement.

Such NL-preprocessor can translate, for example, the following types of queries:

Which rivers are tributaries of Rhein?
Display cities with more than two million population.
Which administrative units have capitals with more than 1 000 000 people?
Show water bodies located in Baden-Württemberg.
Display protected species living in rivers.
Outlets of rivers with protected species.
Which rivers have parts located in administrative units with capitals having more than one million people?
Which rivers have parts with protected species in Baden-Württemberg?
Indicate rivers flowing into the Rhein.

The output of the preprocessor, i.e., the result of translating the query is its representation in the SQL-like language. This output is then passed for execution to the DBMS.

There is a strong opinion that natural language access would be particularly effective in so called metainformation systems. In their context, a user is expected to enter the system without precise knowledge of the structure of the subject domain. The user's behavior could be characterized as a kind of study which simultaneously clarifies both the subject domain and the user's intentions. One of the typical queries therefore would be like "What is known about ...?"

One example here is the bibliographical database which corresponds to a part of the metainformation package for the Environmental Information System of the state Baden-Württemberg. In this package, the metainformational domain is viewed as a collection of texts describing certain aspects of environmental data. Among such texts one can distinguish reports, articles, books, files, databases, programs, etc.

Another example which concerns metadata access relates to the Environmental Data Catalogue (EDC) [6]. Here, the database which describes ecological information suppliers contains such attributes as:

the identification of an information supplier,
the classification of a pollution,
pollutants,
the region (town),
the beginning of the data gathering,
the end of the data gathering, etc.

To illustrate the style of queries within the NL shell made for the EDC system, we use the EDC-object with data related to Novosibirsk region.

Examples of queries to this database are as follows:

What information suppliers gather data on the atmospheric pollution in Novosibirsk and Krasnoobsk?
In which towns does the atmosphere contain the following wastes: nitrogene dioxide, benzapyrene, dust?
Display information on water pollution.
Give me the data on radiation pollution.
Is there information on the water pollution from the February 1990?
Indicate rivers and pollutants.

An example of a full cycle of query processing, when queries are translated by the linguistic processor into an SQL-like representation and then executed by the FoxPro database.

The query: *Where is the atmosphere polluted with NO_2 and CO?*
The answer:

CLASS_POL	atmospheric pollution
SUBSTANCES	sulphur acid, sulphuric anhydride, carbon oxide, carbon monoxide, nitrogene dioxide, nitrogene oxide, benzapyrene, dust, formaldehyde
REGION	Novosibirsk
CLASS_POL	atmospheric pollution
SUBSTANCES	benzapyrene, dust, nitrogene dioxide, carbon oxide
REGION	Iskitim
CLASS_POL	atmospheric pollution
SUBSTANCES	sulphur acid, sulphuric anhydride, carbon oxide, nitrogene dioxide
REGION	Berdsk
CLASS_POL	atmospheric pollution
SUBSTANCES	carbon oxide, nitrogene dioxide, benzapyrene, ammonium
REGION	Karasuk

A more general view of accessing metadata is possible. As long as the metainformation is primarily used to help the user in the search for relevant facts in a huge array of data, we can only treat metadata as a suitably selected and organized data concentrate. When compared with data itself, this concentrate is much smaller in volume, and its structure is considerably simpler. In this quality, the metadata on the base level can be supported by the traditional DBMS facilities. It is assumed also that all links between objects are eventually traced and controlled by the users themselves. These facilities are, however, insufficient in the following cases.

First, the space of environmental metadata may well turn out to be so broad and complex that it will be necessary to help the user to get oriented in it. This support can be provided by some version of a simple expert system.

Second, the metadata can perform some functions that are essentially beyond the scope of the "cardfile" metaphor. In particular, it can do consistency checking, exception handling, serve as a dispatcher to ensure timely "data supply," provide some elements of logical inference on the data, etc.

Third, the ultimate purpose of data objects is to perform certain computational procedures on them, in order to solve certain application problems within the framework of some models. In this quality, objects must allow an exact structural and operational specification, including the possibility of organizing a computational network over them. Functions of the level "simple expert system" can be supported, to a large extent, by the linguistic processor described above.

3. Integration of the NL-shell into an industrial geoinformational system

In the environmental domain, a considerable part of the user access to the data is expected to be conducted within a certain geoinformational system (GIS). Now we describe our approach to elaborate a practical architecture for integrating a natural language shell into the industrial GIS.

The choice of the well-known GIS MapInfo was influenced by the following reasons.

- MapInfo is described as a typical representative of modern commercial GIS. It enables one to represent on the map various data from statistics, ecology, planning, land usage, etc. MapInfo combines numerous means for working with maps and other graphic forms with data processing facilities of DBM Systems. In particular it includes the SQL language extended by spatial data types and operations.
- MapInfo has an open architecture with built-in means of programming and user interface construction (the MapBasic environment), which makes it easy to build applications and use them.

The MapInfo query language enables one to combine graphic and alphanumeric queries, and provides a graphic representation of the output. This is important for spatial databases when they are used in interactive mode. Similarly to all such languages, the MapInfo query language is oriented to professional users. For instance, a query which displays all cities in the states with population of more than 4 million looks like this:

*select * from BIGTOWNS where (obj within any*
(select obj from GERMANY where Population > 4000000))

In this case, an NL-interface could simplify essentially access to data for a non-professional user.

The implemented strategy of integration of a NL shell into the MapInfo follows the GIS data processing technology. All data in MapInfo are stored as tables, each consisting of several files. Non-spatial attributes are represented as separate files. The GIS enables browsing maps, lists and pictures, and supports automatic correspondences between the various data representations. In particular, as soon as an object has been selected in one of the representations, it is marked (e.g., by color) in the other ones.

An SQL query generates an output in the form of a list which is then universally processed as a temporary table. This proves that natural language access can also provide all manipulation facilities supported by MapInfo.

As an example, we have chosen a map of districts which belong to the Novosibirsk administrative unit ("oblast"). They are described by a table which contains, in particular: capital, population, air pollution, water pollution.

The resulting NL interface processes, for example, the following queries.

Where is the maximal atmospheric pollution?
Display the districts with minimal atmospheric pollution.
Show the districts with maximal water pollution.
Are there towns with population more than one million?
Give the biggest towns.
Display the districts with average atmospheric pollution.
Display the districts with average water pollution and average atmospheric pollution.
Indicate the biggest towns with average atmospheric pollution.
Show districts with population more than 50 and air pollution more than 4.

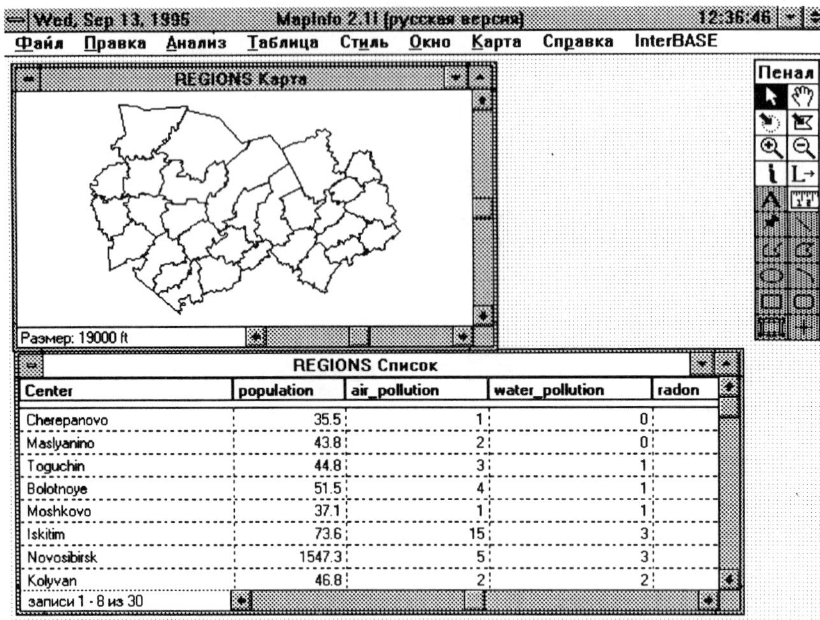

Figure 2

Natural language queries are processed by a MapBasic program which runs in the MapInfo environment as follows. The first picture (Figure 2) demonstrates the MapInfo panel displaying a map of the Novosibirsk oblast with its districts and a table which reports certain data about each district. Natural language queries are entered via the dialog box activated by an InterBASE menu item (see Figure 3).

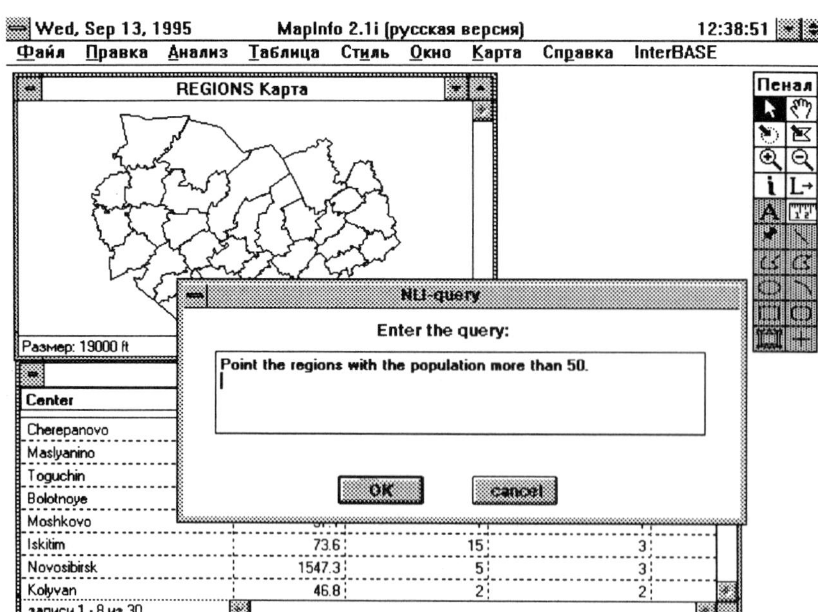

Figure 3

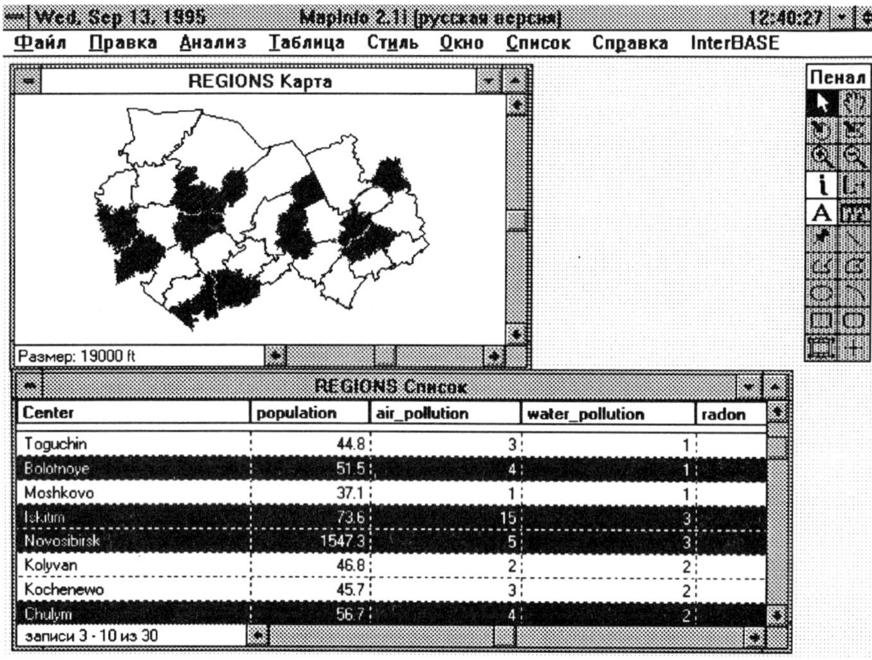

Figure 4

The query is then passed to the InterBASE system. The output is displayed in the form of a MapInfo list and a map where the selected districts are indicated (Figure 4).

One more example is given in Figures 5, 6.

The use of the NL-interface within an industrial GIS essentially enhances the end-user access to environmental data and thus justifies the application of this kind of interface. On the other hand, it provokes some new types of user behavior and implementation issues.

One of them concerns the use of words with exact mathematical semantics, e.g., *average, maximal, minimal,* etc. When the user asks the system to show the districts with the average atmospheric pollution he or she does not expect that sometimes the answer will be empty. However, it's very probable that there are no districts where the atmospheric pollution is exactly equal to the average value calculated for all districts. To make the interface more friendly, we use text substitutions which include the corresponding intervals of values.

Another feature relates to possibilities for direct indication and choice of objects on the map. This means that the system must support processing of "mixed" queries which include deixis like

*What is water pollution in **this** district?*

where ***this*** stands for indication of a certain part of the map made by a mouse or joystick.

Other examples are:

*What is the average population in **these** regions?*

where ***these*** stands for several parts of the map or

*What pollutants are found in **this** lake and in **this** river? or ... both in **this** and **this** regions?*

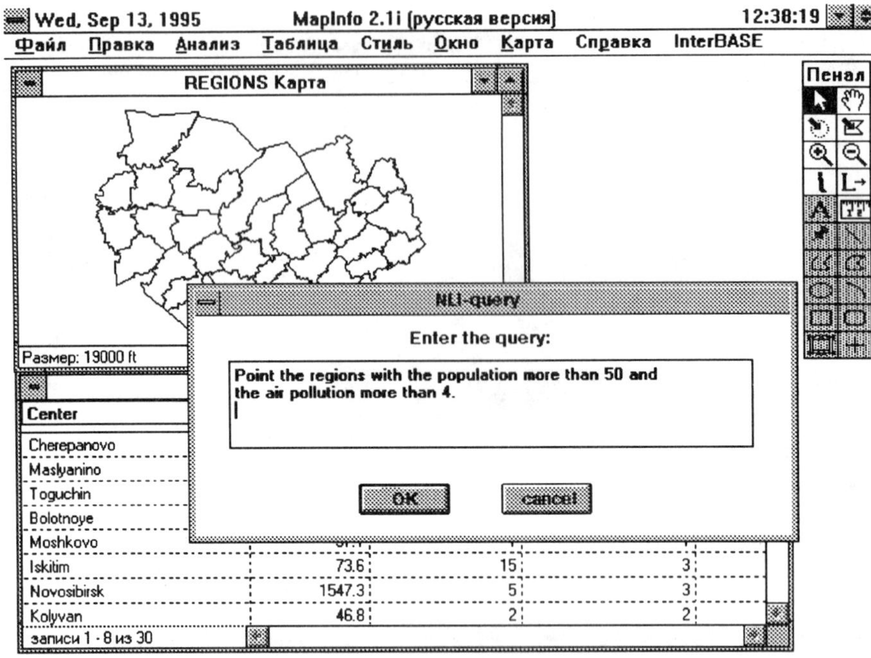

Figure 5

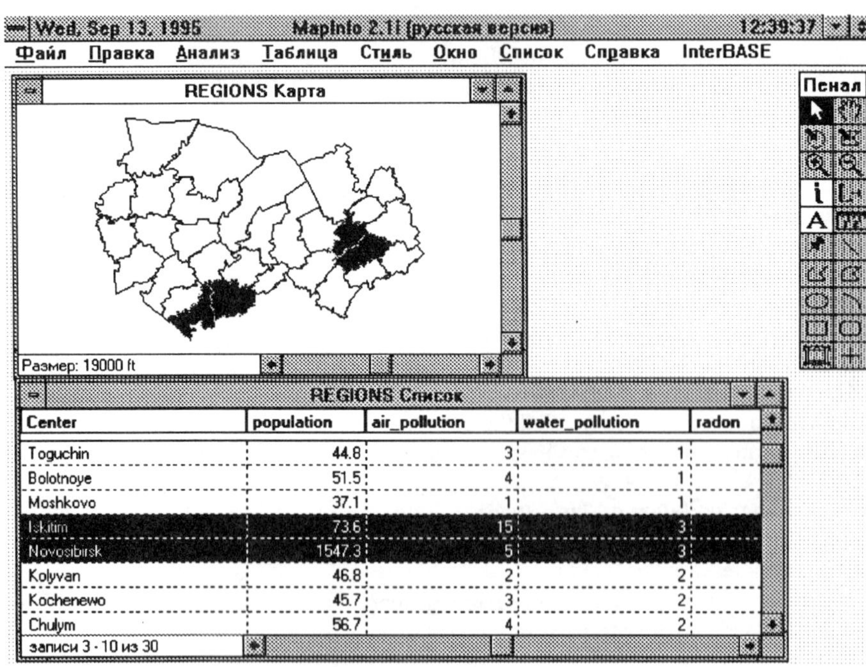

Figure 6

4. Brief characteristic of the InterBASE technology

The InterBASE technology and the implemented InterBASE system are based on:

- semantic-oriented (SO) analysis,
- process of automatical constructing of the initial working version of the L-processor by extracting its components from the database and
- means aimed to support, if necessary, the process of preprocessor improvement.

The SO-parser as applied to (relational) data base distinguishes several types of semantical items. They include attribute and table names, attribute values, relations, predicates, functions, etc. Each item is associated with one or several semantical orientations which could be quite often specified in terms of attribute values. For instance, once the item "35" is met in the query related to a personal data it is initially attributed with a set of semantical orientations such as {age, house_number, group_number, salary}. In principle, the (artificial) query like "2500 age salary 35" could be then successfully processed according to pure SO-analysis scheme by integrating of items for which the intersection of their semantical orientations is not empty. In practice, to eliminate arising multiple variants some parsing rules used in the InterBASE system involve certain pieces of word order or word adjacency.

To describe it very briefly, the automatical process of initial constructing includes the following steps.

The InterBASE system determines and establishes joins of tables using equal attribute names. Then it scans data files and automatically identifies data items.

The numerical items which are met in a certain column of a table are used to determine numerical data intervals. Thus, for example, by scanning the POPULATION column the system can infer and then store the fact that the population of a capital can be, say, from 200,000 to 2,000,000.

The non-numerical items are automatically processed and put into the vocabulary. Roughly speaking, the vocabulary description for the item from the attribute column A is "a value of A." For instance, suppose that while scanning the SPECIES column the system finds the item *trout*. It is put into the vocabulary with semantical identification as "a value of SPECIES." Each vocabulary item can have more than one semantical identification, e.g., *Stuttgart* could be described both as a land capital and an ordinary city.

Simultaneously, the system detects some part of lexical structure for the attribute values. Thus, if the system scans the attribute PHONE_NUMBER it can find that a set of values can correspond to one of the patterns: DDD-DD-DDD, DD-DDD-DDD, ... where D means "any digit."

Having extracted the words from the data files, the system extends the informational part of the constructed system, i.e., the vocabulary. To this end, it combines the set of "universal" or "a priori known" words with the words extracted from the data files. For example, universal words include *more, maximum, less than, find,* etc.

Having extracted the numerical boundaries and lexical patterns, the system extends the operational part of the system, i.e., extends the set of "universal" or "a priori embedded" production rules of parsing (the rules of translation).

Here is an example of actions which are fulfiled by a very simple universal rule for query processing:

"An attribute name AN followed by an attribute value AV should be transformed into AN EQUALS AV under the condition that AN and AV have the same semantical identification."

After all of the above-mentioned steps of automatical processing are completed, the system generates a preprocessor ready to be integrated into the DBMS.

An experienced user can, of course, improve the quality of this preprocessor by defining new words, by supplying some types of additional information about structural properties of the subject domain, etc.

5. Conclusion

Along with queries translation described in this paper, the natural language shells for environmental and ecological domains will include other types of technologies and systems (also based on semantic-oriented analysis) which had been implemented earlier in our works and applied for several subject domains.

The first one is intended to translate short natural language descriptions of the field observations into the data base contents. In this case local syntactic analysis is involved, in particular, for the recovery of ellipsis, for certain kinds of anaphora resolution, for the determination of arguments for the symmetric semantic predicate, etc. On the other hand, the semantic-oriented analysis not only simplifies syntactic irregularities processing but falicitates transition from the single-sentence analysis to the analysis of narratives [7].

The second system InText relates to processing of queries addressed to textual data such as ecolological state reports, environment descriptions, laws and regulations, etc. Here, the NL interface can work upon previously indexed fragments. This indexing — manual or automatical — is performed by the special InText component which simultaniously transfers the associated key-words into the NL shell and integrates them into the linguistic preprocessor. This results in a possibility for end-users to put their queries in natural language and get answers in a form of corresponding textual fragments [8].

Due to social and other reasons environmental information and communication systems practically require easy access to data and therefore this field gives a good possibility for building of applied system with the highest level of the user interface. In addition, the complexity and specific problems of environmental field give new challenges for researches in natural language processing.

References

[1] Narin'yani A.S., Interaction with a limited object domain — ZAPSIB project. In: Proc. of COLING-80, Tokyo, 1980.

[2] Narin'yani A.S., Intelligent Software Technology for the New Decade. Commun. ACM 34, 6 (Jun.1991), pp. 60-67.

[3] Trapeznikov S.P., The System for the Development of Linguistic Processors. In: Artificial Intelligence II. Methodology, Systems, Applications. Amsterdam, North-Holland, 1987, pp. 332-339.

[4] Dinenberg F., Trapeznikov S., Kuchin S., InterBASE — Natural Language Interface System for popular Commercial DBMSs. In: Proc. of East-West Conference on Artificial Intelligence, Moscow, 1993, pp.189-193.

[5] Günther O., Riekert W.-F., The Design of GODOT: An Object-Oriented Geographic Information System. IEEE Data Engineering Bulletin, Aug. 1993.

[6] Schütz T., Der Umwelt-Datenkatalog Niedersachsen — Informationsmanagement für den Umweltschutz. In: Workshop "Integration von Umweltdaten", Kernforschungszentrum Karlsruhe, Bericht KfK-5187, pp. 20-30, August 1993.

[7] Kononenko I.S., Text typological features and understanding model. In: Proc. of International Workshop on Computational Linguistics and its Applications, Kazan, 1995, pp.159-164. (In Russian)

[8] Neverov I.V., Construction of information systems by means of the InText technology. In: Methods and Tools of Program Development, Novosibirsk, Institute of Informatics Systems, 1994, pp.173-180. (In Russian).

Applications of Natural Language to Information Systems
R.P. van de Riet et al. (Eds.)
IOS Press, 1996

Capturing Information on Behaviour with the RADD-NLI: A Linguistic and Knowledge Based Approach

Edith Buchholz *Antje Düsterhöft* *Bernhard Thalheim*
Department of Computer Science
Technical University Cottbus
Cottbus, Germany
{duest,thalheim}@informatik.tu-cottbus.de

Abstract. In this paper we illustrate how information on behaviour can be captured from natural language with the RADD-NLI. The behavioural information contained in verbal descriptions of processes is transformed into the RADD-NLI process model of characteristic processes. This process model is then integrated into the knowledge base of the RADD-NLI. Although taken from a specific domain this model is abstract enough to form the basis for further applications with synonym relations. Processes coming up in the user dialogue will be matched against the knowledge base. A dialogue control is activated if a mismatch occurs or for the detail discussion of captured processes with the user. Linguistic knowledge, especially antonymous verb pairs, is considered to decide whether a captured process will be integrated into the structural database design and/or the process list of the design.
Keywords: Natural Language Interface, Conceptual Database Design

1 Introduction

In most cases a database will be used for complex processes. In order to be able to maintain the database we have to define transactions. The *behaviour* of the database can help to make the system more efficient and faster and thus to save time and money. So, the acquisition of prospective processes of the application and their operating conditions is one of the important aspects in designing databases.
Behaviour has been studied for several years, especially the aspects of behaviour modeling. The aim of this paper is to illustrate how information on behaviour can be *captured* from natural language utterances as a first step towards a complex behaviour modeling process.
Some approaches have shown the possibility of extracting structural (e.g.[TjoB93]), semantic (e.g.[GolS91]) and behaviour information (e.g.[BurR95], [KenW91]) from natural language. Because of the ambiguity and fuzziness of natural language all these approaches result in a vague design which has to be validated. For that reason our aim of a natural language design interface is *a first rough design*. But on the other hand the natural language gives designers which have no experience with database design and are not familiar with formal constructions the possibility to learn how to work with the model. In addition a natural language description of a database contains complex information on structure and semantics as well as behaviour which can easily be seen.

The task, therefore, is to develop a natural language tool that can discover this information and transform it into a database design.

The Natural Language Design Tool. We have implemented a knowledge-based *Natural Language Interface* ([BucCDMT95]) for the developement of a skeleton design as one component of the workbench *Rapid Application and Database Design* (RADD) ([AlbABDT95]). (RADD has been developed on the basis of the extended, *Higher-order Entity-Relationship Model* (HERM) [Tha96]).
The RADD-NLI analyses natural language utterances syntactically, semantically (in the linguistic sense) and pragmatically. The results of the syntax analysis are syntax trees. The semantic roles of a given input will be defined within the semantic analysis. The pragmatical interpretation is a transformation of the syntax trees and semantic roles into a database design. In general a compiler construction approach is the basis for the natural language interpretation. A German lexicon [BucD96] is used which contains German words, semantical items, common sense entries and synonym as well as antonym entries.
In the RADD-NLI, processes are the basis - the statics - for the structural design. Processes are mainly represented by verbs ([Bie88], [Jac83]) and are used to identify the structural elements within a sentence. Semantic roles ([BucMT96]) like theme or cause are defined on the basis of a *verb classification* and are used to initialize heuristics to interpret the different words/ phrases of a natural language utterance [Due96].
The design dialogue with the user focuses on missing elements in the design. That means, a special dialogue control [DueLT96] analyses the given design as well as user characteristics and initializes questions for clarifying details of the design. For the dialogue an inside-out design strategy [Tha93] is used.
In a natural language dialogue the designer describes the application as a first step in the design process. The results of this description will be a structural skeleton and a candidate set of semantic constraints as well as information on behaviour. The designer can validate these results by means of other RADD-tools (e.g. a graphical editor, a semantics checker or a behaviour handler) via a Data Dictionary.
The prototype implementation of the RADD-NLI has been developed in Prolog.

Capturing behavioural information with the RADD-NLI. Information on behaviour is represented within the RADD over possible rows of database states and the conditions of database states on the basis of a given structural design. Therefore, we focuse within the RADD-NLI on the follwing aspects:

1. the acquisition of comprehensive information on possible processes of an application,
2. the definition of the operating conditions of processes,
3. the decision whether a process will be 'materialized' and (Materialized is used to express an integration of a process into the structure *and* the process list of the design. If a process is not materialized it is entered into the process list only.)
4. the integration of our behaviour approach into the existing structural and semantical interpretation. [1]

[1] [Ort83] subdevides the natural language used in the construction context into 'structural words' and 'theme words'. The RADD-NLI interpretation focused on 'structural words' in order to acquire a structural and semantical database design. The strategy for getting information on behaviour is concentrated on the 'theme words'. So we have to show how specific knowledge about theme words

In general, we handle the processes in an abstract manner without direct relations to the prospective database system.

Our approach. The acquisition of information on behaviour with the RADD-NLI is based on the following ideas:

- The starting point for capturing behavioural information for the database design process are *characteristic* processes of an application.
- An identified process of a natural language input is *used for matching* with the RADD-NLI process model within the knowledge base.
- The knowledge base will be developed *starting from one application* and can then be applied to other applications.
- Linguistic knowledge is used to define *decision constraints for materializing processes*, i.e.including them into the structure and the process list of the design.
- An *intelligent dialogue control* decides whether the details of assumptions about processes will be discussed with the user or not.

The following sections deal with the general demonstration of the ideas resulting from special linguistic knowledge: *synonymous* and *antonymous* entries in the RADD-NLI dictionary. [2]

2 The development and use of a knowledge base

The first step in building a knowledge base for capturing information on behaviour is to identify processes within the natural language input of the user. Abstracting from these processes we can define a common process model. The analysis of processes in natural language utterances starts with a specific application. But we also show relations to other related applications.

2.1 How do the processes occur in natural language utterances?

The user describes in natural language utterances the application; he/ she gives a representation of the application. It is well-known that *verbs* are used for describing processes as well as for characterizing things. Our verb classification is used to classify *verbs of movement (location/ possession)* [BucD96] which form the main verb group within the process context of database design. This verb group is characterized by the change of objects.

It is a fact that different users will describe the same process in different words (e.g. 'signieren' (sign)/ 'kennzeichnen' (marking); 'einordnen' (put in order)/ 'einstellen' (arrange)). This is also valid for different applications. One and the same process can have different verbal representations. So, we 'rent a car', 'lease a house', 'hire a car' etc., i.e. we pay money for something in order to be allowed to use it. These three processes have the

can be integrated.

[2]Our verb classification is only used to decide which class of verbs are interesting or not in the context of behaviour modeling. In reason of capturing rows of database states we use a rough verb classification and we do *not* focuse on a more specific (one-) word classification. We are concentrating on verb pairs, verb groups and speech acts (cf. [Due96]).

Figure 1: A part of the library process model

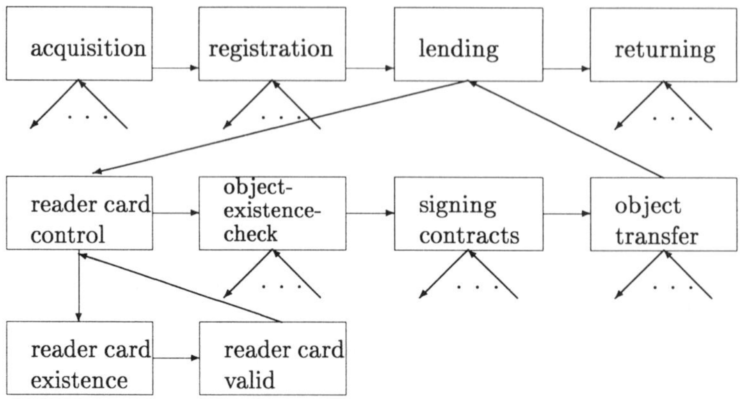

same characteristics but their verbal representation is different.
In the following we choose one expression for naming a process. The other synonymous expressions we find in the synonym dictionary of the RADD-NLI.

2.2 Integration of the process model into the knowledge base

There are several approaches for describing process models (e.g. [HarSJHK94]) and process flows (e.g. [SchuJKB94]). We are *not* interested into an general and abstract way of representing processes like e.g. *Troll* [HarSJHK94]. We only use the term 'process model' in order to describe *characteristic processes* coming *from natural language utterances* of our *specific application area.* Characteristic processes, in our sense, are processes which are usually executed in an application class and which can identitfy an application. Each application of an application class has specific processes and general (characteristic) processes.

The RADD-NLI process model is integrated into the knowledge base and includes the abstract processes, the objects possible in the processes and the representations.
We do not distinguish for modeling between a process and the condition for a process. All such processes of the process model are 'and-connected' (*sequential*). We represent a condition of a process as a process. The time aspect (the time connection of processes) is defined by the order of the processes. The processes order is described by *pre* and *post relations* of the process. *The process model represents the positive case of a process flow only.* That means a process has to be finished in order to start the next. Negative flows will be seen as non-characteristics of the application. The user dialogue can initiate a question which will be used to capture these details.

We classify the following abstractions: *main* and *sub*ordinated processes. An application has different main processes which consist of processes. A sub process can again subordinate several ordered sub processes. Sub processes are seen as detailed descriptions of the relevant process. The resulting process model is useful to consider as a hierachy of processes.

Figure 2: A part of the German frame representation of the library process model

```
Process -Frame: acquisition
          ID: acquisition
          TYP: main
          PRE: acquisition
          POST: registration
          REP: [ erwerben, kaufen, akquirieren]
          OBJ: [lending-object(OBJ)]
Process-Frame: registration
          ID: registration
          TYP: main
          PRE: acquisition
          POST: lending
          REP: [ aufbewahren, verwalten, erschliessen, katalogisieren,
                 signieren, eintragen, aussondern, magazinieren]
          OBJ: [lending-object(OBJ)]
Process-Frame: lending
          ID: lending
          TYP: main
          PRE: registration
          POST: returning
          REP: [ausleihen, entleihen, einsehen, benutzen, durchblättern]
          OBJ: [lending-object(OBJ), lending-subject(OBJ2)]
Process-Frame: reader card control
               ID: reader card control
               TYP: sub
               PRE: lending
               POST: object existence
               REP: [existieren, haben, vorzeigen, kontrollieren]
               OBJ: [reader card, lending-subject(OBJ2)]
Process-Frame: reader card existence
               ID: reader card existence
               TYP: sub
               PRE: reader card control
               POST: reader card valid
               REP: [existieren, haben, [vorhanden,sein]]
               OBJ: [reader card, lending-subject(OBJ2)]
Process-Frame: reader card valid
               ID: reader card valid
               TYP: sub
               PRE: reader card existence
               POST: reader card control
               REP: [prüfen, kontrollieren]
               OBJ: [reader card, lending-subject(OBJ2)]
Process-Frame: object existence check
...
```

Each process has one or several *basic objects.* [3] The objects which are necessary for an action are integrated into the model as variables. Figure 2 shows a part of the frame representation of the library process model. (The representations of the processes are given in German.) The object variables can be exemplified in a design dialogue by the semantic roles belonging to a verb.
The connections between main and sub processes are shown by the objects. A sub process has to have at least one object of the corresponding main process.

A process is identified if a presentation of the process is found and the basic objects are matched. In this case we have to assume subordinated processes and have to discuss them with the user (see section 4).

Figure 1 shows a part of the library process model. The frame representation of the processes is directly transformed into facts of the Prolog knowledge base.
The application type 'library' has 4 main processes: acquisition, registration, lending and returning. So, the process 'Rückgabe' (returning) will only be initialized if the process 'Ausleihe' (lending) has been executed. The condition and, in our case, the process 'Ausweiskontrolle' (reader card control) implies a test of the existence and an expiration date-test of the identity card.

2.3 Adapting the process model to other applications

We have illustrated a library process model which is integrated into the knowledge base as a starting point. The acquisition of behavioural information depends on the knowledge base.
It is not realistic to assume that we can make knowledge available in this way for all applications. We can use our approach only for such *applications as are characterized by the class of main processes* illustrated in the library process model. Similar processes are:

Lending processes. One class of adaptation are lending processes. The class of lending processes includes the video library, the costume agency or the rent-a-car business, among others. For the database design only the objects of the processes are different. The lending object can be 'book', 'microfich' (in the library case) or 'car' (in a rent-a-car application). The main processes within this class of application are the same. The specific verbs identifying a process can be matched using synonymous representations; e.g. 'borrow' (in the library case) or 'rent' (in the rent-a-car application).

Storing applications. Another adaptation is the class of storing applications. In contrast to the class of lending applications the storage and sale applications do not have a returning process. The central process is a change of a possession or a local movement of objects.
For the identification of processes synonyms of verbs and nouns are used. So the library process 'Ausweiskontrolle' (reader card control) is 'Vertragskontrolle' (the control of a contract) in connection with a storing application . A synonymous relation of 'Ausweis' (reader card) and 'Vertrag' (contract) has been identified.

[3]Our general approach is functional oriented. But it is possible to focus on the basic objects for an object-oriented view (cf. [Due96]).

Administration applications. Another kind of abstraction is the registration process. So we can specify the class of administration processes including e.g. address administration. Synonyms can be defined for the identification of related processes in natural language utterances.

Each adaptation of the library knowledge base is a generalization. Processes of a specific application can only be assumed in a general way. The dialogue with the designer is used to clarify whether a specific process is relevant for the application or not.

3 Decision constraints for the materialization of processes

The complex acquisition of behavioural information comprises the following aspects. The information about the processes has to be identified from the natural language. Otherwise the identified knowledge has to be discussed with the user and integrated into the design. The aim of the discussion is to find out wether a process has to be inserted into the structural design *and* the process list of the design (materialzed or not). In the latter case, a process has to be inserted into the structure or the process list of the design.
In natural language complementary processes are often expressed by antonyms.

3.1 Linguistic characterization of antonymous verbs

In the developement of the knowledge base we make use of a class of words called *'antonyms'*. Antonyms are words of contrastive or opposite meaning. These words can be nouns, adjectives but also verbs. For the analysis of processes we are interested in *antonymous verbs.* This class is characterized by word pairs. Antonymous verbs are connected by the *same main object(s)* where the one verb (called basic verb) represents the pre-condition of another verb. That means one process can only be executed if the other process have happend. This process class is called *reversible.*

- 'immatrikulation' (to check in) - 'exmatrikulation' (to check out)
  main objects: subject (e.g. guest or student), locative object (e.g. hotel or university)
- 'ausleihen' (lending) - 'zurückgeben' (returning)
  main objects: subject (e.g. user), theme (e.g. book), locative object (e.g. library), temporal object (e.g. lending time)
- 'hinsetzen' (sit down) - 'aufstehen' (get up)
  main objects: subject (e.g. boy), locative object (e.g. couch)
- 'aufbauen' (build) - 'abreissen' (demolish)
  main objects: subject (e.g. building contractors), theme (e.g. building)
- 'kaufen' (acquire) - 'verkaufen' (sell)
  main objects: subject (e.g. library), theme (e.g. books)
- 'einstellen' (put in) - 'herausnehmen' (put out)
  main objects: subject (e.g. user), theme (e.g. book), locative object (e.g. shelves).

Many of these verb pairs are basically domain independent. Nevertheless, domain dependent verb pairs can be defined.

The natural language lexicon plays an important role within the RADD-NLI. Words, phrases, semantic units, synonyms and antonyms are stored in the lexicon. An antonymous word pair can be identifyied in two different ways.
Many of these verb pairs can be identified by using construction rules of the German language. Prefixes like 'zurück', 'ex' or 're' indicate these words [Bie88]. A antonymous verb pair will included if a contrastive prefix has appeared and the possible objects of each verb are the same. Self-defined antonymous pairs can also be included.
Each captured verb will be matched with possible contrastive verb pairs and checked for the objects.

3.2 The handling of antonymous verb pairs in the context of database design

For the illustratiion of the database design handling of antonymous verb pairs we use the following design example:

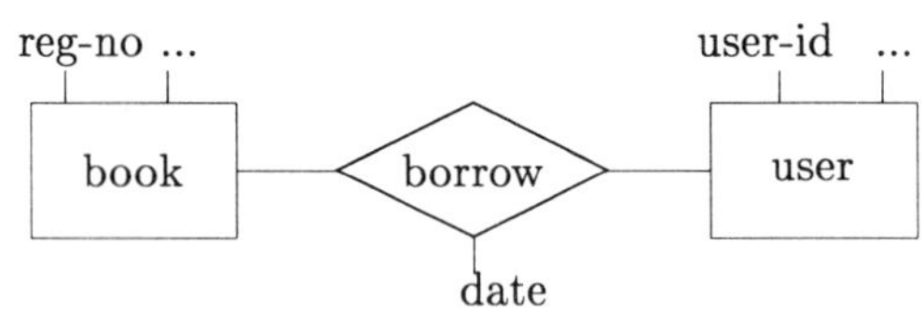

The example presents a structural design of the fact that *user borrow books*. The corresponding relational database could be contain the following table:

borrow	reg-no	user-id	date
	1969	123	270596
	1846	456	290596

The antonymous verb of 'entleihen' (borrow) is 'zurückgeben' (returning).
Using the linguistic knowledge illustrated above we know that both verbs 'work' with the same objects and that one verb of the pair is the prerequisite for the other verb. So, if the basic verb is given the operations resulting from the other verb of the verb pair have to be included in the same table. Besides, the operations are *insert*, *modify* or *delete* operations.
In the case of the process *'zurückgeben' (returning)* a delete operation for the *'entleihen' (borrow)* table has to be initiated.

Therefore, we handle the occurance of antonymous verb pairs in the following way:

- *Verbs of verb pairs are complements.*
  The occurance of one verb of the verb pair indicates the presence of both verbs. A special dialogue control is needed (see Section 5).
- *The basic verb will be materialzed.*
  The results of the pragmatic interpretation of the basic verb will be included into the structural design and the process list of the design.

- *The other verb of a verb pair will be inserted into the process list of the design only.*
  If the basic verb of a verb pair is given the other verb is only included into the process list. Otherwise, the natural language input is analyzed using the pragmatic strategy. The resulting objects are included into the structural design. The direct pragmatic interpretation of the verb (only) is not included into the structural design. A question about the missing basic verb is used to replace the interpretation of the antonymous verb.

4 The acquisition of behaviour in the RADD-NLI

For a given application a knowledge base including the process model (as shown above) is integrated into the RADD-NLI. In addition we can use entries within the German lexicon which refer to synonymous verbs and antonymous word pairs.

Within a dialogue the user will be ask to give a natural language description of the application. A natural language input is first analyzed linguistically (syntax, semantics). Within the pragmatic interpretation the acquisition of information on structure and semantics as well as on behaviour will be started. The dialogue control checks the resulting design and the resulting user characteristics in order to build a design task catalogue. A new question concerning the task with the highest priority will be initiated.

The behaviour interpretation cycle. Each natural language input is checked for verbs which match with a knowledge base representation. In this case tasks concerning the pre and post processes are put into the dialogue control.
In a next step the verb is tested whether it is part of an antonymous verb pair. If it is a basic verb of a contrastive word pair it will be inserted into the structural design (using the pragmatical heuristics) and into the process list of the design.
The following interpretation cycle is used:

```
input:    natural language utterance (NLU)
          knowledge base (KB)
          task catalogue (TC)
          German lexicon (GL)
input/ output:   structural design (SG)
                 process list (PL)
cycle:    FOR each NLU DO
          BEGIN  linguistic-analyzes(↓NLU, ↑SynTree, ↑SemRoles)
                 search-verb(↓SynTree, ↑VERB)
                 IF verb-matches-kb(↓VERB, ↓KB)
                 THEN new-task(↓VERB, ↑↓TC)
                 prag-interpretation(↓↑SG, ↓↑PL)
                 IF verb-in-verbpairs(↓VERB, ↓GL)
                 THEN   IF not-basicverb(↓VERB, ↓GL)
                        BEGIN  change-design(↓VERB, ↓↑SG)
                               new-task(↓VERB, ↑↓TC)
                        END
          END.
```

Figure 3: Realization of the RADD-NLI process models via Higher-order relationships

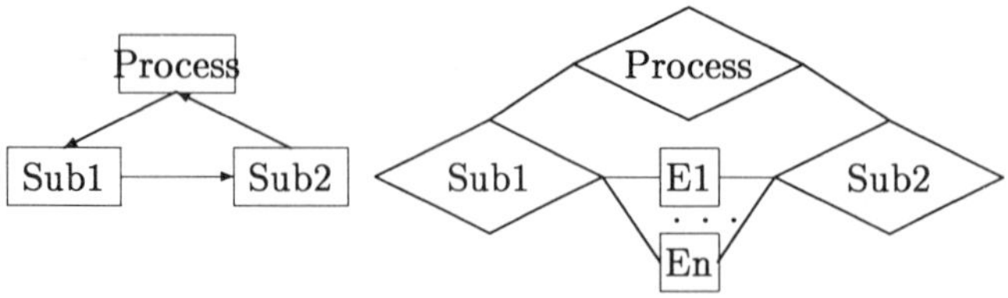

RADD-NLI process model Design using higher-order relationships

HERM constructs as the basis of the design. The execution of the interpretation cycle results in a structural design, the process list of the design and further design tasks. For the description of the structure and the processes special HERM contructs will be used.

So, the materialization of the sequential and subordinated library processes is realized with *higher order relationship* (see figure 3). Higher-order relationships are describing relationships over relationships. The difference to the representation into the knowledge base is the missing order of the processes.

The process list is described by a logical form of the process flow.

The HERM description of the structural design and the process list will be inserted into the RADD-Data Dictionary.

The behaviour handler [Ste94] checks and validates theses results.

The behavioural tasks within the task catalogue. The dialogue design task catalogue contains different kinds of tasks. One of these kinds are behavioural tasks. The behavioural tasks can be classified into tasks which are necessary and tasks which are optional. The necessary tasks include questions about missing processes, e.g. missing basic verbs. The optional questions will be initiated by the user characteristic to discuss details of processes. Optional behavioural task are including e.g. questions about subordinated processes or specific processes of the application which do not match with the knowledge base.

5 Conclusion/ Future work

We have shown the general approach to the acquisition of behavioural information with the RADD-NLI. The approach is based on linguistic knowledge and a process model integrated in the knowledge base. We have introduced an abstract process model which has been developed on the basis of one application and can be used for further applications. A process identified in a natural language utterance will be matched with the knowledge base over the possible natural language represenations of processes in the knowledge base. We see the power of the mechanism especially for user which have no database design experiences in getting complex information using one natural language verb.

Antonymous verb pairs are used to identify reversible processes which will be interpreted in a special way.

The dialogue control of the RADD-NLI will be used for the discussion of the processes and the process assumptions from the knowledge base as well as from the antonym lexicon. So, meaningful extensions of the design can be suggested to the user.
Future work will concentrat on two topics. Firstly, linguistic research on sentence structure and meaning concerning other applications is needed. The approach to behavioural information implies the easy adaptation to other applications. The question is whether the syntactic and semantic characteristics of the library application can be used for similiar applications.
Secondly, the user describes processes of application which are not integrated in the knowledge base. The dynamic updating of the knowledge base could be learned if a special user characteristics is developed.
Last, we will integrate linguistic knowledge on speech-acts into the system.

Acknowledgement. The authors are grateful to Meike Albrecht and Andreas Heuer for their helpful suggestions and clarifying comments.

References

[AlbABDT95] Albrecht, M.; Altus, M.; Buchholz, E.; Düsterhöft, A.; Thalheim, B.: The Rapid Application and Database Developement Workbench - A Comfortable Database Design Tool. In: Proc. Int. Conference on Advanced System Engineering (CAiSE), Finnland, 1995

[Bie88] Bierwisch, M., Motsch, W., Zimmermann, I. (Hrsg.): Syntax, Semantik und Lexikon. Berlin, Akademie Verlag, 1988

[BucD96] Buchholz, E., Düsterhöft, A.: The linguistic backbone of a natural language interface for database design. Forthcoming in: Literary and Linguistic Computing Vol.11, No. 4, Oxford University Press, 1996

[BucCDMT95] E. Buchholz, H. Cyriaks, A. Düsterhöft, H. Mehlan, B. Thalheim: Applying a Natural Language Dialogue Tool for Designing Databases. In: Proc. Int. Workshop on Applications of Natural Language to Databases (NLDB), France, 1995

[BucMT96] Buchholz, E.; Mehlan, H.; Thalheim, B.: Zur Interpretation von Possessiv-Beziehungen im RADD-NLI. In: Tagungsband Workshop 'Natürlichsprachlicher Entwurf von Informationssystemen', Tutzing, Germany, 1996

[BurR95] Burg, J.F.M.; van de Riet, R.P.: COLOR-X: Linguistically-based Event Modeling: A General Approach to Dynamic Modeling. In: Proc. Int. Conference on Advanced System Engineering (CAiSE), Finnland, 1995

[Due96] Düsterhöft, A.: Zur Natürlichsprachlichen Interaktiven Unterstützung im Datenbankentwurf. Dissertation, Fakultät für Mathematik, Naturwissenschaften und Informatik, Technische Universität Cottbus, 1996

[DueLT96] Düsterhöft, A.; Lewerenz, J.; Thalheim, B.: Datenbankentwurf im natürlichsprachlichen Dialog: Zur Dialogsteuerung im RADD-NLI. In: Tagungsband Workshop 'Natürlichsprachlicher Entwurf von Informationssystemen', Tutzing, Germany, 1996

[GolS91] Goldstein, R.C.; Storey, V.C.: Commonsense Reasoning in Database Design. In: Proc. Int. Conference on Entity-Relationship Approach (ERA), USA, 1991

[HarSJHK94] Hartmann, T.; Saake, G.; Jungclaus, R.; Hartel, P.; Kusch, J.: Revised Version of the Modeling Language Troll (Version 2.0). Informatik-Bericht 94-03, Technische Universität Braunschweig, 1994

[Jac83] Jackendoff, R.: Semantics and cognition. MIT Press, Cambridge Mass., 1983

[KenW91] Kensing, F.; Winograd, T.: The Language/ Aktion Approach to Design of Computer Support for Cooperative Work: A Prelimary Study in Work Mapping. In: Stamper,

R.K. (Eds.): Collaborative Work, Social Communications and Information Systems, Elsevier Science Publisher B.V., North Holland, 1991

[Ort83] Ortner, E.: Aspekte einer Konstruktionssprache für den Datenbankentwurf. S.Toeche-Mittler Verlag, 1993

[SchuJKB94] Schuster, H.; Jablonski, S.; Kirshe, T.; Bussler, C.: A Client-Server Architecture for the Implementation of Workflow Management Systems. In: Proc. Int. Conference on Parallel and Distribute Information Systems, USA, 1994

[Ste94] Steeg, M.: From E-R to Optimal database schemes. Reihe Informatik I-7, TU Cottbus, 1994

[Tha96] Thalheim, B.: The Higher Order Entity Relationship Model. Forthcoming, Springer Verlag, 1996

[Tha93] Thalheim, B.: Database Design Strategies. Preprint 1993, Institut für Informatik, TU Cottbus

[TjoB93] Tjoa, A.M., Berger, L.: Transformation of Requirements Specifications Expressed in Natural Language into an EER Model. In: Proc. Int. Conference on Entity-Relationship Approach (ERA), USA, 1993

Applications of Natural Language to Information Systems
R.P. van de Riet et al. (Eds.)
IOS Press, 1996

NL Structures and Conceptual Modelling: The KISS Case

J. Hoppenbrouwers* B. van der Vos† S. Hoppenbrouwers*
*Katholieke Universiteit Brabant
Infolab, Dept. of Economics
Tilburg
The Netherlands
†Vrije Universiteit
Dept. of Computer Science
Amsterdam
The Netherlands
e-mail: hoppie@kub.nl, ajvdvos@cs.vu.nl, stijn@kub.nl

Abstract. As conceptual models are both the result of and subject to communication between domain experts and information analysts, it is of the highest importance to relate conceptual models to the language in which they are communicated. This relation requires the existence of a way in which elementary notions taken from conceptual modelling can be recognized in a natural language (such as English or Dutch). In this paper we show that it is possible to establish such a relation, providing an illustration concerning a limited set of concepts taken from semantic theory. We then propose to apply natural language analysis to some phases in the modelling process, and show that we can use morphosyntactic surface structures to identify concepts useful to (Object Oriented) conceptual modelling.

1 Introduction

An issue in the fields of Information Systems Design and Business Administration is the development of Information and Communication Systems. During the development of these systems, conceptual models (CM) are constructed and validated by both the information analysts and the domain experts involved in the development project. The models describe system structures independent of the implementation environment, and determine the functional properties of the systems to be developed. As the models are vital to the rest of the development project, it is crucial to find methods and techniques that can help us construct high-quality conceptual models.

A qualitatively good conceptual model yields a description of a certain domain that is sufficiently detailed, comprehensive, and accurate. When the properties of the domain are understood and discussed in natural language (NL), the model has to be related to the domain's NL description rather than to the domain itself. This is manifested through the use of NL forms characterizing the modelling primitives used by the method. For example, an object labeled *Library* refers to a particular physical or mental institution since the term *Library* is commonly accepted to refer to this institution. The same holds with respect to the relation between objects modeled. For example, a *Loan* is the result of a specific action on a particular *Book* also involving the *Library* and a particular *Member*.

It seems possible to achieve a tighter relation between CM and NL by using relations shared by the two, without the need for common knowledge representation as dealt with in CYC [15] and without the immediate need for a full-blown NL processing device.

The research described in this paper is part of the LIKE project [26, 27], which focuses on the application of linguistically oriented techniques in the area of Information and Communication systems. A subproject within LIKE is the *Grammalizer* project.[1]

The next section gives an overview of theory about relations between CM and NL. Section 3 briefly describes the KISS method. Section 4 shows useful parallels between CM and English. The potential application of these parallels is presented in Section 5. Finally, in Section 6 some conclusions and suggestions for future work are presented.

2 Related Work

Conceptual modelling is an essential phase in system development. Nowadays domain specialists and analysts together construct such models using interactive methods. These methods often depend in one way or another on NL. The elicitation of the CM from the domain specialist, the creation of the CM by the analyst, and the validation by both of them together are usually combined into one homogeneous process.

According to Mazza *et al.* [18], verification and validation must be done in close cooperation between analysts and domain specialists. During this procedure they check all quality aspects [16] of the CM, which thus causes the model to fulfill its communication, specification and documentation functions [30] properly. Correct use of NL in the context of the conceptual models improves the understandability of the models [3].

More and more approaches consider NL a useful aid; several heuristics are available to derive parts of an ER model [5] from a NL specification, and NIAM [19] is based on semi-formal analysis of sets of elementary NL sentences as a basis for CM construction. In [8] a somewhat similar procedure is proposed.

Other methods are directly based on NL analysis. DEMO [6] and SAMPO [1] study the communication taking place in the Universe of Discourse (UoD) and are defined on the basis of Speech Act Theory. KISS [14] offers a large set of both heuristics and procedures to extract model information from NL sentences, and directly uses some NL constructs to model the UoD.

A completely different approach to the use of NL as a modelling basis is shown in CPL [7]. Here a formal specification technique is proposed which makes use of NL constructs as defined in Functional Grammar (FG) [9], an NL representation formalism. COLOR-$\mathcal{X}$ [2] defines an informal diagram technique based on CPL.

The problem with most of the above approaches is that they do not identify any explicit relation between the CM and NL. To improve interaction with, and validation and comprehension of the model, it is necessary to identify bi-directional relations between (a subset of) NL and the model. An explanation facility or paraphrasing tool, which maps model constructs on NL structures [12], is a first step towards such an approach. Semantic validation [28, 29] is another way.

To achieve the mapping of all possible model constructions on NL constructions, one needs not only definitions of the modelling primitives that can be related to linguistic notions, but also definitions for the relations between them. Such relations are defined in, for example, Rhetorical Structure Theory [17]. This particular theory recognizes different relations between (parts of) texts. Based on binary relations such as *interpretation, condition*, and *evaluation*, a text can be structured. This mechanism is used as a basis for the explanation facility mentioned above.

[1]This project is financially supported by Senter, DIB508313.QID.

Other relations as seen in a linguistic environment can be found in conceptual graphs [24]. Here different concepts are connected by semantically oriented relations, which provide some restrictions imposed on the structure by real world knowledge of relations between concepts.

3 The KISS Approach to Conceptual Modelling

KISS [14] is a conceptual modelling method that heavily depends on NL analysis of texts that are supplied by domain specialists. Starting with textual real-world descriptions, KISS performs a grammatical analysis to extract subject, object, and action specifications that are subsequently used for lower-level modelling. During the whole modelling cycle, NL is used to communicate with the domain specialist.

Currently the KISS method depends on manual grammatical analysis by an experienced analyst. This often leads to a mix-up between information elicitation (by a specialized interviewer) and information modelling (by the analyst), because the analyst has ample room for interpretation of often unclear specifications.

Experience shows that the texts as produced by the domain specialists, even in cooperation with an interviewer, contain many sentences that are grammatically correct but either irrelevant for information modelling or semantically wrong due to a lack of understanding of the real world. Improving domain understanding is one of the obvious targets of information analysis, so a continuous process of backtracking and remodelling is inherent in the KISS approach. It does not aim for immediate correct coverage of the domain, since often the domain experts themselves do not have a sufficiently comprehensive mental model of their domain yet.

KISS information analysts cannot be required to have a firm background in linguistics; familiarity with secondary school grammar must be sufficient. As a consequence, the KISS method has been built on simple grammatical notions and a set of simplified heuristics. Despite these simplifications and generalizations, KISS is effective in knowledge extraction, and because of the rigid framework that contains numerous internal coherence checks, the resulting models quickly converge to a workable UoD description. These UoD descriptions are formal and can be used for automatic prototype generation, which is currently in production.

Because of the simple grammatical analysis required, it seems feasible to build a support tool for KISS analysis of NL sentences. Such a 'Grammalizer' should be the textual equivalent of traditional graphical CASE tools. As such, it should first provide a framework to embrace the KISS method, followed by support for heuristics and simple grammatical analysis to cover a part of the routine work.

4 Finding Parallels between Conceptual Models and Natural Language Structures

Both conceptual modelling and NL paraphrasing are used to describe a domain by means of their respective primitives and concepts. When relating the two methods of description, we need to differentiate between meaning and form in either approach. In (written) NL, form is laid down in word stems combined with morpho-syntax which in a more traditional context is often called *grammar*. FG explicitly separates semantics from morpho-syntactic expression rules. With respect to the CM techniques more

Relation	Definition	KISS expression
Result	The first concept, typically an action or activity, has the other concept as a result.	Gerund
Precondition	The first concept serves as a precondition for the other concept, typically an action or activity.	See text
Specialization	A hyponymic relation between concepts, not the same as the a role relation. [31]	'is a'
HAS_A	The traditional possessive relation.	—
PART_OF	Also known as the aggregation relation and perhaps the most prominent of meronymic relations [25].	—
Property	Indicates an attributive relationship.	Adjectives, adverbs

Table 1: Some candidate basic relations

or less the same holds. The arrows, boxes, etc. make up the syntax; the concepts and relations indicated by these graphical items are essential for interpretation of the model: determining its semantics.

As a preliminary expression of the underlying model semantics, an illustrative set of *candidate* concepts and relations is presented. These basic relations, shown in Table 1, will be used for purposes of examplification. The list can roughly be divided in two sections: an action-oriented part with basic concepts that are commonly used to describe actions, results, etc., and a structure-oriented part containing some concepts that tend to be used for describing e.g. properties. The *specialization* section has some features that call for a closer analysis; it appears that there are two types of ISA, with one type belonging in the action-oriented part and the other in the structure-oriented part.

Though clearly not a relation, we will need the concept *state* in the discussion of some of the relations mentioned in Table 1. In KISS [14], states are absent. The KISS method models the actions *between* states, and a state can thus be deduced from the known activity history of an object. Implementational restrictions (mainly on performance) may call for an explicit record of the last known state of an object, but KISS is a conceptual modelling language, not an implementation language.

4.1 Result

In the context of CM, we assume that every result has an associated action which caused it. Often this associated action is not contained in the same sentence as the result, but the action has to be present in the text at hand. Results without an associated action are considered to be of no value for conceptual analysis.

One of the ways of expressing results is through clauses, e.g. 'John forgot to buy food, so we had nothing to eat', where 'having nothing to eat' is the result. *Result* is defined in [9, p207] as 'a State of Affairs (SoA) presented as being established as a consequence of the SoA presented in the core predication.'

Another common way to describe a result is to use a nominal form, e.g. 'starvation'. Some nominal forms used to express results are directly derived from their initiating actions and can therefore be used to 'track down' those actions (e.g. 'to insure – the insurance')

Results of actions can be a number of things in KISS. Some actions only set a certain attribute of an object, others trigger a procedure, for example to calculate the sum of some numbers, and still others create new objects. Especially the last type of action is of interest to us. For example, the result of '**the library lends a book to a member**' is the fact that now a certain book is linked to a certain member, which determines or enables some future actions of both the library and the member. KISS models this type of result as a *gerund*, in this particular case '**the lending**'. A *lending* is a special kind of object, existence-dependent on two other objects (the book and the member), that has its own life cycle and applicable actions: it can be renewed, possibly even several times, and be ended.

A typical way of expressing a result using only a single word and maintaining an explicit link with the initiating action is, indeed, the *gerund* (also verbal noun) of a verb (cf. [20, 15.12n, 7.15-9, 17.54], [22, 1.78-83]. Many nominal forms derived from a verb are relevant in principle, though not all of the forms below are *typical* gerunds: *-ing* (the insuring), *-ance/ence* (the insurance), *-age* (the storage), *-ment* (the payment), *-al* (the refusal), *-ure* (the departure), *-(at)ion* (exploration) *-NONE* (the end), *-IRREGULAR* (the sight).

But we have also: *-er/-or* (driver/actor), *-ant* (inhabitant), *-ee* (employee). Neither of these three word forms are gerunds, and though they are clearly related to verbs, they are not straightforward nominalizations but (deverbal) agentive nouns [20, 17.52]. We have to be careful not to mix up nominalized verbs with just any nominalization.

4.2 Condition

We have the choice of extending an action with a proposition and to state that this proposition must necessarily be true before the action may be executed. This particular relation between action and proposition is commonly called a *precondition*. The same holds for postconditions, which entail that if a proposition is found to be true, some result must be evident (independent of the question how this result came to be).

In KISS, a condition can have either a dynamic nature (involving procedural structure: 'which set of actions can occur in which phase of the procedure?'), or a static nature (in which case a proposition is explicitly formulated). Since the latter type of condition is not all that prominent a feature of the KISS method, the less explicit dynamic conditions represent the bulk of KISS (pre)conditions. Most of these are contained in a submodel and have no specific linguistic vehicle to express them.

In NL, the typical form a precondition takes is that of an 'If ... then ... ' construction [20, 15.33ff], [22, 8.26]. There is an abundance of variations on the theme, however, including conditional markers with a semantic content richer than that of 'if', such as '**given that, as long as, assuming that, while,**' etc. NL actually includes conditions in a more uniform way than does KISS, which is possible because of the enormous flexibility of NL which enables it to apply general, clause-based forms to all sorts of clauses.

Triggers are a specific combination of a proposition and an action, in such a way that when the proposition (asynchronously) becomes true, the action must necessarily be executed. In procedural programming languages that support the trigger concept there is usually a tendency to use 'if ... then (... else)' for simple preconditions, and to use 'when ... do' for triggers. The linguistic difference between *if* and *when* in English also suggests this usage.

4.3 Specialization

Generally, a *specialization* of a (super) type is a more specific type than the super type: all properties of the supertype are also applicable to the specialized type. A specialization therefore adds properties, but a property can also be an additional constraint, effectively *restricting* some features of the specialization.

Contrarily, a *generalization* of a few types is created in hindsight, when some common properties seem interesting enough to isolate them and make them explicit. It is generally not true that the reverse of a specialization can be called a generalization; both are distinctly different ways of classifying object types. The keyword in both approaches is *property inheritance.*

Essential to both specialization and generalization is the fact that a certain instance of the subtype cannot change between the various subtypes. For example, a *potato* and a *tomato* are both *vegetables*, but a potato cannot change into a tomato. The subclass of an object is fixed when the object instance is created. Contrarily, a *person* can be both a *student* and a *library member* and switch between these roles at will. Taking on a role is an action that an object can perform. Roles that are played therefore are *not* a case of generalization/specialization and have no relation to inheritance.

Unfortunately, KISS mixes up some of the concepts presented in the former paragraphs. The role playing mechanism is called *specialization* (a *student* is a special *person*), and the inheritance mechanism that enables polymorphism is called *categorization.* KISS then confuses terminology even more by introducing the term *class* for a set of object instances that share an attribute value, and by using the same ISA symbol for both specialization and role playing. On top, these are by no means the only concepts which can be expressed by means of 'is a'.

'Is a' can be used for many predications of the subject, in which case the particular form of 'to be' is a copula (cf. [20, 2.16n]). Some related copular verbs are: 'to become, to look, to remain, to seem' (there are many other forms) [20, 16.21]. All copular verbs except 'to be' carry some extra information, so they cannot be simply swapped with 'to be'. The copular verb 'to become', for example, denotes the infinitely small moment in time where the state described in the predication begins. Thus, the extra semantic information in 'to become' is of a temporal nature. The KISS method only uses the one 'pure' copula: 'to be'.

Note that 'is' is such a common word that almost *any* relation can be formulated by means of it. A prominent example: meronymic subrelations need a typification (e.g. 'a part of') in addition to 'is'. In the case of a KISS ISA relation, we always talk about those cases in which only 'X is a Y' needs to be expressed (so without any extra relational specification like 'part of').

4.4 HAS-A

In its most specific, basic sense, a HAS-A relation is interpreted as 'x is the owner of y.' This is an often occuring relation between two objects which arguably is semantically parallel to any other property or relation. Whether or not the possessive is considered a relation of special importance is a matter of choice. Fact is that natural languages typically have specialized forms to express the possessive, which is a good indication that to NL users it is perhaps more basic than 'just any odd relation.' In a KISS context, however, the possessive is not considered any more relevant than any other attributive relation/property, and thus no special expression device is put forward.

In NL, 'to have' as a static verb ([20, 3.34]) often expresses 'possession of', but also, in a more general sense, 'association with' some object or property type (see Section 4.6; [11]. However, a number of other constructions can be used to express such relations [20, 17.38ff.], most prominently genitive (-*'s*) and *of* constructions (e.g. 'the change of affairs').

Note that 'has a' is also rather easily used as an alternative expression of the PART-OF relation (Section 4.5). We will have to decide whether such synonymy is acceptable in an analytic context, and would suggest it is not. It may seem a good idea to abolish the use of 'has a' in CM methods altogether, since it appears to contribute little to the analytic framework. Unfortunately, 'has a' is so common and pervasive that its use cannot be avoided in all cases. For example, expressing a property type without using 'has a' would force us to use rather unusual forms; there is no good alternative (see 4.6).

A useful rule of thumb could be: *If* 'X [to have] Y' is encountered in a sentence, it is best expressed by means of a structure parallel to 'Y [other verb] X'. For example: 'People have names' may be replaced by 'Names identify people'. It seems not a good idea to just make 'to have' passive, leading to '* is had by' cf. [20, 2.21n], and then replace this expression by the common to belong to, because this does not convey any information about the *specific* relationship between the two nouns. Unfortunately, there seems to be no sure-fire method yet to determine the verb to replace 'to have'; this is highly context-dependent.

4.5 PART-OF

PART-OF relations indicate meronymy, along with such relations as 'component of' and 'member of' (see below; for a comprehensive treatment of meronymy in database design, see [25]).

The KISS method includes no specific expression of PART-OF relations. However, general structures normally indicated by PART-OF relations occur throughout the KISS paradigm; it is just that they need not be made explicit.

The only way to put one's finger on meronymic relations in an NL context is to scan for one of its explicit key words, of which 'part of' is the most prominent. Admittedly, this is hardly a viable method. Meronymy in its generic sense is not a relation which can be *marked* in any way by the use of the very words *naming* the relations, such as 'part of', 'member of', and 'place in'. These specific words directly correspond to a number of sub-types of meronymy, which indicates that these subtypes, unlike their generic 'mother' meronymy, do have very direct parallels in natural language. The words identified with subtypes of meronymy according to [32, 4] are: *component of* (object), *member of* (collection), *portion of* (mass), (object) *made of stuff/material*, *phase of* (activity), *place in* (area), and *feature of* (event). Note that many of these expressions could be replaced by a simple 'part of' relation, which would decrease the information content of the expression considerably. Furthermore, note that it is not the 'is a' in 'is a part of' which is relevant; see 4.3.

4.6 Property

First a brief reflection on the difference between properties and attributes. If such a distinction is made at all, it must be sought in the difference between *static* attributes[2] and *dynamic* properties[3]. If we do maintain this distinction, *red* is a typical attribute, whereas *explosive* is a typical property. Viewed in another way, attributes represent the extension of what an action can accomplish. For the sake of clarity and relevance, in this paper we will call both static and dynamic modifiers *properties*.

Secondly, we have to be aware that CM generally aims for type level description, where expression of properties in NL often concerns identification or description at instance level. In such cases, the analyst will have to realize that 'red' is a 'COLOUR', which is a *type* of property.

KISS devotes a whole sub-model to properties, namely the attribute model (which, as the name implies, is restricted to static properties). The attribute model provides more means of property representation than can be dealt with here. Essentially, attribute types are identified by a schematic symbol, with possible addition of a dimension of measurement (e.g. weight) and measuring units (e.g. kilogram). However, these mechanisms deal with highly explicit, static, physically real properties. Note that dynamic as well as more abstract and structure-related properties are not presented as such, but are implicitly incorporated in the model; in fact, they *are* the model.

There are so many ways of expressing properties in NL that one cannot begin to describe them all. In fact, it could be argued that all communication which includes a predicate entails the conveying of some property or another. The question is when to use which form. One of the many ways of expressing $P(x)$ in NL is to say, for example, '**John has red hair**' (Section 4.4) which is actually parallel with '**John is red-haired**'. However, note that it is debatable whether any structure like '**John is red-haired**' is semantically the same as an ISA-relation, which would in this case be '**John is a red-haired person**' (Section 4.3) since a hyponymic hierarchy must be expressed in which John can be differentiated from other persons exactly because his hair is red.

Another prominent means of expressing a property is a possessive form, e.g. '**John's hair is red**' or '**The hair of John is red**' (Section 4.4). Clearly, use of such structures causes a semantic build-up which leads away from elementary sentences and therefore is not recommendable in analytic contexts. The same goes for yet another typical NL way of expressing properties, the use of adjectives or adverbs ([20, 7.1ff], [22, 2.2ff]. The possibility to identify attributes by spotting the relevant adverbs, adjectives, and clauses is explicitly acknowledged by KISS, but in practice reliable recognition of properties from a text is a rather messy business, boiling down to detailed interpretation rather than the recognition of specific forms. Paraphrasing is less tricky because one typical, straightforward form may be chosen, in which case the choice for a standard predication like '**Cars are black**' or (at type-level) '**Cars have a colour**' seems recommendable.

5 Applications

The various parallels between NL and CM, of which we discussed a few in the preceding sections, offer interesting opportunities for integration of linguistic and analytic

[2]Attribute: quality or feature that someone or something has [21, *attribute* 4, p.82]

[3]Property: way in which a substance or object behaves in particular conditions [21, *property* 3, p.1152]

concepts. The next sections will elaborate on a few basic phases of normal system development, and suggest some possible applications of a lexicon in these phases.

5.1 Elicitation of Conceptual Models

Elicitation of facts, opinions, vocabulary, etc. from domain experts is one of the areas in which NL can and should play an important part. The reason natural language currently is not so readily used for information analysis input is twofold. First, analytic methods are still largely based on technical (data storage/retrieval) principles instead of on pure modelling principles; technical structures are rarely compatible with NL structure and categorization principles [14]. Second, language may be a great means of every-day communication, but it is generally felt that for exact, deterministic and unambiguous description NL is not optimally fit by nature [10]. However, if NL is used only for *factfinding* on which further analysis is based, nothing stands in the way of using formal methods alongside NL-based elicitation. In fact, the combination of an optimally communicative elicitation method with an optimally accurate method of analysis seems ideal.

The main problem then is to minimize (if not eradicate) ambiguity from the NL structures taken in via the elicitation procedure and, on the other hand, make sure concepts (and implicitly the relations between them) are covered comprehensively for a particular context. This requires two main sets of restrictions on NL input. One set imposes formulation by means of those (standard) NL structures/forms (see Section 4) which are best fit to unambiguously capture the particular analytic concept called for (definition of such a set is language specific but further holds for any domain). The other restrictions uncover the intricacies of the specific domain vocabulary, i.e. sort out exactly what particular people working in the domain mean with a particular word, whether there is consensus on this, and whether the terminology used is in fact optimally deterministic and unambiguous (this set of restrictions therefore enforces highly domain-specific results).

5.2 Paraphrasing of Conceptual Models

Efficiency and correctness of communication between analyst and domain specialist can be greatly improved when domain specialists can be immediately confronted with NL phrases exactly expressing the whole of consequences of a change of the conceptual model. The various generic relations as presented in Section 4 could be a starting point for explanatory phrase generation. Such a mechanism should be capable of performing a two-way interaction. It should be possible to immediately generate NL sentences reflecting the elicitated conceptual relations as a whole, thus enabling the domain specialist to closely monitor the construction of the model and respond forthwith to possible conceptual flaws.

5.3 Verification of Conceptual Models

Verification and validation as currently supported by most tools is restricted to the syntax. The techniques described in [23, 33] adopt rule-based verification and validation approaches that ignore the semantic contents of the labels used. Souveyet uses the

$$
\begin{array}{lll}
(1) & \text{Meta-Model} & \Leftrightarrow M_1(prim_1(Label_1), prim_2(Label_2)) \\
(2) & M_1 \Rightarrow \{ \begin{array}{c} E_1 \\ \vdots \\ E_n \end{array} \Rightarrow & \Downarrow \\
(3) & & E_i(Label_1, Label_2) \\
 & & \Downarrow \\
(4) & E_i \Rightarrow \{ \begin{array}{c} L_1 \\ \vdots \\ L_m \end{array} \Rightarrow & \Downarrow \\
(5) & \text{lexicon} & \Leftrightarrow L_j(Label_1, Label_2)
\end{array}
$$

Figure 1: Mapping CM relations to NL notions

labeling as if the different submodels, such as the static and dynamic part, are complete and consistent with each other. The label is only used as a primitive identifier.

The presented mapping between linguistic relations and conceptual relations allows us to see whether the relations in a model, usually expressed with arrows and lines, are compatible with those present between the words used as labels. The mapping of conceptual relations and lexical relations on a set of relations which are considered essential reduces the problem to a rewriting problem, as is shown in Figure 1.

Initially (1) is a clause description of a model. It can be verified against the meta model as is indicated in the figure by the '$\Leftrightarrow$'-sign. The model primitives denoted by a label are connected. Using the mapping of the modelling relations (M) (2), which also contains some kind of selection restriction, this can be rewritten to an essential relation (E) between the labels (3). This relation, again, can be rewritten using the mapping between the essential relations and natural language construct (L) (4). In this case there will also be some selectional restriction. The result of the transformation is a lexical relation between the concepts denoted by the labels (5). This relation may be verified in a lexicon storing all the relevant information. This information includes relations between different concepts and selection restrictions on various other relations. If all the transformations succeed, the model is linguistically correct. The semantics of the model then is consistent with that in the lexicon.

5.4 Generation of Conceptual Models

When we take the linguistic approach one step further, we might be able not only to *verify* an existing model, but also to *generate* a complete or partial model directly from NL input. Clearly, this will require much more elaborate linguistic processing and especially the metamodel and the lexicon will need to contain an overwhelming amount of both lexical and semantic information. A machine that offers model generation should, in fact, also be able to translate texts between languages. Achievements in automated translating so far have been disappointing, and we do not claim to solve any of its problems here.

However, when we have a set of *typical* sentence frames available that could be based on Section 4, we should be able to extract some basic structures directly out of NL. Skillful assistance by an experienced analyst will still be required, but basic factfinding might become significantly faster. Additionally, such an automated tool could isolate potential analytical problems and help rephrasing their representations in unambiguous NL.

The effectiveness of such a generation approach is dependent on the availability of a well-constructed lexicon. It might be possible to scan for basic structures without a lexicon, but this will not yield very dependable results without human assistance. A combined approach where generation, paraphrasing, and elicitation are combined into one single module that can both read from and write in the lexicon, seems promising.

6 Conclusions and Evaluation

In this paper, we argued that the explicit usage of linguistic information, often already available to us, can improve the conceptual models we are building and facilitate their construction. We presented some examples of basic relations known in information semantics, and showed possible ways of mapping those relations onto both formal models and NL. Despite the explorative character of this research, these mappings show that what may appear to be a rather random choice of representational forms has more to it than meets the eye, and consequently that there are real and detailed parallels between CM and NL, which help bridge the gap between domain specialist and analyst.

Two ways of using the linguistic information, paraphrasing and verification, need an already filled lexicon. Elicitation and (manually assisted) generation on the other hand could start off with an empty lexicon that is gradually filled up as the process evolves. In practice, most work will be done with an at least partially filled lexicon, so that some frequently recurring concepts and relations are already available.

In the future, we aim to to offer much of the functionality described above by means of an automated lexicon storage module and several model-specific markup and analysis engines. In an approach similar to that taken for construction of a DBMS in a database context, we plan to build a Lexicon Management System (LMS). For a detailed description of the LMS, see [13]. The markup and analysis modules for the KISS method are currently under development in the *Grammalizer* project.

References

[1] E. Auramäki, R. Hirschheim, and K. Lyytinen. Modelling offices through discourse analysis: the sampo approach. *The Computer Journal*, 35(4):342–352, August 1992.

[2] J.F.M. Burg and R.P. van de Riet. Color-x: Object modeling profits from linguistics. In N.J.I. Mars, editor, *Towards Very Large Knowledge Bases: Knowledge Building & knowledge Sharing (KB&KS'95)*, pages 204–214, Enschede, The Netherlands, 1995. IOS Press, Amsterdam.

[3] J.F.M. Burg and R.P. van de Riet. The impact of linguistics on conceptual models: Consistency and understandability. In *First International Workshop on Applications of Natural Language to Data Bases (NLDB'95)*, pages 183–197, Versailles, France, 1995. AFCET.

[4] R. Chaffin, D.J. Herrmann, and M. Winston. An empirical taxonomy of part-whole relations: Effects of part-whole type on relation identification. *Language and Cognitive Processes*, 1(1):9–36, 1988.

[5] P. P. S. Chen. The entity-relationship model: Towards a unified view of data. *ACM transactions on database systems*, 1(1):9–36, March 1976.

[6] J.L.G. Dietz. Subject-oriented modelling of open active systems. Technical Report 92-018, University of Limburg, 1992.

[7] F. Dignum. *A language for modelling knowledge bases: based on linguistics, founded in logic.* PhD thesis, Vrije Universiteit Amsterdam, 1989.

[8] A. Dijk, V. van Sweden, and S. Else. *Taalkundige Informatiesysteem-ontwikkeling.* Pandata uitgeverij, 1989. (in dutch).

[9] S.C. Dik. *The Theory of Functional Grammar Part I: the Structure of the Clause.* Foris publications, 1989.

[10] L.F.T. Gamut. *Logic, Language, and Meaning,* volume 1. University of Chicago Press, 1991.

[11] Nicola Guarino. Concepts, attributes, and arbitrary relations: Some linguistic and ontological criteria for structuring knowledge bases. In R.P. van de Riet and R.A. Meersman, editors, *Linguistic Instruments in Knowledge Engineering,* pages 195–211. Elsevier Science Publishers B.V., 1992.

[12] J. A. Gulla. *Explanation Generation in Information Systems Engineering.* PhD thesis, University of Trondheim, 1993.

[13] J. Hoppenbrouwers. *Structure and Usage of Lexicons for Storage of Domain Models.* PhD thesis, Tilburg University, The Netherlands, forthcoming.

[14] G. Kristen. *Object Orientation: the KISS Method—From Information Architecture to Information System.* Addison-Wesley, 1994. especially chapts. 4; 12.6.

[15] D. B. Lenat and R.V. Guha. *Building large knowledge-based systems: representation & inference in the CYC project.* Addison-Wesley, 1989.

[16] O. I. Lindland, G. Sindre, and A. Sølvberg. Understanding quality in conceptual modeling. *IEEE Software,* 11(2):42–49, March 1994.

[17] W.C. Mann. Rhetorical structure theory: A theory of text organization. Technical Report ISI/RS87190, USC ISI, June 1987.

[18] C. Mazza, J. Fairclough, B. Melton, D. de Pablo, A. Schewffer, and R. Stevens. *Software engineering standards.* Prentice Hall, 1994.

[19] G.M. Nijssen and T.A. Halpin. *Conceptual schema and relational database design: a fact oriented approach.* Prentice Hall, 1989.

[20] R. Quirk et al. *A Comprehensive Grammar of the English Language.* Longman, 1985.

[21] J. Sinclair et al., editors. *CoBUILD English Language Dictionary.* William Collins Sons & Co, London, 1987.

[22] J. Sinclair et al., editors. *CoBUILD English Grammar.* HarperCollins Publishers, London, 1990.

[23] C. Souveyet and C. Rolland. Correction of conceptual schemas. In B. Steinholz, A. Sølvberg, and L. Bergmann, editors, *Proceedings of the Second Nordic Conference on Advanced Information Systems Engineering (CAiSE'90),* pages 152–174. Springer Verlag, May 1990.

[24] J.F. Sowa. *Conceptual Structures.* Addison Wesley, 1984.

[25] V.C. Storey. Meronymic relationships. *Journal of Database Administration,* 2(3):22–35, 1991.

[26] R.P. van de Riet. Linguistic instruments in knowledge engineering, a research proposal and some experiments. In K.Fuchi and T.Yokoi, editors, *Knowledge Building and Knowledge Sharing, Proceedings of the 1993 Conference,* pages 200–207. IOS Press, 1994.

[27] R.P. van de Riet and R.A. Meersman, editors. *Linguistic Instruments in Knowledge Engineering, proceedings of the 1991 workshop on LIKE,* Tilburg, 17-18 January 1991. LIKE, North-Holland.

[28] A. J. van der Vos, J. A. Gulla, and R. P. van de Riet. Verification of conceptual models based on linguistic knowledge. In *proceedings of the First workshop on Applications of Natural Language to Data Bases,* 1995.

[29] A. J. van der Vos and R.P. van de Riet. A first semantic check based on linguistic information for state transition diagrams. Technical Report IR-372, Vrije Universiteit Amsterdam, 1994.

[30] R. Wieringa. Three roles of conceptual models in information systems design and use. In E. D. Falkenberg and P. Lindgreen, editors, *Information System Concepts: An In-depth Analysis,* pages 31–52. IFIP, North-Holland, 1989.

[31] R.J. Wieringa and W. de Jonge. The identification of objects and roles – object identifiers revisited. Technical Report IR267, Vrije Universiteit Amsterdam, December 1991.

[32] M.E. Winston, R. Chaffin, and D. Herrmann. A taxonomy of part-whole relations. *Cognitive Science*, 11:417–444, 1987.

[33] R. Wohed. Diagnoses of conceptual schema. In R. A. Meersman, Z. Shi, and C.H. Kung, editors, *Artificial Intelligence in Databases ans Information Systems (DS-3): Proceedings of the IFIP TC2/TC8/WG2.6/WG8.1 Working conference on the role of Atrificial Intelligence in Databases and Information systems*, pages 437–456. North-Holland, July 1988.

Applications of Natural Language to Information Systems
R.P. van de Riet et al. (Eds.)
IOS Press, 1996

A Basis for Natural Language Analysis of Part-Whole Relationships in Fact-Based Conceptual Modelling

Pramila Gupta
prom@stan.xx.swin.edu.au

James A. Sykes
jsykes@lucy.swin.edu.au

Centre for Information Systems Research
Swinburne University of Technology
P. O. Box 218, Hawthorn
Victoria 3122, Australia

Abstract. The conceptual modeller concerned with information systems development has few procedural guidelines for dealing with part-whole relationships in an organized way. Some modelling techniques provide partial notational support, but for initial discovery and classification the modeller has to rely mainly on intuition and experience. The part-whole relationship has been studied in other disciplines and there is also some research in information systems development based on those studies. In some work the forms of natural language used to express part-whole relationships have been studied. This paper draws on these ideas and investigates their connection with the use of natural language in fact-based conceptual modelling methods such as NIAM and FORM. It is proposed that natural-language analysis of the sentence types encountered in fact-based modelling can be extended to deal explicitly with part-whole relationships.

Keywords: Part-Whole Relationships, Fact-Based Conceptual Modelling, Natural Language Analysis.

1 Introduction

Conceptual modelling is an important activity in information systems (IS) development. In this activity a model of the information considered to be conceptually relevant in some problem domain or Universe of Discourse (UoD) is developed. This model is expressed as a conceptual schema that describes the grammar of the information to be stored in the corresponding information base. Principles of conceptual modelling (the 100 percent principle and the conceptualization principle), requirements of a conceptual schema and definitions for related terms are described in an ISO report [11].

Conceptual modelling consists of four main tasks, *knowledge acquisition, conceptualization, validation and evolution management* [19]. In this paper we are concerned with the first two tasks. The main objective of knowledge acquisition and elicitation is to get information from the users of a system. A natural language such as English is the most common way of expressing and communicating this information. In the task of conceptualization, UoD concepts such as entities and their related aspects are structured and described using constructs of the modelling method. Validation by the users is normally an essential feature of knowledge acquisition and conceptualization.

There are many conceptual modelling techniques well-established in practice. When selecting one of these for IS development, some important issues should be considered. We prefer a technique that distinguishes clearly between real world concepts and their representation, results in an implementation- independent schema, adopts a fact-based discovery of entity types and their aspects, and emphasizes both the process and the product aspects of conceptual modelling [8].

Conceptual modelling techniques belonging to the so-called fact modelling family, also known as object- role modelling (ORM), are fact-based. ORM techniques provide set procedures for developing conceptual models. Well-documented accounts of ORM may be found in [16] for NIAM and in [9] for FORM, a revised form of NIAM.

The starting point in ORM is acquisition of information about the UoD, based partly on natural language analysis. This analysis helps in the discovery of object types and the roles played by object types in their relationships with each other. We use the term *relation* or *relationship* interchangeably for associations between things existing in the real world. In ORM all relationships are represented at the type level, with the construct of a fact type, irrespective of their semantic nature, and without any necessity for discovering and modelling their specific kinds explicitly. The state of the art and the existing use of natural language analysis in ORM are described in section 2.

Researchers in linguistic semantics, e.g., Leech [12], have suggested that componential or feature analysis helps in understanding the full semantics of sentence components and their relationships. Some linguists and psychologists have used these suggestions to distinguish various kinds of semantic relations and to describe their taxonomies ([24]; [1]). Winston et al. [24] have used forms of natural language expressions as a way of explaining the taxonomy of part-whole (PW) relations. Winston et al. have acknowledged that English language expressions do not solve all problems for recognizing different kinds of PW relations. Nevertheless, the prominence of the natural language aspect in their studies is attractive to the users of ORM, which makes considerable use of natural language.

Relationships have been discussed at length in the context of computerized knowledge and information systems, e.g., for knowledge base modelling [14] and for modelling of databases [20]. Advances in object-oriented technology have lead to an increased interest in studying the semantics of PW relationships in IS development. In section 3 we discuss the importance of PW relationships in IS development, particularly in conceptual modelling. In the same section, we also briefly review the theories developed by Winston et al. [24] and Chaffin et al. [1] for PW relations and how their theories have been used in research by the IS community.

From a review of literature stemming from research in conceptual and object-oriented modelling, we find that some modelling techniques provide notational support for modelling PW relationships. However, none of the techniques provides a suitable procedure that could be paralleled to suggestions by Winston et al. [24] for discovery of these relations via analysis of natural language expressions. We are particularly interested in ORM procedures for handling PW relationships. Although there have been some developments in modelling PW relationships with representational notations and role names (reviewed in section 2), there are no provisions available for assisting in the discovery of these relationships from ORM fact types. Thus it is left to a modeller's experience and intuitions to decide what kind of a relationship a fact type represents.

Even though PW relationships are difficult to discover, they are conceptually important. Therefore, it is worthwhile to attempt to provide guidelines for their discovery. This need and the notion of using natural language to differentiate the kinds of PW relations illustrated by Winston et al. [24] were the motivation for the study described in section 4. The aim was to investigate links between their approach and ORM, and to assess whether it would be beneficial to extend the analysis of fact types in ORM by adopting some of their suggestions. The outcome of the study is discussed and evaluated in section 5. The resulting benefits from the study and the proposals for future research are summarized in section 6.

2 Natural language analysis in ORM and scope for extensions

Information is that part of knowledge that can be communicated by some means. Knowledge that can not be communicated does not constitute useful information [25]. In an information system, this communication has to take place in a language that can be understood well by the users and developers of the system. A natural language such as English is one of the most common means of this communication.

In the acquisition phase of conceptual modelling, information is communicated by users in textual descriptions in natural language or in forms and reports. Fact-based conceptual modelling techniques have their major strength in *processes for discovering* from communicated information the aspects to be modelled. Information examples occurring in these communications are transformed into declarative elementary sentences that can be verbalized in the style of ORM. Similar types of sentences are grouped into a sentence type. In the process of arriving at sentence types, entity types, their unique identifiers (reference types), their other label types, and the roles that object types (entity types and label types) play in relationships with each other are discovered. A sentence type is represented in graphical notations with a construct called a fact type that comprises one or more object types and their roles. Interconnected fact types constitute an ORM schema. The sentence types of ORM can be unary, binary or n-ary. Instances of a sentence type are expressed in the following style:

Entity-type with label-type “label” role name entity-type with label-type “label”
Example:
Person with person-name “John” drives car with registration No. “ASD 2345”

Two points to be noted about this style of sentence from an IS perspective are:

- Each entity type should have a reference scheme for identifying each of its instances uniquely. This requirement arises from the need to be able to communicate with an information system regarding individual instances.
- Entity instances represented with proper names (labels) are classified in their respective entity types and thus a context is added to the natural language sentences by stating the entity types involved. This avoids referential ambiguities that may be misinterpreted by human beings and which can not be solved by computer systems ([9], pp. 46).

Besides what has been explained above, not much use is made of an ORM sentence type. The remaining components of the sentence type are recorded as a “sentence with holes". That is, the entity types with their labels are treated as the arguments of the rest of the sentence type, which is termed a predicate. In this paper our concern is with extended analysis of predicates for discovering various kinds of semantic relationships that are presently not differentiated in ORM. In most ORM techniques the only kind of relationship that is given a different notation is the "is-kind-of" relationship. An ORM schema is a one- level (flat) schema except for subtype and supertype hierarchies of "is-kind-of" relationships. An extended notational support for grouping abstraction (power set) built on "is-member-of" relationships has been described in [10]. The modelling of composites and their parts through schema object types is described in [23]. The naming of roles as *has part* is proposed for "part-of" relationships in [5]. None of these proposals for extensions in ORM offers procedures for assisting modellers to discover situations in which the proposed notations should be used.

Generally, ORM sentence types are grammatically well-formed natural language sentences. It is shown in [22] that NIAM sentence types correspond to the seven types of clauses (SV, SVO, SVC, SVA, SVOO, SVOC, and SVOA)[1] of English grammar [18]. In practice one may find that some ORM sentence types do not follow the rules of English grammar. In English [18] a simple sentence is a single clause, i.e., there is one finite verb (or verb phrase). However, a sentence that is considered simple in the grammatical sense is not necessarily elementary in the sense in which this term is used in ORM, where it is not uncommon to split sentences on the grounds that this can be done without "information loss". The motivation for doing so comes from the requirements of relational database design. One also finds "sentence types" in ORM where there is no finite verb at all (arguments against this practice have been put forward in [22]).

In view of the differences between ORM sentence types and the clause structures of English, we propose that in the initial steps of ORM, every candidate sentence type should be subjected to a grammatical check. This will ensure that each sentence has an English clause structure. We should also try to validate that the verbalization of a sentence type reflects as accurately as possible the situation being modelled (for example, avoid over-use of the word "has" for a role name). The validated sentence type should be labelled with the corresponding clause type. There can be difficulties in choosing the appropriate clause structure for a sentence type. This should be sorted out by applying *paraphrasing* (moving and changing the clause's components and verifying with the client that the meaning remains the same) and by asking relevant questions as suggested in [18] and [22].

Once each sentence type has a well-defined natural language form it is possible to analyze it further for what it expresses. We think that this can (and should) be done in an organized way by applying natural- language-related knowledge from other disciplines to ORM sentence types. One potential area is the taxonomic classification of different kinds of semantic relationships. This has received much attention in linguistics and psychology and is the main concern of this paper.

3 Part-whole relationships

The literature in semantics, e.g., ([12]; [6]), has classified *semantically* different relations into various categories. Class inclusion (is-kind-of), part-whole (that includes is-part-

[1] In Quirk et al. [18] type of a clause is decided based on identifying which parts of a sentence perform the functions of a subject (S), verb (V), object (O) (direct and indirect), complement (C) and adverbial (A).

of and is-member-of), attribution (is-characteristic-of) and ownership (is-owner-of) are some of the kinds of semantic relations. One theory about relationships is that they are complex concepts characterized with distinct features. Another theory is that they are primitive concepts that explain other concepts, e.g., entity types, but are not explained themselves. The experience that most people easily perceive and conceptualize the semantic distinctions between the various kinds of relationships tends to support the first theory [3].

Differences in semantic relationships that are acknowledged and studied in semantics and psychology are not very well recognized in modelling for IS. One reason for this is that implementation technologies have been limited in their capabilities to implement relationships. Another reason is that the distinction between semantic relationships at the basic level and higher level abstractions is not always clearly understood. By *semantic relationships at the basic level* we mean the relations at the observable level where a mental image of a concept is usually most easily formed. By *higher level abstractions* (i.e., composition, grouping, aggregation and generalization/specialization) we mean concepts that are built up from relationships at the basic level. Higher level abstractions hide the underlying relationships and entities.

In IS literature, the term "part-whole relationship" is used sometimes to mean a relationship that exists between two entity types or their instances at the basic level, i.e., the simple binary link, and sometimes to mean a higher level abstraction. In this paper we use the term "part-whole relationship" in the former sense only. Two kinds of higher level abstractions based on PW relationships are recognized. One is *composition* that is based on the underlying "is-part-of" relationships and the other is *grouping or collection* based on "is-member-of" relationships.

3.1 Importance of part-whole relationship in conceptual modelling

Any entity or any relationship that is perceivable, recognizable and conceptualizable in a UoD is potentially of importance in conceptual modelling. A PW relationship is a link between an instance of a *part* entity type (constituent or component) and an instance of a *whole* entity type. Whenever we think of how things are constituted, we are using the notion of PW relationships. The concept is semantically important as it makes a problem domain more understandable. Our mental picture of the structuring of entities and of the behaviours contributed by their respective parts can be clearer and more precise. Not only physical and concrete entities, but also logical and abstract entities have parts.

A relationship between an entity and a naming or characterizing entity (i.e., attribute or feature) does not contribute to the entity's constitution. In this sense parts are different from attributes that only describe entities. A clear distinction between parts and features of an entity is made by Guarino [7]. The distinction is based on the ontological notion of *foundation*, which has some similarities to the data-modelling notion of dependence of one entity on another.

3.2 Theory of part-whole relations

Winston et al. [24] and Chaffin et al. [1] give a good account of PW relations. Their studies, based on theories in linguistics, logic and cognition, have attracted the attention of researchers in IS development. The main features are:

- PW relations are considered to be different from other semantic relations such as spatial and class inclusion (subtype and supertype relationship), attribution, ownership and attachment.

- Based on the different terms for expressing PW relations used by ordinary English speaking people, a taxonomy of PW relations is developed. Examples using different English terms for each kind are given. The taxonomy includes Component-Integral Object, Stuff-Object, Portion-Mass, Place-Area, Activity-Phase, Member-Collection and Event-Feature PW relations. It is a result of different combinations of four properties of relations: functional/non-functional, homogeneous/non-homogeneous, separable/non- separable and contemporary/non-contemporary. The taxonomy corresponds to different semantic domains such as concrete, abstract and collection entities. A hierarchical structure of PW relations is common. All PW relations exhibit the logical property of "connection" and furthermore this connection must be transitive[2], irreflexive[3]and antisymmetric. Relation Element Theory [2], that has roots in feature analysis theory of linguistics, is used to explain the taxonomy.

- The studies show how the recognition of PW relations and their particular kinds is made difficult by ambiguous use of English surface lexical terms. The main problem is found with the use of the generic term "part-of" that is appropriate for all kinds of PW relations, but makes an expression vague. Based on the results of empirical studies [1] it is suggested that sorting of PW relations is possible via the use of specialized terms and that part terms could be selected to express different relations. To validate the selection of a term paraphrasing is suggested.

- The empirical studies [1] also showed that a PW relation is only fully understood in the context of the entities involved in it.

Although the above theories are not specifically directed towards IS development, they are relevant and it is therefore not surprising that they have been used by some researchers in conceptual modelling and design. Motschnig-Pitrik [15] has reviewed the aspect of transitivity in the taxonomy for PW relations [24] and has proposed that stuff-object and member- collection relations are not transitive. Civello [4] has differentiated the semantics of composition at analysis and design levels. Storey [21] has reviewed the taxonomy for its treatment in database design.

The issue of discovering PW relationships is not considered in any of the above research. In our opinion, no conceptual modelling technique or object-oriented analysis method provides procedural guidelines to analysts for discovering PW relationships at the basic level. As a result, the analysts are forced to work at a higher level, and to proceed intuitively. Therefore it is worthwhile seeking some definite guidelines for modellers. We propose starting from sentence types as a way of doing this in ORM.

4 Investigation

The study described in this section is an investigation of the links between the approach of Winston et al. [24] and ORM. It was thought that some of the suggestions made by Winston et al. could be adopted in analysis of ORM sentence types.

[2]For relations of the same type, e.g., both are Component- Integral part-whole relations.
[3]Not all researchers consider is- part-of relation reflexive, e.g., see [13].

The taxonomy of Winston et al. [24] is based on the idea that ordinary English speaking people use different terms for expressing different kinds of PW relations. On this basis, it can be proposed that the use of natural-language expressions can help the analyst to discover and classify PW relations, thereby providing a direct link with ORM procedures where sentence types similar to English clauses are analyzed.

On the other hand Winston et al. acknowledge that surface lexical features of English language are not the best guides to differences among PW relations. In ORM also we have similar cautions [22] for the use of term like "has" as a role name.

To investigate these ideas two strategies that we adopt are as follows:

A. Examples of each kind of PW relation from [24] are expressed in the style of ORM sentence types. Corresponding English clause structures are also identified for these sentence types. Where examples from Winston et al. are at the instance level, an attempt is made to paraphrase to the type level (without the reference type), although in some cases this results in a doubtful expression (marked with ??). We do not include all the examples given in [24].

   The results from strategy A should indicate whether it would be possible to adopt research by Winston et al. [24] in ORM.

B. From the ORM literature, some examples are selected that have corresponding expressions in [24] and the kind of PW relation expressed by each is identified.

   The results from strategy B should indicate whether PW relations occur in ORM, even though they might not be modelled explicitly.

4.1 Investigation applying strategy A

Examples for general part-whole relations

Examples by Winston et al.	*ORM sentence types*	*English clauses*
The X is part of the Y	Class X is part of Class Y	SVC
X is partly Y	Class X is partly Class Y	SVAC
X's are parts of Y's	Class X is part of Class Y	SVC
X is a part of Y	Class X is part of Class Y	SVC
The parts of a Y include the X's	Parts of Class Y include Class X	SVO
Y has X	Class Y has Class X	SVO

The six examples in the left column from [24] illustrate that there are many generic lexical units for PW relations, some with very similar meanings. Examples by Winston et al. are at the instance level. When we express their examples at the type level in ORM style, we lose information about multiple instances of *parts* and *wholes.*

Examples for specific kind of PW relations

Component/Integral Object

Wheels are parts of car	Wheel is part of car	SVC
Chapters are parts of Books	Chapter is part of book	SVC
Belgium is part of NATO	Country is part of organization	SVC
Plays have acts	Play has act	SVO

The specialized term for this kind of PW relation is "is-a-component", whereas the terms "is-a-member" and "is-a-portion" are not acceptable. The example *Belgium is part of NATO* is included here because Winston et al. so classify it. It can be argued that it is a case of Member/Collection because *Belgium is member of NATO* is also acceptable.

Member/Collection or Group

Examples by Winston et al.	*ORM sentence types*	*English clauses*
A tree is part of a forest	Tree is part of forest	SVC
This ship is a part of a fleet	Ship is part of fleet	SVC

The phrase "is-a-member" specializes Member/Collection PW relation. The term "some-of" can also be used in a count sense. The term "is-a-portion" is not acceptable.

Portion/Mass

The slice is a part of a pie	Slice is part of pie	SVC
A yard is part of a mile	??length is part of length	SVC
This hunk is part of my clay	??	SVC

We do find some cases (marked ??) here for which expression is difficult or impossible in the style of ORM sentence types. The difficulties have to do with setting the context (i.e., choosing the entity types) and establishing a referencing scheme. The distinguishing characteristic is that there is a mass sense in these relationships. Winston et al. propose to replace "part-of" with "some-of" and verify if the meaning is preserved.

Stuff/Object (Constituency)

The bike is partly steel	Product is partly material	SVAC
The lens is made of glass	Object is made of stuff	SVC

An object may be involved simultaneously in Component/Integral Object and Stuff/Object relations. When an object is made of a single stuff then the term "made-of" reflects this kind of relation as illustrated with second example above.

Phase/Activity

Paying is part of shopping	Phase is part of activity	SVC

This relationship does not have the form of "X has Y" but the form "the parts of activity include phases" is possible.

Place/Area

The Everglades is part of Florida	Place is part of area	SVC

4.2 Investigation applying strategy B

From ORM sentence types to English clauses and examples by Winston et al.

Cases that seem to be probable PW relations are selected from the literature[4].

Examples using the term "has" for Component/Integral Object PW relationships

ORM sentence type	*English clause*
Formula has formula	SVO
Document has chapters	SVO
Document has keyword	SVO

There are examples found in ORM literature with *part of, used in* and *composed of* role

[4]The ORM examples shown have mainly been drawn from research reported in [17].

names, that can be considered cases of Component/Integral Object PW relationships.

Examples of Member/Group PW relationships

ORM sentence type	*English clause*
Employee works for department	SVC
Convoy has ship	SVO
Person is a member of a team	SVC
Department belongs to faculty	SVC
Manager is committee member for project	SVC

The last example is a case in ORM where an analyst or a user may not conceptualize a Member/Group relationship. With the predicate *is committee member* it may not be modelled as a member of relationship.

Examples of Stuff/Object and Place/Area PW relationships

Product contains chemical	SVO	Stuff/Object
City is situated in country	SVC	Place/Area

5 Discussion and evaluation

The results of the investigation in the previous section show that generic terms for PW relations are not the best guides to the differences between various PW semantic relations. The need for caution concerning the use of some common terms like "has" and "part-of" and suggestions for paraphrasing of sentences with specific terms has previously been observed in both the work of Winston et al. and in the ORM literature.

PW relations are obvious if the domain is understood well and the contexts of entity types are known. ORM sentence types meet this need for setting the contexts that made it easy to identify the type of PW relation for examples from the ORM literature.

The examples given by Winston et al., and those used from the ORM literature, when expressed as English sentences, have clause structures of SVC, SVO, or SVA but not SV. Sentence types with SV structure are not candidates for PW relation as two noun phrases are necessary for this relationship.

While transforming an example by Winston et al. [24] to an ORM sentence type, all the information is not retained as we lose information for cardinality, optionality and sharability. This is not a serious matter as we can model the information with suitable constructs for constraints in later steps of ORM.

We do not come across examples in [24] where a PW relation is not applicable at the type level. A referencing scheme for each entity type is not a concern in [24] and for some examples of Winston et al. we find it difficult to think of a referencing scheme for ORM. This may require more investigation in the context of IS development.

In the ORM literature we do come across sentence types that are similar to the ones obtained by mapping examples in [24] for PW relations. In the absence of an explicit modelling for PW relationships, the sentence types are modelled as any other fact types in ORM. Sometimes role names indicate PW relationship, at other times not. There is no attention given during analysis to naming the roles in a way that could reflect a PW relationship. Usually the term "has" or "has part" is used to indicate that a whole has a part. However this may be confused with other relationships.

When grammatical structure of the fact types for PW relationship is of SVxx type, the recognition of a PW relation depends on the user's conceptualization of the noun phrases appearing in the xx components. This was observed for the example *employee is committee member for project.*

On functional PW relationships

There are cases in IS modelling (especially for object-oriented implementation) where an exact functional relationship between a *part* and a *whole* is expressed with a verb/verb phrase instead of "part-of" or a related term. Winston et al. [24] do not provide any such examples.

An example from [4] for a functional PW relation is "Gate releases bottle on bottling plant". In ORM also there are examples where the role names reflect the functional role played by a *part* with respect to its *whole.* It is necessary to develop a way of first identifying a functional PW relationship with grammatical analysis of an ORM sentence type and then paraphrasing the sentence with "part-of" term. Good knowledge of a problem domain and knowing the contexts of entity types will contribute to this analysis.

6 Conclusions

The work discussed in this paper has indicated how ORM might be extended to deal with categories of semantic relationships, at least for the case of PW relationships. These are important in IS development but difficult to discover.

The possibility of extending ORM arises from its use of natural language sentences, which are capable of expressing all the varieties of PW relationships.

The investigation discussed in this paper showed that it was possible to apply the taxonomy of Winston et al. [24] to examples of ORM sentences. For this to be more useful in practice it will be necessary to express the taxonomy and the corresponding natural language terms in the form of guidelines for the ORM analyst. Validation, possibly via paraphrasing should form part of the guidelines.

In this paper our intention has not been to propose these guidelines but to derive a beneficial contribution to ORM procedures by establishing links between the proposals from Winston et al. [24] and ORM. Once an ORM procedure is modified for discovery of PW relationships at the basic level, the bases for developing rules and definitions for higher level abstractions would also then seem possible.

Suggestions for future research

ORM procedures should be modified to help analysts in discovering different semantic relationships and their taxonomic classification. The proposals in [24] are based on the lexical units of "is part of", "has/have" and "is partly" rather than on grammatical analysis. There is scope for extending the analysis of ORM sentence types, based on their respective English clause structure. Specifically, functional PW relationships require further investigation with grammatical analysis of sentence types. In some parallel research we are investigating how static roles can be differentiated from dynamic roles based on the verb/verb phrase. We propose to set this investigation also in the context of functional PW relationships.

Development of a lexicon with two sets of words, i.e., one related to *part* terms and the other for the verb/verb phrases that indicate the functional role of a *component* in relationship with its *whole*, should be undertaken.

References

[1] R. Chaffin et al. An Empirical Taxonomy of part-whole Relations: Effects of part-whole Type on Relation Identification. *Language and Cognitive Processes*, 3(1), 1988.

[2] R. Chaffin and D. J. Herrmann. Relation Element Theory: A New Account of the Representation and Processing of Semantic Relations. In D. Gorfein and R. Hoffman, editors, *Memory and Learning: The Ebbinghaus Centennial Conference*, Erlbaum, 1987.

[3] R. Chaffin and D. J. Herrmann. The Nature of Semantic Relations: A Comparison of Two Approaches. In M. Evens, editor, *Relational Models of the Lexicon: Representing Knowledge in Semantic Networks*, Cambridge University Press, 1988.

[4] F. Civello. Roles for Composite Objects in Object-Oriented Analysis and Design. In *Proceedings OOPSLA'93*, 1993.

[5] P. N. Creasy and H. A. Proper. A Generic Model for 3-Dimensional Conceptual Modelling. Technical Report 342, Department of Computer Science, University of Queensland, Australia, 1995.

[6] D. A. Cruse. *Lexical Semantics*. Cambridge University Press, England, 1986.

[7] N. Guarino. Concepts, Attributes, and Arbitrary Relations: Some Linguistic and Ontological Criteria for Structuring Knowledge Bases. In R. P. van de Riet, and R. A. Meersman, editors, *Linguistic Instruments in Knowledge Engineering*, Elsevier Science Publishers B. V., 1992.

[8] P. Gupta and J. A. Sykes. Towards a Framework for Assessing Object Discovery Capabilities of Object- Oriented Analysis Methods for Information Systems Development. In *Proceedings of 6th Australian Conference on Information Systems*, 1995.

[9] T. A. Halpin. *Conceptual Schema and Relational Database Design*, Second Edition. Prentice-Hall, Australia, 1995.

[10] A. H. M. ter Hofstede and Th. P. van der Weide. Expressiveness in Conceptual Data Modelling. *Data & Knowledge Engineering*, 10(1), 1993.

[11] ISO. *Concept and Terminology for the Conceptual Schema and Information Base*. J. J. van Griethuysen, editor, International Organisation for Standardisation, Publication no. ISO / TC97 / SC5 - NIAM 695, Switzerland, 1982.

[12] G. Leech. *Semantics*. Baltimore: Penguin Books, 1974.

[13] L. Liu. Exploring Semantics in Aggregation Hierarchies for Object-Oriented Databases. In *Proceedings of the Eighth International Conference on Data Engineering*, IEEE Computer Society Press, 1992.

[14] N. M. Mattos. Abstraction Concepts: The Basis for Data and Knowledge Modelling. In C. Baitini, editor, *Proceedings of the Seventh International Conference on Entity Relationship Approach*, North-Holland, 1989.

[15] R. Motschnig-Pitrik. The Semantics of Parts vs. Aggregates in Data/Knowledge Modelling. In *Proceedings CAiSE'93*, Lecture Notes in Computer Science, No. 685, Springer, 1993.

[16] G. M. Nijssen and T. A. Halpin. *Conceptual Schema and Relational Database Design: Fact Oriented Approach*. Prentice-Hall, Australia, 1989.

[17] ORM. T. A. Halpin and R. Meersman, editors, *Proceedings of First International Conference on Object-Role Modelling*. Held at Magnetic Island, Australia (to be published), 1994.

[18] R. Quirk et al. *A Comprehensive Grammar of the English Language*. Longman, 1985.

[19] C. Rolland and C. Cauvet. Trends and Perspective in Conceptual Modelling. In P. Loucopoulos et al., editors, *Conceptual Modelling, Databases, and Case: An Integrated View of Information Systems Development*, John Wiley & Sons Inc., NY, 1992.

[20] J. M. Smith and C. P. Smith. Database Abstractions: Aggregation and Generalization. *ACM Transactions on Database Management Systems*, 2(2), 1977.

[21] V. C. Storey. Meronymic Relationships. *Journal of Database Administration*, 2(3), 1991.

[22] J. A. Sykes. English Grammar as a Sentence Model for Conceptual Modelling using NIAM. In E. D. Falkenberg et al., editors, *Proceedings of the IFIP International Working Conference on Information System Concept: Towards a Consolidation of Views*, Chapman & Hall, 1995.

[23] O. de Troyer. Schema Object Types: A New Approach to Modularisation in Conceptual Modelling. In G. Sakke and A. Sernadas, editors, *Information Systems-Correctness and Reusability, Workshop IS-CORE'91, Selected Papers*, Technische Universitt Braunschweig Informatik-Berichte 91-03, , Braunschweig, 1992.

[24] M. E. Winston et al. A Taxonomy of Part-Whole Relations. *Cognitive Science*, 11.

[25] J. J. V. R. Wintraecken. *The NIAM Information Analysis Method: Theory and Practice* Kluwer, Deventer.

Applications of Natural Language to Information Systems
R.P. van de Riet et al. (Eds.)
IOS Press, 1996

NTS-based derivation of KCPM cardinalities: *From natural language to conceptual predesign

G. Fliedl, Ch. Kop, W. Mayerthaler, H.C. Mayr, Ch. Winkler
Universität Klagenfurt

Abstract. This paper reports some recent results on the extraction of conceptual design knowledge out of natural language requirements. In particular we will focus on determining the cardinalities of relationships and attributes based on natural language sentences. This is done by a specific linguistic approach called NTS ("Natürlichkeitstheoretische Syntax") and by using, as a (target) interlingua, a particular conceptual modeling approach, i.e., the Klagenfurt Conceptual Predesign Model (KCPM). The work in question has been carried out in a joint project of linguists and computer scientists at the university of Klagenfurt.

Keywords: Conceptual Design, Conceptual Predesign, NTS, Requirements Analysis, Natural Language Requirements, Natural Language Processing, Cardinality

1 Introduction

Since a couple of years there are attempts to merge, within software life cycles, the phases of requirements analysis and of conceptual design. Object oriented analysis (OOA, e.g. [1], [2]) is the actual buzzword and its proponents argue that the models they use work very fine as a communication medium between designer and enduser. This means, that the designer's work results, i.e. a conceptual scheme reflecting the analysed requirements, could immediately be understood and validated by the "requirements", i.e., the endusers. Practical experiences, however, often show another picture: The use of relatively abstract modeling notions, that is common to OOA approaches, makes the design of complex information systems more intransparent to endusers as it is pretended in theory.

Another important reason for that discrepancy is the fact that (similar to the classical ER-based conceptual modeling aproaches) OOA Methods force the designer to early design decisions on what specific modeling notion has to be associated with a given aspect of the universe of discourse (UoD) in question. I.e. one has to distinguish between formal concepts like classes (objects), association-types (relationships), attribute types (values) etc. within an analysis stage the main objective of which should be to "capture", as completely as possible, the relevant aspects of the given UoD. Moreover, if such a decision turns out to be inadequate in a later analysis step, changes with more or less complex local and global effects will become necessary. On the other hand, the designer has to formalize the collected information and to validate his perception of

*The research results published in this paper are part of the NIBA project which is sponsored by the anniversary fund of the "Österreichische Nationalbank" (project-no. 5513).

things in collaboration with the endusers.

To overcome these problems we propose, in accordance to [3], to place in front of the conceptual design a phase which we call *conceptual predesign*[1] [4], [5] where UoD relevant information is collected mainly in natural language form and "translated" into a glossary-like predesign schema. This predesign schema then works as a very detailed scratch pad for a given UoD.

To allow for an efficient design process the necessary schema transformations between the several life cycle phases should be automated as far as possible. [6] presents a set of rules for the transformation of KCPM-schemas into an extended entity-relationship model (EERM+), actually we are investigating rules for the mapping of KCPM-schemas onto the three models (static, dynamic and functional model) of the Object Modeling Technique OMT [2]. However, our goal is not only to simplify the mappings between conceptual predesign and conceptual design, but also to automate the process of getting the predesign schema itself. This means, that we would like to extract the predesign schema entries from the enduser's natural language requirements statements and thus to automate the early design phases as far as possible.

For that purpose we (the authors) started the project NIBA [2]. The NTS (Natürlichkeitstheoretische Syntax), developed at the department of linguistic, gives the fundamental for analysing natural language. Using NTS, the designer's rather intuitive decision process in extracting the relevant information becomes explicit, based on the linguistic knowledge about sentences, phrases, words and their internal structure. We attempt to transform that knowledge into rules in order to automate the process by a parser. In [7] we presented, as a first stage, the finding of elementary information, i.e. of those UoD aspects that are specified within our predesign model by using the notions *thing(-type)* and *connection(-type)*.

In the present paper we are going one step further and focus on finding adequate cardinalities for *perspectives* (these correspond to *roles* within the ER model) of *connections*, i.e. relationships. [8] derive cardinalities from natural language text mainly by studying special determiners and quantifiers (e.g. *a*, *the*, *every*, *several*). Furthermore, cardinality constraints are detected, if plural words are used without articles. To overcome the problem of disambiguity "the most plausible" among all the interpretations of such determiners is selected. This principle also is followed within our approach.

Section 2 gives an short overview over KCPM, our model of conceptual predesign, section 3 introduces the idea of NTS. In section 4 we explain the NTS-based derivation of cardinalities.

2 Conceptual predesign with KCPM

An important aim for the development of KCPM (Klagenfurt conceptual predesign model) was to harmonize the developer's and the end-user's view of a given UoD, i.e.,

[1]This phase again is called *conceptual* since it works with a - though less abstract - conceptual model.

[2]NIBA is an acronym for the German expression "**N**atürlichsprachliche **I**nformations**b**edarfs**a**nalyse" or in English "natural language information requirements analysis".

to provide for an interface for their mutual understanding. The approach was influenced by the DATA-ID model [3] which we extended and specialized to provide at least the same semantic expressivness as modern approaches to object oriented analysis do. The most important modeling notions of our approach are: **thing-type**, **connection-type**, **perspective**, **event-type**, **operation**, **constraint**. We shortly explain these notions by relating them to the known conceptual models (e.g. entity-relationship model, object-oriented models):

Thing-type is a generalization of the notions class (*entity-type* or *entity-set*, respectively) and *attribute* on the other hand. Thus, typical *things* (instances of thing-types) are

- natural or juridical persons,
- material or immaterial objects,
- abstract notions

as well as descriptive characteristics of the above mentioned examples (e.g. a customer-name, a product-number, a product-description). This is also an important difference between DATA-ID and our model, since the DATA-ID approach distinguishes between entitytypes and attributes: We did not want to force a requirement engineer to decide on that at an early stage of the analysis.

Apart from the simplification this generalization induces for the end-user (in whose world everything just continues to be a "thing"...), it also provides for more flexibility during linguistic analysis. For, although there are heuristics and rules (see [9], [10]) to find attributes [3] in natural language sentences, these do not work in all situations. In undetermined cases, however, using KCPM we can defer the decision to later transformation steps [5]. Moreover, the known conceptual models have different conceptions concerning which relations between attributes and classes, between two or more classes, and between attributes they permit. Hence, design decisions often depend on the particular modeling concept of the model in use. The generalized KCPM approach allows to separate these model specific aspects from the linguistic analysis because there is no a priori restriction.

Things are related within the real world. To capture this, we introduce the notion of **connection-type**. Two or more thing-types can take part of a connection-type. To define a connection-type completely, it must be described from the point of view (**perspective**) of all of the thing-types involved. Note that this approach corresponds to that of conceptual object/role models like NIAM [11].

Sentences leading to connections (and perspectives) are e.g. the following: [4]

(S1) *Ein Flug hat Passagiere* (perspective of *flight*)
("a flight has passengers")
(S2) *Ein Passagier bucht einen Flug* (perspective of *passenger*)
("a passenger books a flight")

[3]In cases were the decision, if an UoD element should be modeled as a conceptual class or attribute, may be made immediatly, we mark the respective thing-type. This information then is used when mapping the KCPM schema to a conceptual one.

[4]Since our NTS-parser (sect. 4) has been developed for the analysis of German sentences, examples are given in German.

The **abstractions generalisation** ("is-a", with set inclusion on the instance level) and **aggregation** ("is-part-of") are treated as specific connection-types.

Things can perform activities in order to fullfill tasks, tasks again relate to things. Such activities are described using the notion of **operation**. An operation can be simple (e.g. *read flight number*; evaluate and/or modify one ore few connections) or complex (e.g. *to book a flight*; evaluate and/or modify a set of connections). The second example also shows that *"to book"* can be seen from two points of view. First, one might interprete it as a connection for the static UoD-schema. Secondly, someone could interprete it as a dynamic UoD aspect thus modeling it as an operation.

The execution of an operation is supposed to be provoked by an event, operations in turn can provoke events. Therefore KCPM provides the notion of **event-type** to capture that kind of real world dynamics. Event-types mainly are characterized by preconditions and postconditions (bound to the "happening" of their instance events) and by the operations they provoke.

UoD aspects that cannot be modeled using these notions (and their characteristics, see below) are captured by (textual) constraints. The notation of KCPM schemas is glossary-oriented and thus similar to that of the DATA-ID approach. The glossaries form the basis of an information ressource dictionary for the application in question and emphasize the scratch pad character. Traceability between all the entries and source natural language sentences is given through so-called sentence references. To model one of the above-mentioned notions in detail, meta-attributes of the notion are presented as glossary columns. For example, to model a thing-type in detail, meta-attributes of this thing-types are a thing-description, references to synonymes, examples, expected number of examples etc. (see Figure 1).

Since we concentrate within this paper on extracting cardinality information, we restrict ourselves on an outline of the thing-type and the connection-type glossary columns:

Relevant thing-type meta-attributes

th-id#: holds an unique thing-type identification number.

classification: holds information about the conceptual "equivalent", e.g. entity-type, value-type, if extractable from the text (see above); will be successively be filled during the mapping process from predesign to design schema.

quantity: holds the expected amount of instances of the resp. thing type, e.g.

> **(S3)** *Wir haben 500 Angestellte. ("we have 500 employees")*

examples: holds instances of the resp. thing-type (e.g. *Klagenfurt airport* for the thing-type *airport*).

value constraint: holds natural language descriptions [5] of the legal value domain, e.g.

> **(S4)** *Das Alter eines Kapitäns muß über 30 Jahre sein.*
> *("the age of a captain must be over 30")*

[5] The formalization of consistency constraints is subject to a subsequent study.

synonym: references synonyms (e.g. *passenger*, *customer* in an airport UoD).

description: holds narrative text on the resp. thing-type.

sentence ref.: holds the numbers of the sentences of the natural language text that refer to the thing-type in question.

uod-area: airport		uod: airport	department: ---					
id#	name	classification	quantity descriptor	examples	value constraint	synonym	description	sentence reference
D001	Flughafen			"Flughafen-Klagenfurt				S7
D002	Passagier					D300		S1,S2
D003	Kunde					D200		
D004	Flug							S1,S2,S5, S8,S9
D005	Kapitän							S3
D006	Angestellter		500					S4, S7
D007	Alter				über 30			S3
D008	Gepäck							S7, S5
D009	Bodenpersonal							S6
D010	Zuordnung							S6
D011	Flugzeug							S8, S9

Figure 1: Thing-type glossary

Relevant connection-type meta-attributes

c-id#: holds an unique connection-type identification number.

connection descriptor: holds the id# and name of a thing-type which represents an "objectification" of the resp. connection-type (if any). For example, lets have a look on the sentences

(S5) *Das Gepäck wird dem entsprechenden Flug zugeordnet.*
("The baggage is assigned to the corresponding flights").
(S6) *Das Bodenpersonal prüft die Zuordnung.*
("The ground personnel checks the assignment").

In (S5), the perspective *"zugeordnet"* (*assigned*) could be seen as a verbal description of the whole connection. In (S6), the end-user speaks about the word *"Zuordnung"* (*assignment*) and about a part of a connection between the thing-type *assignment* and the thing-type *"Bodenpersonal"* (*ground personnel*). It seems that assignment also points to the connection with the verb assign. In this case, the relation between *assignment* and *assign* should be made explicite. This is done using the connection descriptor.

per perspective:

perspect#: holds an unique perspective identification number.

envolved thing-type: thing-type connected via the resp. perspective.

cardinality (min, max): holds a relation qualifier similar to numerous conceptual models: Each cardinality has a lower and an upper bound. The lower bound can rage between *zero* and a definite number. The upper bound must range between the lower bound (must have at least the value *"1"*) and an indefinite value *"N"*.

p-descriptor: circumscribes the envolved thing-types of a connection, e.g.

(S7) *Einige Angestellte arbeiten auf Flugäfen als Bodenpersonal.*
("some employees work on airports as ground personnel").

In this case employee and airport are the envolved thing-types. The thing-type ground personnel describes a kind of employees qualifying the connection. Thus *ground personnel* is seen as a perspective descriptor.

A more detailed description of the glossaries and of further KCPM-notions can be found in [6], [12], [13], [4].

3 The NTS approach

NTS stands for **N**atürlichkeits**t**heoretische **S**yntax. This is a grammar model based on generative syntax. The descriptions of grammatical phenomena are represented by trees expressing both constituency and dependency relations. These trees are unfoldings/projections of lexical base-categories. The maximal unfoldings of the respective categories (verb, noun etc.) are markedness theoretically parametrized: the less umarked, the higher the unfolding. The syntax theoretic language of NTS is two-fold. It provides a formal syntactic description and markedness theoretic evaluation thereof.

We distinguish between dominant and subdominant percolation/heritage. Every tree has just one head and accordingly just one dominant heritage line. The head of a construction usually is a lexical category. So called functional heads normally belong to the area of subdominant heritage. Given our framework, we do not use abstract theta-grids, but specified semantic roles for instance AGENT/PATIENT/OBJECTIVE/ INSTRUMENT/GOAL/LOCATION etc.

As in valency or dependency grammar the verb is the head of the whole sentence. Within uod-area: airport uod: airport department: ---

c-id#	name	descriptor	descr.	perspective					sentence reference
				p#	envolved thing-type	name	min:max	p-descriptor	
C001				p001a	D004 Flug	hat			S1, S2
				p001b	D002 Passagier	buchen			
C002				p002a	D006 Angestellter	arbeiten		D009 Boden-personal	S7
				p002b	D001 Flughafen				
C003		D010 Zuordnung		p003a	D008 Gepäck	zuordnen			S5
				p003b	D004 Flug				
C004				p004a	D010 Zuordnung	prüfen			S6
				p004b	D009 Boden-personal				
C005				p005a	D004 Flug	durchführen	1:1		S8, S9
				p005b	D011 Flugzeug	einsetzen	0:N		
...									

Figure 2: Connection-type glossary

the noun phrase, the noun is the only permissible head. Functional elements like definite articles, auxiliaries and non-governing affixes are generated under a specifier-node (**SPEZ**).

A markedness-theoretical evaluation of the generated phrase-structures is given according to the principles of naturalness theory [14].

Knowledge processing, as required in conceptual predesign, requires a high degree of efficiency from a computerlinguistic model for the analysis of language. We just quote [15]:

> "This requires an information base for the language itself and necessitates the exact formal definition of linguistic knowledge about the natural language. This implies
>
> - a linguistic dictionary,
> - a concept lexicon which represents word meanings,
> - a computational grammar,
> - a process capable of determining the meaning with respect to grammatical values and to the context."

The aim of the NTS approach is to comply with those requirements with regard to praxis oriented computerlinguistic work. However, there are the following additional requirements in the field of NTS:

- the lexicon should be structured context-oriented,
- basic concepts of the meaning of words should be included in this (restrictive) lexicon,
- the determinating parameters *grammatical values* and *context* should be made explicit by a markedness-theoretic evaluated system.

Computational grammar is considered as the *missing link* between a sector of the UoD and the schemes applied/defined in the KCPM. In other words, syntactic structures can be translated directly into the KCPM modeling concepts, the input being any German sentence related to the chosen segment of reality. The analysis planned contains the following steps:

- In phase 1 the words of a text are compiled in a lexicon. This means categorial, semantic and contextual specification of words.
- In phase 2 word- and morphosyntactically interpreted microstructures are assigned to words and verbgroups (e.g. verbcomplex).
- Phase 3 is dedicated to the analysis of (sentence)syntax according to the specific X'-mechanism of NTS [14]. This mechanism is a generator of phrase-structures defining wordphrases as unfoldings/projections from lexical entities. These unfoldings are defined with regard to the respective categories. A table in the appendix shows the maximal unfolding of categories in German. Given the present state of the art, complex sentences have to be split up into primary structures in terms of the NTS-model.
- In the last phase linguistic concepts (syntactic and morphosyntactic patterns) are mapped to concepts of the conceptual predesign (*thing-type*, *connection-type*, *event-type*,*operation*, *constraint*, *perspective*).

4 Determination of cardinalities

In a former paper [7] we have shown how to derive (identify) thing- and connection-types. Now we are going to fill the blanks in the *min,max* -column standing for cardinalities in the connection-type glossary. Cardinalities provide information on lower and upper bounds to instance sets of those thing-types that are connected via the perspectives in question. For instance, we use the usual definition instead of the extended one presented in [16]. [8] focus on the determination of certain cardinalities in relation to special determiners. From a NTS point of view, cardinality information may be expected in sentences that refer to connection (connection-types). Within sentences like those, given a subject perspective, the cardinality of the subject-NP is determined by the denotation set of $NP_{obj}/\text{-}PP_{obj}$ or PP_{adv} in primary structures. These primary structures are $SUBJ - P^2(obj/adv)$-relations with unmarked verbs as their heads.

For our analysis let's have a look at the following sentences representing primary structures:

(S8) *Ein Flug wird mit genau einem Flugzeug durchgeführt.*
("A flight is carried out by exactly one aircraft").
(S9) *Ein Flugzeug kann für mehrere Flüge eingesetzt werden.*
("An aircraft can be used for several flights").

Cardinalities are assigned according to the structure of the phrase marker. We start with the subject position, hereby presupposing that the most general case is [0,n]. We denote that assumption by [0?,n?] indicating that it is not yet verified. The cardinality determination process then tries to verify the assumption or to modify it adequately. Ideally, this modification is a disambiguating process that depends on structural relations as defined by the phrase marker. So we get a sequence of disambiguated cardinalities whose last element is the one to be filled into the connection-type glossary (see Figure 2). If the ultimate cardinality contains a question mark, the system designer should contact the user in order to get further information, because the disambiguating process did not succeed completely. Note, that natural languages contain, among others, the following cardinality designators (see also [8]):

- suffixes encoding number, e.g. Pilot**en** (pilots)
- elements encoding modality like *können* (*can*), *möglich* (*possible*)
- adjectives restricting extension like *eindeutig* (*unique*), *genau* (*exactly*)
- adverbs of time and space, e.g. *gestern* (*yesterday*), überall (*everywhere*)
- indefinite pronouns like *ein* (*a*)
- quantifiers like *ein* (*one*)

The cardinality of *Flug* in relation to *Flugzeug* (S8) now is determined by the following steps (for a visualization see Figure 3):

- determining the primary structure of the sentence $= SUBJ + P^2(obj, adv)$.
  (A primary structure/sentence is an *atomic sentence* in the sense of [11].
  These are sentences which can not be split up without loss of information.)
- assigning the natural (default) cardinality [0?,n?] to N^3_{subj}.
- adapting the cardinality step by step with regard to inherent values of cardinality designators **[0?:n?]** $= (1) \Rightarrow$ **[1?:1?]** $= (2) \Rightarrow$ **[_!:_!]** $= (3) \Rightarrow$ **[1:1]**;
  $= (1) \Rightarrow$: induced by cardinality-designator *"einem"* (see Figure 3),
  $= (2) \Rightarrow$: induced by cardinality-designator *"genau"*,
  $= (3) \Rightarrow$: result.

Note: The cardinality of the element with maximal node distance to the primary head is dominant for determining the result. "_" are place-holders. The cardinality of *Flugzeug*

in relation to *Flüge* (*flights*) (S9) is determined by the following steps (for a visualization see Figure 4):

- determining the primary structure of the sentence $= SUBJ + P^2(obj, adv)$.
- assigning the natural (default) cardinality [0?,n?] to N^3_{subj}.
- adapting the cardinality step by step cardinality with regard to inherent values of cardinality designators **[0?:n?]** $= (1) \Rightarrow$ **[0!:_]** $= (2) \Rightarrow$ **[_:n!]** $= (3) \Rightarrow$ **[0:n]**.
  $= (1) \Rightarrow$: induced by cardinality-designator *"kann"* (see Figure 3),
  $= (2) \Rightarrow$: induced by cardinality-designator *"mehrere"*,
  $= (3) \Rightarrow$: result.

To sum up, in NIBA we embed cardinalities into constituent structures in order to give the designer the possibility of a *structure dependend* determination.

5 Conclusion

As has been shown within this paper, cardinality information may be extracted from natural language sentences by evaluating cardinality designators that are embedded

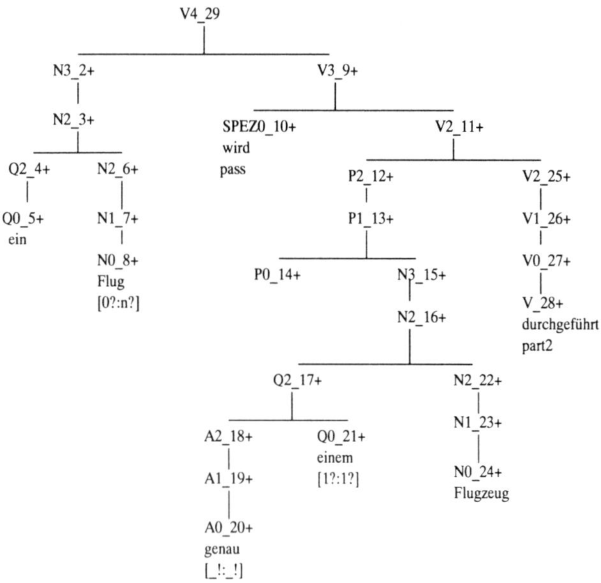

Figure 3: Unfolding structure including carinalities for (S8)

within the constituent structure of these sentences. Thereby we start with the most general cardinality [0?,n?] as a default value for each perspective. Given an exhaustive requirements analysis, the cardinality determination process should eliminate all question marks from the cardinality entries within the connection-type glossary. If there is still a "?", which is easily detected by the designer due to the glossary structure, additional information has to be gained from the enduser.

Technically, we have developed a "syntax tree driven" approach to determine the most specific cardinalities for a given perspective. I.e., we parse the syntax tree of a sentence from left to right. As the parser's work goes on, actual cardinality information specializes or replaces the previous one until the parser reaches the right most node of the syntax tree.

Next NIBA steps will consist in

- the extraction of information classifying thing-types, i.e. if they should be mapped onto classes or attributes,
- the extraction of entries for the operation glossary and for the event glossary,
- the automatic decomposition of complex phrases,
- the verification of our hypotheses concerning sentence-syntax within a subproject that focusses on textlinguistic issues.

References

[1] Coad, P.; Yourdon, E.: Object-oriented Analysis. Prentice Hall 1991.

[2] Rumbaugh, J.; Blaha, M.; Premelani, W.; Eddy, F.; Lorensen, W.: Object-oriented modeling and design. Englewood Cliffs, NJ, Prentice-Hall, 1991.

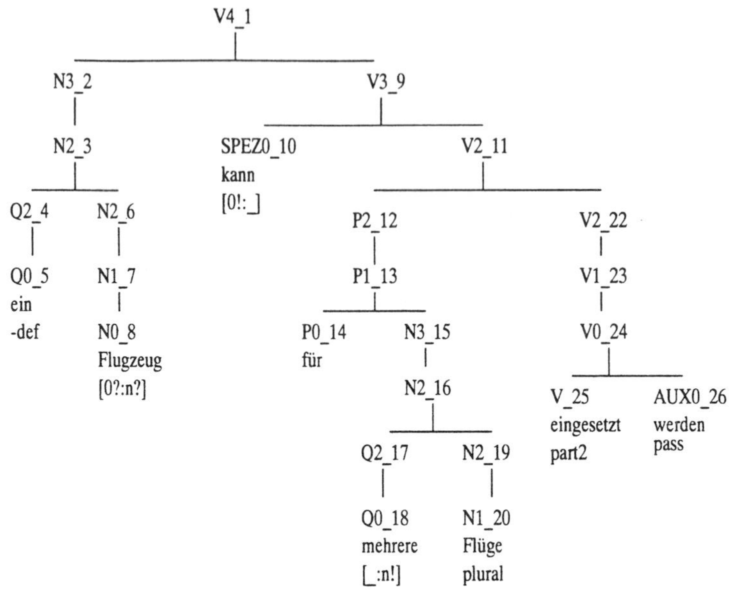

Figure 4: Unfolding structure including cardinalities for (S9)

[3] De Antonellis, V.; Demo, B.: Requirements Collection and Analysis. In: [17], pp. 9-24.

[4] Kop, Ch.; Mayr, H.C.: Reusing Domain Knowlegde in Requirements Analysis. In: (Györkös, J. et al.): Proc. ReTIS'94, 3rd Conf. on ReEngineering of Information Systems, Bled, 1994.

[5] Kop, Ch.; Mayr, H.C.: Objektorientierte Analyse und konzeptueller Vorentwurf. In: [18] pp. 103-110.

[6] Kop, Ch.: Herleitung von EERM+-Schemata aus Ding-, Zusammenhangs- und Operationsverzeichnissen. Diplomarbeit, Universität Klagenfurt 1993.

[7] Fliedl G.; Kop, Ch.; Mayerthaler, W.; Mayr, H.C.; Winkler, Ch.: Dinge und Zusammenhänge: NTS gestützte Ableitung konzeptueller Vorentwurfschemaeinträge aus natürlichsprachlichen Anforderungsdefinitionen. Appears in: Workshop Natürlichsprachlicher Entwurf von Informationssystemen Tutzing, Mai 1996.

[8] Albrecht, M.; Bucholz, E.; Düsterhöft, A.; Thalheim, B.: An Informal and Efficient Approach for Obtaining Semantic Constraints using Sample Data and Natural Language Processing. In: [19] pp 1-11.

[9] Chen, P.P.: English Sentence Structure and Entity Relationship Diagrams. In: Int. Journal of Information Siences, Vol 29, 1983, pp 127-149.

[10] Tjoa, A, M.; Berger, L.: Transformation of Requirement Specification Expressed in Natural Language into an EER-Model. In: [20] pp 106-217.

[11] Nijssen, G.; Halpin, T.A.: Conceptual Schema and Relational Database Design - A fact oriented approach. Prentice Hall Publ. Comp., 1989.

[12] Schnattler, M.: Herleitung von Ereignisschemata aus erweiterten Operations- und Ereignisverzeichnissen. Diplomarbeit, Universität Klagenfurt, 1993.

[13] Mayr, H.C.; Schnattler, M.: Vorkonzeptuelle und konzeptuelle Dynamikmodellierung.

[14] Fliedl, G.; Mayerthaler, W.: Natürlichkeitstheoretische Syntax. In: [21], pp. 610-635.

[15] Herzog, O; Rollinger C.-R. (eds): Text Understanding in LILOG. Integrating Computational Linguistics and Artificial Intelligence Final Report on the IBM Germany LILOG-Project. Lecture Notes in Artificial Intelligence 546. Springer Verlag, Heidelberg 1991.

[16] Burg, J.F.M. and Riet, van de, R.P., COLOR-X: Object Modeling profits from Linguistics, Technical Report IR-365, Vrije Universiteit, Amsterdam, 1994.

[17] Ceri, S. (ed.): Methodology and Tools for Database Design, North Holland, 1983.

[18] Oberweis, A. (eds): Proceedings EMISA Fachgruppentreffen 1995, Requirements Engineering für Informationssysteme - Karlsruhe Oktober 1995.

[19] Thalheim, B. (ed.): Proceedings of the Workshop Semantics in Databases, Prague, Jan. 13-16, 1995.

[20] Elmasri, R.A.; Kouramajian, B.; Thalheim, B (eds.).: 12th International Conference on Entity Relationship Approach. Arlington, Texas. New York, Springer 1993.

[21] Jakobs, J.; v. Stechnow, A.; Sternefeld, W.; Vennemann, Th.. (eds.): Syntax. Ein internationales Handbuch zeitgenvssischer Forschung. DeGruyter, Berlin.

Appendix

$$
\begin{array}{lll@{\qquad}lll}
V^{max} & = & V^4(mainclause) & ADV^{max} & = & ADV^2 \\
V^{max} & = & V^3(subordinateclause) & P^{max} & = & P^2 \\
N^{max} & = & N^3 & PT^{max} & = & PT^0 \\
N[\text{+präd}] & = & N^{max} - 1 = N^2 & INT^{max} & = & INT^0 \\
A^{max} & = & A^2 & ART[-def] = Q^{max} & = & Q^0 \\
Q^{max} & = & Q^2 & SPEZ^{max} & = & SPEZ^0 \\
 & & & AUX^{max} & = & AUX^0
\end{array}
$$

$$\boxed{X^n \rightarrow X^n/X^n - 1}$$

X^n in case of recursion of categories $X^n - 1$ in other cases, $X^n - 1 =$ head

$0 \leq n \leq 4$[V (main clause)] $0 \leq n \leq 3$[N, V (subordinate clause)] $0 \leq n \leq 2$[A, ADV, P, Q] $n = 0/$[SPEZ, INT, PT, AUX]

X is a variable over the wordclasses {V (verb), N (noun), A (adjective), ADV (adverb), Q (quantifier, P (preposition), PT (particle), INT (interjection), ART (article), SPEZ (specifier), AUX (auxiliary)}

Specifiers are linguistic signs, that point to grammatical categories; e.g. in *Diese Firma exportiert viel nach Italien ("this enterprise exports a lot to Italy")* the verb exportiert (exports) specifies the sentence, since it indicates the category "main-clause". In each German main-clause the finite verb fills the position of the second constituent. The degree of unfolding is limited according to the respective categories. Frequently used and more flexible categories reach a higher unfolding, the general principle being: "The more natural the higher the unfolding". Since a verb is more "useful" than for instance an adverb, the verb's degree of unfolding is higher than that of the adverb; since the main clause is more verbal than the subordinate clause, its maximal unfolding is V^4. The V^3-unfolding of the subordinate clause reflects the less verbal/more nominal character of the subordinate clause.

Applications of Natural Language to Information Systems
R.P. van de Riet et al. (Eds.)
IOS Press, 1996

Linguistic Tool Based Information Elicitation in Large Heterogeneous Database Networks

Stephen Milliner, Mike Papazoglou

School of Information Systems
Queensland Univ. of Technology
Brisbane, QLD 4001
Australia

Hans Weigand

Infolab, Tilburg University
P.O.Box 90153,
5000 LE Tilburg
The Netherlands

Abstract. In this paper a logical model to facilitate pro-active elicitation of schema information from multiple heterogeneous information sources is presented. This is achieved through high-level descriptors – constructed using the WordNet linguistic tool – whose aim is to provide a consistent, logically organized view of information across multiple discrete heterogeneous sources. The model dynamically clusters databases into clumps located in a logical space, so that the elements within a cluster have a high degree of semantic correlation. Thus, interactions between remote database sites are focused, irrelevant information is filtered out and searches are accelerated.
Keywords : Large Scale Heterogenious Database Network, Linguistic Tool, Relationship Discovery, Information Elicitation, Dynamic Database Clustering.

1 Introduction

The multitude, diversity and complexity of on-line information sources makes discovery of appropriate information a significant obstacle to a large-scale distributed information infrastructure. Regrettably, the standard approach to multi-database querying naively assumes that the user is to some extent explicitly aware of the existence, structure and contents of (exported) schema elements in each of the autonomous databases. While this approach to querying might be feasible when the number of nodes[1] is small, it can be potentially intractable in the presence of a large number of information sources. There is a clear requirement for powerful and responsive tools for locating, retrieving, cross-correlating and combining the right pieces of information across large database networks, with a minimum effort by the end-user. Such tools must establish a common linguistic basis so that diverse systems may agree on the meaning of the information that is to be shared.

In our view the first step in sharing and exchanging information in a large multi-database system is to ascertain what data sources exist, how they are related, and what

[1] A database node may contain a collection of databases. As we are interested in the interaction and relationships between nodes we occasionally use the terms database and node interchangeably. Where confusion may arise the differences are made explicit.

kind of schema information they provide. This step is followed by posing a meaningful request formed on the basis of the information obtained. System size, complexity and the dynamic nature of the system (and interactions) precludes an explicit logically centralized a priori specification of the entire inter-database schema space and schema inter-relationships. This dictates against the use of a network-wide global directory such as in the case of the Carnot project which uses the Cyc common-sense knowledge-base as an extensive global context and federating mechanism [1]. In order to be effective, distributed information elicitation schemes should rely on content-specific agreements for the sharing and use of information originating from disparate data sources. This results in establishing common *ontologies* for semantically common domains. This paper describes the use of dictionaries and linguistic tools to aid the process of information elicitation in large networked information sources. The proposed approach promotes the semi-automatic (self) organization of database node interactions, clumps databases in logical space, and enables the automatic discovery of new relationships between network-wide information resources.

In the following related work section existing distributed system architectures are discussed. Section-3 discusses the system organization while section-4 presents higher-level abstraction constructs for clustering databases around them, while conclusions and future work are presented in section-6.

2 Related Work

Our approach to eliciting information from disparate information sources is related to work on multi-databases and information retrieval. In multi-database systems and federated databases the focus has mainly been on sharing of distributed information and not on information discovery. Distributed information management is performed by means of a common language and is assumed that users know the information of interest. A particular database may choose to export parts of its schema and import schema portions from remote databases. All exported database elements are registered in a federal dictionary. A requesting database consults the federal dictionary for existing databases and available schemas, and then imports schema elements it requires. While this approach might be appealing for a small number of interconnected databases it clearly not scalable. Locating the right information in a large unstructured network of data dictionaries is extremely cumbersome, has limited potential for success and, more importantly, is error prone.

Some of the issues relating to the identification of semantically related chunks of information – in the context of multi-database systems – can be found in [2]. This publication describes an approach that relies on an abstract global data structure to match user terms to the semantically closest available system terms. This allows users to form imprecise queries when accessing data rather than being forced to use system-specified terms. However, this approach tends to centralize the search within a single logical index thereby introducing performance limitations for large networks.

In most information retrieval systems, the emphasis is usually on how to build an indexing scheme to efficiently access information given some hints about the resource [3]. Most of the distributed information retrieval systems are designed to work in a homogeneous environment. There has been some work to extend schemes to a network of heterogeneous information retrieval systems [4]. In [5], an approach is described that relies on *external indexing* for finding information in a network of information systems. Each node of the index contains a network address along with a set of condensed descriptions called *skeleton*. Resource providers are added to the index using knows-about relationships. This approach tends to centralize the search in a single index and is used for the actual resource discovery. Potentially (if users make queries about all existing information space), all nodes would have the same index. It is not clear from the above references how the actual node selection is performed.

3 Database Clustering and the Three-tier Organization

To help establish database node inter–relationships a logical cross-correlation of disparate information sources at a higher level of inter-node interaction is introduced. This is achieved by creating logical objects *Generic Concepts* (GCs), which achieve explicit semantic clustering between relevant pieces of information. Generic concepts pertain to and abstractly describe a certain area of interest. Databases are then linked to these GCs by means of a weighting factor which reflects their own interests. Generic concepts essentially represent centroids of the inter-node relationship space around which databases cluster, and are engineered to span the universe of discourse.

Figure 1 shows the three tier inter–database node organization. The bottom level depicts a simplified view of diverse database nodes (ovals) and their schemas in relational form. The middle level represents meta–data for the database schemas. Meta–data contains a description of the schema items' structure (eg. relations, attributes, fields, references). The top most level corresponds to the meta–schema or generic concept, level. This level contains abstract dynamic objects which implement the clustering of related portions of the underlying component schemas. A GC is thus, unlike a global schema, a logically decentralized construct dynamically defining "islands of related information". A single database may be simultaneously involved in several clusters of databases. This approach enables the construction and maintenance of (abstract) sub-spaces of the universe of discourse (UoD), so that resource elicitation is structured. The advantage of forming such database clusters, is that searches are goal-driven[2] and the number of potential inter-database interactions is restricted substantially.

Although we may normally cluster database nodes around "areas of interest", other clustering features, such as geographical location, access authorization and usage roles

[2]A goal-driven search accepts a high-level request indicating what a user requires and is responsible for deciding where and how to satisfy it.

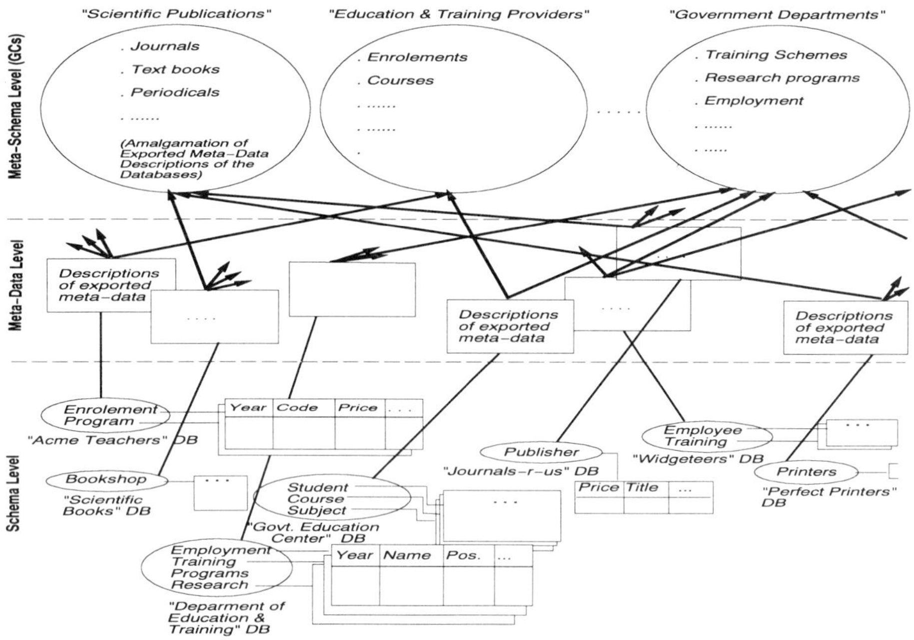

Figure 1: Levels of abstraction in the Three–tier Inter–database Organization

– reflecting different levels of responsibility within an organization – corporate term usage, and domains of applicability and so on, can be introduced. Consequently, several different logical groupings of the data resources may be possible, based on a combination of various criteria. To create GCs we categorize and group related collections of schema elements by way of descriptions that abstractly delineate a particular concept, and apply them to the entire collection of members of a GC. In order to produce this description a common linguistic tool, WordNet [11], is used. GCs dynamically clump databases together based on common areas of interest into a single atomic unit. This generates a *conceptual space* which has a specific content and a scope. GCs in fact define ontologies for semantically common domains. In the context of multiple database nodes a common ontology, materialized through a specific GC, can serve as a knowledge-level specification of the ontological commitments of a set of participating databases.

To achieve a logical sub–division of the distributed information space, we arrange our database cluster space in a form that resembles a cluster-based *associative network* [7]. This type of network is a variant of semantic networks [8] which uses numerically weighted similarity links. In this way we can define cluster of nodes relevant to any given node by calculating weighted association links between the nodes, based on average of contextual "closeness" in several feature dimensions, including in the relevant cluster only those nodes linked with a weight over a certain threshold. The cluster structure is derived from the values of terminological node descriptors and only semantically very similar nodes are clumped together in the same cluster. Hence by clustering database nodes around GCs, the relationship space is logically sub–divided, and searching is implemented via reference to weights that are ascribed to the links between database nodes and generic concepts. The links being discussed here define a conceptual relationship organization upon which physical data sharing may be pursued. How searching is pursued, how physical data sharing is organized, and how the conceptual organization described here ties in with it, is discussed in [9] and [19].

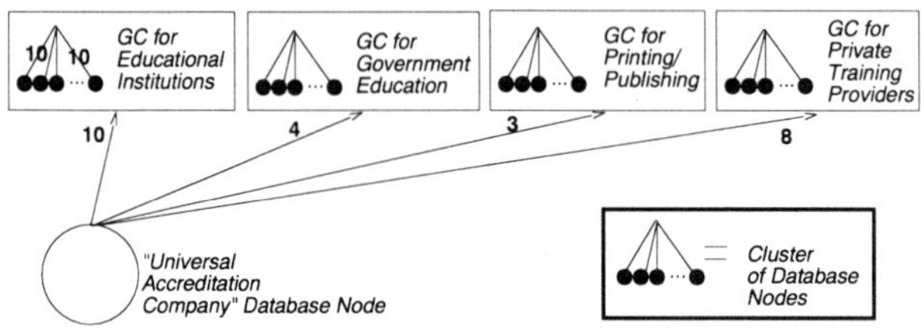

Figure 2: Connecting a Database Node

Consider for example, the case of the *Universal_Accreditation_Company* database which is being set up to provide accreditation of courses and subjects between institutions and various private educational training providers. The *Universal_Accreditation* database, will maintain information on various education service providers, their courses and subjects, and how these inter-relate. In order to be able to source appropriate information from remote database sites, the node must determine which areas are of interest, and then establish strong links to GCs implementing these, cf. Figure 2. This process may occur over time, as database nodes may dynamically specify the degree to which they participate in various database clusters. By *strongly linking* to a certain GC (eg. ranking it 10/10 say), nodes agree to associate with each other and thus inter-node organization is achieved implicitly. Each of these same database nodes may also link less strongly (eg. ranking of 8/10) to other GCs which have their own associated cluster of database nodes.

During initialization of the system GCs are created and link weights to them are established. This is essentially a pre–clustering process, where groupings of database nodes are established on a tentative basis only. During execution link weights to GCs are updated over time, new GCs may be formed, and existing GCs may disappear. Generic concept initialization relies on the assumptions that databases (associated with individual nodes) were formed in relation to a specific area of interest, and that these *areas* may be defined and generalized to form an *appropriate* number of *abstract meta-objects* (i.e., generic concepts).

4 Constructing Generic Concepts

In order to initially cluster databases a high level description must first be developed by each administrator. To demonstrate this consider the previous example of the Universal_Accreditation database, which deals with academic institutions and accreditation processes. This database will contain entities such as *courses*, *committees*, *accreditation_processes*, etc.

The administrator must provide an object-oriented (OO) view of the component schema contents. This is essentially based on an object-oriented analysis model of the information domain such as the OMT [10] in conjunction with the *subject-oriented* development methodology [6]. The subject-oriented approach supports the packaging of related classes (such as schema classes) into subjects. Each subject views its domain in its own, subjective abstract way. Subjects can be used to flatten, reorganize and aggregate their underlying class hierarchies to contain just those features and details used by the subject itself. The combination of the OMT and subject-oriented methodologies is consistent with our view of the logical clustering process and leads to further flexible semantic enrichment of the data domain descriptions.

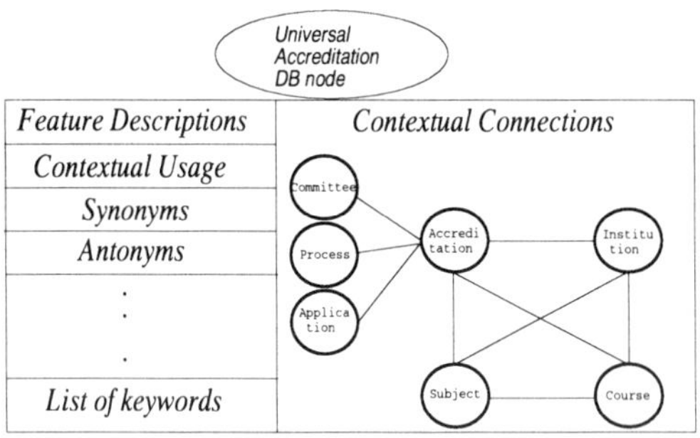

Figure 3: Description of an Abstract Descriptor Class

This methodology results in composing *abstract descriptor classes* (ADCs) which are defined with the information they maintain, e.g., descriptions of their features and any constraints they comply with. As part of the description the administrator may also choose to include certain details such as: remarks about the meaning of attributes, geographical location, infrastructure information (eg. department a database node is associated with and its position within the organization or institution), a general description of the class's application domain and so on. These details are not required by the initial clustering process but are useful to remote users wanting further details about an information resource, and during link weight updating (i.e. re–clustering).

An abstract class (as shown in figure 3) comprises two essential components: a section containing details provided by administrators for viewing by users (both local and remote), and a section containing a graph structure derived from the administrators

OO view of the database's domain. The nodes of the graph are descriptions of the classes depicted in the OO design. The class descriptions and the link structure are used in the initial clustering of databases to form the generic concepts.

4.1 Class Node Descriptions

Comparison of graph nodes cannot be based solely on the single term names given to the OO classes from which the database node description graph has been derived. A common semantic and syntactic platform must be used to provide a common terminological/ontological framework. In order to achieve this, we make use of the massive semantic network WordNet, which yields less discontinuous matching than simple keyword matching approaches.

The clustering similarity metric is then based on the meaning of a term (polysemy and homography), several terms with the same meaning (synonyms), and the "semantic level" of a term (specifications and generalizations [2]). Hence each graph node class description comprises a matrix $a_{n,m}$ of (noun) terms. A particular term, $a_{i,1}$ say, will correspond to the name of the class in the OO diagram. The synonyms of this term will be $a_{i,2}$, $a_{i,3}$ ... $a_{i,m}$ (some may be null terms). Terms $a_{i-x,j}$ (x 0) will be more general than terms $a_{i,j}$, and terms $a_{i+x,j}$ will be more specific.

An example of the GUI output for the class label "course" is depicted in Figure 4. The first step after entering the term is to choose the *senses* from the list WordNet provides. The sense number returned is then associated with the term (as is the case with all other words in the class description), thereby avoiding problems of polysemy (words with many senses) and homography. For example, Figure 4 shows that the term "course" has eight senses in WordNet, but once the domain of discourse is limited to study, then only one of the eight can occur. In the next step more general terms and more specific terms for the class label are generated. In the final step, all synonyms for these terms are generated to produce the node's class label description matrix $a_{n,m}$.

We can distinguish between two distinct approaches to the study of word meaning: primitive-based versus relation-based [18]. Relation-based approaches, such as adopted by WordNet, stay in the realm of natural language. Although circularity is a lurking problem, one avoids the problem of establishing "the" set of primitives as well as inconsistency caused by different interpretations of these primitives by different users. Although the kind of relational semantics in WordNet is quite useful in a clustering and matching context, it also has certain limitations. WordNet does only consider concepts that correspond to one word – thus where necessary, multiple terms are linked together. Certain important semantic relations, such as "purpose" are not accounted for – instead these aspects of a database node are included as separate "fields" within the description (left hand side of Figure 3). To avoid an "explosion" of closely related senses, some kind of generative theory might be useful [17]. In addition, when class names have been chosen badly, the method may break down. Linguistic correctness is

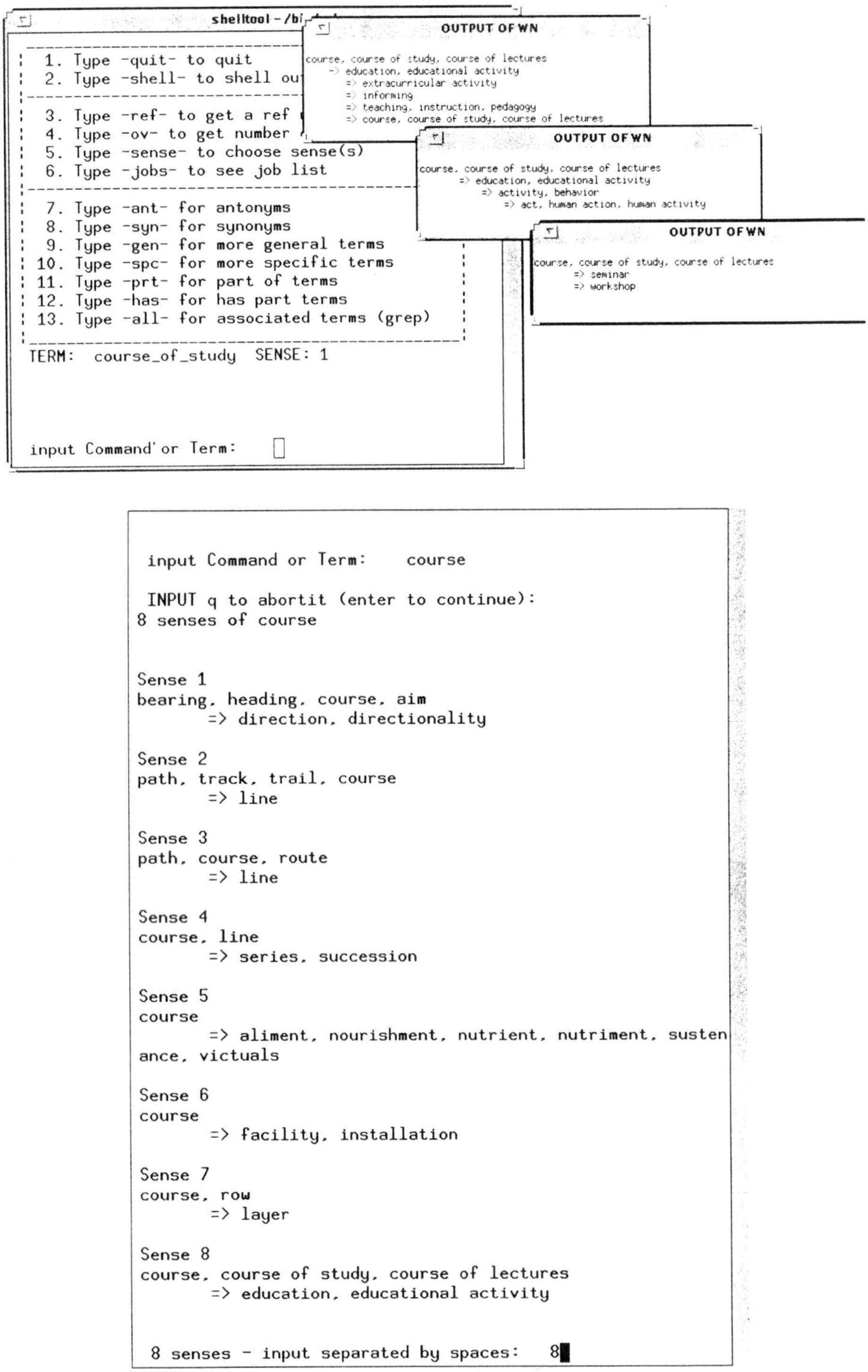

Figure 4: Semantic Network Output

a feature of data schemas that grows in relevance when databases tend to be used more over the boundaries of local contexts. See [20] and [21] for the integration of linguistic tools in information system design.

By generating a semantic hierarchy for each ADC, we maximize the probability that relationships between nodes in two independently constructed database descriptions, will be identified in the clustering process. In this way, users may be provided richly semantic descriptions of the disparate data resources in a network of databases, while maintaining a common context (i.e. the massive semantic network). This context is not exhaustive, but can be extended to cater for specific domains.

4.2 Conceptual Similarity Metrics

During clustering, the similarity between two graphs (representing two different database schemas) is calculated in two steps. Firstly, the nodes in one graph are compared with those in the other graph. From this a initial "pairing" of the nodes is determined. In the second step a comparison of the structure of two graphs is made based on the inter–node pairings and a semantic distance value is calculated. This essentially corresponds to a grouping of information sources based on their specialized domain seeding knowledge.

4.2.1 Comparing Nodes Within Description Graphs

A key aspect of handling information elicitation is defining the degree of similarity (see [12]) between two discrete schema elements represented as nodes in two discrete graphs. This is mainly based on statistical co-occurrences of descriptors in objects, and has been successfully used for automatic thesaurus generation of textual databases [13]. In order to cluster description graphs we first convert graph node terms into a matrix of inter-individual similarity. Pseudo code for the comparison of two database description graphs "X" against "Y" containing class description matrices (within graph nodes) of the form $C_{n,m}$ is as follows:

```
For (i = 0; i <number of nodes in Graph X; i++){
    For (j = 0; j < n /* matrix i_{n,m} */; j++){
        For (k = 0; !found && k < m /* matrix i_{n,m} */; k++){
            Search for X-node item i_{j,k} in each of Y-node class descriptions. Increment hits matrix H_{i,p} if
            item found in one of Y-node's "p", set found to TRUE, mark row of "p" where match was found
            (i.e. do not perform any more comparisons with elements of "p's" row, or current "i" row).
        }
    }
    /* find which node "p" in Y's graph "i" should pair with - n: rows in "i", q: rows in Y's node "r"*/
    For (r = 0,max = 0; r <max(p) in row H_{i,p} && H_{i,r}! = 0; r++)
        If (max < (H_{i,r}/(H_{i,r} + n + q) max =(H_{i,r} /(H_{i,r} + n + q)
}
```

Node similarity s_{ij} between node "i" in graph "X", and node "j" in graph "Y" is symmetric, and is used in the derivation of the distance between the two graphs.

There are two "phases" in the semantic comparison of database node descriptions. Firstly, there is the comparison of graph nodes containing synonyms, generalizations and specializations of "area of interest" terms (as produced by WordNet). Secondly, there is the comparison of how nodes from different graphs relate to each other in terms of their respective graph structures. Hence, we consider localized equivalence of graph nodes, with respect to the global structures of their respective graphs.

4.2.2 Comparing Description Graphs

When pairwise similarities have been established between all relevant term pairs, a hierarchical agglomerative cluster generation process can be adopted [14]. To determine the structural and semantic similarity between two graphs we base our assumptions and algorithm regarding conceptual similarity between terms in different WordNet instances representing abstract classes, on heuristics-guided spreading activation algorithms, and on work in the information retrieval (IR) area presented in [15], [16]. These approaches have developed algorithms which take advantage of the semantics in a hierarchical thesaurus representing the "is-a" relationships between index terms. The algorithms calculate the conceptual closeness between a document and a query, interpreting the conceptual distance between two terms as the topological distance of the two terms in the hierarchical thesaurus. In these, terms semantic relatedness is based on an aggregate of the interconnections between two nodes (representing concepts) in a semantic network. Based on the above results we can define a conceptual distance metric as follows:

$$DIST_{IR}(X,Y) = 1/l \sum_{t_j \in X}^{l} min_{t_i \in Y}(d_{ij})$$

where:

$DIST_{IR}$(X,Y) = distance from graph X to graph Y

d_{ij} = shortest path between node t_i and any node t_j in graph X

l = number of nodes in graph X; and assuming edges weights of 1.

The above formula measures conceptual distance by mapping pairs of index terms [16], whereas [15]estimates the average minimum path length over all pairwise combinations between two nets. In both cases comparisons are performed in relation to a weighted hierarchical thesaurus. In the case here, we simply merge the two graphs being compared (around the node pairings - i.e. based on the WordNet structure) to produce a "local" thesaurus graph. In addition, no weights are assigned to graph edges, instead the conceptual distance between two graphs are qualified by the (maximum) node similarity value obtained in the previous step. In essence, the IR technique is concerned with conceptual distance only. Hence, more attention is paid to the number of edges separating nodes, rather than the actual graph structure. This results from the fact that only 'is-a' hierarchical graphs are considered. When node similarities (s_j) are included, we can define the distance between two graphs as follows:

$$DIST_{ADC_{IR}}(X,Y) = 1/l \sum_{t_j \in X}^{l} min_{t_i \in Y}(D_{ij})$$

where:

$DIST_{ADC_{IR}}$(X,Y) = distance from graph X to graph Y

$D_{ij} = d_{ij} \times \frac{1}{max_{s_j}}$

In order to further differentiate graphs from each other, a second factor based on the number of edges branching out from a node is included in the distance metric. The database description graph distance metric may thus be re–defined as:

$$DIST_{ADC}(X,Y) = 1/l \sum_{t_j \in X}^{l} min_{t_i \in Y}(D_{ij} + B_j)$$

Where:

$DIST_{ADC}$(X,Y) = distance from graph X to graph Y

$B_i = \frac{|b_{X_j} - b_{Y_j}|}{l+k}$

b_{Z_u} = number of edges from node "u" in graph Z

k = number of nodes in graph Y

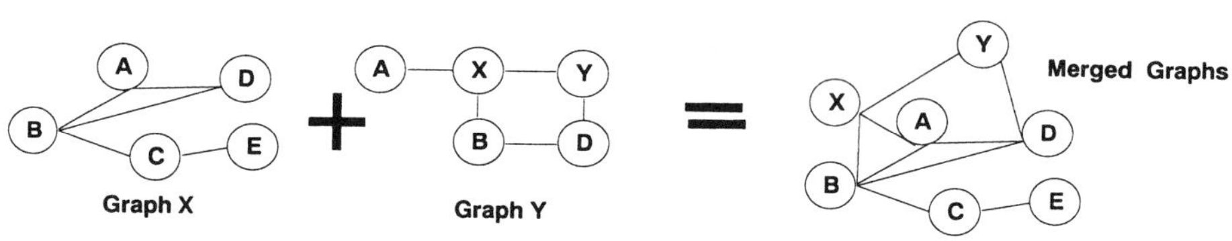

$1/l \sum_{t_j \in X}^{l} min_{t_i \in X}(D_{ij}) =$ 1/5 (0 + 0 + 0 + (1*1/1+1/6) + (1*1/1+1/6)) = 0.467 = Distance from Graph X to Graph Y

Figure 5: Example Distance Calculation from Graph X to Graph Y

As an example of a distance calculation, consider the two graphs and their merger shown below in Figure 5.

Assume that initial comparison of the graph nodes (see section 4.2.1) has resulted in the pairs : X_A–Y_A, X_B–Y_B and X_D–Y_D, with similarity values of 1.0, 0.8 and 0.9 respectively (for example). Based on the above definitions and these valuse, a summary of the distance calculation between graphs X and Y is presented in the lower half of Figure 5.

We then apply the initial clustering process which makes use of these inter–graph distance values and organizes database schema partitions. This results in the clustering of database node graphs around GCs. The subject-oriented programming methodology can also be applied at this stage as it provides primitives (in the form of *composition expressions*) which facilitate the composition of abstract classes by specifying how to combine details from the various constituent abstract classes and reconcile any different points of view between the abstract classes.

5 Conclusion

In this paper we have described a methodology for organizing inter-node relationships in large collections of networked databases in order to elicit schema related information. The proposed form of interaction results in the creation of dynamic clusters of database nodes centered around around areas of interest or expertise (viz the generic concepts). Generic concepts support navigation and the process of information elicitation in large networks contextually interlinked schema terms originating from diverse information sources. Unlike other distributed architectures based on static segregation and indexing, this database clustering approach ensures that data items within the space are never completely segregated (logically) from each other. This results in a dynamic distributed system organization comprising a large number of fully logically interconnected database nodes.

This architecture fulfills three fundamental tasks : it provides a common ontology to which participant databases may contribute; it specifies a relatively small set of databases/nodes for interaction (viz. the database clusters); and implicitly provides local nodes with a model of other systems (via weighted links). The stronger the correlations between services offered at disparate nodes, the more similar their area of interest and the more closely the link weights to various global concepts will resemble each other. This restricts the potential number of database nodes which must be searched and interpreted. In future work we will be evaluating the ability of the clustering process to provide a good initial defining of the database node inter–relationships – this will provide some evaluation of the possible short comings of the system outlined in section 4.1. Other methods for updating of link weights and searching of the system are to be developed and evaluated. In addition, we will be incorporating further "layers" on top of this initial platform to promote data sharing.

References

[1] M.N. Huhns et al. "Integrating Enterprise Information Models in Carnot", *1st Int'l Conf. on Intelligent and Cooperative Information Systems*, Rotterdam, May 1993, M. Huhns, M. Papazoglou, G. Schlageter (eds), pp. 32-42.

[2] M. Bright, A. Hurson, S. Pakzad "Automated Resolution of Semantic Heterogeneity in Multidatabases" ACM ToDS, vol. 19, no.2, June 1994.

[3] G. Salton and M. J. McGill. "Introduction to Modern Information Retrieval", McGraw Hill Computer Science Series, New York, 1983.

[4] P. Simpson "Query Processing in a Heterogeneous Retrieval Network", 11th International Conference on Research & Development in Information Retrieval, ACM SIGIR, Grenoble, June 1992.

[5] R. Alonso and D. Barbara and L. L. Cova "Data Sharing in Large Heterogeneous Information Network" Workshop on Heterogeneous Databases, IEEE-CS TC on Distributed Processing, Dec. 1989.

[6] H. Ossher et. al "Subject-Oriented Composition Rules", Procs. OOPSLA'95, Austin Texas, 1995.

[7] N.V. Findler "A Heuristic Information Retrieval System Based on Associative Networks", in *Associative networks*, (N.V. Findler, Ed), Academic Press, 1979.

[8] F. Lehmann (Ed) "Semantic Networks in Artificial Intelligence", Pergamon Press, 1992.

[9] S. Milliner, A. Bouguettaya, and M. Papazoglou "A Scalable Architecture for Autonomous Heterogeneous Database Interactions", 21 Int'l Conference on Very Large Databases, Zurich, Switzerland, Sept. 1995.

[10] J. Rumbaugh et al. "Object–Oriented Modeling and Design", Prentice Hall international editions, 1991.

[11] G. Miller "WordNet: A lexical Database for English", Communications of ACM, vol. 38, no. 11, Nov. 1995.

[12] B. Everitt "Cluster Analysis", Heinemann Educational Books Ltd., Great Britain, 1981.

[13] H. Chen, K.J. Lynch "Automatic Construction of Networks of Concepts Characterizing Document Databases", IEEE Transactions on Systems, Man and Cybernetics, vol. 22, no. 5, Sept. 1992.

[14] G. Salton "Automatic Text Processing", Addison-Wesley, Reading Mass., 1989.

[15] R. Rada et al. "Development and Application of a Metric on Semantic Nets", IEEE Transactions on Systems, Man and Cybernetics, vol. 19, no. 1, 1989.

[16] Y. W. Kim, J.H. Kim "A Model of Knowledge Based Information Retrieval with Hierarchical Concept Graph", Journal of Documentation, Vol.46, No.2, p113-136, 1990.

[17] J. Pustejovsky "The Generative Lexicon", Computational Linguistics, vol. 17, no. 4, p409-441, 1991.

[18] R. Jackendoff "Semantics and Cognition", Cambridge MA: The MIT Press.

[19] S. Milliner, M. Papazoglou "Reassessing the Roles of Negotiation and Contracting for Interoperable Databases", International Workshop on Advances in Databases and Information Systems, p144-157, Moscow, May 1994.

[20] H. Weigand, "Linguistically Motivated Principles of Knowledge Base Systems", Foris, Dordrecht (Mounton-De Gruyter, Berlin), 1990.

[21] H.Burg, Color-X Event Model: Integrated Specification of the Dynamics of Individual Objects", 14th International Conference on Object–Oriented and Entity–Relationship Modeling, p146-157., Dec. 1995.

Applications of Natural Language to Information Systems
R.P. van de Riet et al. (Eds.)
IOS Press, 1996

Correspondence Analysis of Dynamic Schema Constructs Using Case Grammar

Sari Hakkarainen
Swedish Institute for Systems Development and
SYSLAB Stockholm University and
Royal Institute of Technology,
Electrum 212, S-164 40 KISTA, Sweden
sari@sisu.se

Abstract. The problem of determining correspondence assertions in schema comparison is addressed focusing at the analysis of the dynamic schema constructs. Schemas are semantically enriched using a method of linguistic instruments. A heuristic method for determining the correspondence assertions between semantically enriched dynamic schema constructs is proposed. Results of a limited case study of requirements specifications for telecommunication services, imply the proposed approach to be a promising line of research in integration of schema dynamics.

1 Introduction

In semi-automatic schema integration the most problematic issue is the comparison phase of the process. Schema comparison consists of correspondence detection and conflict analysis among the combined schemas. The problems arise because a UoD can be modelled in many different ways and the comparison concerns the semantic interpretation of models created by different people for different purposes. During the last years, several heuristic methods for schema comparison have been proposed. These methods can be classified along a dimension according to the knowledge sources they make use of. Some methods focus on the static information contained in a conceptual schema, such as the names of object types and attributes and the relationships between object types, as in [1,2,3]. Other methods take into account more of the information in a schema, such as constraints and update semantics [4,5].

The above methods only consider the knowledge contained within the schemas to be compared. Recently, a number of techniques for semantic enrichment have emerged. *Semantic enrichment* involve using alternative sources than the schema describe additional knowledge about the UoD. A semantic enrichment technique can take many different forms, e.g.; concept hierarchies [6], shared ontology [7], linguistic knowledge [8], fuzzy terminologies [9], domain abstractions [10] or extension analysis [11]. However, the existing techniques provide poor specifications of how, in practice to acquire and apply the proposed additional knowledge from the UoD to a schema. Another problem is that the schema parts which specify the dynamics of an application system are seldom considered in the existing methodologies. [12]

In the research area of knowledge representation there exists several formalisms for representing general expert knowledge. The issue has been studied from the psychological, linguistic and computational point of view and much effort has been put in the development of semantic networks, often referred to as relational or conceptual graphs. A semantic network offers an intuitive representation of knowledge since it represents the linear semantics of logic and natural language as a structure of interconnected nodes and arcs. [3]

There are various case systems, i.e. sets of deep cases available for describing actions denoted by verbs in all sentences in a particular UoD, for instance [14, 15, 16], which have been applied in knowledge representation and natural language processing. However, these systems vary not only in notation but also in the contents of the set of cases and in the deep case structures for actions. It seems there is no universal set of deep cases nor an universal agreement on their usage. Thus, we conclude that yet using the case grammar and an established case system for general knowledge representation, a deep case system has to be application domain dependent.

During the last years there have emerged a number of techniques for comparison of conceptual graphs. The techniques may approach the comparison from several usage perspectives but often have the theories of conceptual dependency [15] or structure mapping [17] as theoretical basis for the comparison. These techniques consider the conceptual graphs related to the static information of a schema and rely heavily on construction of a classification structure. In the context of this thesis, none of the existing techniques is quite adequate. The introduction of dynamics into the comparison implies that the time aspect has to be taken into account. A dynamic rule specifies conditions to a system state *before* an event occurs, and conclusions the system state *after* the event has occurred. Thus, a structure mapping algorithm, such as [18] or measurement of semantic distances, such as [19] are not applicable here. For comparison of dynamic parts of component schemas a novel method needs to be developed.

In this paper, we address the problem of schema comparison in determining correspondence assertions and conflict predictions focusing at analysing the dynamic schema constructs. The purpose is to propose a method for how to compare dynamic schema constructs with the intention to provide user a set of correspondence assertions among several local schemas. We apply a case grammar to schemas specifying a real world application domain of telephoning optional features. The studied schemas are defined in Delphi, a conceptual modelling language for specification of data and processes. We modify the linguistic knowledge technique [20] to match the application domain as a method for semantic enrichment. An algorithm for comparing semantically enriched Delphi schemas is proposed and applied in the case study. Finally, we compare the results with control schemas, i.e. the integrated schemas used in the same domain.

2 Application System Specification in Delphi

2.1 Overview of the Language and the Tool

As the analytical starting point for this paper we describe Delphi, a conceptual modelling language and tool environment, developed at Ellemtel Utvecklings AB. A Delphi schema consists of a static and a dynamic part. The static part specifies possible states of the system while the dynamic part specifies the possible state transitions between these states. Delphi has a graphical representation of the static schema components expressed in DCML. The graphical representation of Delphi corresponds to a linear representation, which is expressed in (slightly modified) first order logic. [21] presents a more detailed description of the logical interpretation of graphical Delphi schemas. The Delphi tool does not support integration of schemas. It is complemented with a simulation technique which may be used for validation of a specification and a technique for consistency control which may be used for verification of a specification.

2.2 Specification of Static Aspects of a UoD

In the static part of a Delphi schema all possible states of the system are specified. A system state is described by stating which entities with specified properties and static constraints there exist, which attributes and data types these entities possess, and which are the relationships among the entities. It is also possible to specify invariants, static rules which apply to the schema in any system state. We illustrate the usage of static Delphi schema components as applied to a telephoning case, which is provided by Telia Research [22], here adapted from the case study in [23].

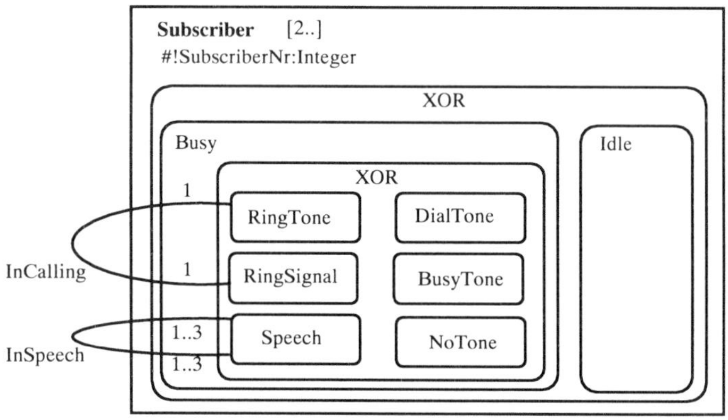

Figure 1: An example of a static Delphi schema

The static part of basic functionality for telephoning is graphically specified in fig 1. There is one entity type, a *Subscriber*. The cardinality constraint for the entity type subscriber is [2..] which means that at least two *Subscriber* instances have to exist but there is no limit to how many more subscribers there may exist. The subscriber in this telephoning system has only one attribute, the *subscrNr* (tel.), denoted with the '#' in front of the attribute name, followed by :integer, the specification of data value type for the attributes range. There are two entity states, *Busy* and *Idle* which may hold for a subscriber. The logical connective *XOR* means that these entity states are mutually exclusive, i.e. a subscriber can not be both busy and idle at the same time. The specification language Delphi also includes the logical connectives of *AND*, *OR* (inclusive or), ≤ 1 (at most 1), and / (not). The entity state *Busy* has six, also mutually exclusive, sub states, which describe the tone which can be heard in a telephone hook. There are two relations, *inCalling* and *inSpeech*, denoted by arrows. The mapping constraints in Delphi are declared as relative amounts. In the example an instance of the entity type subscriber while being in the state of speech has to be in speech with at least one and at the most three other subscriber(s) in the same state.

2.3 Specification of Dynamic Aspects of a UoD

In the dynamic part of a Delphi schema all possible state transitions between the above states are specified. The required state transitions which may occur in the specified system are described by stating which dynamic rules apply. A dynamic rule states which preconditions hold in the initial system state, which (external) events occur in that system state, and which post conditions hold for the system state after the transition. Note, that only the rules specified in the post conditions are affected by a dynamic rule; the rest of the system stays in the state prior to the event.

In fig. 2 we illustrate a dynamic schema part, i.e. the specification of the event *dialsTo* from the specification of call waiting, an optional feature in the telephoning case. Precondition in the first dynamic rule of the event in fig. 3 describes the system state when the fact of a subscriber being in call waiting with another is to be concluded. The preconditions in the second and the third dynamic rules describe which system states lead to a busy tone to be heard by a subscriber who is dialling. The fourth dynamic rule specifies that when the event *dialsTo* occurs the relationship *inCalling* should apply between the dialler and the one being dialled to only if the other subscriber is idle. Finally the fifth dynamic rule specifies that the dialling subscriber should receive a busy tone also if the other subscriber does not have the sub feature call waiting available.

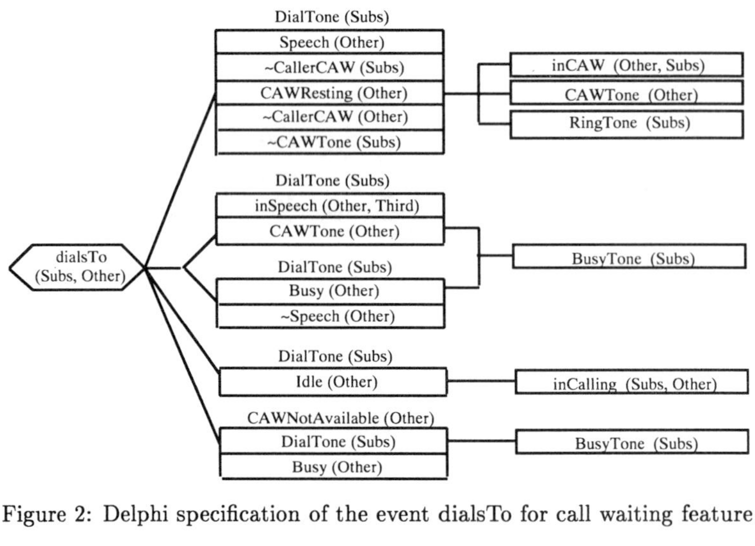

Figure 2: Delphi specification of the event dialsTo for call waiting feature

3 Framework for Schema Comparison

3.1 Correspondences and Conflicts

Here, we describe a framework for analysing schema comparison methods as introduced in [12]. The framework is here used as guidelines in development of the schema comparison method.

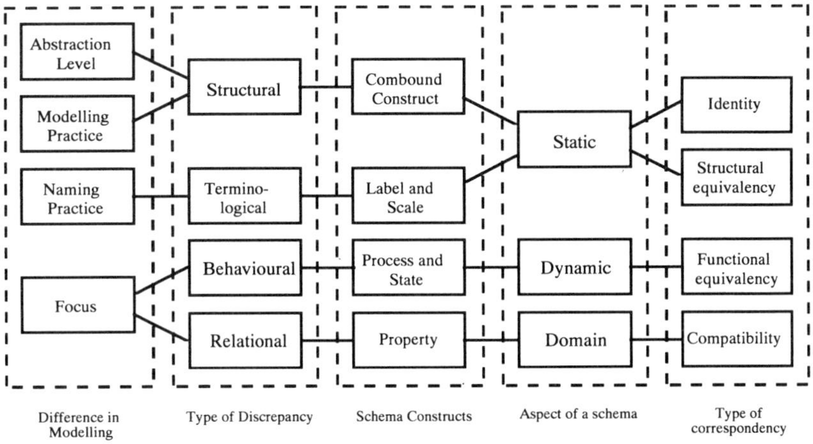

Figure 3: Dependency relationships describing similarity and conflicts

In figure 7, we summarise the central parts of the classification framework by showing which dependency relationships there exist between the distinct parts of the framework. The arrows connecting the boxes in the figure should be interpreted as "affects" when followed from left to the right and as "is inherent in" when followed in the inverse direction. For example, dynamic aspects of a schema affect the functional equivalency type of correspondence whereas the functional equivalency is inherent in the dynamic aspects of a schema.

Four types of conflict situations which arise and five types of correspondences which occur are identified when comparing concepts in the component schemas. The types of conflicting situations among schemas modelling the same UoD are: conflicting terminology, structure, behaviour, and relation. The types of knowledge used for comparison are considered according to the dimension of static information and rules, dynamic information and rules contained in a schema, and the knowledge sources outside the schemas to be integrated. An important objective of the framework is to make precise what types of knowledge that occur within the different sub processes in schema comparison. In schema comparison, two concepts A and B which are compared are assigned a correspondence assertion, semantic relationship that exists between the representations of A and B. A measure of the degree of correspondence is defined, because it is an important support when competitive assertions are compared. For more details see the above mentioned article where a definition of the nature of such relationship is given.

3.2 Enrichment of Semantic Schema Properties

A semantically enriched schema expresses more of the semantics of an application than the original schema by introducing additional (general) information about the objects. We illustrate this in fig. 4, where the starting point is that two conceptual schemas, CM1 and CM2, describing two application systems are compared to each other and the problem is how to establish correspondences between concepts between the two schemas. Now, when the schemas are semantically enriched using some mechanism for domain knowledge modelling, we obtain a single schema of domain knowledge, denoted DK, to which all or a subset of objects in both schemas are connected. Thus a semantic relation between the compared models is established and can be used in determining correspondence assertions among the concepts.

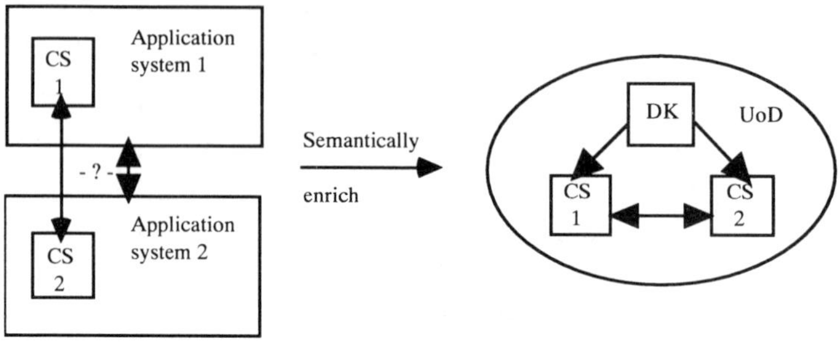

Figure 4: Semantic enrichment of two schemas

3.3 Linguistic Instruments

In a case study [23] we use a modified version of linguistic instruments, a semantic schema enrichment method adapted from [20] as the basis for semantically enriching the compared Delphi specifications. The method of using linguistic instruments has not been previously tested on dynamic schema constructs.

In linguistic instruments, a conceptual modelling approach is formalised using first order logic and a theory based on linguistics. Two types of cases are distinguished in case grammar, one of the theoretical foundations of conceptual graph theory. The two cases are; *surface case* meaning the classification of nouns according to their syntactic role in a sentence and *deep case* referring to categorising of the noun phrases according to the conceptual role they play in the action described in the sentence. Conceptual graph theory [16] is used and extended by language constructs for specifying constraints.

In natural language there are typically three ways of marking the cases on the surface level: marking by other words like particles and prepositions, marking by word order, and morphological marking. However, the marking is neither comprehensive nor homogeneous, which is basically the reason for defining case grammars in natural language understanding in the first place [14]. The word classes are considered easier to interpret and identify syntactically. In the examples below we use the English classification of words.

4 Applied Linguistic Instruments

4.1 Deep Case System for Schema Analysis

In the development of the application specific case grammar we followed [20, 24]. In the case grammar proposed as a deep case system, a deep case is defined for relationships, entity type relations, and events only. A *deep case system* consists of a complete set of deep cases available for describing actions denoted by verbs in all sentences in a particular UoD. A deep case consists of an action and a set of semantic roles:

An *action* of a deep case is any of the above objects which describes an activity of any kind. A syntactic restriction for objects which may be actions is, that they have to be classified as verbs, where a verb is an object that indicates the occurrence or the performance of an action.

A *semantic role* of a deep case is defined for the schema objects of the type entity type (in a specific entity state), attribute, and data type. A syntactic restriction for objects which may be bearers of semantic role associated to a deep case action is that these objects have to be classified as nouns, where a noun is an object or a group of objects that refer to an animate (living thing), place (physical/logical) or artefact (physical/logical thing). Generally, a noun can have the grammatical characteristic of being substantive, adjective (assigning a characteristic to the noun), pronoun (replacement for a noun), numeral (a symbol used to express a number), or the present or past participle (adjectival/noun usage of verbs) verb forms. In the proposed deep case system there are five semantic roles associated to actions in the telephoning case:

agent	usage:	"instigator of the action, the most general case of an actor in an action"		
	argument(s):	{entity type}	word class:	{noun}
	schema object:	{animate}	preposition:	{-}
	surface case:	{subject}		
co-agent	usage:	"represents shared instigator ship of the action (applied also when the instigator is not known in a co-operative action)"		
	argument(s):	{entity type, attribute}	word class:	{noun}
	schema object:	{animate, artefact}	preposition:	{with}
	surface case:	{subject}		
sender	usage:	"agent from whom/which activity comes (comp. source - the object from where the action comes)"		
	argument(s):	{entity type}	word class:	{noun}
	schema object:	{animate, artefact}	preposition:	{from}
	surface case:	{subject, direct object, indirect object}		
object	usage:	"thing that is acted upon or that changes, the most general case of an object acted upon in or changed" by an action"		
	argument(s):	{entity type, entity state, attribute}		
	schema object:	{animate, artefact}	word class:	{noun, adj.}
	surface case:	{direct object}	preposition:	{-}
recipient	usage:	"object affected by the action"		
	argument(s):	{entity type, attribute}	word class:	{noun}
	schema object:	{animate, artefact}	preposition:	{to}
	surface case:	{dative}		

To apply case grammar to a static schema, we proceed in two steps. The first step is to identify actions (grammatical predicates) as candidate to become actions of deep case concepts. As defined above the constructs which may take the role of a action have to be classified as a verb. Also following the above rules, in the static part of a Delphi schema only relationships are possible targets for that particular world class. In the dynamic part of a Delphi schema only event types and its subordinate schema concepts are possible targets for that particular world class. The second step is to identify roles (grammatical subjects and objects) as candidates to become semantic roles to the deep case structure. The schema structures which may take a semantic role are classified as nouns. In the static part of a Delphi schema the arguments in entity, entity state, and attribute structures are possible targets for semantic roles. In the dynamic part of a Delphi schema the arguments in events and dynamic rules referring to schema structures in the static part are possible targets for semantic roles. In the following section, we exemplify the usage of the deep case system.

4.2 Semantic Enrichment of Static Aspects

In the schemas describing the static aspects of the telephoning case only a few schema constructs are assigned the classification of verbs, all being relationships between two entities of the same type. In fig. 5 we present these static case structures.

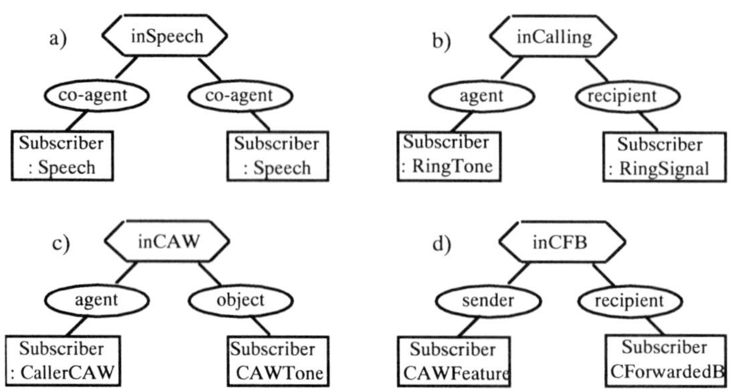

Figure 5: Semantic enrichment of the relationships using the deep case system

The relationship *inSpeech* exists between two subscribers and it is said to be equally directed. Therefore, as depicted in fig. 5.a, both subscribers share the role of a co-agent in the action of being in speech. In the relationship *inCalling* between two subscribers the one, currently receiving a ring tone, is the instigator of the action and the one receiving the ring signal is the object of the action, more specifically the one affected by the action. Hence, in fig. 5.b we have assigned the roles of an agent and a recipient to the involved subscribers. In a relationship *inCAW* there is one subscriber trying to reach another, identified as the instigator of the action and another as the one being acted upon, i.e. receiving the CAW tone while being busy. In fig. 5.c the subscribers are assigned the most general roles agent and object. The semantics of being *inCFB* means that in a particular system state, there are four subscribers; one trying to reach another, which is in speech with a third and also has forwarding to a fourth subscriber. The relationship *inCFB* is then between the second and the fourth subscriber, where the second is the actor from which the forwarding action comes from and the fourth is the object affected by the action. Hence, in fig. 5.d the subscribers are assigned the roles of a sender and a recipient.

4.3 Semantic Enrichment of Dynamic Aspects

We assume that the dynamic schema constructs are expressed as events specifying the possible state transitions, with reference to static schema constructs as in section 2. In the following examples, we use the graphic notation developed in [23]. To specify the enriched structure of a head of an event we draw the hexagon, for the involved entities with assigned variable names we draw the rectangle, and the role is drawn in an oval connecting the event with the entities. To specify the enriched structure of a body of an event we simplify the graphic notation in that we enumerate the belonging semantic rules and draw them all in the same event. Thus we do not repeat the structure of the head of the event, and may leave empty those dynamic rules which do not specify new semantic roles.

Here, we exemplify the usage of the case grammar within the structure of an event. In fig. 6 we describe a quite simple deep case structure of an event in the call waiting schema. Recall the Delphi specification of the event in section 2, fig. 2.

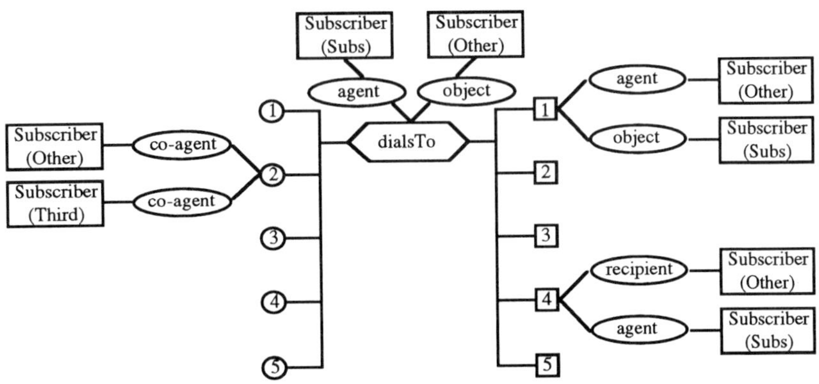

Figure 6: Semantic enrichment of the event dialsTo for call waiting feature

In the head of the event *dialsTo (Subs, Other)*, we have identified *Subs* to be the agent and *Other* the object for the event to occur. The interesting semantic rules are the first, second and fourth, whereas the rest do not introduce any semantic roles to the event and are therefore left empty. The conclusion part of the first semantic rule states that the relationship *inCAW* will hold between the other subscriber and the subscriber which was the instigator of the event after the semantic rule is executed. This means that the subscriber *Subs* is assigned the semantic role of an object and the other subscriber *Other* the semantic role agent. The precondition part of the second semantic rule states that the relationship *inSpeech* between *Other* and *Third* should hold during the time of the event for the rule to be executed. This means that the role of *Subs* remains unchanged, *Other* is assigned the semantic role of an co-agent, and a third entity, *Third*, is introduced to the semantic enrichment structure and assigned the semantic role of an co-agent. Finally the conclusion part of the fourth semantic rule states that the relationship *inCalling* will hold between *Subs* and *Other* after the semantic rule is executed. This means that *Subs* is assigned the same semantic role as in the head of the event and Other is assigned the semantic role of a recipient in the semantic enrichment of the event.

5 Comparison of Semantically Enriched Dynamic Schema Constructs

5.1 Heuristics for Comparison of Events

We propose a simple heuristic algorithm for comparing dynamic aspects of a schema. In order to apply the algorithm the component schemas should fulfil two conditions. The component schemas should be semantically enriched by use of linguistic instruments as described in above section, or an equivalent case system, and specified in a modelling language containing dynamic schema constructs, such as the events in Delphi.

The algorithm takes as input a conceptual graphs specifying semantically enriched events of a schema and produces as output for a user recommendations of possible correspondences. There are two central components in the algorithm: 1) computation of correspondences between dynamic rules based on a measure of correspondence degree and 2) determination of which recommendation on compatibility to suggest to a user based on the partial ordering of combined correspondences between dynamic rules.

In the comparison algorithm proposed in [23] we use the above concepts to define the following three sub processes to semi-automate comparison of two semantically enriched dynamic parts of Delphi schemas:

I Compare the deep case roles of preconditions

- Identify absolute diversity of single structures and remove found structures from the comparison lists
- determine correspondence degree for pairs of enriched structures of post conditions from the compared events in the compared schemas

II Compare the deep case roles of conclusions

- Identify absolute diversity of single structures and remove found structures from the comparison lists
- determine correspondence degree for pairs of enriched structures of post conditions from the compared events in the compared schemas

III Compare the correspondence degrees of dynamic rules

- Compare the degrees of preconditions with the degrees of conclusions for a pair of semantic rules and assign a degree for each dynamic rule
- Form a partial order relation for the weighted dynamic rule pairs and determine a suggestion for the user

In the determining correspondence the time aspect is considered in that the enriched structure of an event (called head of an event) is used as the context for comparison of the enriched structures of conditions and conclusions of its dynamic rules. A *correspondence degree*, Cd between two conditions or conclusions is to be interpreted as relative to the deep case structure of the head of the event. We introduce five degrees of correspondence, Cd, denoted $\sim$, $\neq$, $-$, $+$ and & with the numeric values of 0.00, 0.25, 0.50, 0.75, and 1.00, respectively. The Cd of $\neq$, $-$, $+$ and & are assigned to a pair of structures. The pair can be a pair of conditions or a pair of conclusions, each being a part of a dynamic rule in an event in different component schemas. The degree $\sim$ is assigned to single structure of a event head, condition or conclusion.

Cd $\sim$, means that the structure introduces new roles for the involved entities and there does not exist a matching structure in the compared event. Cd $\neq$, means that there is a mismatch between introduced roles in the structures. Cd –, means that there is no change in one of the structures but there is a structure introduced in the other matching the structure of the head of the event (new entities may also be introduced). Cd +, means that there is no change of role, relative to the head of the event in either of the structures. Cd &, means that there are new structures introduced both having exactly the same matching grammatical structures.

A user recommendation (suggestion) is assigned to dynamic rules of two events and based on comparison of conditions and conclusions in context of their event heads. We propose four types of suggestions that a comparison system may make, namely suggest ignore, notify, weak, strong, and merge. A suggestion is derived from comparing the correspondences computed for pairs of conditions and conclusions of a dynamic rule in two events as a computation of a combined correspondence degree (combCd). Given the numeric values of a Cd above, a *combined correspondence degree*, combCd of two semantic rules, R1 and R2 is, given a correspondence degree, Cd1 for a pair of condition (R1) and condition (R2), and a correspondence degree, Cd2 for a pair of conclusion (R1) and conclusion (R2), is the mean of Cd1 and Cd2, i.e. combCd (R1, R2) = (Cd1 + Cd2) / 2).

5.2 Experimental Results

We have run an experiment with the comparison algorithm using material from the case study at Telia Research AB. As mentioned earlier, the application domain of the case is optional features to traditional telephoning services. It consists of a schema for basic call which standardises the basic concepts and events generic to all the functionality in the telephoning system, a schema for call waiting which is an optional feature involving knocking tone for the subscriber when being called to while being busy, a schema for call forward on busy which is an optional feature involving forwarding for the subscriber when being called to while being busy, and a schema which specifies an integrated view to the three specifications. The integrated schema was verified through the Delphi simulation functionality and validated through proving its consistency in the Safe Guard system [22]. Thus, it was used as a control case in this experiment.

The local schemas were semantically enriched on both static and dynamic aspects. We compared dynamic parts solely on the basis of case grammar structures using the correspondence analysis. The case consists of 16 event definitions with totally 42 semantic rules, 84 precondition and 56 conclusion logical constitutes, giving 255 candidate combinations for correspondence assertions.

combCd	.11 – –	.22 + –	.22 – +	.33 & –	.33 – &	.44 + +	.66 & +	.66 + &	1 & &
Prec	nm	.64	.67	nm	nm	.96	1	1	1
Rec	nm	1	1	nm	nm	1	.52	.18	.11

Table 1: Precision and recall by decreased scope of combCd of correspondence assertion types

In tab. 1 we have captured the results of using the comparison algorithm on the three semantically enriched schemas relative to the control schemas. A detailed documentation of the outcome is given in [23]. The columns of the table denote possible combinations of correspondence degree for a dynamic rule. The rows of the table show precision (|correct proposed| / |proposed|) and recall (|correct proposed| / |existing correct|) values from the three sets of correspondence assertions. The values vary between one and zero where one denotes the best precision/best recall and zero a comparison with no precision/recall at all. The 'value' nm in the cells denotes inability to any measurements, when there were no occurrences of the particular combination in the test situation.

The table shows that the algorithm captured all the correspondence assertions assigned to the control schema (existing correct). The table also strongly suggests that the algorithm has the capacity to reach both perfect precision and recall. Note also that the exclusion of $\sim$ and $\neq$ assertions at early stage in the comparison procedure has correctly removed a proportion of .72 from the total set of assertions, where 27 percent were excluded by the $\sim$-assertions and 45 percent by the $\neq$ assertions.

6 Concluding Remarks

We addressed the problem of determining correspondence assertions and conflict predictions in schema comparison focusing at the analysis of the dynamic schema constructs. The main contribution of this paper is that we specify how the linguistic knowledge is taken into account in correspondence detection and conflict analysis. We develop and apply a novel heuristic method for determining the correspondence assertions. The applicability of our method is tested on case from a real world application domain consisting of formal requirements specifications for telecommunication services. Our belief is that there has to be comprehensive rules with examples from the UoD specific application domain in any practical case of semantic enrichment. The linguistic knowledge technique is modified to match the application domain of the case study as a method for semantic enrichment. We have applied the case system to specifications of telephoning services and compared the results with a control schema used in that domain.

The results of the case study imply the proposed approach to be a promising line of research in integration of schema dynamics. Results of the experiment show that the algorithm provides user with sound, explanatory suggestions to correspondence assertions. However, until more extensive empirical studies are made we can not claim any universal characteristics nor applicational power of our approach. Yet compared to other existing approaches it has the advantage of being easy to comprehend and in a large extent, homogeneous in how it will be applied in practice. The method provides a comprehensive explanatory ground for practical usage situations, and also for further development and testing of the algorithm.

Acknowledgements

The case study [23] was financed by KRAV-laboratory at Telia Research AB as a part of the SDeLphi project, conducted at Logikkonsult AB. Some of the practical issues of the case study have been solved in co-operation with the SISI project at the Department of Computer and Systems Sciences, SU/KTH. Some of the theoretical work for this study has been carried out in the Effective IT, phase III project at the Swedish Institute for Systems Development, SISU.

References

1. J. A. Larson, S. B. Navathe, and R. Elmasri, A Theory of Attribute Equivalence in Databases with Application to Schema Integration, IEEE Trans. on Software Eng. 15 (4), pp 449 - 463, April 1989
2. S. Hayes and S. Ram, Multi-User View Integration System (MUVIS): An Expert System for View Integration, Proc. of the 6th Int. Conf. on Data Engineering, Feb. 1990
3. S. Spaccapietra, C. Parent and Y. Dupont, Automating Heterogeneous Schema Integration, VLDB J., 1(1), pp 81-126, Aug. 1992
4. M. Bouzeghoub, and I. Comyn-Wattiau, View Integration by Semantic Unification and Transformation of Data Structures, Proc. of the 9th Int. Conf. on Entity-Relationship Approach, Lausanne (CH), Ed. H. Kangassalo, Oct. 1990
5. V. Vidal, and M. Winslett, Preserving Update Semantics in Schema Integration, N. Adam (Ed.), Third Int. Conf. on Information and Knowledge Management, Maryland, IEEE Press, 1994
6. C. Yu, B. Jia, W. Sun, and S. Dao, Determining Relationships among Names in Heterogeneous Databases, ACM SIGMOD RECORD spec. issue on Semantic Issues in Multidatabase Systems, 20 (4), 1991
7. G. Spanoudakis and P. Constantopoulos, Similarity for Analogical Software Reuse: A Computational model, A. Cohn (Ed.), Proc. of 11th European Conference on Artificial Intelligence, John Wiley & Sons, 1994
8. P. Johannesson, Linguistic Instruments for Schema Integration, M. Bouzeghoub (Ed.), First International Conference on Databases in Natural Language, Versailles, 1995
9. P. Fankhauser, and E. J. Neuhold, Knowledge based integration of heterogeneous databases, D. K. Hsiao, E. J. Neuhold, and R. Sacks-Davis (Eds.), Interoperable Database Systems (DS-5), North- Holland, 1993
10. N Maiden, and A. G. Sutcliffe, Requirements Critiquing Using Domain Abstractions, Proc. of IEEE Symp. on Requirements Engineering, pp 110-117, IEEE Computer Society Press, 1994
11. M. Castellanos, A Methodology for Semantically Enriching Interoperable Databases, M. Worboys and A. F. Grundy (Eds), Advances in Databases (LNCS 696), Springer-Verlag, 1993
12. S. Hakkarainen, Analysing and Evaluating Heuristic Support for Schema Comparison, Proc. of 5th European-Japanese Seminar on Information Modelling and Knowl. Bases, Sapporo, 1995
13. J. F. Sowa, Semantic Networks, S. C. Shapiro (Ed.), Encyclopedia of Artificial Intelligence, pp 1011-1024, Wiley and Sons, New York, 1987
14. C. J. Fillmore, The case for Case, E. Bach and R. Harms (Eds.), Universals in Linguistic Theory, Holt, Rinehart & Winston, 1968
15. R. Schank, Conceptual Information Processing, North-Holland, Amsterdam, 1975
16. J. F. Sowa, Conceptual Structures: Information Processing in Mind and Machine, Addison-Wesley, London, 1984
17. D. Gentner, Structure Mapping: A Theorethical Framework for Analogy, Cognitive Science vol. 7, pp 155-170, 1983
18. G.-C. Yang, Y. B. Choi, and J. C. Oh, CGMA: A Novel Conceptual Graph Matching Algorithm, H. D. Pfeiffer, and T. E. Neagle (Eds.), Conceptual Structures: Theory and Implementation, 7th Ann. WS, Springer-Verlag, 1993
19. P. E. Maher, A Similarity Measure for Conceptual Graphs, Int. J. of Intelligent Systems, 8, pp 819- 837, 1993
20. P. Johannesson, Linguistic Instruments and Qualitative Reasoning for Schema Integration, N. Adam (Ed.), Third Int. Conf. on Information and Knowledge Management, Maryland, IEEE Press, 1994.
21. Wideb\u00e4ck, F., The Graphical Notation of Delphi, Logikkonsult NP AB, 1992
22. G. St\u00e5lmark, L. Ekenberg, S. Berg, I. Olsson, and F. Nordberg, F\u00f6rstudie i formell analys av tj\u00e4nsteinteraktion, validering och verifiering (in Swedish), Telia Research AB, 1994
23. S. E. Hakkarainen, Using Case Grammar for Comparison of Dynamic Aspects in Delphi Schemas, - a Case Study, SYSLAB-Report Series, The Royal Institute of Technology and Stockholm University, Dec. 1995
24. K. Brown, Linguistics Today, Fontana Paperbacks, 1984

Applications of Natural Language to Information Systems
R.P. van de Riet et al. (Eds.)
IOS Press, 1996

Implementation of a Third Generation View Integration Tool

Elisabeth Métais (1), Zoubida Kedad (1),
Isabelle Comyn-Wattiau (1)(2) and Mokrane Bouzeghoub (1)

(1) Laboratoire PRiSM, Université de Versailles,
45, avenue des Etats-Unis, 78035 Versailles, France.
(2) ESSEC, av B. Hirsch, BP 105, 95021 Cergy-Pontoise Cedex, France.
email: Elisabeth.Metais@prism.uvsq.fr

Abstract. This paper addresses the problem of view integration in a CASE tool environment aiming at the elaboration of a conceptual schema of an application. The previous integration tools were mainly based on syntax and structure comparisons. A new generation of intelligent tools is now arising, assuming that view integration algorithms must also capture the deep semantics of the objects portrayed in the views. Dealing with the semantics of the objects is now a realistic objective, thanks to the research results obtained in the natural language area. This paper presents the implementation of a view integration algorithm enhanced by the use of linguistic knowledge. This algorithm mainly consists of a semantic unification of views described using an extended entity-relationship model. It is combined with natural language techniques such as Fillmore's semantic cases and Sowa's conceptual graphs, supported by semantic dictionaries.
Keywords: view integration, linguistic knowledge, semantic distance, conceptual graph, unification, similarity vector.

1 Introduction

View integration is a conceptual design methodology which permits to synthesise in a single global schema different views of the same universe of discourse. This approach is particularly suitable when designers are faced with one of the following problems :

- Merging several existing databases in a single centralised (or virtually centralised) information system,
- Gathering the different parts of a distributed system into a unique centralised view to insure global consistency,
- Designing very large databases by integrating several partial designs corresponding to different user groups,
- Designing very large databases by stepwise refinement including progressively more and more information,
- Providing data through a data warehouse system.

In all these different situations, the integration process basically consists in (1) matching the different partial structures to detect possible conflicts, (2) merging the consistent views into a single global schema. In this paper, we mainly address the first point.

The main problems occurring during the design process can be summarised as follows: different terminologies, differences in class definition, use of equivalent structures, conflicts between constraints and redundancies of concepts and constraints. Some of these problems (mainly terminology and class definition) are obviously linguistic. They occur in the view comparison step and can be summarised as: "Do two given conceptual fragments of data types represent the same concept in the real world ?".

1.1 Previous work in view integration

View integration is a difficult but important research area where significant results have already been achieved. A comprehensive state of the art in the domain is made in [4], [5] and [9]. The recent evolutions of integration tools lead us to classify them into the following three generations.

- First generation tools

The first significant results in view integration mainly consisted in the definition of methodologies in which the designer is often or always solicited, due to the high level of semantic information required for the integration process [18], [33], [28] and [3].

In [6] view integration is discussed in the framework of a formal model, which serves as a theoretical basis for a clear definition of several operations involved in the integration process (e.g. comparison of information content, local schema transformation, and schema merging).

- Second generation tools

Two main features characterise the second generation approaches. First, they refer to expert system or knowledge based system techniques to provide a view integration tool. Second, they suggest comparing structures by defining measures of similarity. A few approaches offered some aids to help the designer in making integration decisions [36], [35], [12].

The expert system approach described in [12] makes the designer's task easier by providing him with friendly interfaces in order to specify assertions between views which are candidates for integration.

Schema Integration System (SIS) tries to quantify the similarity between each pair of constructs. Consequently the designer is presented with lists of pairs, ordered by this measure of similarity, which he can use to assert equivalences, introduce modifications or generate mappings [36]. At the most elementary level, object properties, particularly names and data types, are compared. Moreover the definition of the weight associated to each criterion and the form of aggregation of those criteria are left to the designer. [35] uses such an aggregation defined by the ratio of equivalent attributes to the total attributes of two objects. The underlying integration methodology is described in [34].

[22] also refers to this methodology using the Semantic Data Model [21] and extending the methodology to the integration of composite objects. The objects are compared in a pairwise fashion in order to determine their equivalence. The comparison results in the definition of a degree of similarity or dissimilarity. These similarities are combined as independent probabilities and integration takes place as soon as a threshold value set at 0.8 is achieved.

[17] uses neural network technology to determine categories of objects : objects in the same category may overlap. The view integration process concentrates then on the comparison of objects inside the categories.

• Third generation tools

Some researchers have proposed the use of linguistic instruments in the integration process. This stream of thinking offers us a new method for solving persistent problems by enriching the correspondence between the real word concept and its conceptual representation. [11] shows how linguistic knowledge can be used to enhance conceptual design.

[25] and [26] introduce a modelling formalism for view integration which utilises case grammar and speech act theory and can be used in a heuristic method for identifying schema correspondences. [27] proposes a method based on partial orders and Galois lattices.

[29] and [1] suggest the use of semantic electronic dictionaries storing concept hierarchies and canonical graphs to retrieve the semantics of the views. [32] defines a model of fuzzy thesaurus drawn from linguistics tools. This thesaurus aim is to deal with the meaning of words. It also gives a fuzzy semantic-nearness coefficient between concepts.

[30] notices the use of linguistic tools in the management of heterogeneous information systems. [13] uses the CYC knowledge base [20] as a global schema for consistency checking. [7] builds a concept base on the top of each system to be integrated in order to enrich their description with more semantic information.

The main idea of the third generation approaches is to bring solutions to the problem mentioned above (i.e. "Do two given conceptual fragments of data types represent the same concept in the real world ?") assuming that the real world is quite well portrayed by some models or thesaurus or dictionaries issued from a long research in the linguistic domain.

1.2 View integration approach in the Khéops CASE tool

The general principle of view integration (for a complete description, see [14], [10] and [15]) is based on two main concepts : the similarity vector and the unification process.

The view integration process begins with the comparison of view components. Each comparison results in the computation of a **similarity vector**. For example the confrontation of two attributes leads to a two component vector $\mathbf{Sim}_{att}\mathbf{(name, domain)}$ where *name* specifies whether the two attributes have the same names. The *domain* component evaluates whether the two attributes have identical, included or different domains.

The view integration proceeds as a **unification process**. The two views are considered as complex objects. The integration process aims at matching the patterns of these objects in order to build a complex integrated object.

1.3 Enhancing the integration process with linguistic knowledge

As shown in the state of the art, view integration is still an evolving research area and benefits from the results of research in other domains. The arising of expert systems and reasoning methods in the eighties permitted the development of tools integrating some of the designer's know-how. But the limitation with which all algorithms where confronted was always the lack of semantic information concerning a given schema. In the nineties, the results obtained in the linguistic area dealing both with syntactic and semantic aspects of words give us the opportunity to go a step forward in automatic view comparison.

The Khéops integration tool produces good results with respect to the syntactic information and the constraints, but may have some limitation when two different concepts are portrayed in the conceptual schemas by very similar structures. For example, an entity PERSON with the attributes name, address and telephone may be considered as similar to an entity WAREHOUSE with the same attributes name, address and telephone.

Another problem of this algorithm is the number of computed comparisons due to the "Cartesian product" aspect of the algorithm, although some heuristics aim at reducing it. This high number of comparisons is time consuming and it may even lead to absurd comparisons, which could succeed. For example, the previous case PERSON and WAREHOUSE should never have been confronted, because they are concepts from different categories (human being and building).

An extension of the approach toward the exploitation of linguistic knowledge should avoid some of the previously mentioned problems. The comparison criteria treated by the initial algorithm were mainly syntactic, but the basic philosophy was to consider the result of the comparison of two objects as a set of different values. Each of these different values results from a facet of the evaluation, materialised by a similarity vector. Adding the use of linguistic tools to the algorithm is then quite naturally accomplished by adding new components in the vectors, or by modifying the evaluation of existing components.

This paper deals with the enhancement of the view integration algorithm in the Khéops CASE tool [8], and more precisely with the views comparison step of the algorithm. We introduce typing to improve the unification process efficiency. Section 2 describes the generic linguistic knowledge used by Khéops. In Section 3, we will mention the improvements obtained by the insertion of this linguistic knowledge in the view comparison process and we will define the concept of confidence measure to deal with the different levels of knowledge introduced in the process. These new functionalities and the resulting prototype are illustrated using a session sample in Section 4.

2 Description of the generic linguistic knowledge

The linguistic knowledge we use is described by three different structures, namely *semantic cases* of Fillmore, *canonical graphs* of Sowa and *semantic relations*.

2.1 Semantic cases

Semantic cases were introduced by Fillmore [19], and later expanded and used by Sowa [37] in the definition of the canonical graphs. They express the role played by each noun in a sentence (e.g. in the sentence "Workers manufacture shoes with leather", "Workers" has the semantic case "agent", "shoes" has the semantic case "result" and "leather" plays the role of "material"). These cases are more semantic than the usual syntactic cases (subject, direct object, adverbial phrase of place, etc.) in that they are not dependent upon the surface structure of the sentence (i.e. the syntactic construction of the sentence).

2.2 Canonical graphs of Sowa

The canonical graphs of Sowa [37], [38] are structures that specify both the relationships expected between concepts, i.e. the "semantic cases" of Fillmore (called "conceptual relations" by Sowa) and the "semantic constraints" of the expected concept (also called "selectional constraints" by Sowa). Semantic constraints may also be considered as a semantic typing. Figure 1 is an example of a canonical graph, where "agent", "object" and "location" are the "semantic cases", and "Human", "Physical-object" and "Place" are the "semantic constraints". This means that when we have a sentence like "X delivers Y", X is the one who delivers (the agent of the action) and must belong to the "Human" semantic category, Y is the thing to be delivered (the object of the action) and must be a "Physical object".

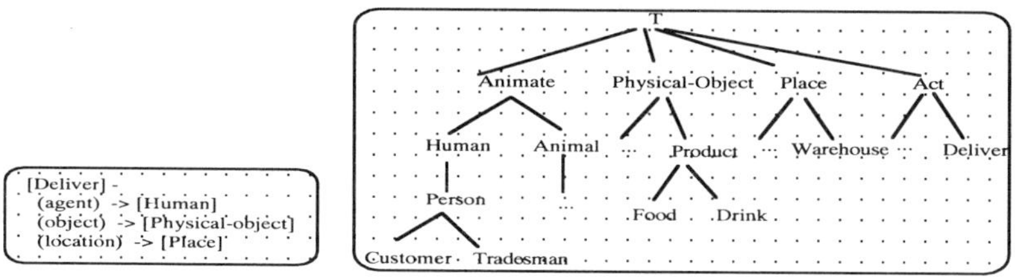

Figure 1: *Sample of a canonical graph and a concepts hierarchy*

2.3 Semantic relations

Semantic relations establish links between words or word meanings (concepts). An extensive discussion of relation types is presented in [39]. They include relations of synonymy, antonymy, hyponymy/hypernymy (is-a), and meronymy/ holonymy (part-of). Each relation defines a graph establishing the fact that this relation exists between the different words or word meanings.

The concepts are organized as a hierarchy. Figure 1 gives an example of a hierarchy whose top is "T". The concepts contained at the first level of this tree (e.g. Animate) may be considered as "semantic categories".

2.4 Semantic dictionaries

The linguistic knowledge described above is stored in two complementary dictionaries: (1) the morphological and syntactic dictionary and (2) the semantic dictionary. The *morphological and syntactic dictionary* contains knowledge such as the word roots, the word nature (e.g. noun, verb, preposition, article), attributes such as gender of nouns or nature of verbs (e.g. transitive), and some relational links between words. The *semantic dictionary* contains the canonical graphs of Sowa, the concepts hierarchy and the other semantic relations between concepts. Another dictionary stores linguistic knowledge concerning the application. It may be informed by the natural language parser during the analysis of a natural language specification.

From an implementation point of view, several projects aiming to build such electronic dictionaries are presently in progress : the CYC American project [20], the EDR Japanese project [24], the GENELEX EUREKA project [2], the MULTILEX ESPRIT

II project [23]. WordNet [31] has the particularity to be currently available and free in the public domain.

3 Introducing linguistic knowledge in the view integration algorithm

In this section, we show how the previously described general linguistic knowledge is treated in the view integration algorithm, and how this knowledge can enhance both the reliability and the efficiency of the object comparison process.

There were two main problems due to the lack of semantics in the Khéops initial algorithm. First, was the possible unification of two different concepts portrayed by two objects (e.g. entities) characterised by the same structure (e.g. same attributes). Second, was the large number of computed unifications. In the first subsection, we will explain how some information about the concepts represented by the objects could sometimes solve these two problems.

Whereas the initial algorithm was based on mainly syntactic criteria organised as a similarity vector, the modified algorithm is based on the cohabitation of syntactic and semantic criteria in the vector. The second subsection describes these new similarity vectors, with their components and their evaluation rules. In the third subsection, we discuss the usefulness of linguistic information.

3.1 Contributions of linguistic knowledge

The comparison step is difficult to automate mainly because this task requires a lot of knowledge which is not modelled within the schema, but which is in everybody's brain. This knowledge may concern the meaning of a name, a generalisation between two concepts or any other link. The two examples presented below illustrate how the algorithm can deduce such a knowledge, mainly from the concepts hierarchy and the canonical graphs.

• *Example 1: Detection of hidden generalisations*

Generalisation is now a widely admitted extension of the entity/relationship model. Most view integration algorithms have some solution to integrate an entity coming from one view and a different entity coming from a second view if they have explicitly the same generic in the two views, or if one of the two entities is a generic concept of the second.

The contribution of natural language techniques happens each time this hierarchy is not explicitly specified by a generalisation arc. That is because this arc is not meaningful when each view is considered alone. Some generic can be found using the concepts hierarchy of the semantic dictionary. Figure 2 shows an example of this process. The two relationships "repair" differ in the object component which is "Motorcycle" in the first view and "Car" in the second one. The concepts hierarchy generalises the two concepts in a "Vehicle". Thus the integrated view can be enriched by this new generic concept.

Without the concepts hierarchy of the semantic dictionary, this example could not have been resolved automatically.

• *Example 2: Selection of the pair of entities to be compared within relationship unification*

In order to unify two relationships, the algorithm has to unify their participating entities. Until now, the system had to compare each pair of elements of the Cartesian

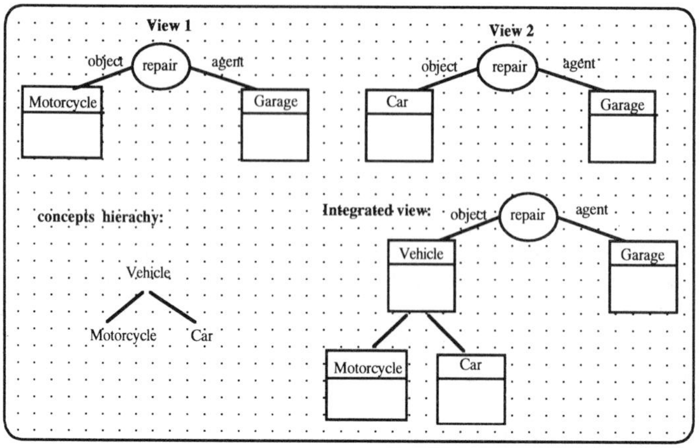

Figure 2: *Detection of hidden generalisation*

product of the two sets of entities. On the example of Figure 3, to unify the relationship "buy" of view 1 and the relationship "buy" of view 2, the primitive algorithm needs between 3 and 9 comparisons. This process may be time- consuming because recursively, each of these comparisons may imply a Cartesian product of the attributes of the compared entities.

If we can deduce the semantic roles (agent, object, time and location) from the linguistic knowledge dictionary, we can reduce significantly the number of comparisons. Indeed, these cases lead us to compare only couples of elements which are linguistically equivalent or close. In the example of Figure 3, using the role informations, it is obvious that only the couple (Person, Customer) which plays the role of "agent" and the couple (Car, Vehicle) which plays the role of "object", are interesting to be compared. So we have now only two comparisons to do, and we can expect fewer wrong unifications.

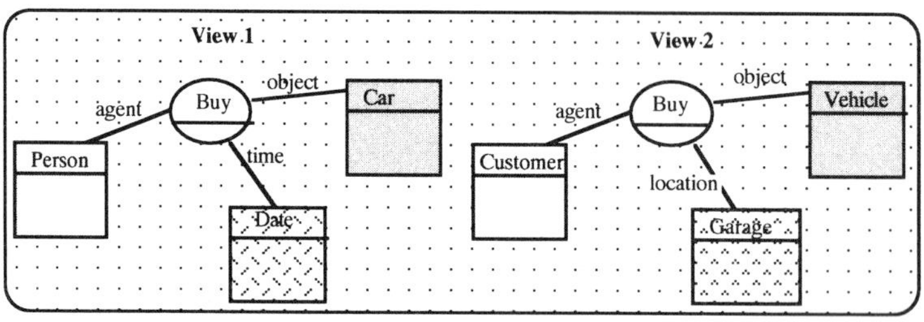

Figure 3: *Selection of pairs of entities using linguistic cases*

Thus, the contribution of the linguistic tools is to deduce the semantic role played by each entity in a relationship. To deduce the roles, we need to use the two kinds of information stored in the semantic dictionary: the canonical graph of the relationship and the concepts hierarchy (Figure 1). The system tries to put each entity in correspondence with a semantic case of the canonical graph. In order to establish this correspondence, the entity has to meet the semantic constraints linked to the cases by referring to the concepts hierarchy to make sure that the constraint is a generic of the entity. Thus, at the end of this process, if there is a one-to-one correspondence between the entities and the selected cases, then the process is successful.

We illustrate this technique with the help of the example drafted at Figure 4. In the canonical graph, among all the semantic constraints ("Human", "Physical-object" and "Place"), "Tradesman" only verifies the first one, i.e. "Human" (as "Human" is a generic of "Tradesman" in the concepts hierarchy). So, "Tradesman" can only play the role of "agent". In a similar way, "Product" can only play the role of "object" as the only semantic constraint verified is "Physical-object" which is one of its generic. And "Warehouse" can only play the role of "location". As each entity plays a different role, there is no ambiguity. The results obtained are shown in Figure 4.

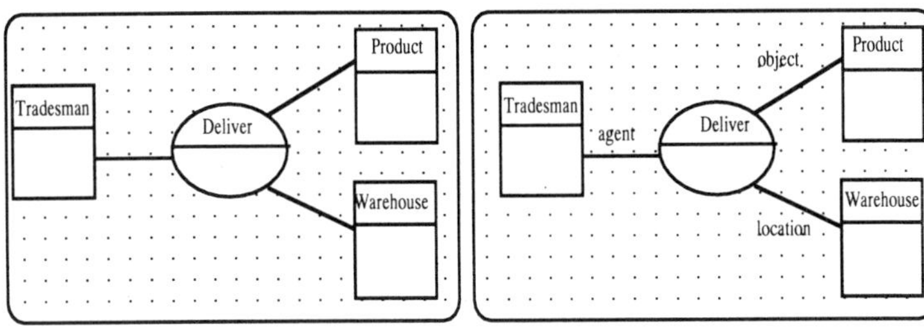

Figure 4: a. *Example of conceptual schema* — b. *The schema enriched with linguistic information*

3.2 Similarity vectors involving linguistic knowledge

As mentioned above, linguistic tools are mainly helpful in the comparison of two objects (relationship, entities or attributes). In our algorithm, the result of the comparison of two objects is reported in a "similarity vector". Thus we have included a new component. In this section we will first describe this new component. Then we will define the concept of confidence used to deal with the different levels of knowledge included in the comparison process. Finally we will describe the evaluation process.

• *The similarity vectors*

The comparison of two concepts leads to elicit common characteristics and different ones. The difference between two concepts is a semantic distance [16] in the sense that the more characteristics two concepts share the closer they are. The similarity vectors represent this closeness between concepts. They have two kinds of components: (1) syntactic components related to the syntactic characteristics of objects such as names and domains, (2) semantic components related to the meaning of objects, and derived from semantic relations and concepts hierarchy.

A new component has been added to integrate the linguistic knowledge contained in the semantic dictionary, namely the semantic relations of synonymy, antonymy, hyponymy/hypernymy ("is-a") and meronymy/holonymy ("part of"). The concept hierarchy (Figure 1) portrays a particularly interesting "is-a" semantic relation, including the semantic categories of the concepts (according to [16], the existence of a category or more to which the two objects belong states on their similarity). Thus, we arbitrarily define a semantic component called sem_sim between two object types of the conceptual schemas as follows :

sem_sim(C1,C2)=1 iff C1 and C2 are related by a synonymy relation, or they refer to the same concept in the hierarchy of concepts.
sem_sim(C1,C2)=0.75 iff C1 is a direct supertype of C2 in the hierarchy of concepts.

sem_sim(C1,C2)=0.6 iff C1 is an indirect supertype of C2 in the hierarchy of concepts.
sem_sim(C1,C2)=0.5 iff C1 and C2 are directly related to a common supertype of concepts.
sem_sim(C1,C2)=0.25 iff C1 and C2 are indirectly related to a common supertype of concepts.
sem_sim(C1,C2)=0 iff C1 and C2 have no common supertype except the root "T" of the hierarchy of concepts.

The numerical values must be considered as forming a scale characterizing similarity. The minimum value "0" is the dissimilarity case (the two object types portray concepts belonging to incompatible semantic categories, according to the concept hierarchy) while the maximum value "1" represents the equivalence case where two object types portray the same concept (either with the same denomination either because of a synonymy link). We qualify these values with the adjective "arbitrary" because a 0.5 similarity is not two times as similar as a 0.25 value. These numerical values are arbitrary in the sense that they only define a total order between the different cases of similarity.

- *The confidence measure*

Real problems of view integration are very various. For example, in some situations, the designer knows that the names attributed to the different components of views refer to a common and validated data dictionary. In other cases, on the opposite, he knows that a lot of terminology problems exist. In order to improve the view integration algorithm, we have associated each similarity component with a confidence measure. Thus, each component of a given similarity vector has a weight, modifiable by the designer. In standard situations, mean weights are used. In specific situations otherwise, the designer is allowed to define the right weights according to the reliability of the different informations he gets about syntactic and semantic aspects of views.

- *Evaluation of similarity vectors of attributes*

The similarity vector of two attributes contains three components : the name component resulting from the names comparison, the domain component and the semantic similarity between the two corresponding concepts. Two names are identical (name = 1) if their identifier strings are identical. Two domains are identical if their intentional or extensional specifications are equivalent. The determination of the corresponding concepts for the two attributes allows the evaluation of the semantic similarity between two attributes as explained above.

The result of the interpretation of the similarity vector Sim_{att}(name, sem_sim, domain) is a value which ranges over [0,1]. Let wn, ws, wd be the weights assigned to *name*, *sem_sim* and *domain* respectively; the global value is defined by the following rules:

REA1: If sem_sim = 0 Then sim = 0.
REA2: If sem_sim = 1 Then sim = 1.
REA3: If sem_sim $\notin$ {0,1} Then
sim = ((name*wn)+(sem_sim*ws)+(domain*wd))/(wn+ws+wd)

The rule REA1 corresponds to the *category* criterion. If two concepts have no common supertype except the root "T" of the concept hierarchy, that means that they belong to different categories. It is not necessary to compare their other components, and we can directly induce that they are not equivalent.

- *Evaluation of similarity vectors of entities*

The similarity vector defined for entities is defined as : Sim_{ent}(name, sem_sim, structure, constraints). The evaluation of this vector consists in the evaluation of each component. In this paper, we limit ourselves to the first three components : the *name* component, the *sem_sim* component and the *structure* component. The evaluation of the *constraint* component is detailed in [15]. The name component is evaluated as it was for attributes. The *sem_sim* component corresponds to the semantic closeness between the two entities. Its determination obeys to the same rules as the *sem_sim* component of attributes.

The *structure* component is computed from the set of similarity vectors associated with the set of attributes [10]. From this set, a similarity matrix is built as follows : let E1 and E2 be the two compared entities, Ai ($1 \leq i \leq n$) the attributes of E1 and Bj ($1 \leq j \leq m$) the attributes of E2. The similarity matrix M is [n,m], and Mij contains the result of the evaluation of the similarity vector corresponding to attributes Ai and Bj. This similarity matrix is itself interpreted according to the maximum number of attributes in each entity (respectively n for E1 and m for E2) and with respect to the number of equivalent attributes (p). The following rules describe the interpretation procedure :

RES1: If $p = n$ and $n = m$ Then structure = 1
RES2: If $p = n$ and $n < m$ Then structure = 0.75
RES3: If $p = 0$ Then structure = 0
RES4: If $p = n/2$ and $n = m$ Then structure = 0.5
RES5: If $p > m/2$ and $n \leq m$ Then structure = 0.66
RES6: If $n/2 < p < m/2$ and $n < m$ Then structure = 0.33
RES7: If $p < n/2$ and $n \leq m$ Then structure = 0.25

As for the similarity vector of attributes, a weight is associated with each component. The interpretation is driven by the following rules; let wn, ws, wst be the weight of the *name*, *sem_sim* and *structure* respectively:

RES7: If sem_sim = 1 Then sim = 1
RES8: If sem_sim = 0 Then sim = 0
RES9: If sem_sim $\notin \{0,1\}$
Then sim = ((name*wn)+(sem_sim*ws)+(structure*wst))/(wn+ws+wst).

The RES8 rule expresses that if two entities have different categories (sem_sim=0), their other components are not comparable and therefore we can conclude that they are not equivalent.

- *Evaluation of similarity vectors of relationships*

The similarity vector corresponding to relationships is defined as : Sim_{rel}(name, sem_sim, structure (ent,att), constraints). In this paper, we limit ourselves to the first three components, the constraint component is described in [15]. The evaluation of *name* and *sem_sim* components is the same as for entities and attributes. The latter represents the semantic similarity between the two concepts corresponding to the compared relationships.

The structure component has two values, which are both evaluated using rules RES1 to RES7. The first value (*ent*) is computed from the set of similarity vectors resulting from the comparison of pairs of participating entities. However the process performance is improved in the sense that we restrict the pairs of entities to those in which entities play the same role in the relationship (as illustrated in Section 3.1).

From this set of vectors, a similarity matrix is built as follows : let R1 and R2 be the two compared relationships, Ei ($1 \leq i \leq n$) the participating entities of R1, and E'j ($1 \leq j \leq m$) the participating entities of R2. The similarity matrix M is [n,m]. Mij contains the evaluation of the similarity vector corresponding to Ei and E'j, if the two entities play the same role within the relationship. The similarity matrix is interpreted using rules RES1 to RES7.

The second value of the structure component, (*att*) is computed from the set of similarity vectors resulting from the comparison of all possible pairs of attributes characterizing the relationship, in the same way as for entities.

Let wn, ws, we, wa be the weights associated with *name*, *sem_sim* and *structure* respectively. The interpretation of the similarity vector is done according to the following rules :

RERL1: If sem_sim = 1 Then sim = 1
RERL2: If sem_sim = 0 Then sim = 0
RERL3: If sem_sim $\notin$ {0,1} Then
S=(name*wn)+(sem_sim*ws)+(structurent*we)+(structuratt*wa)
sim = S/(wn+ws+we+wa)

3.3 Scale of usefulness of linguistics

As seen above, both linguistical and structural aspects are used to establish the similarity of two objects. Furthermore, we can remark a preponderancy of one of these two aspect, depending on the nature of the considered objects.

- *Comparison of two entities*

The extraction of the semantics of an object (i.e. to which concept does the entity name refers) is indispensable when comparing two entities. Indeed, as portrayed in Figure 5, when the views come from different departments of a company, we can expect that they address different properties (i.e. different attributes). For example, the medical service will store physical properties on an employee, while the human resource department will store intellectual characteristics. Considering that in the real word the set of properties is quite infinite, and the number of attributes of an entity usually very limited, searching the concepts portrayed by the two entities is expected to be more efficient than comparing their structures (i.e. their participating attributes).

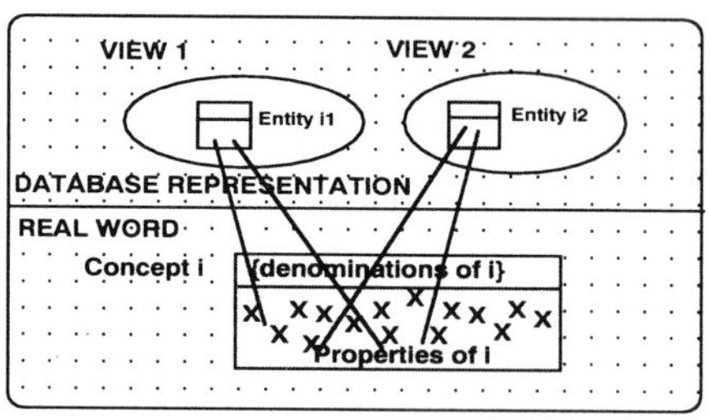

Figure 5: *Two entities portraying the same concept may share few properties*

- *Comparison of two relationships*

Concerning the comparison of two relationships, it may be useful to know to which concepts they refer in order to compare them, especially if the dictionary detects converse verbs (e.g. to buy and to sell). Indeed, if the two relationships refer to different concepts, we can deny their similarity. For example, a relationship "buy" and a relationship "build", both between a employee and a car, can't be integrated. But the structure of the entity is as important as the concept, because two relationships referring to the same concept are not necessarily similar. For example, a relationship "assign to" between an employee and a project corresponds to the same concept ("to assign to", which means "to transfer to another") than the relationship "assign to" between a product and a warehouse. A relationship is intrinsically defined by its component entities. Thus, comparing the structures of relationships (that is their participating entities) is not less important than searching to which concept they refer. Nevertheless, linguistic knowledge is very helpful for the participant entities comparison by providing their semantic roles in the relationship.

4 Implementation in a case tool

The work described in this paper is part of the Khéops CASE tool [8] ongoing prototype. Khéops is a database design environment which helps the designer to elaborate the conceptual schema of an application, and then to translate it into an operational database schema. In this prototype, natural language is used among other languages (graphical and formal) to enter or to generate information, as well as to make documentation, validation and reverse engineering possible. Moreover, the knowledge used by natural language analysis is exploited as often as possible at all of the design levels.

4.1 The view integration prototype

The view integration approach is integrated in an incremental object oriented database methodology. The view integration process can be summarized in three steps : the schema comparison step, in which the similarity vectors are computed, the validation step where the user can validate the comparison result, and the merging step which produces the resulting schema.

The view integration prototype is composed of three modules, corresponding to the integration steps mentioned above. The three modules are the following :

- *The comparison tool*

The inputs of the tool are the specifications of the two views to integrate and the linguistic knowledge stored in the dictionnaries. The result of the comparison is a set of similarity values produced by the interpretation of the similarity vectors.

The similarity vectors are produced by comparing pairs of objects belonging to the cartesian product of the two compared views. The interpretation of these vectors is done using the confidence measure defined by the designer for each vector's component. It generates the similarity values associated to each object pair.

- *The validation tool*

This tool allows the designer to validate or to modify the similarity values resulting from the comparison step. This validation is done through the similarity editor. The similarity values corresponding to the pairs of objects are displayed, controlled and possibly modified by the designer.

- *The merging tool*

This tool produces as output the resulting schema. The inputs are mainly the two compared views and the validated similarity values. The designer is also asked to specify a threshold value above which objects will be considered as equivalent and integrated in the resulting schema.

4.2 Example

The following example shows the resulting schema produced by the integration tool from the specifications of two views. Two samples of graphical specifications to integrate are shown in Figure 6.

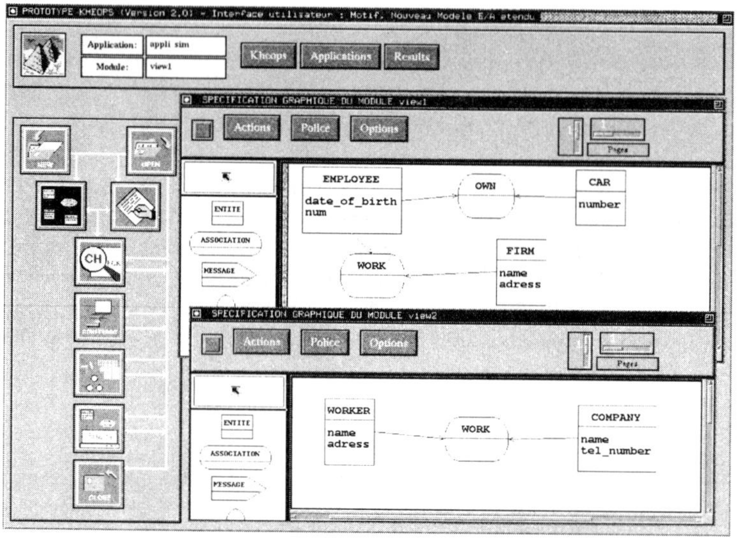

Figure 6: *Graphical specification of two views*

The resulting unified schema and the similarity values are shown in Figure 7. These values take into account the meaning of objects by the mean of the semantic similarity component.

The similarity editor shows a similarity value of 0.60 for the pair ("Firm","Company"), and a similarity value of 0.40 for the pair ("Firm","Worker"). "Firm" and "Company" are considered equivalent in spite of their different structures while Firm and Worker are not considered equivalent although having the same structure. We can also notice that the objects "Worker" and "Employee" have been merged in spite of their different structures and different names.

• The two objects "Firm" and "Worker" have the same structure and different names. They belong to different categories. The corresponding simlarity vector is : sim_{ent} (name = 0, sem_sim = 0, structure = 1). The global similarity value between the two objects is 0.4. This value has been computed with the following confidence measures : $\mathrm{w}_{name} = 1/5$ $\mathrm{w}_{sem\_sim} = 2/5$ $\mathrm{w}_{struct} = 2/5$

• The objects "Firm" and "Company" have different names and not exactly the same structures. They refer to the same concept. The corresponding similarity vector is : $\mathrm{sim}_{ent}(\mathrm{name} = 0, \mathrm{sem\_sim} = 1, \mathrm{structure} = 0.5)$. The global similarity value between the two objects is 0.6. This value is computed using the confidence measures mentionned above. Although having different names and some differences in their structures, they can be considered as equivalent.

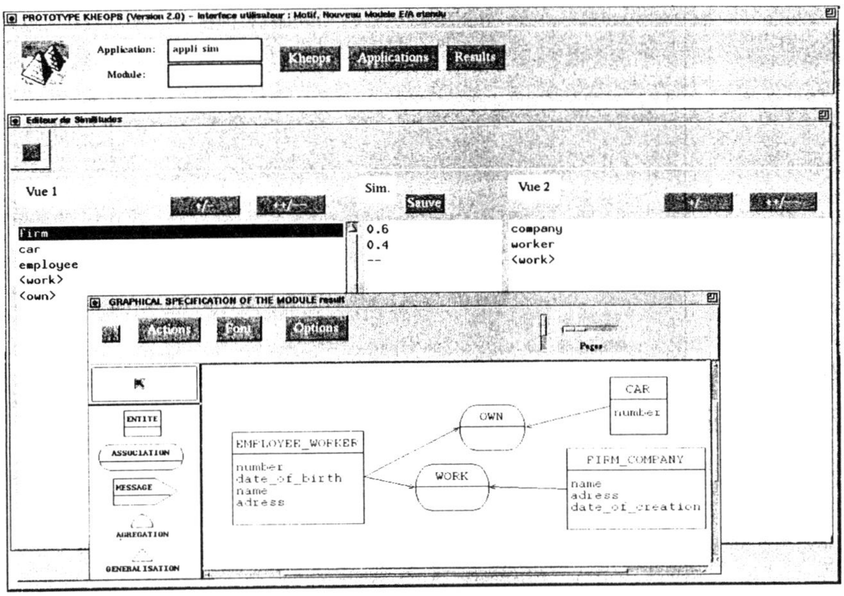

Figure 7: *The integrated view*

5 Conclusion

The first papers about view integration used to conclude on the need of semantic information about the conceptual schemas, whatever source it comes from. Now electronic semantic dictionaries provide large deposits of information on the meanings of the words, thus the issue is now to define when this knowledge is useful, that means for which objects, with what kind of limitations.

The benefits of introducing linguistical criteria in the comparison of two object depends on two factors: the type of the objects to be compared and the adequacy between the application and the dictionary. Concerning the types of the objects - as shown in section 3.3 - searching the concepts portrayed by two entities is expected to be more efficient than comparing their structures (i.e. their participating attributes). Concerning the comparison of two relationships, comparing their structures (i.e. their participating entities) is not less important than searching to which concept they refer. Nevertheless, linguistic knowledge is very helpful for the participant entities comparison by providing their semantic roles in the relationship. The adequacy between the application and the dictionary depends on each specific situation. To deal with this point, we introduced a confidence measure - described in Section 3.2 - attributing a weight to each criterion before starting the integration process.

Just as natural language is not the best way for the user to specify everything in his application, so too some assertions need not any linguistic help to be compared. For example, the integrity constraints on attributes can be very helpful in the comparison step: several very similar objects, with incompatible constraints may evoke a partition of a super class. But the most adequate tool to extract their semantics is still the logical calculus.

• *Further works*

The integration approach described in this paper may be integrated in an incremental database design methodology, such as the implementation in the Khéops case tool. Our work can also be fruitfully used in the current trend of Data Warehouse building. In order to provide data coming from different sources, these systems invariably induce DBMS interoperability. Thus an integrator is required to provide an integrated view of local heterogenous schemas. Until now, such integrators are mainly based on human interaction because the objects to be integrated are from very different kinds. Comparing the structures is not often possible due to the variety of models (Relational model, Object Oriented various models). Comparing the denominations is also weakened because of the variety of languages (local language or English, common language or jargon). Thus an approach based on the word semantics by the mean of multi-languages semantic dictionaries should be appropriate and would allow more automation in the integration process.

Acknowledgment

The authors wish to thank Jessica Barros, Gilles Levreau and Jean Noel Meunier for their kind collaboration during the course of this work.

References

[1] Ambrosio A.P., Metais E. and Meunier J.N., "The linguistic level of the Khéops CASE Tool", First International Workshop on Applications of Natural Language to Data Bases, NLDB'95, June 1995.

[2] Antoni-Lay M.H., Francopoulo G. and Zaysser L., "A Generic Model for Reusable Lexicons: The Genelex Project"5"Le projet GENELEX : EUREKA pour les dictionnaires génériques" in "Literacy and Linguistic Computing", Vol 9, No.1, 1994.

[3] Batini C. and Lenzerini M., "A Methodology for Data Schema Integration in the E-R Model", IEEE Transactions on Software Engineering, Nov. 84.

[4] Batini C., Lenzerini M. and Navathe S.B., "A Comparative Analysis of Methodologies for Database Schema Integration", ACM Computing Surveys, 15, 4, Dec. 86.

[5] Batini C., Ceri S. and Navathe S.B., "Conceptual Database Design", The Benjamin/Cummings Publishing Company, Inc., 1992.

[6] Biskup J. and Convent B., "A Formal View Integration Method", Proceed. of the ACM-SIGMOD internat. conf., Washington, May 1986.

[7] Bonjour M. and Falquet G., "Concept Bases: A Support to Information Systems Integration", CAiSE'94, 1994.

[8] Bouzeghoub M. and Métais E., "Semantic Approach For Object Oriented Database Design", Proceed of VLDB conference, Barcelone, VLDB Barcelone, 1991.

[9] Bouzeghoub M., Comyn I. and Richard D., "Conception de Bases de Données: Etat de l'Art sur la Modélisation Conceptuelle, l'Intégration de Vues et la Conception Physique", Rapport de recherche MASI, Université Paris VI, July 1987.

[10] Bouzeghoub M. and Comyn I., "View Integration by Semantic Unification and Transformation of Data Structures", Proceed of the 9th ER Approach conf, Lausanne, 1990.

[11] Buitelaar P. and Van de riet R.P., "The use of a lexicon to interpret ER diagrams: a LIKE Project", Proceed of the ER Approach conf, Karlsruhe, 1992.

[12] Civelek F., Dogac A. and Spaccapietra S., "An Expert System Approach to View Definition and Integration", Proc. of the 7th ER conf, Rome, 1988.

[13] Collet C., Huhns M.N. and Shen M.N., "Resource Integration Using a Large Knowledge Base in Carnot", IEEE Computer, December 1991.

[14] Comyn-Wattiau I., "L'intégration des vues dans le système expert SECSI", Ph.D. thesis, University of Paris VI, June 1990.

[15] Comyn-Wattiau I. and Bouzeghoub M., "Constraint Confrontation : An Important Step in View Integration", Proc. of the 4th CAiSE Conference, Manchester, UK May 1992.

[16] Delughach H.S., "An exploration into semantic distance", Lecture Notes in Artifical Intelligence, 1993.

[17] Ellmer E., Huemer C., Merkl D. and Pernul G., "Neural Networks technology to Support View integration" 14th International Conference on Object-Oriented and Entity-Relationship Modelling (OOER'95), Dec. 95.

[18] Elmasri R. and Wiederhold G., "Data Model Integration Using the Structural Model" Proceed. ACM-SIGMOD internat. conf., Boston 1979.

[19] Fillmore C., "The case for case", universal in linguistic Theory, Bach et Harms, Holt, Rinehart and Winston, New York, 1968.

[20] Guha R.V. and Lenat D.B., "CYC : A Midterm Report", dans "Knowledge acquisition and learning", ed. B.G. Buchanan et D.C. Wilkins, 1993.

[21] Hammer M. and McLeod D., "Database description with SDM : a Semantic Database Model", ACM Transactions on Database Systems, Sept 1981.

[22] Hayne S. and Ram S., "Multi-User View Integration System (MUVIS) : An Expert System for View Integration", IEEE 6th International Conference on Data Engineering, Los Angeles, February 1990.

[23] Heyer G., Waldhr K. and Khatchadourian H., "Motivation, goals et Milestones of ESPRIT II project MULTILEX", in "Génie logiciel et langage naturel", vol. 1, EC2, Versailles, France, 1991.

[24] Hiroshi Uchida and Takahiro Kakizaki, Electronic Dictionary Project in "Machine Translation Summit" Editor M. Nagao. published by Ohmsha Eds. 1989.

[25] Johannesson P., "Logic Based Approach to Schema Integration", 10th Entity/Relationship Approach, San Mateo (California U.S.), 1991.

[26] Johannesson P., "Using Conceptual Graph Theory to Support Schema Integration", 12th International Conference on Entity-Relationship Approach, Springer-Verlag, Dallas, 1993.

[27] Johannesson P., "Supporting Schema Integration by Linguistics Instruments", First International Workshop on Applications of Natural Language to Data Bases, NLDB'95, Versailles, France, June 1995.

[28] Mannino M.V. and Effelsberg W., "Matching Techniques in Global Schema Design", Proceed. IEEE COMPDEC conf., Los Angeles, CA, 1984.

[29] Métais E., Meunier J.N. and Levreau G. "Database Schema Design, Validation, and View Integration : a Perspective from Natural Language", "XII International Conference on Entity/Relationship Approach", ER'93, Dallas, December 1993

[30] Meunier J.N., "Apport de la linguistique à l'atelier de conception de bases de donnes Khéops", Ph. D. thesis University of Versailles France, 1996

[31] Miller G.A., Beckwith R., Fellbum C., Gross D., Miller K. and Tengi R., "Introduction to WordNet: An On-Line Lexical Database, technical report, Cognitive Science Laboratory, Princeton University, August 1993

[32] Mirbel I., "Semantic integration of Conceptual Schemes" First International Workshop on Applications of Natural Language to Data Bases, NLDB'95, 1995.

[33] Navathe S., El-Masri R. and Sashidar T., "Relationship Merging in Schema Integration", Proceedings 10th VLDB Conference, 1984.

[34] Navathe S., Elmasri R. and Larson J., "Integrating user views in database design", IEEE Computer, January 1986.

[35] Sheth A.P., Larson J.A., Cornelio A. and Navathe S.B., "A Tool for Integrating Conceptual Schemas and User Views", Proc of the 4th int. conf. on data engineering, Los Angeles, Feb 1988.

[36] de Souza J.M., "SIS- A Schema Integration System", Proc. BNCOD 5 conference, 1986.

[37] Sowa J.F., "Conceptual structures : information processing in mind and machine", in Addison Wesley publishing company, reading Mass, 1984.

[38] Sowa J.F., "Knowledge Representation in Databases, Expert Systems and Natural Language", in "Artificial Intelligence in Databases and Information", North-Holland, Amsterdam, 1990.

[39] Storey V.C., Goldstein R.C., Chiang R.H.L. and Dey D., "A Commorsense Reasoning Facility Based on the Entity-Relationship Model", Entity-Relationship Approach Conference, December 1993

Author Index